LASTING
Impressions

Weaving Literature into the Writing Workshop

SHELLEY HARWAYNE

DIRECTOR
The Manhattan New School

HEINEMANN
Portsmouth, NH

HEINEMANN EDUCATIONAL BOOKS, INC.
361 Hanover Street   Portsmouth, NH 03801-3959
Offices and agents throughout the world

Published simultaneously in Canada by
Irwin Publishing
1800 Steeles Avenue West   Concord, Ontario, Canada L4K 2P3

Acknowledgments for borrowed material begin on page vii.

Every effort has been made to contact the copyright holders and the children and their parents for permission to reprint borrowed material. We regret any oversights that may have occurred and would be happy to rectify them in future printings of this work.

Library of Congress Cataloging-in-Publication Data
Harwayne, Shelley.
     Lasting impressions : weaving literature into the writing workshop
/ Shelley Harwayne.
          p.   cm.
     Includes bibliographical references.
     ISBN 0-435-08732-0
     1. English language—Composition exercises—Study and teaching
(Elementary)—United States.   2. Literature—Study and teaching
(Elementary)—United States.   3. Reading (Elementary)—United
States.   I. Title.
LB1576.H28   1992
372.64′044–dc20   92-24369
                                                              CIP

Canadian Cataloguing in Publication Data
Harwayne, Shelley
     Lasting impressions : weaving literature into
the writing workshop
     ISBN 0-7725-1957-9
     1. English language—Composition and exercises—
Study and teaching (Elementary).   2. Literature—
Study and teaching (Elementary).   3. Reading
(Elementary).   I. Title.
LB1576.H37   1992   372.64′044   C92-095184-8

Designed by Mary C. Cronin
Cover photo by Kas Wilson
Printed in the United States of America
92 93 94 95 96   10 9 8 7 6 5 4 3 2 1

For my mother, Ann,
who has magical hands

CONTENTS

PERMISSIONS

ACKNOWLEDGMENTS

Throughout the writing of this book and the living attached to it, I have been surrounded by many small circles of support.

First, my family. My husband, Neil, worked hard to make my writing life easier. He kept my office well-stocked with yellow legal pads and my favorite black pens. He ran to post offices, fax machines, and duplicating shops. He read what I wrote and admired it, even when it was mostly raw edges. He served me cappuccino to wake me up and coffee ice cream to calm me down. But Neil hasn't just made my writing life easier, he's made all of my life easier and lovelier, richer and more rewarding. This book is published as we celebrate our twenty-fifth wedding anniversary. My gift to him will be time—time once again to do the things we love— go to the theater, travel, host dinner parties, and wander around flea markets and antique stores.

My family thank-you extends to my children, my son Michael and my daughter J.J. I've always been a proud mama, showing their pictures, telling their stories, admiring their successes, and they in turn have now returned the favor. I thank them for being proud of me, for helping me keep my priorities straight, for reading an occasional chapter and smiling at the right places, for allowing me to share so many stories from their lives. And I thank them for all their long distance calls, which pulled me away from my desk at just the right moments. They always made me laugh.

Next, my friends. I suppose I should thank all those friends who over the last several months forgave me when I didn't return their phone calls, answer their letters, or meet them for dinner. But there are a few very special friends who not only forgave me for being so busy, but were also there to help me with this project. Hindy List's energy and enthusiasm for the work I do has always inspired me to accept big challenges. She was a thoughtful and gentle reader of the early drafts of this book, as she has been a thoughtful and gentle friend for so many years. I can't thank her enough for her steadfast commitment to this book, her important insights, and all her long, comforting phone calls. Joanne Hindley's friendship has also been essential to me as I wrote this book. She graciously read chapters, tried out ideas, and shared her own teaching moments. We spent countless hours talking about children, and literature, and teaching. I thank her for her clear, original, and brilliant thinking and her willingness to share. More than this, I thank Joanne for joining me at the Manhattan New School. The building is graced by her presence.

There are also a few clusters of faraway friends, who in a very special way have pushed me to think new thoughts. Teachers in Denver, Colorado, hold a very special place in my heart. I always appreciate their kind words, their correspondence, and their occasional baked goodies. They also introduced me to the most beautiful bookstore in the world. I will always be grateful to Laura Benson, Ellin Keene, Steph Harvey, Liz Stedem, Phoebe Sophocles, Helene Willis, and all the wonderful educators at Regis University and the Public Education Coalition.

And then there are my friends in Gothenburg, Sweden. I spent five summers teaching public school teachers there, and they taught me to slow down—not just to talk more slowly but to take time out for island picnics, beautiful sunsets, and wild strawberries. I say "Tack" to Ann Boglind, Abbä Carlquist, and Kerstin Palmquist.

Of course, the Teachers College Writing Project has also served as an important support system for my teaching and learning. I thank Lucy Calkins for introducing me to the writing-process approach and for creating the structure that over the years has enabled so many wonderful teachers, writers, and staff developers to get together on a regular basis to think through wise ways to make change in the New York City schools. No doubt, much of what I believe in today has its roots in the roundtable discussions that took place every Thursday morning over yogurt, coffee, and bagels. I also thank Lucy for reading the beginning chapters of this book and for offering wise suggestions about its shape. And I particularly want to thank those members of the Writing Project community who helped flesh out my own thinking on the place of literature in the writing workshop.

That conversation began in the very early days of our project with the help of Georgia Heard, Martha Horn, and JoAnn Curtis. It continued as Jenifer Hall, Ralph Fletcher, Elizabeth Henley, Karen Howell, Suzanne Gardinier, Drew Lamm, Mary Savage, Susan Radley, Carmen Colon, Richard Courage, Kathy Bearden, Jim Sullivan, and Elizabeth Servidio joined our staff. The voices of Dorothy Barnhouse and Vicki Vinton, fine writers and fine teachers, were particularly helpful in sorting out the relationship between reading and writing. I especially want to thank my colleagues Andrea Lowenkopf and Martha Serpas. Their gentle, graceful talk and their compassion for New York City children inspired all of us to work even harder. And another thank-you to Joanne Hindley, who not only brought her passion for children's literature to our weekly meetings but also reminded us all to treat one another with respect and honesty. A special thank-you goes to Georgia Heard. I continue to be inspired by her poetry and her teaching ideas.

On Thursday afternoons the Writing Project became home to a fine group of public school staff developers. Their presence was an integral part of our efforts to effect change in the city schools. Each week I looked forward to meeting with Mimi Aronson, Joan Backer, Kathy Barabas, Lydia Bellino, Llewelyn Burke, Kathy O'Connell Cunningham, Ralph Gioseffi, Ellen Goldberg, Lesley Gordon, Joëlle Murphy, Shirley McPhillips, Roseanne Palamero, Laurie Pessah, Lettie Smith, Cheryl Stroud, Sharon Taberski, Arty Voigt, and Edie Ziegler. I thank this close-knit circle of educators for always pointing me in the right direction. Time and again, they reminded me to think about real children and real teachers in real classrooms. I thank them as well for always having more confidence in me than I deserved.

I especially want to thank Lydia Bellino whose Thursday afternoon presence was so frequently reinforced by a long heart-to-heart phone call or an overstuffed letter filled with journal articles, newspaper clippings, and children's writing. I also need to add a special thank-you to Laurie Pessah, who was not only an important member of our Thursday afternoon network but also made it possible for me to do research at her warm and wonderful schoolhouse, P.S. 148 in Queens, New York. Laurie introduced me to many fine teachers, but I'm especially grateful to her for helping me connect with Antoinette Ciano, the teacher who graciously shared her fifth graders with me.

This book is primarily the story of my work with Antoinette's students. It is not the story of Antoinette or other fine New York City teachers. Those stories deserve, I think, to be told by the teachers themselves, and I hope one day to read their books.

Making change in any city school is a tremendous challenge. Those of us in New York City owe a debt of gratitude to our friends and colleagues who are in the position to make the big decisions that support our efforts. A respectful and admiring thank-you for their wisdom and leadership goes to Charles R. Chew, Director of Communication Arts and Social Sciences for the New York State Education Department, Steve Tribus, Director of Academic and Instructional Support, and my dear friend and colleague Francine Ballan, Director of Professional Development. I am also grateful to my colleagues in Community School District #2, where so much ground-breaking research has taken place over the last few years. I consider myself fortunate to work alongside Anthony Alvarado, Superintendent, Hindy List, Director of Curriculum, Tanya Kaufman, principal extraordinaire of P.S. 183, and Judy Davis, a teacher's teacher.

And of course, I have had a great deal of production help. Surprisingly perhaps, I wrote this book by hand. My basement is cluttered with eighteen cartons filled to the brim with sheets of yellow paper. Most are illegible. My thanks go to Julie Pierce, the most patient, diligent, and enthusiastic typist one could ever dream of. I also thank her close friend Timberly Whitfield for getting the permissions for this book off to a good start and for passing the project on to Leslie Klein.

I also owe thanks to Kas Wilson, the photographer whose classroom scenes have brought life and warmth to this text. Kas is not only a gifted photographer, she is also the mother of young Stephanie, first grader and resident natural scientist at the Manhattan New School. And of course, I thank the dedicated and patient people at Heinemann, Philippa Stratton, Joanne Tranchemontagne, and Melissa Inglis, who turned this seemingly impossible project into a reality.

And finally, there is my most recent circle of support. I now call the Manhattan New School home, and I offer loud, proud, and heartfelt thanks to the faculty of our brand-new school: Joan Backer, Tara Fishman, Layne Hudes, Joanne Hindley, Julie Liebersohn, Eve Mutchnick, and Elizabeth Servidio, not just for joining me on this incredible journey but for carrying so much of my load as I attempted to complete this book during the same autumn months in which we opened our little schoolhouse. I thank them for their enthusiasm and humor and brilliance. I thank them for taking care of me, and each other and, most of all, our beautiful New York City students.

Making a Lasting Impression

*You have to read in order to write . . . art is a
seamless web, and we all latch into it where we
find a loose end.*

Archibald MacLeish

We do it in September, and we're still doing it in June. We line the walls of our writing workshops with the finest in children's literature.

It's as if we've taken lessons from Quintilian, a wild animal preserve. Workers there know that if you want to attract hippopotami, you prepare mudholes. Teachers too know that if you want to attract children to the joys of a writing workshop, you must prepare fertile ground and do what the experts suggest: "Bathe, immerse, soak, drench your students in good literature."

Fill them up. Read aloud, read silently, recite, do choral readings, tell stories, dramatize, sing. Fill them up some more. Then step back and watch what happens.

Over the last several years, as co-director of the Teachers College Writing Project, I've been doing just that, stepping back and watching New York City teachers and staff developers surround young writers with the finest in children's literature.

I've watched Isabel Beaton read picture books aloud to her bilingual kindergartners as her assistant Ida Rivera softly echoes each line in Spanish. I've watched Isoke Nia and her fourth graders wallpaper their writing center with beautiful book jackets, floor to ceiling. I've watched Elizabeth Henley fill students with poetry, then drape huge sheets of paper across the playground fence and invite young writers to compose poems al fresco.

So too, I've stood in awe as Joanne Hindley shared her collection of grandparent picture books and then inspired students to write their own. I marveled at the way Martha Horn pointed out to students how the architecture of their writing resembled that of professional writers. I watched children become spellbound when Georgia Heard shared her own poems and JoAnn Curtis offered "challenge" books to encourage writers to meet new goals. Time and again, I wondered how Dorothy Barnhouse could pull out just the right book, at just the right moment, to help a student understand point of view, or use of time, or sense of scene.

As I watched these wondrous teachers and children at work, I became increasingly jealous. I yearned for those books, those students, those classrooms. And so, during the last year and a half, I've done more than watch. I've nudged my way into classroom after classroom throughout New York City to nourish my own spirit, to try out some playful ideas, to begin to understand what it is that those dog-eared texts do for the young writers in our classrooms.

New York City teachers have been more than generous. They've shared with me their precious students and libraries and workshop hours. More than that, they've shared their ideas and insights about the ways literature informs students' writing.

They've let me teach. They've let me watch them teach. And together we have watched the students teach us—and themselves and each other.

And we've talked. We've talked at early breakfast meetings, at in-service courses, at evening network meetings.

I've continued that talk at our Thursday staff meetings at the college. Together with Lucy Calkins and a cadre of writers and expert teachers, we've tried to burst the cliché of "the reading-writing connection." How does the literature we read inform the literature we write?

Above all, I've discovered that over the course of a school year, literature has the potential to follow a vibrant and dynamic lifeline in a writing workshop. What literature does for young writers early in the year differs from what it can do for writing communities later in the year.

This should come as no surprise. After all, over the course of a school year, most things in the writing workshop change. The sixty-four sharp points in the crayon box become broken and blunt. The white-out dries up, the Scotch™ tape runs out, the markers lose their covers.

But there is good news. If we've created the right environment, many students move from safe topics to risky ones. Those who at first could only write for ten minutes now groan when the writing hour is over. Students who rarely shared now can't get enough of the author's chair. And yes, students do improve their handwriting, eliminate their spelling demons, and outgrow their editing checklists.

It should come as no surprise that over the course of a school year the role of literature changes as well.

When I was a young child watching Saturday afternoon television, I saw a commercial for the Vega-Matic. A fast-talking man in a business suit demonstrated how this gadget could chop, slice, mash, shred, or dice any vegetable right on your kitchen counter. Literature is like that Vega-Matic. It's a good, hard, versatile worker. There is different work to be done in the fall than in the spring. Our goals may change, but literature remains a constant friend.

This book, therefore, falls into two main parts.

The first is like a wide angle lens and corresponds to the beginning of the school year. I've discovered that if our students don't care about reading and writing, if they don't care about one another, their school, and their world community, it doesn't matter how brilliant our December mini-lessons are or how clever our March conferences. Students need to value listening to good literature, talking about good literature, and owning good literature before they are asked to have a good lead or to use surprising details. Early in the school year we need to cultivate fertile ground for writers. During the autumn months we can use literature to help build supportive communities for readers and writers, to get to know what our students bring to us as readers and writers and help them lead a writerly life. We can use literature to help students view reading and writing as lifetime pleasures and to nurture their own images of good writing. We can also use literature to help students discover the important issues in their own lives.

The second part of the book zooms in on the quality of students' writing. During the winter and spring we find ourselves laying literature alongside our students' drafts to look closely at literary techniques and genres and mentor relationships. The final chapters are filled with ways to use literature within the familiar workshop structures of conferences, mini-lessons, author studies, and reading response groups. In the closing chapter I explore the issue of how to design schools so that literature can be at the heart of all we do.

What follows are stories from New York City classrooms in which students not only have favorite writers and texts, they have also discovered ways to learn from them. The book is filled with practical classroom techniques, what Wallace Stevens might have called "not ideas about the thing but the thing itself." These classroom activities are not meant to be sought after end products; rather, they suggest an array of classroom techniques that can help students and teachers reach important goals. Some of the activities fit into traditional workshop structures, others require new classroom routines and rituals.

Throughout the book I have tried to practice what I preach, to "beware of the cute idea." That's the advice I most often give to teachers who are attempting to develop literature-based classrooms. Our mailboxes fill each day with cute commercial ideas in the name of whole language. But cute ideas alone are not good enough. The work we do is too important.

When I select or design teaching strategies, authenticity is the filter that helps me sift through the dozens of ideas wandering through my mind and coming across my desk.

I'm interested in ways of teaching that have authentic, real world, life-long implications. I'm interested in ways of using literature that make a lasting impression on students' lives and on their writing (hence, the title of this book). When Peter Stillman, a noted writer, teacher, and editor, heard the title, he handed me a sketch he did several years ago (see Figure 1).

FIGURE 1

What do They make there, Daddy?

The building in that sketch could, I suppose, be a factory or a library or a museum, but it needs above all to be a schoolhouse. If we do things right, if we surround children with the finest literature and handle those children and that literature with care, we will be making lasting impressions. We will be doing our part to make life-long readers and writers.

Becoming Passionate About Literature

2

The Camaraderie of Language and Literature

The greatest thing to be gained from the reading of books is the desire to truly communicate with one's fellow man. To read a book properly is to wake up and live, to acquire a renewed interest in one's neighbors, more especially those who are alien to us in every way.

Henry Miller

I love the beginning of the year. When I was a little girl and my family celebrated the Jewish New Year each September, I had no idea that the whole world didn't mark the beginning of the year in September. It seemed the most natural time for new beginnings. After all, I always had a new teacher, a new classroom, and a new Howdy Doody lunchbox (if I was lucky).

Today I realize that you don't have to be Jewish to celebrate the New Year in September. For those of us in the teaching profession it is a time to make New Year's resolutions, to have new commitments and new priorities.

I love walking into school buildings in September. I love seeing teachers smuggle cushions past the custodians and cart in huge cardboard displays scrounged from neighborhood shopkeepers. I love seeing teachers return the classroom plants and small animals they've carefully tended over the summer and once again smuggle them past the custodian's office. I also love the fresh helping hand charts and the little signs on the doors that tell you the location of each class. Mine were always made with a brass fastener and a little cardboard arrow, but today we have velcro. And the signs themselves are wonderful. My favorite is a bushy-tailed squirrel ready to hold one of those velcro-backed acorns, each one announcing, "We're in the gym," "We're at the library," or "We're at home."

Beginning-of-the-year stories are also memorable.

I heard on the radio about a new policy at a high school in Massachusetts. Juniors and seniors have a new semester option. They can take physical education or they can sign up for a reading class to read about physical fitness.

On an October flight to Buffalo I met a West Point plebe. She told me what her new life was like in a military academy. "We're only allowed four responses until March—Yes sir (or ma'am); No sir; No excuse sir; or Sorry sir, I do not understand. Each day we have to know every headline story in the *New York Times* as well as the sports page. We can be drilled at any moment. We're only allowed three miscellaneous items at a time on our desk. And," she went on, "the hardest part of all, we can't have music in our rooms until Christmas."

Perhaps my favorite beginning-of-the-year story comes from my colleague Joanne Hindley. Her close friend, teacher Isabel Beaton, sent her the following note after the first week of school:

Dear Jo,
On Tuesday the first day back I came home and cooked rice pudding from scratch. I boiled the rice in milk and baked it with eggs, more milk, and sugar. I topped it with whipped cream and ate it.
  On Saturday, after the first week back, I ate two-thirds of an Entenmann's cheese-bun coffeecake in one sitting. How was your week?

Love,
Isabel

And I also love September, the beginning of the school year, because it's the one month when you can more easily set aside big blocks of time. Schoolwide specials and pull-out programs haven't begun. Text books haven't been distributed. Test sophistication materials haven't reared their ugly heads out of those locked cabinets. And, after the two-month break, students haven't as yet been programmed to expect a subject shift every forty-five minutes.

September is the best time to be dramatically different, to create new rituals, new emphases, a new tone in the room. September is the perfect time to dream the impossible dream, to luxuriate in big blocks of time devoted to language and literature.

All I needed was a classroom and a gracious teacher. And I found them at P.S. 148 in Elmhurst, Queens. Antoinette Ciano agreed to share her fifth-grade students with me. Together we'd study the power of literature during those first weeks of school.

Having an Image

"My class" ran from nine o'clock to twelve o'clock, with an occasional early morning fire drill and once a week a morning gym period. The only frequent interruption was the arrival of a new student. By month's end Antoinette's register had risen to thirty-five students. Each time the door opened, heads turned and I lost the web of intimacy I was hoping to create. At the lunchbreak, I returned class 5-409 to their teacher and claimed a corner of the school library to interview students individually.

"What goes through your mind when a new student enters?" I asked the fifth graders. "Does he speak English?" was their most common response.

No surprise. Ten native languages are spoken in this classroom, including Arabic, Korean, Urdu, and Portuguese. When a new student entered, I didn't worry about language. I worried about space. Each day, the aisles were further swallowed up with the arrival of more desks, more chairs, more ten-year-olds.

Peter, a Laotian child with dark quill-like hairs crowning his broad face, was in charge of rolling the rugs. Each morning precisely at nine-thirty, after fifty minutes of independent reading time, the class would gather in the meeting area. Peter knew which desks to shift in order to make space for the rugs to be spread in the back of the room. Most of the students sat on the floor, but others had assigned spots on benches and desk tops that bordered the rugs, creating our back-of-the-room bleachers. Then our "together-time" began.

Our work kept us huddled in the back of the room for well over an hour each morning. The work there was joyful and spirited and celebratory. It wasn't the kind of classroom work you could easily define or squeeze into those minuscule square blocks in a teacher's planbook. No, I had a different image of classroom work in mind. I wanted the children to join me in caring passionately about language and literature, and caring passionately about one another and the community around us.

Several years ago I led a week-long writing institute in Norway. At the closing dinner party, the teachers, seated around a long u-shaped table, stood in turn and toasted one another, sang Norwegian drinking songs, and cheered one another on as they told stories from their rich family traditions. That was the mood, the feeling of camaraderie, I was trying to create in the beginning of the year in room 409.

Reading Aloud to Build Community

When he was Secretary of Education, William Bennett remarked that "the teaching of humanity begins with 'once upon a time.' " New York City teachers know this to be true. That's why they weren't surprised when, after several teenagers were found guilty of defacing a synagogue, a local judge sentenced them to read *The Diary of Anne Frank* and Elie Wiesel's *Night* and to meet to talk about their responses. The teachers weren't surprised because they believe in the transformational power of story. They know shared stories can build classroom communities, change relationships, and get students caring about one another.

And so we huddled in the back of the room and honored stories, those from our own lives and those from literature. I told them about the empty nest syndrome I was muddling through, about my childhood in Brooklyn, about the loss of my brother, about my husband's obsession with facts and figures. And they told me about growing up Chinese in New York City, about missing the Dominican Republic, about watching their mom remarry, about attending their first funeral.

I also shared some of my favorite language stories, ones I usually reserve for teachers. I wondered if ten-year-olds could appreciate the brilliance, humor, and poignancy in young children's language learning, but they loved stories about very young writers. First-grade teacher Julie Liebersohn asked her students for the opposite of "out." One child responded, "safe." Elizabeth Servidio asked for the difference between a pound and a yard and a child responded, "The pound keeps the dog in, the yard lets the dog loose." They sensed the cleverness in the child who defined "gritty" as "baby rocks," the one who asked, "Is singing cursive talking?" and the one who called the back of her knee her "leg-pit."

They laughed as hard as teachers do when I told the story of a Bronx teacher who was reading aloud a book about twins. She asked the children if they knew the term for three babies born at the same time, and she continued with four, five, and six. When she asked if anyone knew what you call seven babies born at the same time, one child volunteered, "Dwarfs?"

They understood the sadness attached to Elizabeth Servidio's story about a young preschooler who came to school vowing never to go to the zoo again. He explained to his teacher that he heard on the news, "The guerrillas have no arms."

Then, of course, we spent a lot of time honoring stories from literature. We weren't studying any genre or any author's literary technique, but I read aloud a lot in order to get students caring about one another, about their community, and about reading and writing.

P.S. 148 prides itself on its fine school and class libraries. Laurie Pessah, the staff developer in the building, and Pat Nevins, the school librarian, know children's literature. They read journals, attend conferences, hang out in bookstores. They know how to juggle textbook allotments, use PTA donations, and search out discount supply houses.

Classroom libraries are well stocked, and the teachers are fussy about the books in their rooms. Rumor has it that at P.S. 148, if you get Ms. Ciano, you also get Gary Paulsen, Katherine Paterson, Langston Hughes, and Lois Lowry.

I had a rich array of books to choose from, but I didn't reach for just any text on the shelf. I read aloud only those books I cared deeply about. I didn't settle for anyone else's list of favorites. I created my own. Several years ago I heard a reviewer say that the reader's job is to "communicate the prickles at the nape of her neck." On my list of read-alouds, then, are only books the students know I love for real.

I'm fussy about books because I put great trust in literature. I appreciate the veterinarian who recommends Susan Varley's *Badger's Parting Gifts* and Judith Viorst's *The Tenth Good Thing About Barney* to grieving family members whenever a pet dies. I agree with Katherine Paterson that "stories help us to see what is true and that visions of truth are nourishing to the human spirit." I agree with Vartan Gregorian, former president of the New York City Public Library, that "the contents of the books have everything to do with the street out there . . . The library allows one to go five thousand years into the past to try to cope with the present and also to fantasize about the future."

Therefore, I deliberately searched for the kind of books that would help create a caring, supportive, nurturing climate. Each time I read aloud I lit a candle. It was a mushroom-shaped candle covered with an intricate African pattern in deep reds and blues. The shopkeeper in Johannesburg told me that as it melts and the light shines through, it will be as beautiful as a Tiffany lamp. I explained to the fifth graders that "the candle will help create the magical and mystical aura that reading aloud deserves."

The first chapter book I chose to read aloud was Paul Fleischman's *The Half-A-Moon Inn,* a story that takes place in a different century and speaks of beggars, ragmen, thieves, and family curses. I didn't limit my choices to those modern-day, somewhat humorous, somewhat realistic fictional tales the students seem to enjoy so. I chose *The Half-A-Moon Inn* deliberately for several reasons, not the least of which is Paul Fleischman's craftsmanship. But *The Half-A-Moon Inn* is also the story of separation, of a boy from his mother. Even fifth graders still have pangs of separation when the school vacation ends. It's the story of a mute boy, a way, I thought, to get us talking about respect and admiration for those who are different.

I also chose *The Half-A-Moon Inn* because it demonstrates how valuable it is to be literate. The mute boy depends on writing down his thoughts and has incredible difficulty communicating with illiterate adults.

I read the nine short chapters aloud during the first week of school. I had intended to read a chapter a day and was delighted when the students demanded more. It's one of the few occasions when I've welcomed whining: "No, go on. You can't stop now. Please, please. Just one more. You gotta let us know what happens. Just one more chapter, one more page, pretty please."

It's hard to say no when it's a terrific story. In my visits to other New York City classrooms I can recall the same scenario when teachers read aloud Katherine Paterson's *Bridge to Terabithia,* Doris Buchanan Smith's *A Taste of Blackberries,* or Lois Lowry's *Autumn Street.*

During the first weeks of school, I also read many picture books aloud. Fifth graders still love the turning of pages, the moments of marveling at illustrations, and the power of a short, well-crafted story. The books I chose, however, were different from the ones they recalled from their younger days.

I read several that led to ongoing talk about respecting and celebrating people's differences. You can't read Peter Golenbock's *Teammates,* the story of Pee Wee Reese standing up for his black teammate Jackie Robinson in the 1947 baseball season, without considering prejudice, abuse, and hostility, as well as friendship, loyalty, and decency. You can't read Joan Blos's *Old Henry,* the story of a non-conforming neighbor, without talking about how different kinds of people learn to cooperate and get along. If children are eventually to help one another with their writing, there can be no room for students who mock one another's spelling, or handwriting, or dialect, or choice of topic.

I read several books that put listening to one another on the front burner, including Diane Stanley's *The Conversation Club* and excerpts from Randall Jarrell's *The Bat-Poet.* In *The Conversation Club,* a group of mice decide to meet once a week to talk. And talk they do, simultaneously, never realizing that the point is to listen to one another. In *The Bat-Poet,* Jarrell presents a striking critique of listening to form while ignoring content (see page 224). It's hard to run a good reading and writing workshop if students don't really listen to one another's comments, questions, drafts, or finished work.

I also read aloud the kind of literature that gets students delighting in language. Young writers need to be as much in love with words as Pablo Neruda, whose prose poem "The Word" reads:

> It's the words that sing, they soar and descend . . . I bow to them . . . I love them, I cling to them, I run them down, I bite into them, I melt them down . . . I love words so much . . . The unexpected ones . . . The ones I wait for greedily or stalk until, suddenly, they drop . . . Vowels I love . . . They glitter like colored stones, they leap like silver fish, they are foam, thread, metal, dew . . . I run after certain words . . . They are so beautiful that I want to fit them all into my poem . . . I catch them in midflight, as they buzz past, I trap them, clean them, peel them, I set myself in front of the dish, they have a crystalline texture to me, vibrant, ivory, vegetable, oily, like fruit, like algae, like agates, like olives . . . And then I stir them, I shake them, I drink them, I gulp them down, I mash them, I garnish them, I let them go . . . I leave them

in my poem like stalactites, like slivers of polished wood, like coals, pickings from a shipwreck, gifts from the waves . . . Everything exists in the word.

I shared many picture books that highlight the richness of the English language and read books that celebrate unusual words. Marvin Terban's *Superdupers* is filled with explanations of such enticing words as *hoi polloi, hodge podge, hubbub,* and *humdrum.* Nancy LeCourt's clever alphabet book has everything from *Abracadabra to Zigzag,* including *bigwig, creepy crawly, dilly dally, eenie meenie,* and *flip-flop.*

We read Patricia MacCarthy's *Animals Galore* and John Graham's *A Crowd of Cows.* Children delighted in knowing that a group of penguins is called a colony and a group of pigs is called a drift.

We pored over books filled with idiomatic expressions and familiar sayings, including Marvin Terban's *Punching the Clock* and Betty Fraser's *First Things First.*

I pulled Peter Spier's old classics, *Crash! Bang! Boom!* and *Gobble Growl Grunt,* from the library shelf. We loved noting the differences between "vrooms, tingalings and thuds," between "purrs, roars, and grunts."

Our love of language extended beyond picture books. In fact, I also brought in stacks of reference books: guidebooks to trees, shells, flowers, and insects: cookbooks with long glossaries, thesauruses and picture dictionaries. I told the students that writers lead nosy lives. I encouraged them to borrow these reference books and to walk down the street trying to identify dogs, trees, clouds, and vehicles.

I told the students that writers love to know the precise name of things. They want to know the difference between snooker, pool, and billiards. They want to know the difference between a dalmatian, a Great Dane, and a dachshund. They even delight in the sounds of these words.

I asked them to read labels in the supermarket, to know the difference between squash, zucchini, and eggplant. I asked them to pay attention in the kitchen and note the difference between mashing, mincing, marinating, and melting.

I also shared the kind of literature that lingers in students' minds all day and into the night, the kind students can't wait to share with their families over the supper table, the kind that makes them marvel at their world and begin to take responsibility for that world.

I read excerpts from many nonfiction texts, the kind that make the reader say, "Isn't that amazing!" The students loved hearing Royston Roberts's explanation of how velcro was discovered in *Serendipity: Accidental Discoveries in Science.* They admired the man who investigated the cockleburs that stuck to his jacket and later turned his findings into the fabric that closes their sneakers.

They loved hearing Milton Meltzer's explanation of why Smith is such a popular last name in *A Book About Names.* They were surprised to find out that Smith, meaning a craftsperson who works with metal, wood, or stone, is a common name in many languages: Schmidt in German, Herrara in Spanish, Kowalski in Polish, Haddad in Syrian, Ferraro in Italian.

Then too, during those very first weeks of school I wanted our students to know that people play with language. I shared books filled with tongue twisters, homonym riddles, and wordplay poems. We laughed together over Remy Charlip's *Arm in Arm,* William Steig's *CDB,* Richard Wilbur's poetry collection *Opposites,* Eve Merriam's *Chortles,* Fred Gwynne's *A Little Pigeon Toad,* and all of Peggy Parish's *Amelia Bedelia* books. Playfulness with words, ideas, and design will come in handy when these young writers begin to generate topics, shape texts, and revise drafts.

And of course, I read aloud many books that simply took their breath away. I was following Cynthia Rylant's advice:

> Read to them *Ox-Cart Man* and *The Animal Family* and *Birds, Beasts, and the Third Thing*. Read these with the same feeling in your throat as when you first see the ocean after driving for hours and hours to get to it. Close the final page of the book with the same reverence you feel as you kiss your sleeping child goodnight. Be quiet. Don't talk the experience to death. Shut up and let these kids feel and think.

As Rylant goes on to say, "Teach them to be moved and you will be preparing them to move others." I selected Jane Yolen's *Owl Moon,* Barbara Cooney's *Miss Rumphius,* Byrd Baylor's *I'm in Charge of Celebrations,* and Mem Fox's *Wilfred Gordon McDonald Partridge* as "sure-fire-take-your-breath-away" picture books.

And finally, I read aloud picture books that would help students take a renewed interest and pride in their community.

Sometimes when I look out at a sea of city faces I find the children too young to deserve such worried looks and anxious poses. Too many children lead fearful lives. I imagine that in cities throughout our country children are warned not to play in the park alone, not to talk or even look at strangers, not to eat the candy they went trick or treating for. In room 409 we chanted together lines from Douglas Florian's *Street Scenes,* "City street, jumping feet, traffic cop, bus stop." We roared at Debra and Sal Barraccas's *Adventures of Taxi Dog* and took solace in Dynne DiSalvo-Ryan's *Uncle Willie and the Soup Kitchen.* We marveled at the information in Miriam Schlein's *Pigeons* and David Macaulay's *Unbuilding.* We read aloud passages from Swift and Ward's classic, *The Little Red Lighthouse and the Great Gray Bridge,* the story of our own George Washington bridge. To a rap beat we read Leah Komaiko's *I Like the Music* and *My Perfect Neighborhood.*

It's hard for children to do good work when they're feeling hopeless, so we filled the air with the good things about our community. We lifted our spirits not only with picture books but also with poetry and short stories and newspaper articles.

We recited poems about city life. The children loved those by Langston Hughes and Myra Cohn Livingston and Lilian Moore. They decorated the side bulletin boards with Marci Ridlon's "Catching Quiet" and Margaret Tsuda's "Commitment in a City."

Catching Quiet

It's hard to catch quiet
in the city.
You have to be quick.
It isn't around long.
You might find it
after the roar of a truck,
before a jet flies by.
You might find it
after the horns stop honking,
before the sirens start.
You might find it
after the ice-cream man's bell,
before your friends call you
to play.
But when you find it,
stick it in your heart fast.
Keep it there.
It's a bit of the sky.

Commitment in a City

On the street we two pass.
I do not know you.
I did not see
if you are—
fat/thin,
dark/fair,
young/old.

If we should pass again
within the hour,
I would not know it.
Yet—
I am committed to
love you.

You are part of my city,
my universe, my being.
If you were not here
to pass me by,
a piece would be missing
from my jigsaw-puzzle day.

We needed to look out our classroom window and be in awe of the squirrels and oak trees and juniper bushes that dot our concrete playground.

We read and reread Nancy White Carlstrom's short stories in *Light: Stories of a Small Kindness*. The children needed to know about an elderly woman who volunteers at Saint Luke's hospital, rocking the premature babies. They needed to know about a New York City teacher and her second graders who rally round a handicapped boy, celebrating his small victories.

We needed to look out our classroom window and notice the small kindnesses too—the school crossing guard who's always there, the kindergarten child who rides to school in a wheelchair on her father's lap, the old woman who feeds the pigeons in all kinds of weather.

We also searched newspapers for some of the good things happening in our city. The students' favorite was a short entry in the "Metropolitan Diary" section of *The New York Times*. A man wrote about traveling home on the subway from Yankee Stadium. The Yankees had been losing badly so this fan left the game early. The subway car was filled with "a dozen wall street traders, ties at half mast, jackets slung over shoulders." (New Yorkers take Yankee losses very seriously.) Then, the fan writes, "a dude with a radio-cassette player the size of a mini-submarine appeared blasting Stevie Wonder music." Before long the depressed Yankee fans were singing and dancing in the subway car. They even gave the young "dee jay" extra tokens to keep him riding longer.

Of course we didn't just share the happy newspaper articles. These young writers needed to take the problems of their community seriously as well. We read articles about pollution and drugs and poverty. But we needed to take the harsh realities in with a sense of hope and a belief in our future as citizens of New York. We needed to look out our classroom windows and feel compassion for the struggling senior citizens, the homeless family looking for shelter, the panhandler asking for quarters on the street corner.

These young writers will write from who they are, from what they know. Recently there was an exhibition of art and poetry in New York entitled "Subterranean Subjects." All the works were inspired by the New York City subways. That exhibit was my first choice for a class trip.

Our immersion in city-related literature became an ongoing class project. The students began compiling a list of novels they might read on their own. George Seiden's *The Cricket in Times Square,* E. L. Konigsburg's *From the Mixed-Up Files of Mrs. Basil E. Frankweiler,* Sydney Taylor's *All of a Kind Family,* and Jean Merrill's *The Pushcart War* were at the top. Their list also included harsher views of New York City, Felice Holman's *Slakes Limbo* and M. E. Kerr's *Dinky Hocker Shoots Smack.*

We also labeled a basket "City Poems," inviting anyone to contribute new discoveries, and set aside a shelf for nonfiction city texts. Barbara Bash's *Urban Roosts* and Ethan Herberman's *City Kid's Field Guide* were instant favorites.

If I were teaching in a mountaintop school in Denver, in a classroom on the Florida coastline, on an Indian reservation in New Mexico, or in a one-room schoolhouse in rural Kansas, I'd still search for literature that instills pride and awe and compassion for community. And of course, I'd invite children in on that search.

Choral Reading to Build Community

I can recall only one day when the students' attention wandered as I read aloud. It wasn't quite ten-thirty in the morning, but the still summery weather quickly withered us as we sat cross-legged, clammy shoulder to clammy shoulder, in the back of the room. I felt my shirt sticking to my back and I began wishing I hadn't worn stockings. The children, dressed in their new school clothes—bright sweat-shirts and stiff new jeans—started to use their notebooks as fans. I knew it was time to blow out the candle and take a break.

I brought out a small, ragged, black book. "Is it your Bible?" the children asked. "No, but it is a special book. It's where I keep the poems I love. And I think it's a good time to share one with you." I flipped the pages looking for just the perfect poem.

The poems in my black book are in totally random order. I have to flip through all the pages to find a specific poem. I've often thought about redoing my collection, but Scott Elledge's advice in the introduction to his anthology *Wider than the Sky* has changed my mind: "enjoy the random order . . . like the faces of people coming up out of the subway or down the escalator at an airport."

I finally found it, Prince Redcloud's "Now."

> Close the bar-b-que.
> Close the sun.
> Close the home-run-games we won.
>
> Close the picnic.
> Close the pool.
>
> Close the summer.
>
> Open school.

The children repeated each line, quickly learning the poem by heart. Then we read it chorally, giving out lines to clusters of children. We said it softly, shouting out only the last line. We read it in a chantlike rhythm, softly tapping the hard covers of our notebooks. Finally, the children created a rather heartfelt dramatic rendition, moaning each line, as if holding back tears. On this muggy New York morning they really meant it.

The children then went back to their desks where they sat in clusters of six or seven. I gave each child a copy of the traditional poem, "If All the Seas Were One Sea."

> If all the seas were one sea,
> What a *great* sea that would be!
> And if all the trees were one tree,
> What a *great* tree that would be!
> And if all the axes were one axe,
> What a *great* axe that would be!
> And if all the men were one man,
> What a *great* man he would be!
> And if the *great* man took the *great* axe,
> And cut down the *great* tree,
> And let it fall into the *great* sea,
> What a splish splash that would be!

Each cluster of students was asked to prepare a choral performance of the poem. They spread out. One group sat in the front of the room under the chalkboard ledge. Two groups relocated to the corridor outside the classroom. Another sat atop their desks as if in a football huddle. The final group returned to the carpeted area to work out their plans. "Be ready to share in twenty minutes," I announced.

The students didn't know it, but I was setting future response groups in motion. Here was their opportunity, to be repeated many times during the first weeks of school, to come together in small social communities. The students got to know one another. They learned to negotiate and take turns. They learned to revise, critique, and compliment one another. They learned to rehearse, modify, and clarify their ideas. They also learned to encourage one another, to take pride in one another, and to perform in front of one another. All of these were skills they would later need to respond to one another's writing.

Antoinette and I visited each planning group, observing the social dynamics and making mental notes about possible future changes. We also offered suggestions, trying to ensure the success of their first performances. We showed them ways to use pace, volume, phrasing, body movements, gestures, and voice assignments to support the content of the poems.

We shared performance tips we had learned from David Shookoff, the education director of the Manhattan Theatre Club, which apply to dramatic interpretation and reading aloud as well as choral reading. He suggests that students use their eyes to sweep the audience before they begin. He points out the difference between high and low voices and loud and soft voices and suggests that the children also sweep the room with their voices. He works with students on making eye contact with their audience by looking up from the paper during a performance. He tells students to "own the stage" and make the audience believe in the importance of their words. And of course, he insists that they use their bodies to demand attention. "No leaning on furniture. No hiding hands in pockets."

At the end of the twenty-minute period, Yoorak served as messenger, dashing quickly from one group to another announcing "Showtime." Students returned to their seats to watch each group perform at our imaginary stage in the front of the room. And the audience marveled at the variations.

One group turned the poem into a song, and another added a rap beat. A third group added gestures, as if they were members of the Temptations with a lead singer in front. Still another group performed the poem as a round. They thought overlapping voices fit the content of "if all the seas were one sea" just perfectly.

Choral performances became so popular with the students that they led to several other class rituals and projects. Each day for a period of two weeks I ended our "together-time" by passing out a copy of a poem for choral reading. At night I flipped through my "bible" of poems looking for those that were particularly rhythmic and lent themselves to interesting vocal arrangements. Among the student favorites were: Kathleen Fraser's "Marbles," Eloise Greenfield's "Things," Karla Kuskin's "Rules," Nikki Giovanni's "Knoxville, Tennessee," Langston Hughes' "April Rain Song," Myra Cohn Livingston's "Street Song," and Judith Viorst's "Talking."

By piggybacking performances, one day after another, the students became increasingly confident and clever. They borrowed and innovated upon techniques they admired and invented new performance skills. They even created their own closing ritual. Each day after the six performances, inevitably two or three children announced that they now knew the poem "by heart." They would stand in front of their peers, the copy of the poem behind their backs, and begin to recite. Kind friends would coach them through if they got lost.

It's so easy in our hectic classroom lives never to have time to return to an unusually successful, powerful activity. Antoinette and I realized that students were gaining a great deal from these choral reading sessions and we didn't replace them too quickly with other curriculum agendas.

As more and more poems were distributed the students realized that they needed a way to organize them. Many envied my little black book and began pasting the poems into their own special poetry notebooks. Others kept them in envelopes attached to their writer's notebook. Still others designated as "poetry-pots" old pencil cases, cigar boxes, or those small oak boxes meant for filing index cards. One student even brought in an old desktop Rolodex and painstakingly copied poems onto the little cards and filed them alphabetically by the poet's name.

Community building need not remain within the four walls of a classroom. Children need to care for the entire school community. Each day as I drive across the Triboro bridge from P.S. 148 to my office at Teachers College, I pass a huge billboard on 126th Street in Harlem. It reads, "Literacy. Pass it on." Children too can pass it on. All we need to do is ask.

When the students felt at home with their own choral readings they were asked to share their expertise with the first graders. I passed out sheets of rather simple chants, poems, and nursery rhymes. I explained to the students that in a week's time they would be asked to select one, prepare it on appropriate chart paper, and teach it to a small cluster of first graders. We borrowed enlarged texts from the first-grade teachers to study how they were created. The teachers visited and gently critiqued the students' first efforts. The students learned that glitter is distracting, as are multi-colored letters, using symbols for words, uneven spacing between words, inappropriate hyphens, and squashed in words. The students reworked their charts until they achieved near perfection.

Finally the big day arrived. The only thing I had forgotten to talk to the students about was how to teach. The fifth graders turned out to be the most pedantic, impatient, frontal teachers imaginable. They pointed to each word, expecting young first graders to learn to read and recite the poems immediately.

Despite their shortcomings as teachers, the big guys loved the little ones, and vice versa. Each group performed their poems as best they could and a return visit was scheduled. In fact, the teachers and children decided that the fifth graders would return on the first Wednesday of every month to teach new poems to the very same children. In the interim, the fifth graders would sit in on primary shared reading time to learn how to teach.

The next month's visit was much more joyful, although now the fifth graders were in charge of selecting the texts. We had Christmas poems in October, lots of verses from autograph books, and some rather disappointing sexist classics like "Georgie Porgie" and "What Are Little Girls Made of?" After each first-grade visit, the fifth graders were asked to reflect on the experience in a process log and share their thoughts with their newly formed response groups.

Honoring Diversity

During that hour-long "together-time" each morning we continued to read aloud, share stories from our lives, and recite our repertoire of now familiar poems. But the hour was also studded with moments of celebration. We paid tribute to the uniqueness and diversity of the members of our growing community.

We began by honoring the diversity of languages in that classroom. We celebrated autumn birthdays with "Happy Birthday" songs in many languages. We sang short verses in Polish, Korean, Portuguese, Chinese, Hebrew, and Spanish. Alejandro taught us his favorite from Colombia. We sang "Sapo verde para ti, sapo verde para ti . . ." to the tune of "Happy Birthday to You." Literally, it means, "A green toad for you, a green toad for you. . . ."

We toasted one another on grand occasions, again in several languages. When Stacey won the antidrug essay contest, we cheered, "Mazel tov, Brindamos, Goon henay, Bordiachi, Congratulations, Stacey."

Katherine taught us Spanish autograph verses. Her favorite was

"De las islas Puerto Rico	"From the island of Puerto Rico
De los paises el Peru	To the country of Peru
Y de toda mis amigas	Of all my friends
La mas dulce eres tu."	the sweetest one is you."

Jeanine read us Chinese Mother Goose rhymes. Matthew shared *Katz and Maus,* a picture book he had learned to read when his father was stationed in Germany.

Children who spoke only English were not left out. Many told stories of their families' special ways of celebrating, and others taught us family sayings, toasts, or made-up words that had special meaning to their families alone.

We honored not only diversity of language but of background experiences. One morning I asked the students to make a time line of the songs that have been important in their lives. They looked confused, so I told them about my own. The first one I recalled was a little rhyme my mother had sung to me, one of those never-ending ones: "My name is John Johnson. I come from Wisconsin. I work as a lumberjack there. When I walk down the street, all the people I meet say, 'Hello, what's your name?' and I answer, 'My name is John Johnson . . . ,' " and so on and so on. Then I recalled a school song. Each Thanksgiving throughout the elementary grades I had to sing "Over the river and through the woods to grandmother's house we go." I recalled feeling not quite American, since I took a bus to grandma's house. Then there was my father's favorite, the cowboy song "Don't Fence Me In." I explained to the children that my father had died when I was their age, and I never did find out why he liked that song so much. The last song on my list was "He Ain't Heavy, He's My Brother." I explained to my young friends that whenever my brother, who has also passed away, used to call me on the telephone and I'd ask, "Who is it?," he'd respond, "He ain't heavy. . . ." I can't listen to that song today without crying.

The students then sifted through their own memories. Some still drew a blank. Holiday songs, like "Jingle Bells" and a few current radio hits came first to their minds. Only a few, primarily the newly arrived immigrants, had memories of learning songs at home with their families.

When students had jotted down a few titles I asked them to look over their lists and on the next blank page in their writer's notebook to elaborate on the songs that seemed most important.

The students who did have important family songs often had poignant scenes or thoughts attached to them (Figure 2).

FIGURE 2

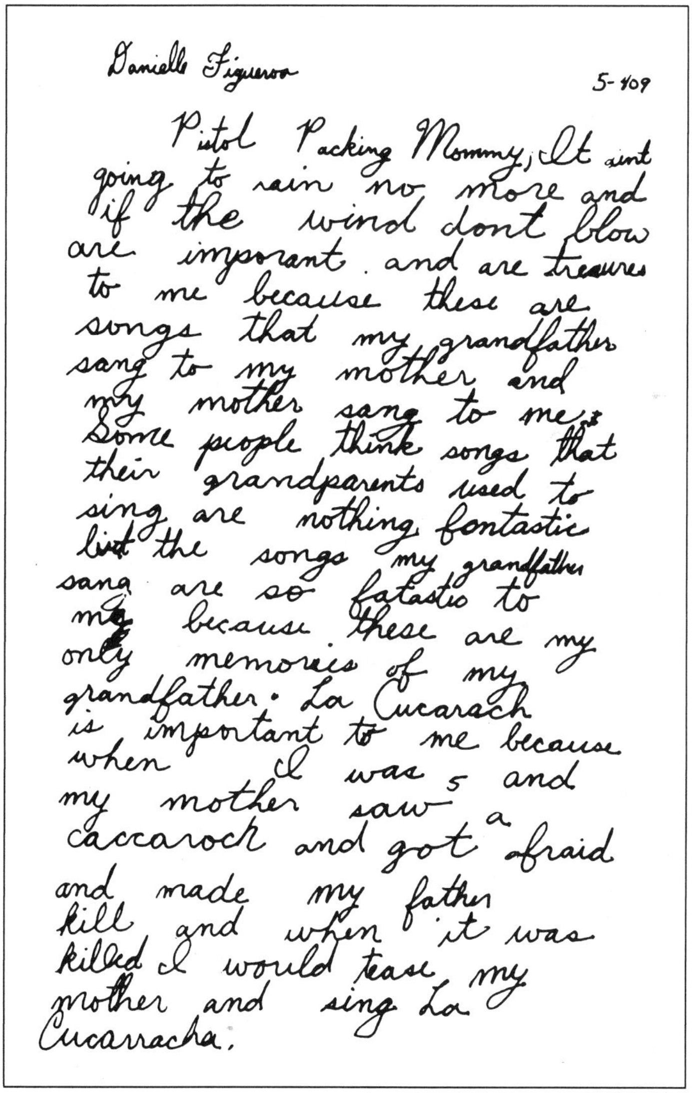

FIGURE 2, continued

Francis Cheng

London Bridge is Falling down.

My dad used to sing it to us as a treat. Now we don't sing we just do our work. I remembes when he was so happy just singing it. He would tell us stories about when he was small and what he did. I heard him talking to my sister about how hard he worked and how tired he was and I remember him singing and it seem- ed as if he would never tire out. When I think of work I think of my dad.

Regrettably, most students said they never sang at home with their families. They were more likely to remember a song or two they had learned at school. But only a few songs, like the one described by Najib (Figure 3), seemed really significant in their lives.

Singing seems to have taken a backseat in our overcrowded curriculum. Perhaps we have carved out too few moments to sing with gusto and to invite students in on choosing songs they'd like to learn.

Sharing song memories was only one of the many ways we celebrated our diverse backgrounds. During those first few weeks of school we also passed around our most cherished "baby" book, the "most read" book in our homes, and even our favorite bookmarks. We marveled at the paper Jeanine used in Chinese school, and we peeked into Alejandro's second-grade schoolbook from Colombia.

We swapped street songs—for playing tag and jumping rope and choosing sides. Antoinette recalled, "Rich man, poor man, beggar man, thief, doctor, lawyer, Indian chief," a childhood chant that helped her count the buttons on her clothes (and was meant to predict whom she would marry). The children then

FIGURE 3

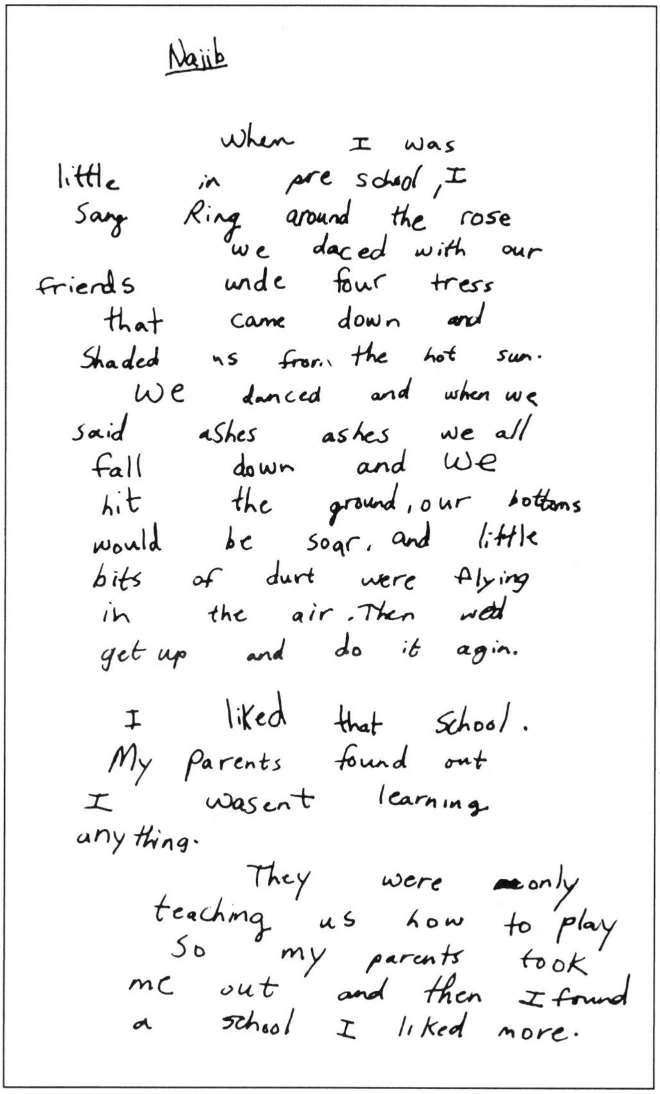

Najib

When I was
little in pre school, I
Sang Ring around the rose
we daced with our
friends unde four tress
that came down and
Shaded us from the hot sun.
We danced and when we
said ashes ashes we all
fall down and we
hit the ground, our bottoms
would be soar, and little
bits of durt were flying
in the air. Then we'd
get up and do it agin.

I liked that School.
My Parents found out
I wasent learning
any thing.
They were only
teaching us how to play
So my parents took
me out and then I found
a school I liked more.

recited their 1990s version. We also talked about unusual literary traditions in our homes and our communities. These appear in the next chapter.

Spending big blocks of time "having a blast" with literature allowed many student voices to be heard. Instead of the usual two or three children whose hands are always raised, many of the shy or withdrawn students and those who often require extra time were able to take part in the community life of that classroom. We were able not only to celebrate the diversity of language and literary experiences, but to applaud students for their hidden talents.

Jessica became known as the class impersonator because she was able to sound just like Holly Hunter's recording of the "Three Billy Goats Gruff," complete with the actress's intonations and southern accent. We had listened to the record during our "together-time" and Jessica asked to borrow it to listen to again and again at home.

Peland, who struggled to make friends in the class, was thrilled that his four-line poem,

> Jobs are a yuk,
> Jobs are not fun
> My boss says hurry up
> But I'm not done.

was turned into a chant during meeting time and performed by his classmates.

Whenever we shared stories in the meeting area, Mary Beth set the mood with one of several chants she had memorized. On some days she'd begin with the native American words:

> Spirits above the ground
> Spirits below the ground
> Spirits gather round.

Students would accompany her chants by tapping softly on stretches of wooden floor.

On other days she'd begin with the African refrain she had discovered in the preface to Gail Haley's *A Story, A Story.*

> We do not really mean, we do not really mean that what we are about to say is true.
> A story, a story; let it come, let it go.

The students appreciated Mary Beth's chanting ritual. Her few simple words set the mood for the storytelling to come and encouraged students to listen just a little bit harder to one another.

One morning I reminded the students that their sharing of literature need not be limited to this morning hour. "No," I continued, "there are wonderful stories and poems that would be appropriate for reading during math or science time, perhaps even during music or art." The next afternoon Edward, a shy, serious-looking child, handed me a handwritten copy of Carl Sandburg's poem "Arithmetic." Antoinette asked Edward to launch the math lesson by reading the poem aloud. In the next few weeks Edward pored over anthologies in the school library gathering several more "math" poems. He quickly became the class "math poet." His classmates demanded copies of Eve Merriam's "Gazinta," Myra Cohn Livingston's "Math Class," Harry Behn's "Circles" and Gwendolyn Brooks's "Computers."

Forming a Bond with a Literate Adult

Early in the year I sensed that the students needed to know that I don't read aloud and do choral reading and tell stories and read silently only when I'm at school. I also do all these things outside of school. I don't engage in literate activities because I'm a teacher but because I'm a human being, and reading and writing are clearly two of life's many pleasures.

New York City kids do know passionate people. Some have parents who are obsessed with tennis or "La Novella," the Spanish soap opera, or gardening, or flea market shopping, or gourmet cooking. But not all of our kids know an adult who is passionate about reading and writing. That's a lovely, teacherly role to fill. And the rewards are great.

Many years ago I was in a car accident and suffered whiplash. I was teaching second grade at the time and found myself frequently creaking my neck, shifting it into place. I still do it today when I'm under stress or the weather is damp. By mid-year, practically all my second graders were creaking their necks. Children, if they like us, will do what we do. That's why teaching is such an awesome responsibility.

I'd therefore begin our hour-long get togethers by talking about my own thrills as a reader and writer. I talked to them about how I was forever joining book clubs and then cancelling so I could get those bargain offers of three books for one dollar each. I told them that I don't always have time to read *The New York Times* carefully every day, but that my husband clips articles he knows I'd hate to miss and leaves them on my pillow. They came to learn how I was carving out regular time in my life to write this book, and they graciously listened to drafts. I talked to them about the book I was currently reading, Oscar Hijuelos's *The Mambo Kings Play Songs of Love,* and they listened as I read the one or two excerpts appropriate for ten-year-olds.

I also brought in and passed around some of the artifacts of my literary life: the T-shirt that reads "Book-Woman," the silver bookmark from Tiffany's, the special pad that clips onto my steering wheel so I can write as I make my way through Manhattan gridlock.

I even shared letters I received from faraway friends, ones I'd never discard. Cheryl Rice from Toronto wrote,

> I have a favour to ask. I'm going to be passing through New York City this summer and I'd like to do some book buying for my vacation collection. Can you recommend a couple of bookstores that have a good selection of literature?

I showed them Laura Benson's letter from Denver, which included the Myra Cohn Livingston poem "Fourth of July" alongside a snapshot of her young son Tim at a holiday celebration. Students need to know that literate people like to visit fine bookshops and to select just the right poem to send to friends.

I filled them up with my literary ways of being because I desperately wanted them to care about reading and writing themselves. I was following Katherine Paterson's advice: "we must love . . . literature . . . so much that we cannot keep that love to ourselves."

My friend Liz Stedem, another teacher of teachers from Denver, Colorado, took a leave of absence to give birth to her daughter. When she returned for a visit with the baby in her arms, the substitute teacher hung a sign: "Welcome Mrs. Stedem and Katherine Reid." One of Liz's second graders protested about the spelling of the baby's middle name. When Liz walked in, the youngster asked her for the correct spelling. "That is how you spell Reid," Liz explained. "Oh, no," complained the child, "I thought you named her Read because you love to read."

That's just how I wanted my fifth graders to think about me, a teacher who loves to read, who loves to write.

At first, talking about myself had seemed self-indulgent. Now it no longer did. The students began to long for literature, yearn for artifacts, and borrow and extend my ways of loving reading and writing.

One day, I brought out the travel photo album I carry in my handbag. Next to each important photo I've put just the right poem or passage that speaks to me of my relationship with the person in the picture.

Next to my husband's photo is Marge Piercy's "Sentimental Poem."

> You are such a good cook.
> I am such a good cook.
> If we get involved
> we'll both get fat.
> Then nobody else will have us.
> We'll be stuck, two
> mounds of wet dough
> baking high and fine
> in the bed's slow oven."

Next to my son's is an excerpt from Anne Beattie's *Picturing Will.*

This is from Mel's journal: "Do everything right, all the time, and the child will prosper. It's as simple as that, except for fate, luck, heredity, chance, the astrological sign under which the child was born, his order of birth, his first encounter with evil, the girl who jilts him in spite of his excellent qualities, the war that is being fought when he is a young man, the drugs he may try once or too many times, the friends he makes, how he scores on tests, how well endures kidding about his shortcomings, how ambitious he becomes, how far he falls behind, circumstantial evidence, ironic perspective, danger when it is least expected, difficulty in triumphing over circumstance, people with hidden agendas, and animals with rabies."

Next to a recent photo of my daughter, Sharon Olds's poem "35/10"

> Brushing out my daughter's dark
> silken hair before the mirror
> I see the grey gleaming on my head,
> the silver-haired servant behind her. Why is it
> just as we begin to go
> they begin to arrive, the fold in my neck
> clarifying as the fine bones of her
> hips sharpen? As my skin shows
> its dry pitting, she opens like a small
> pale flower on the tip of a cactus;
> as my last chances to bear a child
> are falling through my body, the duds among them,
> her full purse of eggs, round and
> firm as hard-boiled yolks, is about
> to snap its clasp. I brush her tangled
> fragrant hair at bedtime. It's an old
> story—the oldest we have on our planet—
> the story of replacement.

Several students began doing likewise, collecting family photos and selecting appropriate poems to tuck into their carrying cases.

Students also longed for a book like my little black book filled with favorite poems I'd clipped and copied over twenty years. Jeanine and Yoorak came to me one day anxious to tell me they had a secret, but of course they couldn't tell. "But you're gonna love it, you'll think its great. We're not gonna tell you until June." By ten-thirty they had shared their secret. They couldn't resist. They had chipped in to buy the biggest spiral notebook they could find, the five-section variety. On the front they wrote, "Our Favorite Poems—collected by Jeanine and Yoorak." On the first page Jeanine had copied Wordsworth's "My Heart Leaps Up," on the second page Yoorak had hand-written William Cole's "Banananananananana," and on it went. Each night they took turns taking the book home and adding one more poem.

I loved their secret book, but I wondered how they would share this one copy after graduation in June. I had visions of them as adults meeting annually on the steps of the New York Public Library and ceremoniously handing over this aging volume for the next year's safe-keeping, much the way countries hand over the America's cup.

The students also wanted to know how grown-ups learn so many poems by heart. "By heart," as Robert MacNeil points out in *Wordstruck,* is such a perfect expression. To commit a poem to memory is to know it by and with and because of your heart. "I learn them because I love them," I explained. "I can't help learning them because I read them over and over again. It helps, of course, to keep them with you at all times and that's why I have my little black book. But that's also why I keep this little lucite frame on my desk." I showed them a small molded plastic frame just right for slipping poems in and out. "Right now I'm learning Richard Le Gallienne's poem, 'I Meant to Do My Work Today.'"

> I meant to do my work today
> But a brown bird sang in the apple-tree,
> And a butterfly flitted across the field,
> And all the leaves were calling me.
>
> And the wind went sighing over the land,
> Tossing the grasses to and fro,
> And a rainbow held out its shining hand—
> So what could I do but laugh and go?

Each time I sit at my desk, I get to read it again and again.

By week's end several students had brought in frames and placed them atop stacks of books on their desks or wedged them between the pencil sharpeners, compasses, and bottles of white-out that border the edge of their desktops. They too slipped in poems they wanted to learn by heart.

Jerry asked for a copy of the Le Gallienne poem. The next time Antoinette asked him "Did you do your homework?" he was quick to respond, "I meant to do my work today, but. . . ." It was hard for Antoinette to be annoyed with a student who had learned a poem by heart and could weave it into his life so naturally. Many more students then asked for a copy of the poem thinking it would be the perfect excuse for not being able to complete assignments. But it only worked once.

Signs of a Literary Universe

One day, at an out-of-town conference, I described to Bernice Cullinan, a leading expert in the world of children's literature, what I was hoping to accomplish in room 409. She said it reminded her of Lee Galda's concept of "Building a Literary Universe." We really were working hard in the back of that room in order to build a literary world for ourselves.

The students knew we were living a different life. We were sharing surprising stories from our lives and from literature, and we were spending surprising amounts of time doing so. There were signs that our literary universe was work-ing, and these too were surprising.

The room filled with inside, literary jokes. One day I had trouble lighting the African candle. A student called out, "You must have told a lie, Shelley!" All the students agreed. They were referring to the curse on Old Miss Grackle in *The Half-A-Moon Inn*. She could never start a fire in her own fireplace because the inn had a curse on it. Only honest people could kindle flames under the roof of the Half-A-Moon Inn.

When literature is woven into the fabric of the school day and teachers and students care about that literature, you can expect it to be used in unexpected ways. The banner on Susan Schiff's door reads, "Some Class." Only if you have read *Charlotte's Web* will you get this inside joke. Only fans of Noisy Nora will understand why, whenever her first graders interrupt her, Elizabeth Servidio says, "But Nora," and they respond with a knowing "had to wait." If you haven't reread *Madeline* in a long while you might not recognize the words Dora Ferri-aulo's children chant as they line up each morning: "In an old school in Queens that was covered with vines lived twenty-four students in two straight lines." Nor will you recognize the words Isabel Beaton's kindergarten students recite before snack time: "We have our bread. We have our butter. But best of all, we have each other." Likewise, you can't appreciate the sign hanging in the back of Bonnie Parella's primary room if you haven't read Joy Cowley's *Mrs. Wishy-Washy*. It reads, "Oh, lovely blocks!"

After Jerry worked "I Meant to Do My Work Today" into his everyday conver-sation, many students wanted to do the same. One day, in fact, we played an impromptu game. The students spread their poems across their desktops and I asked a question that would prompt a poem in reply. "What happens when the wind blows?" I began. The students quickly tried to spot Lilian Moore's "Wind Song" and read it aloud. It begins, "When the wind blows / the quiet things speak." The students caught on and took turns thinking of questions that would make their classmates respond with a particular poem.

From that day on they hungrily waited for occasions they could respond to with a poem. If anyone were to ask any of those fifth graders what time they woke up they'd probably respond with Karla Kuskin's, "I woke up this morning at quarter past seven." If you were to ask them their favorite season, they'd probably recite Nikki Giovanni's, "Knoxville, Tennessee," which begins "I always like summer best." And if anyone ever uttered the words "I'm just going out for a moment," you can be sure the students would spontaneously ask, "Why?" and expect the speaker to respond, "To make a cup of tea." Once again they'd ask, "Why?" and expect the speaker to respond, "Because I'm thirsty." The students would keep on asking "Why?" and wouldn't relent until they had finished every line of Michael Rosen's poem, "I'm Just Going Out for a Moment."

> I'm just going out for a moment.
> Why?
> To make a cup of tea.
> Why?
> Because I'm thirsty.
> Why?
> Because it's hot.
> Why?

Because the sun's shining.
Why?
Because it's summer.
Why?
Because that's when it is.
Why?
Why don't you stop saying why?
Why?
Teatime why.
High-time-you-stopped-saying-why-time.
What?

I recall the line from a song on the radio, "I'm looking for love in all the wrong places." Sometimes I think we've been looking for literacy in all the wrong places. We need to be looking for the inside jokes, for the conversations filled with literary references, for the poems mounted in pretty frames. Perhaps too, we need to be looking outside as well as inside of school. The students learned that I read aloud and tell stories and memorize poems outside of school, and I learned that they too had literary ways of being outside school.

One day I was working with some second graders at P.S. 148 when I overheard two boys going back and forth with Michael Rosen's poem. "Where did you learn that?" I asked. "At home," they explained. Each had a sister in Antoinette's class who shared poems at dinnertime. Now, that's cause for celebration. Sophia and Danielle didn't share poems with their brothers for extra credit or commendation cards or literary badges. They shared them because they loved them so much they couldn't keep that love to themselves. Katherine Paterson would be proud.

When the Australian writer and storyteller Mem Fox visited our project, she mused about why television viewing had become so much more popular than reading. Not only are there no readiness programs, or levels, or competition, or "musts," or "have-to's," Mem explained, but "television viewing is shared family enjoyment."

Sophia and Danielle had found a way to turn their poetry collection into shared family enjoyment. I wondered if more students might be interested in doing the same. I began lending books that were particularly appropriate for joint readings, including Paul Fleischman's poems for two voices, *I Am Phoenix* and *Joyful Noise*, John Ciardi's *You Read to Me, I'll Read to You,* the Dell Young Yearling Share-a-story books, and lots of one-act plays. Every once in a while I'd pull one of these books out of my tote bag and ask, "Would anyone like to borrow this?" I gave no instructions, no suggestions, and of course, no extra credit. Students borrowed books from me much the way my colleagues at the Writing Project would. There were no whole-group assignments, no due dates, no questions at the end of the reading. Instead, students found their own ways to delight in these texts. They shared their family moments with us and returned the books when they were done.

Students also brought in books from home. They lent them to each other and to their teachers and student teacher. Sharing books is part of what it means to be a literate human being. It also became a sign that we were well on our way toward building our literary universe.

An Afterthought

As I reread this chapter, I can't help but think back to a time ten years ago when I launched my writing workshop by gathering the students together, telling them my own personal story created especially for the occasion, and then ushering them back to their seats to quickly record their own personal stories. We've come along way since then.

The writing process teachers I know best have come to realize that leads are not just important to writing, they're important to teaching. Leads set the tone for the school year to come. And just as leads need not be thought of as one-liners, leads to teaching writing need not be thought of as one quick mini-lesson that invites students to pick a topic on the first day of school.

How much better those later self-chosen topics and drafts will be if students begin by honoring stories from their own lives and from literature. How much more that community will thrive if students grow comfortable laughing and crying in front of one another, supporting, comforting, and gently nudging one another.

3

More Than Backpacks and Lunchboxes: Exploring Children's Literary Histories

Early on weekday mornings, I'd read in my bed, I'd feel a mysterious comfort then, reading in the dawn quiet—the blue-gray silence interrupted by the occasional churning of the refrigerator motor a few rooms away or the more distant sounds of a city bus beginning its run.

Richard Rodriguez

On a rainy Tuesday evening in March, my husband and I set off to meet Susan Stires at LaGuardia Airport. She was coming from her classroom in Maine to share her expertise with members of the Writing Project. Her flight was delayed, so we scooted out to The Buccaneer for a late supper, a local diner a few blocks away from P.S. 148.

As I entered I heard a surprising, "Hi, Shelley." I turned my head to greet Stacey, the most grown-up looking of my fifth graders and the only one with double pierced ears. She was sitting at a small round table with an elderly couple, most likely her grandparents. When we left an hour later, Stacey was still swapping stories with her grandma and grandpa.

In the red vinyl booth next to ours was a lively, laughing group of six or seven women. It wasn't hard to eavesdrop on their stories about children, neighborhood, and work. Work turned out to be P.S. 148. They were members of the office staff—secretaries, school aides, and paraprofessionals.

The loudest table was the one over in the corner where several men and women in their late twenties sat with babies and young children on their laps. They were talking in Greek, in English and in a combination of the two. My husband was the first to tune in to their conversation. Amid all the ordering, eating, and care-giving, they were helping one young woman fill out an accident report for her insurance company. "Shelley," my husband whispered in disbelief, "how are they able to do it here? How can they do it in ink?"

An hour in a diner and I had already learned a lot about the students and staff, the parents and grandparents of P.S. 148. Wouldn't I be a better teacher knowing that Stacey has a storytelling family? Wouldn't I be a better colleague knowing that the office workers are friends and love their work? Wouldn't I be a better teacher of reading and writing because I appreciated the fact that literate acts are different in different families?

Several years ago I was having public conferences with some youngsters in Denver, Colorado. I had asked their teacher to jot down background information about each student that might help me in our conference. On a small index card, Justin's teacher had recorded a recent conversation with this second grader.

> Last weekend, I met Justin at a large landscaping shop in town. When I asked him what he was doing he said, "We're buying blankets and blankets of grass."

After I had read Justin's short, factual, and perfectly spelled narrative about eating in an Italian restaurant with his family, I mentioned what I had learned from his teacher. "Can you talk to me, Justin, about that dinner party as if you were chatting with your teacher over the weekend?" Justin forgot about the draft on the table. He went on to tell me about how he and his brother, out of boredom, pressed their noses against the huge glass windows of the restaurant and stared down at the sidewalk below. With much joy, he told me they pretended the lampposts were giant plants, the cars were dinosaurs and all the people were aliens from another planet.

The more we know about our students, the easier it becomes to teach wisely and well. We need to begin the school year by bringing children's lives—their family photos and family stories, their hobbies and their collections—into the classroom. We also need to start the year by getting to know our students' life lines as readers and writers. And just as it's important early in the school year to get to know our students' histories as readers and writers, it seems equally important to know their histories as students who connect their reading to their writing.

In an introduction to his *Collected Stories* Richard Kennedy was asked, "How did you get your ideas?" He answered, "I got the ideas because I was looking for ideas. A person who has it uppermost in his mind that someone is trying to poison him will often find that his food tastes a bit peculiar." In the same way, students will make reading-writing connections when they're looking for reading-writing connections. But are they looking? Do our students know that writers take lessons from their reading? Do our students know that there is such a thing as reading like a writer? We need to find out.

Our students bring more than backpacks and lunchboxes to school. It's not surprising that our project teachers begin their school year not by hanging out in local diners but by building structures into their work that reveal students' histories as readers and writers and as people who have discovered ways to connect the two.

We need to know what individual students' images of good writing are, how they see mentor relationships, if they have favorite genres, writers, and texts, if they "write to please their tastes as readers," as Frank Smith suggests.

When Emily hands us her About the Author page, we need to know what she means by having "a good relationship with literature" (Figure 4).

Last year when Jerry Harste visited our project, he spotted a bumper sticker as we crossed the street. It read, "If you can read this, thank a teacher." Jerry protested, "It should say, 'If you can read this, thank a teacher, and a parent, and a pediatrician, and a next-door neighbor, and a grandparent . . .'" and on he went. We wondered if this was true for our students. We were particularly interested in the literacy events that took place outside of school, in students' homes and community. We wanted to know how students learned to read and write and what role their families played in their literacy learning. We were interested in their attitudes toward reading and writing and their understanding the relationship between the two. We also wanted to probe the images of good writing they were bringing to this year's writing workshop. We were hungry for information because we knew the data we gathered would help us set appropriate goals for the year ahead and inform our teaching and our curriculum.

Although most of the activities involved a combination of talking, writing, and observing as well as a bit of "show and tell," I categorized them under a sub-heading that designates the main avenue of study.

FIGURE 4

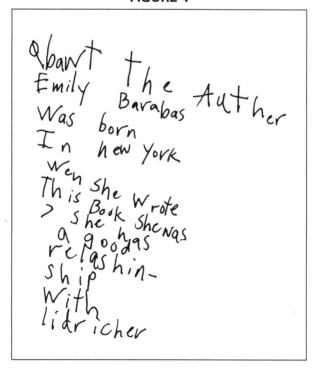

Talking About Ourselves as Readers and Writers

Early in the school year, Antoinette and I spent a lot of time talking informally with the students as we gathered together in the back of the room. As I have described in Chapter 2, much of what we talked about, including our histories, tastes, strengths, and habits, helped us to get to know one another as readers and writers. We reminisced about our first library cards, the first books we owned, our first pieces of writing. We also swapped stories about our families' diverse literary traditions.

There were several ways we initiated these discussions. Perhaps the simplest involved trusting the contagious power of our own stories. When I told the students that my husband clips newspaper articles for me, they talked about their own reading relationships. Kareen and Jennifer always choose the same novel so they can read passages to one another on the telephone each night. Sophia's aunt still sends her books in Urdu as birthday gifts, although she has forgotten much of her first language. Justin's godfather reads "Riki-Tiki-Tavi" to him every Groundhog Day. Long ago they decided that weasels look like groundhogs.

When Antoinette shared the titles of books she was planning to buy her six-year-old son with the class, we found out that some children had never received a book as a gift and that some didn't even know where in the neighborhood to shop for books. When Antoinette and I told stories about the adult reading groups we belonged to, the students speculated on whether they would read together as adults. Some described their parents' church groups, which gathered to read the Bible. Most couldn't imagine their parents reading with other grown-ups.

I also brought in works that helped us learn more about students' literacy backgrounds. Eve Bunting's *Wednesday Surprise* reminded students of illiterate people in their own lives. *The Day of Ahmed's Secret* by Florence Pary Heide and Judith Heide Gilliland led children to share their memories of learning the alphabet and how to write their names. Many of the poems and short prose pieces in Jean Little's *Hey World, Here I Am!* got students talking about their tastes and habits as readers and writers. Florence McNeil's poem "Squirrels in My Notebook" led to a lively discussion about writing research reports.

I went to Stanley Park
to put squirrels in my notebook
My teacher said
write everything you found out
about squirrels

and so I will

I saw a fat one
shaped like a peanut butter jar
attacking my hat
his moustache was made of chips
he ran sideways into the sky

He looked like a ginger cat
with a branch for a tail

he was so mad he ran down again
and I can't write
what he said to me

Lucky for me I had a sandwich
to share with him

He smiled at me till his teeth
weren't hungry
and jumped into the sky
with his jammy legs

he turned into
a kite

Carolyn Mamchur's poem "Together" evoked lots of tender reading together moments.

Lying in bed
next to my mother.
This has to be the best,
the very best thing.
We are reading.
Dad is away
"Want an apple?"
and she bites in.
Crack, crack,
go her jaws
like a hinged fence
that doesn't work right.
I try not to listen
to those hinged jaws
I can't read
I've never noticed
my mother's jaws
doing that before
"Maybe it's the way
she's lying," I think to myself.
"Gee, you eat
apples funny,"
I finally blurt out.
She doesn't say anything.
She just looks at me
awful quiet
and puts the apple
on the bed stead
behind her.

We continue to read
in silence.

That was two years ago.

But it feels like
last night
the two of us
reading in bed

My mother
no longer eating
and I,
wishing, oh, wishing
wishing she were.

After hearing Karla Kuskin's "Being Lost," many students told stories of getting into trouble for reading at the breakfast table or with a flashlight in bed at night.

Being lost
Is the perfect way
To pass the time
On a sky blue day

When it's warm
And the open window
Uncurtains a call
Spiraling up the stairway
Hovering in the hall.
No one comes then
When they call me.
I am not there
Where they look.
I linger alone
In a place of my own
Lost
In a book.

I frequently asked students to do some quick jottings to help gather energy and ideas for class discussions. Some of the activities I use with adults often work well with ten-year-olds. At last summer's writing institute I encouraged people to meet one another by handing out the following questionnaire. The instructions read: "After responding, find someone who matches your five choices exactly."

1. Would you rather read
    ___ on a shady backporch
    ___ stretched out on a beach
    ___ under your bedcovers
    ___ in a wood-panelled library
    ___ on an airplane to Paris?
2. Would you rather be reading
    ___ *The New York Times*
    ___ *Anna Karenina*
    ___ *The Accidental Tourist*
    ___ anything by Danielle Steel
    ___ *Language Arts* magazine?
3. Would you rather receive as a gift
    ___ a gourmet cookbook
    ___ a gift certificate to a children's bookstore

___ a paperback collection of the complete works of Philip Roth
___ a hardcover edition of *The World's Greatest Short Stories*
___ a gift certificate to Heinemann?

4. Would you rather read aloud to your students
   ___ *A Taste of Blackberries*
   ___ *Sarah, Plain and Tall*
   ___ *Journey to Jo'Burg*
   ___ *Charlie and the Chocolate Factory*
   ___ *Where the Red Fern Grows*
   ___ *Charlotte's Web?*

5. Would you rather be able to recite the poems of
   ___ Langston Hughes
   ___ Walt Whitman
   ___ Shel Silverstein
   ___ Gwendolyn Brooks
   ___ Robert Frost?

Teachers then mingled and chatted with one another, searching for someone with the exact five responses. In the class of fifty teachers, no one matched exactly, and the choices stirred up some lively, opinionated conversations.

Last fall I prepared a similar questionnaire for my younger students:

After answering the five questions, try to find someone who matches your responses exactly.

1. Would you rather read
   ___ under your bedcovers
   ___ in the public library
   ___ on your living room sofa
   ___ on a park bench
   ___ at your school desk?

2. Would you rather be reading
   ___ a letter from a friend
   ___ a poetry anthology
   ___ the daily newspaper
   ___ a book by Katherine Paterson
   ___ the *TV Guide?*

3. Would you rather receive as a gift
   ___ a dictionary and a thesaurus
   ___ the complete works of Roald Dahl
   ___ a new encyclopedia
   ___ a subscription to *Cricket, Highlights,* and *Stone Soup*
   ___ a gift certificate to a bookstore?

4. Would you rather read to some six-year-olds
   ___ *The Cat in the Hat*
   ___ *Where the Wild Things Are*
   ___ *Madeline*
   ___ *Amelia Bedelia*
   ___ *Mother Goose Rhymes?*

5. Would you rather be able to recite the poems of
    ___ Langston Hughes
    ___ Karla Kuskin
    ___ Eloise Greenfield
    ___ Shel Silverstein
    ___ Jack Prelutsky?

At first the fifth graders appeared rather awkward at mingling. They didn't have the cocktail party savvy the adults had. I had to encourage them to get out of their seats and work the room. Antoinette and I eavesdropped on their talk.

They were less tactful than adults. Their conversation was filled with "Why would you want to read the newspaper? How could you pick Langston Hughes over Shel Silverstein?" and lots of "Yucks" and "Echhhs." After about fifteen minutes of searching, the students met in their response groups to discuss what they had learned from the experience. This time their talk was filled with tallies of their searches: "Jeanine and I had four the same, Kareen and I none!" The students were surprised at how hard it was to find someone who agreed with their taste. They also suggested that I add a sixth box to each question so they could fill in "other."

Antoinette and I studied the student responses as a whole and individually. We were surprised by how many students liked reading in the library or at their desk in school. We wondered if they lived in noisy households. We were surprised at how many students chose reading a letter from a friend and how few chose the daily newspaper. No one chose magazine subscriptions or gift certificates to bookstores.

We also found it revealing to read the responses of individual students and then to chat with children whose responses intrigued us. There was quite a range of responses in the room. Jerry preferred reading a poetry anthology and the complete works of Roald Dahl. He'd like to be able to recite Langston Hughes's poems, and he'd prefer to do all this in the public library. Marco, on the other hand, wanted to be reading the *TV Guide* on his living room sofa and memorizing Jack Prelutsky's work.

To spark further conversation about our literary backgrounds, I devised a quick survey of student favorites. On a small slip of paper, the students numbered 1 to 10. Then I warmed them up with some sure-fire fifth-grade issues. They quickly jotted down their favorite musical group, school subject, party food, class trip, and television program. Next I proceeded to their literary interests. Many of the students slowed down as I asked them to record their all-time favorite writer, illustrator, poet, nonfiction writer, and a favorite story from literature they knew well enough to tell. When students looked at me with blank faces, I was quick to let them know how astonished I was that they didn't have favorites in the literary world and promised they would by semester's end.

Immediately following the survey, I initiated a whole-class discussion of why the first set of questions seemed easier to answer than the second. Most students admitted spending more time watching TV and listening to music than reading. They also considered why they were more familiar with names of show-business personalities than those of writers. "Their names are everywhere," Stacey explained, "in newspapers and magazines, even on our lunchboxes and sweat-shirts and stickers." "Maybe someone should sell Katherine Paterson T-shirts and pencil cases," suggestion Peland. Not a bad idea we thought. The students then met in small response groups to compare notes on their lists of favorites.

Later that week, two students tallied the answers and posted a bar graph of the results. Antoinette led them in a discussion of how these results might influence life in room 409 in the year to come. The students talked about what genres they'd like to study, which authors they'd like to read, what trips they'd like to take, and of course the food and music that should be at all class celebrations.

Listing their favorites led to some rich conversation, but so did the series of more unconventional questions I asked one day:

1. What kinds of things does your family mount with magnets on your refrigerator door?
2. Whom do you help to read and write?
3. What are the most unusual reading or writing events in your home?

The students again jotted down their responses and then volunteered to sit in the author's chair during the week to elaborate on what they had written. Refrigerator doors turned out to be the key place to hang school correspondence, including announcements, reminders, and schedules. But some of the items mounted also revealed that many of the students were under extreme pressure to do well in school. Parents frequently hung up test papers with high marks or assignments that earned teachers' complimentary stickers. Yoorak's mother puts up Korean newspaper articles to encourage her to read in her first language. She also posts the family's running list of books to borrow from the public library. Only nonfiction texts are allowed. Danielle described a corner of the refrigerator that is reserved for her poems. Once a month she's expected to hang a new one in this magnetic gallery. In December, she writes a poem as a Christmas tribute to her deceased grandparents, whose photo is posted nearby.

Perhaps because so many students are immigrants there were many touching stories about helping other people to read and write. Zanvi taught her non-English-speaking grandmother to recognize on sight the words *free* and *save*. Grandma is now able to clip coupons for the family from newspapers and magazines. Zanvi also taught her to recognize the names of family members so she can sort and distribute the mail. Jeanine discovered a page of sample questions to help her uncle finally pass his citizenship test. She's also responsible for helping family members fill out job and school applications. Kristen regularly visits her Aunt Mary in a nursing home. She entertains her by reading newspaper advertisements, because Aunt Mary misses going shopping.

The children's lives were also filled with individual literary delights. Emil described the pleasure he gets in browsing in an old set of encyclopedias whenever he's bored. He's particularly fascinated with sections on wars, energy, and dinosaurs and studies the photographs and captions closely. Yoorak takes books into the bathtub with her but quickly tosses them into the laundry hamper if her mother enters the room. Every Christmas Jenny takes down a string of lights that hangs in her bedroom window. She drapes them across her headboard so she can read by Christmas light and "watch the rainbows dance across the pages of her novel."

FIGURE 5

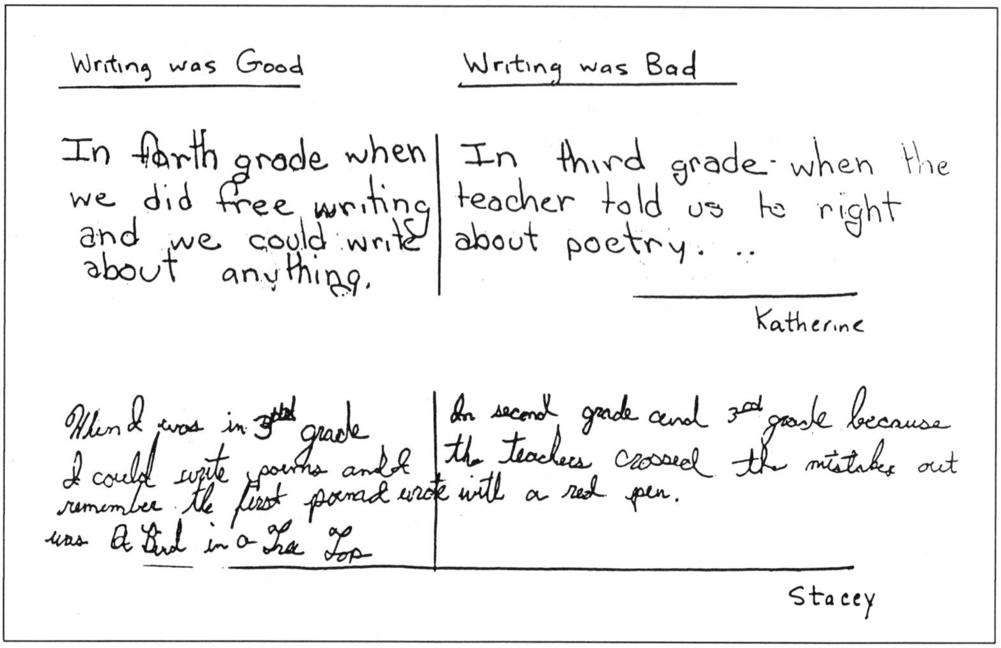

Writing was Good

Writing was Bad

In fourth grade when we did free writing and we could write about anything.

In third grade when the teacher told us to right about poetry. . .

Katherine

When I was in 3rd grade I could write poems and I remember the first poem I wrote was a Bird in a Tree Top.

In second grade and 3rd grade because the teachers crossed the mistakes out with a red pen.

Stacey

The children also shared many unusual family literacy traditions. Several involved religious practices. Kevin described a sign that members of his family hang on buildings in Chinatown. If there's a baby who won't sleep at night, the family writes a note to passersby requesting that they pray for peaceful sleep for their child. Kevin said the passersby know that they should read it three times so the prayer will be answered.

In Zanvi's family, posters of Indian gods hang in the kitchen. At every meal, incense smelling of fruits and flowers is lit. Family members read from a series of prayer books as her grandmother offers food to the gods. Zanvi reports that "the smoke rises and makes a ring around the god's face like a Christmas wreath around Santa." The prayer books are kept in a large tin can. They're read in a set order and then read over again from the beginning. Zanvi recalls that her mom used to sing her "Swami-narshana," a favorite prayer, whenever she couldn't fall asleep at night.

At ten o'clock each evening, Yoorak takes part in a Buddhist ceremony. "The whole family reads words from our Bible and we're all trying to memorize the prayers by January. We have a chart that my father fills out. Each night we put a slash if we recited well and a circle if we didn't." "The minister at our temple," she continued, "gives a prize to the family that practiced the most and another to the family that recites the best."

One final way I used quick jottings to get students talking about their histories as readers and writers was to give them simple two-column tasks. "Draw two columns. On the left, jot down a time when writing was good for you. On the right, jot down a time when writing was bad for you." Responses from Katherine and Stacey appear in Figure 5.

FIGURE 6

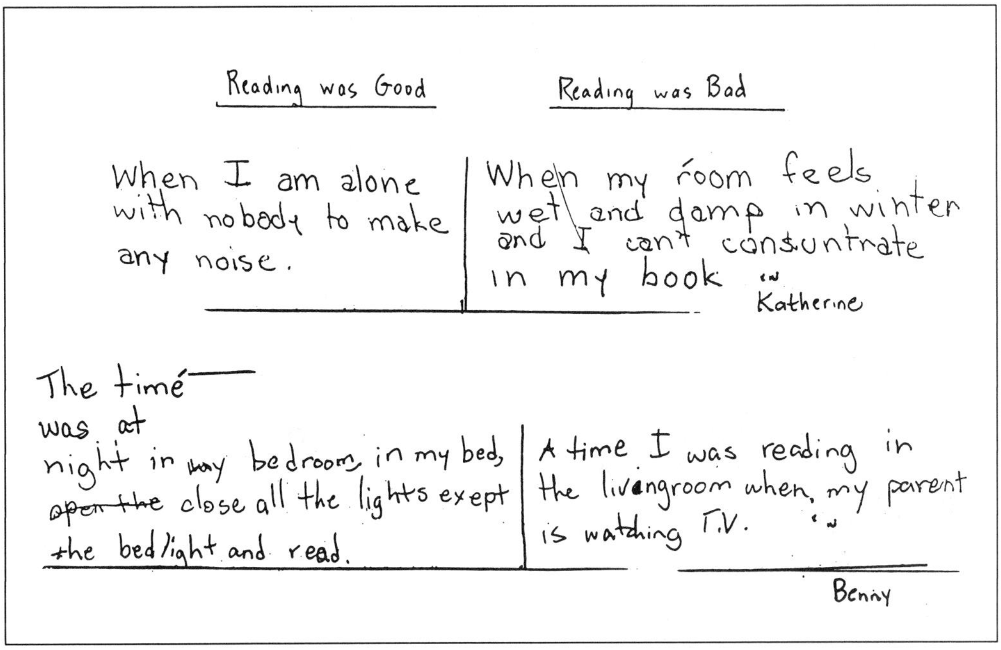

Reading was Good | Reading was Bad

When I am alone with nobody to make any noise.

When my room feels wet and damp in winter and I can't consuntrate in my book
Katherine

The time was at night in may bedroom in my bed, aper the close all the lights exept the bed light and read.

A time I was reading in the livangroom when my parent is watching T.V.
Benny

Students were able to do the same with reading events. Responses from Katherine and Benny appear in Figure 6.

Students then met in pairs to share their experiences, trying to figure out what made these moments so positive or so negative. Eavesdropping on their conversations, Antoinette and I gathered additional data that would inform our teaching. We realized that most of the writing moments students recorded were connected to specific pieces or specific kinds of writing. Most of the reading moments were connected to environmental conditions rather than to a particular text. We wondered if these ten-year-olds felt more successful and confident as readers than as writers. Did they believe they had made it in the world of readers? Were attractions and distractions now outside of themselves? Did writing remain a challenge, dependent on their abilities to handle topic choice, genre, and spelling?

So far, all this quick jotting was intended primarily to get students talking about their histories as readers and writers. But most of these exercises can be adapted in order to get at students' images of good writing and their sense of mentorship. For example, I could have asked children to draw two columns and on the left, to jot down texts they've enjoyed hearing read aloud, and on the right, texts they've found boring to listen to. The students could meet in clusters afterwards to discuss their choices and elaborate on what they think makes for good writing. I could also have directed students to draw two columns and on the left, to list people they've learned from, and on the right, people who've learned from them. Students could then meet to discuss how they went about learning from someone else and/or teaching someone else.

Our talk was not limited to these informal moments of whole-class gatherings, response groups, or author's chair meetings. I also learned a great deal about students by conducting more formal interviews.

Unfortunately, interviews are time-consuming. My role as part-time teacher allowed me greater scheduling flexibility, but classroom teachers don't have this luxury. Most of the teachers I know best don't attempt to have long interviews with all their students during the first few weeks of school. Instead, they begin with a small cluster. They arrange breakfast or lunchtime meetings. They use workshop conference time to interview. They've even been known to pull a couple of children away from their desks during silent reading time and to interview them in the hallway. Teachers are never sorry for time spent in this way. It's always worth it.

Often they begin the interview with broad, open-ended questions. "Tell me about your reading," Louise's teacher says, and the six-year-old responds, "I read my own stories. I try to read the chapter books that my sister reads—she's eight. I read Winnie the Pooh sticker-activity books. I read Merry Christmas holiday books and I read the Bible."

The teacher probes to see how Louise envisions the reading-writing connection. "Have you ever tried to write any books like those?"

"No," says Louise.

"If you wanted to, how would you go about writing an activity book?"

Louise's responses let her teacher know whether she has the essence of the genre down. The teacher continues to elicit information from her about chapter books, holiday books, even Biblical writing. The interview ends when Louise's teacher lets her know that this is a year for her to try new things, perhaps to write the kinds of things she enjoys reading.

Some teachers ask students to bring their best piece of writing to the interview so that the text can serve as a point of departure for the conversation to follow. The piece Carol brings begins

> It was a hot summer day on the banks of the Mississippi. The dreary sultriness in the air seemed to slow down time. The scorching sun beat on May Belle's innocent face as she perched herself on the railing of the second story of the magnificent plantation house set behind a landscape of rather massive oaks on her wealthy father's estate. . . .

It's no surprise to her teacher that Carol's favorite book is *Gone with the Wind.* She is writing to please her taste as a reader. During the year, no doubt, she will revise her work to correspond more closely to her image of good writing. How can her teacher help Carol if she hasn't taken the time to understand where this young writer is headed?

When I interviewed Antoinette's students I asked them to bring more than their best piece of writing. I asked them to bring their entire writing archives. They brought shoe boxes and shopping bags and old overnight bags filled with pieces they and their parents have been saving.

I was interested in understanding the kinds of writing they had done and considered worth doing, but I was particularly interested in using their old pieces as a counterpoint to their current images of what makes for good writing.

Sophia brought in a cloth tote bag covered with small pinecones. She spread the contents on the library table. Most of the items were stapled six-page booklets from first, second, and third grade. Scattered among them were homemade greeting cards and some pages filled with her early attempts to write in cursive.

We spent several minutes admiring her cache. Sophia was particularly amused at the dedication page in a birthday book she had written in grade two. She had crossed off the names of all the friends who have moved out of the neighborhood. I asked her when she had done this editing, and she said, "One day last summer when I was reading this stuff over."

I then asked, "Sophia, if you were to make other kinds of changes in your writing now that you're a fifth grader, what might you do?"

Her first response had to do with mechanics. Now her handwriting was better and she was a better speller.

"What about the quality of the writing?," I continued, "the way you wrote it?"

Sophia juggled her tiny tortoiseshell glasses as she struggled to answer the question, which seemed too abstract. But two things helped. Rather than consider her whole body of work, Sophia selected a particular piece to talk about, a little book called "All About Me." And I reworded my question. "Sophia, if you want people to read this book and say 'Oh, she's such a good writer,' how would you write this book differently?" As she reread the Table of Contents (Figure 7), she said, "I'd certainly change the order of the chapters. It sounds mixed up."

Her new order would read, "When I was born, About myself, My birthday, What I like, What I don't like, My favorite thing to do, What I like to eat." Her revision clearly indicated an internalized sense of chronology, priority, and balance.

I then asked, "What about each chapter? What would you do so they're as good as a book from the library?" This way of wording the question also seemed to make sense to Sophia.

She opened to Chapter 2, What I like to eat (Figure 8).

"Of course I'd make it longer. Chapters aren't that short."

"And how would you go about making it longer?"

"I could write about the three ways my mom makes chicken—bread-crumbed, barbecued, and the Pakistani way with spices from my country."

FIGURE 7

Table of Contents

1. My birthday.
2. What I like to eat.
3. My favorite thing to do.
4. What I don't like.
5. When I was born:
6. What I like.
7. About my self.

FIGURE 8

> 2. <u>What I like to eat</u>
>
> I like to eat chicken and ice-cream because they are so good and I like them very much.

"How do you know that would be better for the reader?"

"Because I've read books, and I got ideas."

The interview continued as Sophia told me about the books she admires, writing with "specific detail," and the challenge of "painting pictures" for readers.

Sophia's tote bag full of writing helped reveal how she sees good writing. I now knew a little bit about what she has learned from the books she has read and from the mini-lessons her teachers have taught.

The next day, Zanvi, who had been eavesdropping on my interview with Sophia, brought in a piece of writing she had done in second grade and her fifth-grade update (Figure 9).

Zanvi explained how "Today was not a good day" had turned into an entire paragraph. She suggested that the writer's job is to answer the reader's questions. "Of course, the kids will ask me why it wasn't a good day. So now I tell them."

During the first few weeks of school, I often used my interview time to prompt students to talk about the connections they made between reading and writing. I asked some students to bring a piece of their own writing and a piece of published professional writing that had somehow influenced them. Of course, some students came empty-handed, explaining that this had never happened to them. One student brought a book on sharks that gave him information for a shark report. Another brought a choose-your-own adventure book whose format she had attempted to recreate. Several students brought picture books, particularly those

FIGURE 9

with distinctive shapes, like those with an alternating pattern of good news-bad news. One child brought Cynthia Rylant's *When I Was Young in the Mountains,* which had given him the idea of writing a collage of memories.

Occasionally I asked students to prepare for an interview by bringing several pieces of professional writing they wish they had written. It's very revealing to have the students explain their choices and it's also revealing to look for threads that cut across all five pieces. Are they all the same genres? All by one author? All gory? All about sibling rivalry? All muddy prose filled with flowery adjectives?

Sometimes I was particularly interested in the students' understanding of mentor relationships and asked them to bring a body of work from an author they admire. "What would you like to do that this writer does?," I would begin. Along the way I would usually ask, "How would you go about learning from this writer?" Sometimes I would even ask the student to select a favorite passage and, as an experiment, to try to imitate the style. Students usually begin asking me questions about the apprentice role. "Do you have to write about the same topic?" "Are you allowed to copy parts?" "Can your friend be your mentor?" "How do you imitate a writer?" The questions they ask me are often as revealing as their answers to mine.

Pat, a third-grade teacher at P.S. 148, gives up her lunch hours during the third or fourth week of school, but she doesn't conduct individual interviews. Instead, she spends the time tape-recording several students talking about the text she has read aloud before lunch. By week's end, she has all thirty students on tape.

The day I visited she had read aloud two picture books. One, *Teddy Rabbit,* by Kathy Stinson is the story of a young boy who drops his stuffed rabbit onto the subway tracks en route to a teddy bear picnic. The second, *I Wonder How the Frog Died,* was written by a first grader named Jemina. It reads,

> I wonder how our class frog died
> The snails are sleeping in their tank
> for they cannot tell
> The newt is busy swimming
> for he cannot tell
> The chameleon is too far away
> for he cannot tell
> The gerbil is too busy running around
> for he cannot tell
> My teacher is not too busy
> so she may be able to tell.

Pat simply asks, "What do you think?" and lets the tape roll. She's listening to the quality of their talk. Do they talk only about the content? Do they include craft? Do they talk about both books at the same time? Is their talk filled with clichés? What information are they bringing to this year's reading-writing workshop? Who doesn't talk? Who doesn't stop talking?

As Pat studies the recording, she learns a lot about individual children. In fact, she keeps a small loose-leaf notebook with a section for each child. Throughout the year, she tries to assemble a portrait of each student as a reader and a writer.

That day she noted that Karen liked *Teddy Rabbit* because she "likes stuffed animals and kids who have security blankets." She doesn't like Jemina's book because she "doesn't like frogs, especially dead ones." Karen could not shift from the content of the story to the quality of the writing, as many of the other students had.

Pedro commented, "I like Jemina's story because it has repetition, but I like *Teddy Rabbit* even though there's no repetition. The students agreed. Pat realized that her students think of repetition only as refrains, repeated words. They did not recognize repetition in the mood, characters, art, or theme in *Teddy Rabbit.*

Pat found José's comments intriguing. He said, "Karen had taste in words, a sweet taste." She also noted that Jessica's talk was filled with "teacher-pleasing" words ("the writer paints pictures and uses colorful language"). She made a note to probe Jessica's use of these clichés.

Ted Chittendom of Educational Testing Services recently visited one of our weekly staff meetings and spoke of story time as an alternative method of reader assessment. Teachers can evaluate a child's attention to, interpretation of, and connection to the story. And they can listen to students' ideas about the quality of the text and note the language the students use to convey those ideas.

Writing About Ourselves as Readers and Writers

When my daughter, J.J., left for college, my sister sewed a patchwork quilt for her dormitory bed. It was made up of squares from the T-shirts my daughter had worn and adored over her seventeen years. The quilt honored every school she had attended, club she had belonged to, city she had fallen in love with, team she had rooted for, and orchestra she had played in. It's a tradition in our family to begin something new by looking back on what you've done before.

In our staff development work at Teachers College we often begin summer institutes, adult reading circles, and semester long in-service courses by looking back on what we bring to who we are as teachers of reading and writing. One effective way to get started is to make time lines of ourselves as both readers and writers. Teacher Susan Woodard recalls her history as a writer (Figure 10).

Sometimes we ask teachers to enrich their time lines by adding turning points, key people who've been influential, either positively or negatively, as well as books that linger in their memories. Then we ask them to elaborate on the most significant moment on their time lines, much the same way I asked the fifth graders to reflect on the songs in their lives.

Judy Davis wrote about recently finding her sixth-grade report card and seeing her teacher's comment, "Finally reading on grade level." Esther Berkowitz

FIGURE 10

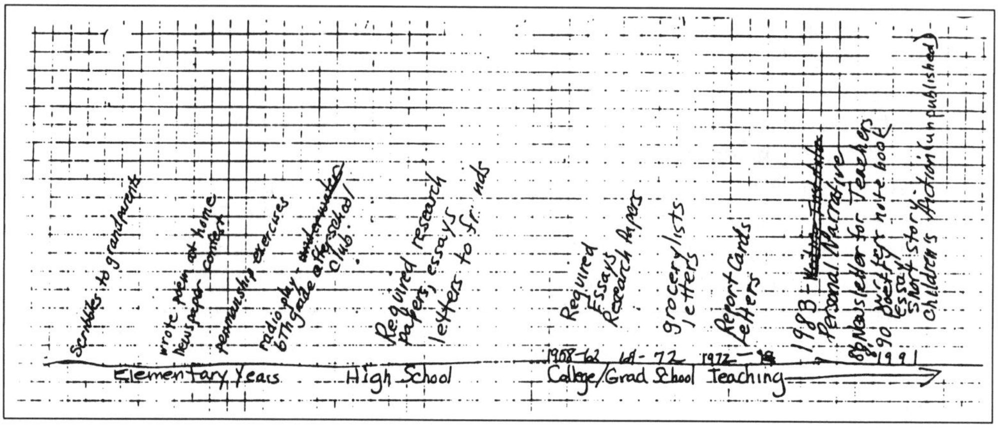

FIGURES 11 and 12

Time line of Learning to Write | Time line of Learning to Read

- When I was 2 I used to write on the walls of my father and my mothers bedroom

- When I was 3 I used to think scribbling was writing.

- When I was 5 years old, I. though that geometric shapes were part of the alphabet.

- When I was in 3rd grade I thought I was a great script writer,

- When I was in 4 th grade. I thought I was a genius in writing. Write better and think my entries are strong and I love writing

- when I was 2 or 3 years old my father and mother read books to me in my bedroom and my brother's bedroom

- When I was 4 years old I read to my brother every and I taught him how to rea

- When I was in 1st grade, I started to get into Judy Blume books.

- when I was in 3rd grade I started to get into thicker books.

- Now I love reading novels about Judy blume and 6 grade.

Jennifer

- In Pre-school, I used to try writing full sentences!

- 1st grade when I started to write cards. Every body loved them.

- 2nd grade - when I published my first book and I thought it was bad. But nobody else thought so.

- 4th grade - I loved doing writing because it was different from 3rd.

- Now, when I cuddle up under the kitchen table and write.

- Kinder garten. Pretending to know read books. Started going to the library.

- 1st grade - I read big books and loved them. I also loved pop-up books.

- 2nd - I read basil readers and hated them.

- 3rd - I started to read road signs and thicker books I loved reading even more

- 4th - I went to the library a lot and took out poem books and regular books.

- 5th - I love reading and I find a lot of words I don't know in my books. I love reading mysteri Nancy Drew, Baby Sitters Sweet Vally Twins.

Danielle

remembered reading *Moby Dick* in a torturous fashion in high school. She recalled tearing the book into pieces at the semester's end and dropping them one by one into a nearby sewer.

One Brooklyn teacher stunned the class by capturing a time when a principal created his own means of censorship. There was a tragedy in the borough. A young boy had climbed the fence of the Prospect Park Zoo and been mauled to death by the bears. The principal, remembering the page in Anthony Browne's *Gorilla* in which the child enters the zoo at night, ordered all copies of the book removed from the building. Later that day, he informed the staff that he had thought of a better solution. He had torn the page out of each copy.

Students too can write time lines and then elaborate on the key moments. Figures 11 and 12 illustrate how Jennifer and Danielle responded.

FIGURE 13

9/12/00

When I was three years old, my mother and father told my folk and faily tales. But when I know the tales by heart but I ask my mother to tell it agin.

When I was four my parents taght me how to write, so I could read my self. Just now I thought of Eills island, and when the place open agin, and people's memoriors of when they came here, and how it feel not to see gold pavement, Candy Cane instead of poles, but they wore happy to see it was free in America.

When I was six, (1st grade) my teacher taght me how to sound out the word out.

When I was seven (2nd grade) I had working books. Than I went to another school, this school. (P.S. 148.)

When I was eight (3rd grade) I had writing prass instead of workbooks.

(Thank God, I hate workbooks!)

Kaity combined her history as a reader and a writer (Figure 13).

As their teachers had done, the students were asked to reread their time lines in order to ask themselves questions and make discoveries about themselves. They were then asked to expand on any moments they thought particularly significant. Kareen tried to capture her earliest memories of learning to read and write (Figure 14).

I was particularly interested in students' memories of having been read aloud to, and at one point I asked them to make a separate time line of those memories, as Yoorak has done (Figure 15). I also asked students to elaborate on moments that were especially significant. Unlike Yoorak, many did have strong memories of having been read to at home (Figure 16).

I was interested in these read-aloud memories because I suspected that there was a strong correlation between the ability to write in literary ways and a rich oral language background. I imagined returning to this data once the students were drafting and revising pieces. Although I did not expect to learn much from their memories at this point, I found that I did. These poignant passages reminded me that even the graduating class derives incredible pleasure from being read aloud to. I was reminded of how crucial it is for students to feel important and for their efforts to be encouraged and celebrated.

FIGURE 14

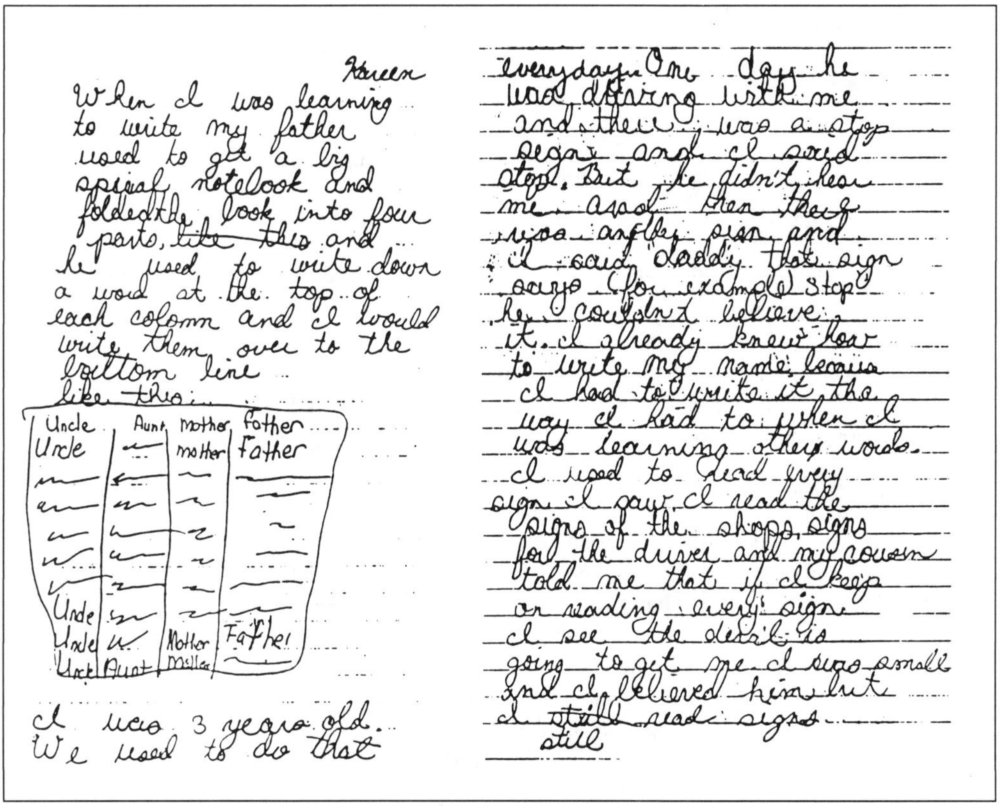
Kareen

When I was learning to write my father used to get a big spiral notebook and folded the book into four parts, ~~like this~~ and he used to write down a word at the top of each colomn and I would write them over to the bottom line like this:

Uncle	Aunt	mother	father
Uncle		mother	Father
Uncle			
Uncle		Mother	Father
Uncle	Aunt	Mother	

I was 3 years old. We used to do that everyday. One day he was driving with me and there was a stop sign and I said stop. But he didn't hear me and then there was another sign and I said daddy that sign says (for example) stop he couldn't believe it. I already knew how to write my name because I had to write it the way I had to when I was learning other words. I used to read every sign I saw. I read the signs of the shops, signs for the driver and my cousin told me that if I keep on reading every sign I see the devil is going to get me. I was small and I believed him but I still read signs still

FIGURE 15

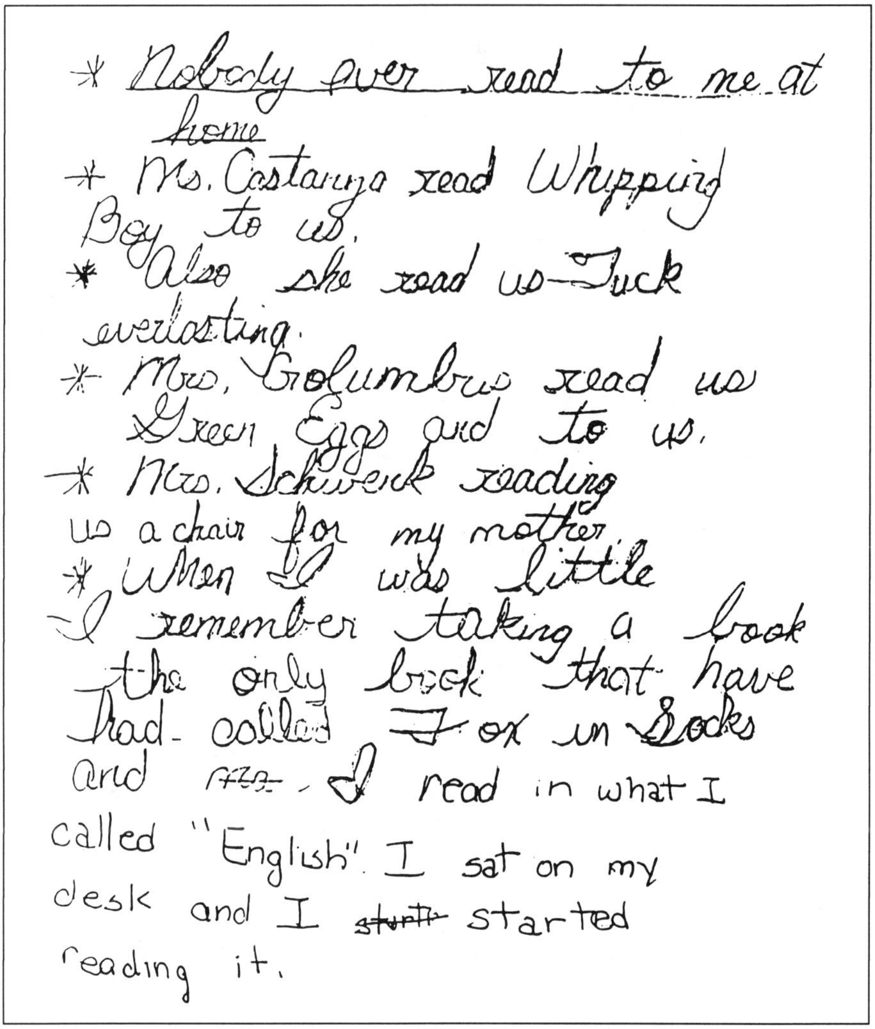

> * Nobody ever read to me at home
> * Ms. Castanza read Whipping Boy to us.
> * Also she read us Tuck everlasting.
> * Mrs. Columbus read us Green Eggs and to us.
> * Mrs. Schweck reading us a chair for my mother.
> * When I was little I remember taking a book the only book that have had called Fox in Socks and ___. I read in what I called "English". I sat on my desk and I ~~stur~~ started reading it.

The students recorded their time line memories along with other crucial scenes from their lives as readers and writers. Antoinette would often ask them to free-write over long weekends on any one of the following topics:

- Thoughts about buying, lending, losing books.
- Games played with reading and writing.
- Moments when you moved an audience with your words.
- Feelings about your earliest published work.
- Pieces you plan to save forever and why.
- Comments on the best writer you know.
- Goals for yourself as a reader, as a writer.
- Times when reading helped your writing.
- Times when writing helped your reading.

FIGURE 16

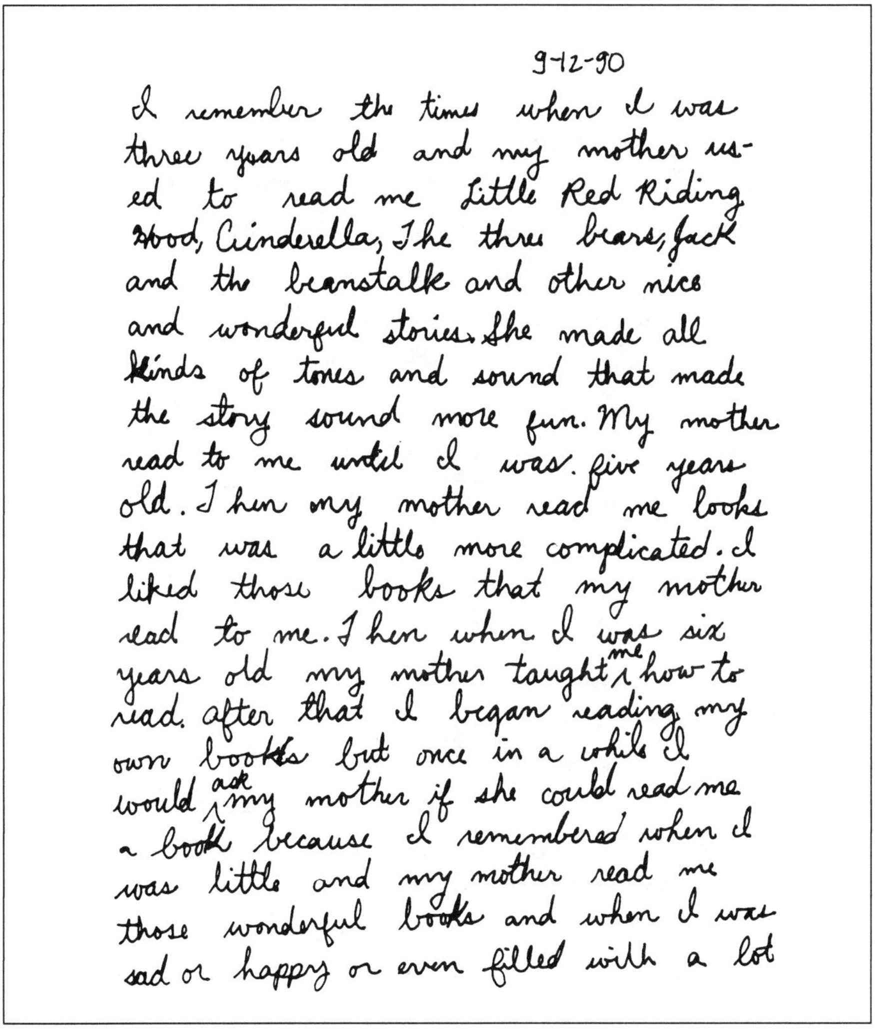

9-12-90

I remember the times when I was three years old and my mother used to read me Little Red Riding Hood, Cinderella, The three bears, Jack and the beanstalk and other nice and wonderful stories. She made all kinds of tones and sound that made the story sound more fun. My mother read to me until I was five years old. Then my mother read me books that was a little more complicated. I liked those books that my mother read to me. Then when I was six years old my mother taught me how to read. after that I began reading my own books but once in a while I would ask my mother if she could read me a book because I remembered when I was little and my mother read me those wonderful books and when I was sad or happy or even filled with a lot

The students also wrote in response to literature that had been read aloud in class (see Chapter 3).

Well-crafted, richly detailed scenes from published memoirs can inspire teachers and students to recall and record their own literacy memories. At teacher meetings I read John Steinbeck's painful description of learning to read from *The Acts of King Arthur and His Noble Knights.* "Words," he writes, "were devils, and books, because they gave me pain, were my enemies."

I read Russell Baker's recollection of writing an essay about "The Art of Eating Spaghetti" in *Growing Up,* Annie Dillard's description of her town library and the books she loved most from *An American Childhood,* and Patricia Hampl's powerful opening scene describing her Czech grandmother's response to seeing an old family album of photographs from Prague in her memoir, *A Romantic Education.*

I also read Eudora Welty's description in *One Writer's Beginnings* of her mother reading aloud "in the big bedroom in the mornings, when we were in her rocker

FIGURE 16, continued

of joy. I loved those great moments and times when I cried. I loved my mom a lot because she did such a wonderful thing for me and I enjoyed it a lot. She made me feel like I could read already. I miss those wonderful times and moments. Now I could read my stories but I will always remember those times. I will never forget them. I love them. Now everything changes in the life. I remember when mom read me those stories and I loved it now I read stories to my mother and she feels the same way. happy, sad, filled with joy or crying or she goes to sleep when I read her my stories like I used to do. I tell her to lie down and I will read her some nice and wonderful stories and she really enjoys them, likes them just the way I did. Now mom makes me feel like I am an important person and that she needs me a lot. And I feel that I am an important person too. I like reading to mom and I enjoy the book too and my job is to help my mother in what ever she needs and to read to her as much as my mother would like.

Edward

FIGURE 16, continued

I remember last Christmas when my mother read a book to me and Matthew called: Love You Forever.

Mommy was sitting on the rocker that was facing the Christmas Tree. Me and Matthew sat on the rocker's arms staring at the Christmas Tree. Then she started reading. My favorite line was:

I'll love you forever
I'll like you for always,
As long as I'm living
My baby you'll be.

The dedication she wrote said this:

Merry Christmas,
To My Two Babies
Who Will always be
My Babies
With All My Heart and
Soul
Forever Love,

Mommy

I felt happy to know that my mother will always love me no matter how old I get!

Danielle

together, which ticked in rhythm as we rocked, as though we had a cricket accompanying the story."

These memories resonate for teachers, who respond not only to the content but also to the style. The personal moments they record themselves seem to take on the same vignette feel.

This procedure also works well with students. I read them passages from the Reading Is Fundamental publication "Once Upon a Time." Judy Blume recalls not wanting to return *Madeline* to the library. Natalie Babbitt describes her love affair with the alphabet. Jean Fritz remembers being sick in bed reading *Peter Pan*.

I also read selected passages from the published memoirs of children's writers. In *Dear Mem Fox* Mem Fox writes about memorizing poetry. In *How I Came to Be a Writer* Phyllis Reynolds Naylor explains how she used her books as toys. In *A Grain of Wheat* Clyde Bulla tells why he loved the books he received for Christmas. I also share Jean Little's description of learning to use a fountain pen in *Little by Little* and Beverly Cleary's memories of her very first picture books in *A Girl from Yamhill*.

Reading these evocative, beautifully crafted scenes aloud to students reminded them of their own memories. At the same time, the writing seemed to influence their writing style. Their notebook entries were often longer, slower, and filled with sensory detail.

Good Writing and Mentorship

Most of the writing tasks so far have revealed a lot about students' backgrounds as readers and writers but little about their sense of good writing or of mentorship. The following are activities that address these issues.

After I read Paul Fleischman's *The Half-A-Moon Inn* to the students I duplicated the first page on eight-and-a-half-by-fourteen-inch paper, even though standard size would have sufficed. I wanted wide margins so that students could free-write about what they noticed in the text.

> Aaron awoke to the sharp cry of sea gulls, suddenly remembered what day it was and burst out of bed as though the sheets were afire. He could hear that his mother was already up, hitching the horse to the wagon. He scrambled into his clothes, scooped up an armload of woolen cloth and shot out the door—for today they'd be traveling to Craftsbury!
>
> "Whoever you are behind all that wool—good morning to you!" called his mother. Aaron smiled and scurried by her, his arms piled high with the wool she'd washed and dyed and spun and woven into cloth. He felt as restless as a chipmunk on the first day of spring, for it was but once every month

The students were asked to "talk about the way Paul Fleischman writes," using the margins to record their thoughts (Figure 17).

It was helpful to look at the responses individually. Benny appreciated precise verbs, while Jerry admired strong imagery and Alejandro pointed out the writer's power to involve the reader in the character's lives. Kareen's reaction to writing about the author's craft was to highlight her favorite parts. Kaity connected the story to her own life. For Luis it was a struggle to respond at all.

It was also helpful to look at the data across the class. Very few children commented on the page as a lead to a book. Those who did respond to Fleischman's style often used clichés. Most students did as Kareen did, reacting to content rather than craft.

FIGURE 17

I think he has a good way of writing "he burst out of bed as though the sheets were afire." It makes you see in your mind how fast Aaron got out of bed.

Jerry

Nothing

Maybe how the Author describes

Luis

Paul Fleischman has a way of describing the things. and D has a way of, making you find the feelings.

Alejandro

_I like to travel to new place or go to that place

I like when Aaron's mother said about Good morning like a kind mother will do.

Kaity

My favorite part is when "Aaron's mother said "Whoever you are behind all that wool— good morning to you," I like it because it sounds like Aaron isn't mute to me because it's like Aaron forgot to say good morning, and just smiled.

Kareen

It was like suddenly he burst out of bed, it's like that he was in a big hurry. What I mean is that instead of jumping out of bed the author wrote he bursted out of bed so he could make the story more excting, same thing with the scrambled his clothes instead she should wrote he got into his clothes

Benny

Antoinette planned to distribute this page several times again during the year to see if children's ability to read like writers changed over time.

We also probed students' understanding of mentors. As a homework assignment, Antoinette asked students to free-write about someone in their lives outside of school who served as a mentor. The results were often surprising. Felix wrote

> My mentor is my stuffed toy called Papito. Because of him I have a stronger imagination. Since I make believe stuff, I need someone to encourage me. Also he encourages me to have fun.

As her mentor Yoorak listed Connie Chung, the television news anchorwoman. From her, Yoorak learned to "always act businesslike, sit with your back straight and head held up high, like you're proud of yourself, always wear a suit, always speak clear, don't mumble, don't let your voice squeak out, and most of all, act like you know what you're doing." Antoinette says knowing this about Yoorak has helped her in working with this very ambitious and diligent student. She also looks at Felix with new eyes, knowing how important his make-believe world is to him. "More than that," she says, "their ideas about mentors inform my ways of introducing authors to them. I want them to have positive feelings about entering mentor relationships."

On yet another morning, I asked the fifth graders to list the questions they'd ask their favorite authors if they had a chance. (Students who didn't have a favorite author were asked to think of any author they admired.) This task was informed by a newspaper article I had read years before in which Beverly Cleary criticized the letters she receives from school children. She wondered why children want to know an author's favorite ice cream, or color, or television program." I hoped that our students' questions would be more targeted, more concerned with the author's writing process.

Early in the year and then again in the spring, Maria listed James Herriot as her favorite writer. In September she wanted to know how many pets he had, how much money he earned, and where he went to school. Later in the year she made the list in Figure 18.

Antoinette also planned to repeat this quick exercise several more times during the year in order to discover whether students' favorite authors changed and what they thought they could learn from an accomplished writer.

As I have suggested, many of these beginning-of-the-year activities would be repeated throughout the year. We planned to turn them into rituals in order to follow students' learning. When students know that the first Friday of the month is a time to write in the margins of a copy of a favorite text and that every Monday morning time is set aside for reflective writing, they come expecting to write and they come prepared. Unless important activities like these become rituals that occur at predictable times, it is too easy for the special events, pull-out programs, and extraordinary curriculum demands to fill our days.

Sharing Personal Artifacts

Props get people talking, touching, marveling, writing. There are glimpses of these moments throughout Chapter 2. We shared the "most-read books" in our homes, newspapers in many languages, even our old report cards. Of course, not everyone brought in items in every category. In fact, students often surprised us by bringing in their own private treasures. They knew they had a captive audience.

FIGURE 18

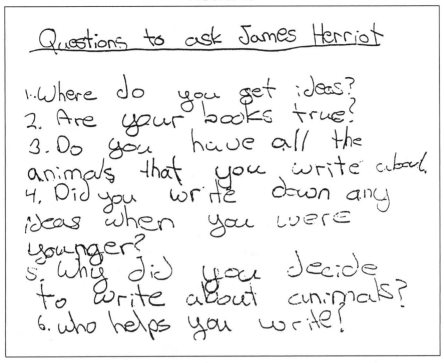

One day Katherine showed us an old Skittles candy wrapper she had ironed, which she had been using as a bookmark for over two years. The next day we had a corner collection of unusual items used as bookmarks—laminated locks of hair, flattened straws, ice cream sticks, and broken bits of garland.

Stacey brought in Eloise Wilkin's *Golden Book of Mother Goose Rhymes* and the next day we had an elaborate collection of our favorite "baby" books—board books, books with zippers and shoelaces, scratch and sniff books, and even books that could survive bubble baths.

Jeanine shared her Chinese printing and the next day we had enough writing samples in Urdu, Korean, Hebrew, and Arabic to fill the back bulletin board.

One day I brought in a poem I had written when I was a seventh-grade math student that only ten-year-olds would appreciate.

> What is
> What is
> What is it to me?
> What really is Geometry?
> I think it is of no use
> To know a triangle from an obtuse

On it went for several sappy rhyming stanzas.

By week's end we had several students' earliest attempts at poetry covering the bulletin board. Some were variations on "Roses are red, Violets are blue." Most were filled with moon and June, flowers and showers. Antoinette suggested that when they had done a poetry course of study in December, they could hang their latest attempts next to these early ones.

Personal artifacts did much more than create beautiful, interesting settings in which to read and write. The items students shared often served as a fulcrum around which other activities developed.

One month before classes begin in September, Cynthia sends a letter of welcome to the incoming students in her fourth-grade class. She tells them a little bit about what their school year will be like and asks them to bring several items with them on the very first day of school. These include the best piece of writing they've ever done, a piece of professional writing they admire (one they wish they'd written) and a piece they'd be comfortable reading aloud to kindergarten students.

On the first day of school, the three pieces become central to classroom activities. During writing time the children share their best piece of writing with a partner and then do a reflective piece explaining their choice. During reading time the students display the professional texts across the chalkboard ledge and then select one to read. Their own favorites form the classroom library for the first weeks of school. The books chosen for kindergarten students launch a class discussion of the importance of reading aloud and sharing their own early childhood memories. Then Cynthia marks the calendar. In two weeks' time the students will be reading to a group of kindergarten children and will continue to do so every two weeks for the entire year.

Cynthia learns a lot from her students on that first day of school. She reads the students' reflective pieces trying to understand their choices. Many select pieces about birthdays and holidays as their best, pieces with the "best" content but not necessarily the best crafting. Some choose pieces because they are their longest or demonstrate their best illustrations or handwriting. Cynthia usually discovers a few students who have chosen a favorite piece because they're proud of its literary quality.

The chalkboard library also gives Cynthia a feel for her students' sense of good writing. Some years she is awed by her students' choices. The finest writers are lined up on the ledge in a wide range of genres—poetry, nonfiction, picture books. Other times their selections are limited to books from a formulaic series. Their contributions help Cynthia decide which books to read aloud that year, which genres to study, and how to stock the class library.

Even the choices for kindergarten listeners reveal a great deal about the students' insights into literature. Some bring in their own favorite bedtime stories. Others select books with content and format that are too sophisticated for very young children. Cynthia is always delighted when fourth graders choose to read their own work to five-year-olds.

Later that first week, Cynthia makes a point of being up front with her students. She lets them in on what she's learning about them and what her hopes for the year are. "As the year goes on," she tells them, "I'm hoping more and more of you will be proud to read some of your own work up and down the corridors of this school. This is a year for us to read literature and to write literature. This is a year for us to let the literature we read help us improve the literature we write."

Now What?

Beginning early and continuing throughout the school year, we collect data on our students. We take notes on their conversations. We read their writing. We marvel at what they bring to share with their classmates. We also watch them at work as they visit the library, attend book fairs, play with puppets, decorate the classroom, and work as teachers' helpers in the kindergarten rooms. We have a folder for each student and we file surveys and questionnaires and interview notes and scraps of paper with random observations. So much data. So what?

Perhaps the only way these data take on any importance is if we allow them to inform our individual work with each student as well as our broader curriculum designs and decisions.

What became essential to both Antoinette and me was studying the data. We wanted to put this information to good use, so we looked at it in several different ways. We looked at each student's folder filled with seemingly unrelated bits and pieces. In his wonderful memoir, *String Too Short to be Saved,* Donald Hall explains the source of his title. "A man was cleaning the attic of an old house in New England and he found a box which was full of tiny pieces of string. On the lid of the box there was an inscription in an old hand: 'String too short to be saved.'"

Sometimes it seemed we had scraps of paper too unimportant to be saved. When we reread Marco's folder, though, we were reminded that he prefers *TV Guide* reading, rarely finishes a book, has no favorite writer, and considers social studies his favorite school subject. Antoinette made some quick notes inside Marco's folder. She would talk to him about historical fiction, readers' theater, and perhaps a reading partner.

We also studied the folders in clusters or cumulatively. As Jerry Harste suggests, the children became our curricular informants. We looked at one issue across all the students and allowed that to inform our teaching. We now had new insights about the place of newspaper reading, letter writing, and reading aloud in the year to come.

We reread the data looking for relationships between different issues. We wondered if students who had a clear understanding of mentor relationships might also be those who were more likely to have favorite writers.

We looked at all the information on just four or five students. We knew we couldn't study all of them equally, and so we chose just a few to study deeply. We then spent additional time interviewing the chosen ones and allowed the portraits we assembled on a handful of students to help us teach the entire class.

When you learn that students attend after-school and weekend classes to learn Chinese, Korean, and Hebrew, you realize how little free time students have for reading and writing outside of school. When you learn that many students are responsible for helping family members fill out applications and follow English instructions, you begin to wonder if those activities should be part of your reading-writing workshop. When you learn that students travel long distances to borrow books in their first language, you rethink your class and school library collections.

The activities described in this chapter took place during the very first weeks of school along with our efforts to build community, play with language, and honor diversity. They also took place along with a gracious invitation to students to write in response to fine literature.

4

Literature as a Seedbed for Discovering Topics

Every man is a borrower and a mimic, life is theatrical and literature a quotation.

Ralph Waldo Emerson

Last autumn, I launched a teacher workshop by suggesting that "the way to begin thinking about our students' reading-writing connections is for us to think about our own." I then read aloud several short, yet powerful texts, including the following *New York Times* editorial.

The Girls Who Had Everything

Fairy godmothers are not distributed equally, but the same witch appears at every birth. Her gift is vulnerability: once delivered into the world no child is ever safe again. Parents know this. That's why they're forever yelling "Don't touch!" and calling the pediatrician and fretting when the baby doesn't finish his bottle. That's why they turn deaf ears when their children beg to walk to school alone, go to the store alone, play in the vacant lot on their way home. That's why parents are such terrible pests.

Parents also know that there's no protection against the lightning bolt, the toppling cornice, the car that comes out of nowhere. Children, however, know none of these things. But if they are ever to find them out, if they are ever to grow up, they have to do it on their own. That's why parents, even when they are very old, shiver when the telephone rings late at night.

Two months ago a girl at whose birth there were many fairy godmothers was strangled in Central Park. This week another girl with many godmothers was killed by a speeding car. Both have been described as "preppies," who moved in the "same wealthy social circle" and hung out in the same "preppie bar." They didn't really, but never mind. What's being created here is not a story but a subtext. It reads, "That's what you get for being so rich."

In that subtext there's an implication: that each of us is weighed on some eternal scale, and that if we are perceived to have "everything" then something must be take away. But all those who have ever raised and loved children know better than to embrace so cruel a doctrine. Instead they curse that witch who attends every birth, whether it be to the rich or the poor, and against whom there is no defense.

I also read this passage from a Harvard guide for freshman.

For parents, the freedom we mentioned is perhaps the hardest thing to deal with. When the medical-student-since-twelve you sent to Harvard tells you that high school teaching is now the plan, or when the sure-to-be-an-Olympic-swimmer you drove through rain and snow to age-group swim meets exchanges varsity swimming for Harvard theatre, or when the one who was certain to major in economics, go to business school and take over the firm, instead decides on English, don't take it as deliberate hurt or as a rejection of all you have done together as parents and children. Almost always it is neither. It is a young person setting out on his or her own life's course. Don't try to hold the course you set and have been sailing together for seventeen years. It is very hard to sail a ship with two pilots. You should come along, but always keep in mind that it is a new voyage, someone else's voyage. This way, college can be the shared and happy embarkation it ought to be.

I ended with this poem written by our friend Arlene Mandell.

Little Girl Grown

Monday I tied blue ribbons in her hair
before she went to school
Tuesday I packed her teddy bear
and she was off to camp.
Friday I drove her to college
with her silver flute.
Sunday she moved to Manhattan with her fiance.

Will the neighbors on East 35th Street
please see that she doesn't dawdle
on her way to work?
She's the one with the flute
and the teddy bear
and blue ribbons
in her hair.

I then gave the teachers a brief period to work on their own writing. "If possible," I suggested, "allow these pieces to inform your own work."

When we reconvened, I referred to the kinds of reading-writing connections Nancie Atwell describes in *In the Middle*. Asking for a show of hands, I surveyed the room.

"How many connected to the genre, were inspired to write a poem or an editorial or a parent handout?" No hands went up.

"How many connected to a stylistic device or a literary technique you admired?" No hands went up.

"How many connected to the topics, to the content of the pieces?" Most of the hands went up.

And I wasn't surprised. After all, all those gathered were teachers, people who cared about children. All were sons or daughters, people who have left home, left families. Some were parents, people who continue to worry about their own sons and daughters. It was no wonder then that their pages filled with old memories and new fears, personal stories as well as professional ones, and even a letter or two to a child away at college.

I understood why the adults made important topic choice connections. The pieces "touched home." They sparked the "shock of recognition" many writers speak of. I also thought I understood why teachers were unable to connect to genre or literary technique. After all, they had only heard me read the texts aloud once. To connect to the form or shape, to borrow a literary device, they'd need to hold those pieces in their hands, to read and reread them, to dwell deeply in them and study them closely.

But my colleague Dorothy Barnhouse has helped me see that there's another reason to explain why connections to topics were so prevalent that day. The teachers hadn't written for a long time. They weren't working on any drafts, they weren't trying to solve any problems in their own work in progress. If one of the teachers had been struggling with ending her poem, perhaps she might think to herself, "Arlene's last line really works. I admire the way she returns to the earlier images. I wonder if that technique would work for me? I wonder if it would have that same powerful effect?"

At adult reading and writing workshops, Dorothy often asks people to begin by reading and responding to a short story. She then directs the participants to "write from their obsession with the piece." Only those who are struggling with their own texts seek to replicate something they admire in the piece. The others make topic choice connections. Perhaps a word, a line, a passage, or their own interpretation of the text suggest ideas for their own writing.

Truman Capote once said, "When I write a book, it is like a seed from which you can grow your own plant." I suppose that's why literature is an especially good friend early in the school year. Students, like the teachers at the workshop, haven't as yet found their stride as writers. They often think they have nothing to write about. Their lives don't seem worth writing about. They don't know they have stories to tell or they don't have the courage to tell them. The late Polish writer Jerzy Kosinski once said that the students at Yale don't write well because they don't believe they have anything interesting to say. It's not just Ivy League students; all our children need to believe they have something interesting to say. Literature plays a key role in helping children's voices take the floor. Literature triggers thoughts, unlocks memories, and helps create the kind of community in which it's safe to tell our stories.

Rethinking the Role of Literature

Literature does indeed play a key role in our writing workshops and yet over the years the teachers I know best have been reluctant to focus on literature as a means of helping students find their own topic for writing. Literature was fine if it helped students study a genre or revise a draft, but it was not supposed to give them topics. That was their responsibility. Suggesting that a piece of literature might help our students find their own topics was somehow connected to "story-starter" activities.

When Tony Petrosky, a noted authority in the field of reader response theory, visited our project several years ago at a time when we were first experimenting with writer's notebooks, he was surprised that students kept separate notebooks for reading and writing. In his own life, he explained, they're all of a piece. Why should it be different for our students? We respond to reading the same way we respond to everything. Reading is just another thing that happens.

Tony was right. Now our stomachs don't tighten when we hear Tom Newkirk say, "Stories enable stories." And we don't shrink in our seats when we hear Jane Yolen say, "Stories lean on stories." Instead, we nod our heads in agreement. We know it to be true. We've not only come to appreciate that responding to literature can help students find their own topics for writing, we've come to value literature as a major resource for generating topics.

In years past if we began the writing workshop by reading a story about a birthday celebration, we used to worry that all thirty students would write about birthday celebrations. We no longer worry. Our new appreciation for the connection between literature and topic choice is grounded in five key changes in our work.

First, most of our teachers and students have made the writer's notebook a regular part of their writing lives. These beautiful blank books are used to gather generative bits and pieces of writing for possible later development. Most notebook entries are not traditional stories with beginnings, middles, and endings. Instead, students use their notebook as a container for free and reflective writing, random thoughts, musings, questions, anecdotes, captions, wordplay, poems, and of course, occasional narrative pieces.

Ideas come from everywhere—from family stories, haunting images, and overheard conversations, from firsthand experiences as well as responses to movies and museums and social studies lessons. And of course, entries are sparked by the novel students are reading at home in bed as well as the birthday story the teacher has read aloud.

Whatever the writer deems significant is grist for the literary mill. Our colleague, writer Vicki Vinton, suggests that "where the ideas come from is never as important as where the ideas lead." When children reread their notebook pages they make surprising discoveries, find recurring themes, and follow new pathways of thinking.

Today, if students choose to respond to a birthday story, we trust that for them the story was in some way significant. For one student the entry may lead to some important thinking and later a finished piece of writing. For others the entry may remain just one of many notebook jottings.

Our teaching has also changed because we've become more acquainted with the research on reader response theory. We now appreciate the fact that individual readers will each have a unique response to a text because of the individual experiences they bring to the act of reading. Readers cannot separate themselves from their reading. They cannot help but read texts their own way.

Although we expect a diversity of responses to any text, our teaching has changed in yet a third way. We've become a lot more selective about which texts we choose to share with students. Now we don't choose just any birthday story.

At an International Reading Association convention in New Orleans, Don Holdaway, in critiquing what has recently been published in the name of Big Books, reminded the audience that the literature we choose must be like the food in New Orleans, "rich, enticing, and full of flavor."

This criterion holds for books throughout the grades. Texts that are rich, enticing, and full of flavor are more often those with layers of meaning and those that will more likely lead to a rich variety of personal responses. If we choose a well-written birthday story, one student might be reminded of how hard his mom works to prepare his birthday parties, another might think about celebrating a birthday after a best friend has moved away, and yet another might begin to wonder what it will be like to grow old. As Ralph Peterson and Mary Ann Eeds suggest in *Grand Conversations,* "If you want grand conversations you need grand books." If you want grand topic-choice connections, you also need grand books.

Fourth, we've come to realize that the "me, too" feeling we often get when we've read something powerful is no small thing. After children listen to a story or poem or newspaper article, if the room fills with "that reminds me . . ." and similar kinds of talk, it's cause for celebration. When a student finds a passage that gives him chills because it sounds so much like his own thinking, that's a terribly important event. When a student feels the blood rush to her cheeks so that she can no longer continue reading because she has become so filled with her own life story, that's a terribly important event. When six-year-old Michael hears his teacher read Bill Martin and John Archambault's *Knots on a Counting Rope,* the story of a young blind boy's triumph over his fears—his dark mountains—and then rushes off to send a note to his parents (Figure 19), that too is cause for celebration. Along with dozens of other New York City youngsters Michael has proven to us that Jamake Highwater is correct when he says that "it takes as much imagination to respond to a text as it does to create a text."

Our new appreciation for the connection between literature and topic choice is grounded in a final change in our classroom work: we've begun to crack open the traditional ways students write in response to literature. When our teachers first

FIGURE 19

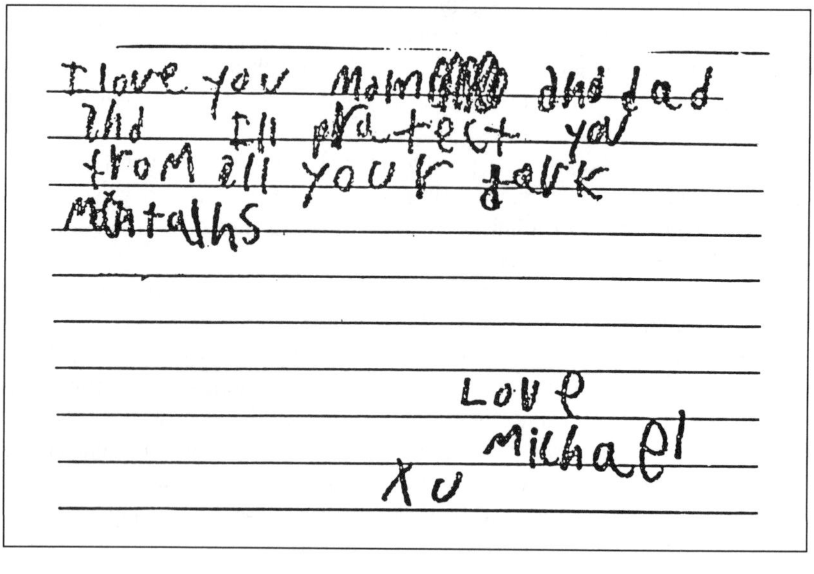

encouraged their students to respond to their reading in their writer's notebook, many were disappointed with the results. Students either retold the entire plot ("This story is about . . .") or wrote in the standard book report format ("I like this story because . . . and hope you do too"). They wrote *about* their reading, not *in response to* their reading.

These concerns were echoed throughout the grades at P.S. 148. In fact, early in the fall semester several teachers and I formed a small study group to explore ways to move students away from such routinized responses. As has become common practice in our work, we began thinking about our students' reading-writing connections by thinking about our own. Teachers brought in their own writer's notebooks and shared entries that had been inspired by their reading. These entries were often the most powerful and most significant. We wondered if there were particular genres, authors, or topics that resonated most deeply in our writing lives. We wondered about the best time for writing—during or after reading. We noticed the variety in our written responses—from quick jottings and long, winding free-writes to narrative passages and occasional poems.

Then we began to think about our students. The teachers asked, "How do we get our students to take risks and stop believing that there's one main idea we want them to write about? How do we get them to trust that it's okay if their writing leads them to surprising places? How do we get them to stop using literature only as a story starter or a model for a parody or sequel? How do we get students to do what we have done and respond to literature in their own unique ways?"

We guessed that the first thing we needed to do was to bring our own notebooks into our classrooms. We needed to demonstrate what a powerful tool literature was in our own writing lives. But we knew this wouldn't be enough. We knew we also needed to nudge young students in new directions.

When Read-Alouds Lead to Diversity of Thought

I began with a picture book, Paul Fleischman's *Rondo in C*. I intended it to be a metaphor for what I hoped would happen in the class whenever we read. A young girl plays Beethoven's Rondo in C and each member of the audience connects to it in an individual, deeply personal way. One remembers a childhood home, another a friend's move far away. After I read the text with the children I suggested, "Just as a piece of music, a smell in the air, or a painting in a museum can jog our brains and get us recalling old memories or thinking about urgent concerns or new ideas, each time you read or are read to you will have your own unique response." I wanted the children to know how much I valued individual responses.

Of course, *Rondo in C* was not a required text. I could have made the same point if I talked about how each member of my family responded to a Broadway play, a television program, a religious sermon, or a presidential speech. "And," I would add, "our responses were not just critical reviews—Yes, I liked it. No, I didn't. Instead, my son began to think about . . . , my daughter about. . . ." There was no one main idea, no one right answer.

Not only do I value diverse responses, I also value responses that are so deeply felt and personal, they help students find their own voices. It's hard to use that teacher-pleasing, question-answering school-voice so many students acquire when you're talking about your grandmother's death or your fears about moving to a new neighborhood.

I explained that sometimes a text touches us so deeply that it gets us thinking about the really important issues in our own lives. "Let your hearts be touched by these writings, let yourselves be moved." "No doubt," I continued, "each of you will respond in a different way. Different parts of the text will stand out for you. Perhaps a character in a story will remind you of someone you know. Perhaps the illustration will get you thinking about a moment in your own life. Maybe you'll connect to the mood of the piece or one word will set you off on a trail of thinking."

Over the next few days I read aloud several powerful texts. These included picture books such as Ann Turner's *Nettie's Trip Down South,* Yukio Tsuchiya's *Faithful Elephants,* Riki Levinson's *Our Home Is the Sea* and short stories from Cynthia Rylant's *Every Living Thing,* Jean Little's poem "Plenty," and Langston Hughes's "Dream Deferred."

After each reading we talked and talked and talked. Students' voices filled the room. I tried not to ignore, critique, or cheer anyone's response. No one was made to feel smarter or slower.

Finally, one morning, instead of talking about the text we wrote.

I had read aloud Kay Chorao's picture book, *Cathedral Mouse,* the story of a homeless mouse that makes friends with a sculptor who is repairing the Cathedral of St. John the Divine in Manhattan. Afterwards, I passed out the biggest yellow-lined stick-on notes I could find. "Instead of talking about our responses," I suggested, "could you each do whatever kind of writing you need to do right now?"

Using their notebooks as lapboards, the students wrote. When they were finished they stuck their yellow stick-ons up on the chalkboard, making a collage that reached clear across the front of the room. Then we all stood back to admire their work, as if viewing an art exhibit in a gallery.

I wanted the students to join me in celebrating their responses. Without even reading their writing we marveled at all the different styles of handwriting, the varied lengths of the responses, and even the doodles on several papers. When we read them we noticed that some students still chose to retell the story or do a quick critique. One student wrote "No Response" as his response.

Those who chose to respond personally to the text displayed a variety of approaches in their content. Most students began with "This story reminds me of . . ." or "My connection to this story is . . ." and then proceeded to share a short personal narrative, the genre they have become so familiar with over the years. Their topics were closely related to the story—finding mice in your apartment, visiting a beautiful church, taking care of a pet, helping a homeless person.

Just as well-crafted, evocative scenes had influenced their style when they wrote about their early literacy memories, so too Chorao's text raised the quality of their notebook writing. Their entries seemed richer and more scenelike than the often bland "the day I found a mouse in my kitchen" pieces I recall so well. Jerry and Jennifer responded with surprising and detailed memories (Figure 20).

Antoinette and I were delighted that the students were becoming so comfortable with this kind of personal writing. Of course, not every story we read resonated for every student, but we never expected that to be true.

After a while, however, we wondered if students weren't being limited by personal narrative. We wondered if their years of writing personal narratives had put them in this rut or if the hours spent telling stories, one bouncing off another, had led them to believe that the only response to a narrative is a narrative.

At the next meeting of our study group we brainstormed ways to challenge students to attempt different kinds of writing when they responded to literature. We invented new writing tasks and selected several genres to read aloud.

FIGURE 20

The story about the mouse reminds me of when I used to be in Elmhurst I lived in a apartment and a old lady lived in the apartment above ours. She used to feed the pigeons. And she had a name for every pigeon, And sometimes you could hear her saying "Don't touch that Ann that's Charlie's food."

Jerry

9-12-90

In the book about the mouse it is like my brothers turtle because when my mom cleans the tank he runs on his feet to go to every room on the second floor and he tries to climb every thing in the bedroom he can find. Also When he is put back in the tank with water he goes on top of the rock and streches out his neck, arms and legs and some times when the sun is out and he is on the rock I say in my mind that he is getting a sun tan.

Jennifer

The next day I shared the poem "Wars" from Jean Little's *Hey World, Here I Am!* and this time I passed out the tiniest yellow stick-on I could find.

> When I was in Grade Two, I said to my father,
> "I think wars are wrong!
> People should be told to stop all this fighting right now.
> If I were crowned Queen of the World,
>   I'd make war against the law."
> My father said I had something there,
> But he didn't seem terribly excited.
> I could not understand him.

> Then I went upstairs and caught my sister Marilyn
> Playing with my new paper dolls without my permission!
>
> We had a war.

When I had finished reading the poem, I said, "Imagine that you are walking home from school with a good friend, someone you can talk to about important things. You've just heard 'Wars.' On this tiny slip of paper, jot down what you would probably talk about."

When they were done writing, I suggested that they open their writer's notebook to the next blank page and stick their yellow note at the very top. Then I said, "Now write to get to the bottom of it." To me, of course, the "it" referred to the issue they would talk about with their good friend. I wanted them to get to the bottom of the idea, to probe it, figure it out. But to the students my words meant something

FIGURE 21

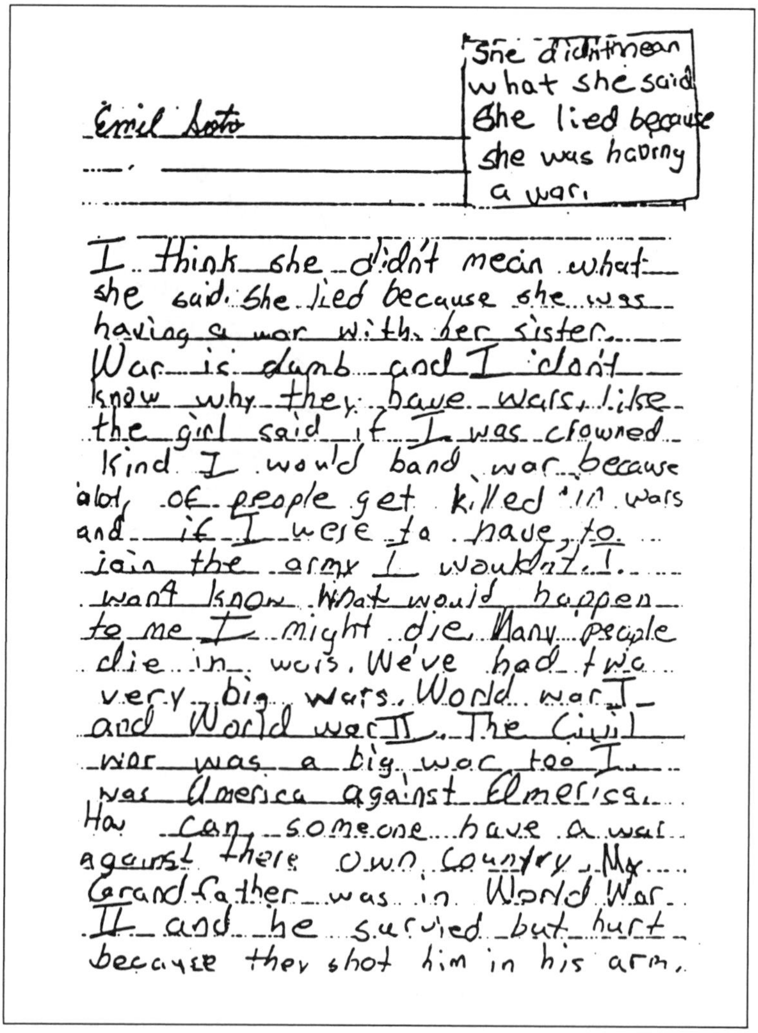
She didn't mean what she said She lied because she was having a war.

Emil Soto

I think she didn't mean what she said. She lied because she was having a war with her sister. War is dumb and I don't know why they have wars, like the girl said if I was crowned Kind I would band war because alot of people get killed in wars and if I were to have to join the army I wouldn't. I want know what would happen to me I might die. Many people die in wars. We've had two very big wars. World war I and World war II. The Civil war was a big war too I was America against America. How can someone have a war against there own country. My Grandfather was in World War II and he survied but hurt because they shot him in his arm.

FIGURE 22

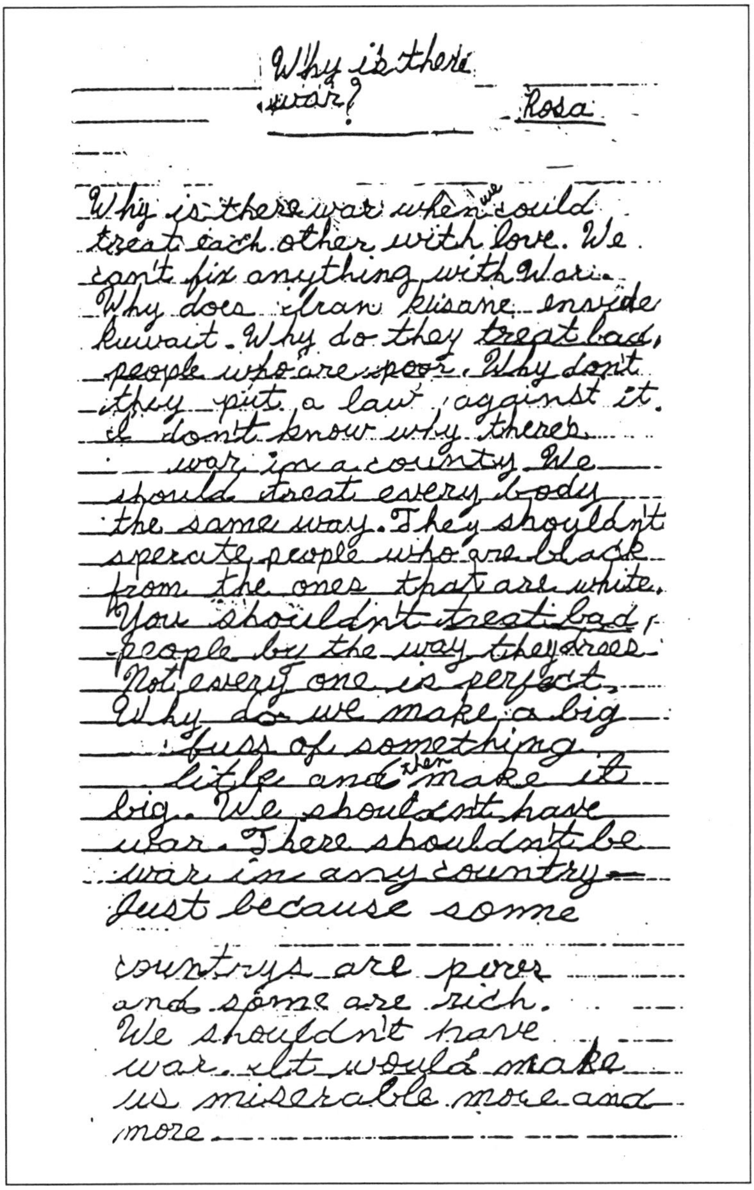

> Why is there
> war?   Rosa
>
> Why is there war when could
> treat each other with love. We
> can't fix anything with War.
> Why does Iran kisane enside
> kuwait. Why do they treat bad,
> people who are poor. Why don't
> they put a law against it.
> I don't know why theres
> war in a county. We
> should treat every body
> the same way. They shouldn't
> sperate people who are black
> from the ones that are white.
> You shouldn't treat bad,
> people by the way they dress.
> Not every one is perfect.
> Why do we make a big
> fuss of something
> litle and make it
> big. We shouldnt have
> war. There shouldnt be
> war in any country.
> Just because some
>
> countrys are porer
> and some are rich.
> We shouldn't have
> war. It would make
> us miserable more and
> more

entirely different. They assumed that "write to get to the bottom of it," meant writing to the bottom of the page. This misunderstanding had surprising results.

Emil's response appears in Figure 21.

On the little yellow stick-on note he talks about the little girl in the poem as a liar. But in his "writing to get to the bottom of it," he addresses a great many more issues. (He had to, since he felt the pressure to get to the bottom of the page.) His thoughts begin to meander. His writing takes on an exploratory feel, one idea bouncing off the last. It conveys a clear sense that Emil is thinking new thoughts.

His writing has moved away from narration toward exposition. The page seems packed with generative one-liners he could elaborate on later in his notebook. Rosa's writing also took off in unexpected directions (Figure 22); her writing has an essaylike quality to it.

Staff developer Randy Bomer is not surprised by the frequent richness of student writing when personal response statements serve as a point of departure. "Partly," he says, "the kids see how significant things can be, and they want to achieve that in their own writing." "I think," he continues, "that it also has something to do with assuming a reflective stance. They've just finished reading and they're pushed to think deeply about what they've read. It's as if that reflective stance carries over into their writing."

I was also able to shift students away from personal narratives when I asked them to begin their responses with a two-column activity. Kareen has labeled the left-hand side "What the story is about" and the right-hand side "What it makes you think about." She is responding to Paul Fleischman's *The Half-A-Moon Inn* (Figure 23).

Kareen knew she could select one of the issues the book had made her think about—illiterate adults, handicapped people—and write to get to the bottom of it, to probe it further. This activity was particularly helpful for students whose responses were primarily plot retellings. They were now able to recall the story and go beyond it.

FIGURE 23

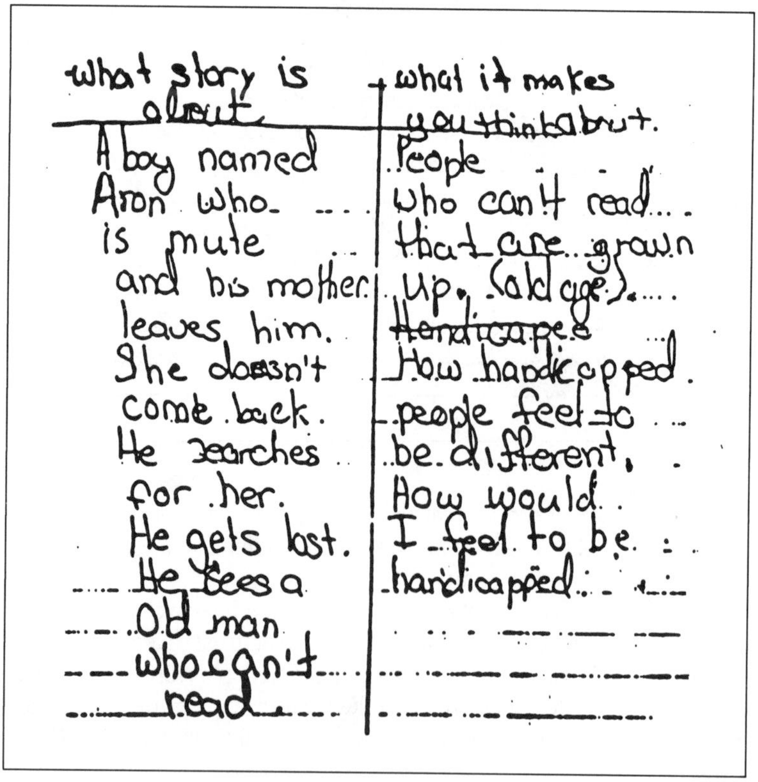

One Friday morning ten minutes before lunchtime I passed out small strips of cardboard. The students were as intrigued by these as they had been by the yellow stick-ons. I explained that I would read four poems aloud and after each one they would do some free-associating. "Jot down any words that come to mind." I read the following four poems:

So Will I

My grandfather remembers long ago
the White Queen Anne's lace that grew wild.
He remembers the buttercups and goldenrod
from when he was a child.

He remembers long ago
the white snow falling falling.
He remembers the bluebird and thrush
at twilight
calling, calling.

He remembers long ago
the new moon in the summer sky
He remembers the wind in the trees
and its long, rising sigh.
And so will I
        so will I.

Charlotte Zolotow

Keepsake

Before Mrs. Williams died
She told Mr. Williams
When he gets home
To get a nickel out of her
Navy blue pocketbook
And give it to her
Sweet little gingerbread girl
That's me

I ain't never going to spend it

Eloise Greenfield

Aunt Roberta

What do people think about
When they sit and dream
All wrapped up in quiet
    and old sweaters
And don't even hear me 'til I
Slam the door?

Eloise Greenfield

Double Dutch

My family says funny things to me.

If I watch my Grannie
When she's making apple pie,

She smiles at me and whispers,
"You're the apple of my eye."

If I look for Mummy's car keys,
When she's running late,
She ruffles up my hair and says,
"You really are my mate."

If I help my Grandad
To prune the cherry tree,
He pats my back and tells me,
You're as busy as a bee."

If I find my father's tape
When he wants to measure,
He hugs me close and then he says,
"You're such a little treasure."

If I let my younger brother kick
My football every day,
He grins at me and mumbles,
"As a sister you're OK."

If I let my little cousin read
The book that I've just brought,
She dances round me cheering,
"You're a super duper sport!"

It's confusing, what they say
But underneath I know.
    It must be that they think I'm great
And want to tell me so.

                    Bronwen Scarffe

After each poem I paused to give the students time to write. But the students paused as well. They didn't have the slightest idea what to do. "Jot down any words that come to mind" just wasn't enough direction for ten-year-olds. Most thought I was asking them to write down favorite words from the poem. I found myself obliged to prompt their responses. "So Will I" speaks of the things a grandfather remembers from his childhood. "I wonder what things you'll probably remember?" "Keepsake" speaks of things we'll save forever. "I wonder what your keepsakes are?" And on it went. "Aunt Roberta" prompted thoughts about people's dreams, "Double Dutch" about people's pet names.

The students asked me if these little cards were bookmarks. "No," I answered, but I realized they could work like bookmarks. "A bookmark holds your place in a book," I told the students, "and these words might hold a special place in you as a writer." The students handed me their cards as they filed out the door on their way to the lunchroom (Figure 24 shows several examples).

When I returned the cards to the students on Monday morning, I suggested that they look them over for any words that seemed significant and use these as points of departure for their notebook writing. "But we don't remember the poems," they complained. "We forgot why we wrote these."

"It doesn't matter," I said, wondering if their writing would be any different if the generative piece of literature was not planted firmly in their minds. I was right.

Not having the original piece of literature in mind didn't matter. The students looked over their jottings and wrote from them much as they had learned to write from a piece of literature.

Najib explained that the word *wallet* got him thinking about other old keepsakes, and he wrote to discover why they are so important in his life (Figure 25).

The teachers in the study group continued to meet every week in order to share our discoveries and critique and revise our structured response tasks. When I shared the students' writing with them, the teachers challenged some of my thinking. They helped me to see that "my prompts"—those tag questions after each poem ("So what will you remember? So what are your keepsakes?")—were limiting. They forced the students to respond in a specific way. They lead students to believe that I was looking for particular things. "Perhaps it was a legitimate way to get started," they suggested, "but now it is time to remove the scaffolding."

During the following week, I once again gave out little slips of cardboard and read aloud several more poems. But this time I asked no tag questions. Instead, I asked the students to simply jot down whatever words or phrases came to mind. This time the students needed no explanation. They were ready to respond.
I read aloud the following three poems:

The Reason I Like Chocolate

The reason I like chocolate
is I can lick my fingers
and nobody tells me I'm not polite

I especially like scary movies
'cause I can snuggle with Mommy
or my big sister and they don't laugh.

I like to cry sometimes 'cause
everybody says "what's the matter
don't cry"

and I like books
for all those reasons
but mostly 'cause they just make me
happy

and I really like
to be
happy

                                   Nikki Giovanni

Bad Day

Johnny was acting
funny today.
I couldn't get him
to come and play.
He just sat there and
picked at a stick
and fooled around with a yellow brick.
he didn't seem to know I was there.
But I don't care.

I might take a walk
and look at cars
or chin myself on
the playground bars
or hang around with
another bunch. . . .
Maybe he'll come out
after lunch.

Marci Ridlon

That Was Summer

Have you ever smelled summer?
Sure you have.
Remember that time
When you were tired of running
Or doing nothing much
And you were hot
And you flopped right down on the ground?
Remember how the warm soil smelled—
And the grass?
That was summer.

Remember that time
When the storm blew up quick
And you stood under a ledge
And watched the rain till it stopped
And when it stopped
You walked out again to the sidewalk,
The quiet sidewalk?
Remember how the pavement smelled—
All steamy, warm and wet?
That was summer.

Remember that time
When you were trying to climb
Higher in the tree
And you didn't know how
And your foot was hurting in the fork
But you were holding tight
To the branch?
Remember how the bark smelled then—
All dusty dry, but nice?
That was summer.

If you try very hard,
Can you remember that time
When you played outside all day
And you came home for dinner
And had to take a bath right away
Right away?
It took you a long time to pull
Your shirt over your head.
Do you remember smelling the sunshine?
That was summer.

Marci Ridlon

FIGURE 24

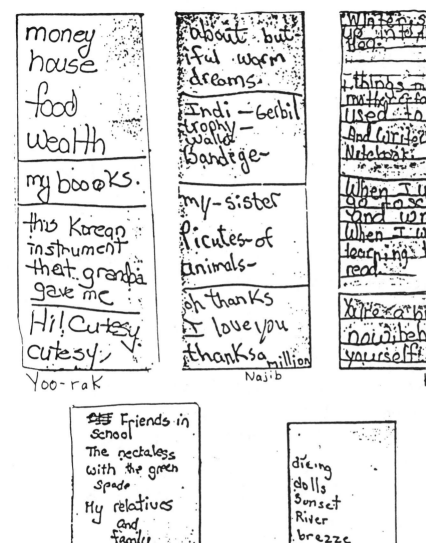

money
house
food
wealth

my boooks.

this Korean
instrument
that grandpa
gave me
Hi! Cutesy
cutesy;

Yoo-raK

about but
iful warm
dreams.

Indi — Gerbil
trophy —
wallet
Bandege—

my - sister
Picutes of
animals—

oh thanks
I love you
thanksa million

Najib

Winter snuggle
up in to the
bed.

things my
mother & father
used to have
And writer
Notebook.

When I used
go to school
and write
When I was
learning to
read.

You're a big girl
now behave
yourself!

Kareen

Friends in
School
The neckaless
with the green
spade

My relatives
and
family
They say I'm
Smart cause
I'm the only one
in the family
that knows
English good,
so I help my
family fill out
forms Jeanine

dicing
dolls
Sunset
River
brezze
flowers
cupcake

Katherine

FIGURE 25

Najib   9/28/90

My favorite posetions are things that give me memories, things that are old.

I love my old horn that was used by the bugle boy in an army an old book from 1895 France, a gun and knife that a pirate used in the 1700s. I love all these things because their old. They don't give me memories but they give me what could of happen ned, And that is exciting all the times that horn was blowed, all the people who rented that book, all the people those weapons killed. All the adventurs those weapons bring back memories for those it belonged to. Now they are dead. And now the immaginary adventures for me the nett owner. I love to collect old items. It makes me feel like I know more about the past, their past. Now my future,

Although these titles could be used as story-starters ("Write about chocolate, the summer, or a bad day you had") the rich content of the poems prevented the students from being pigeon-holed into limited topics. In addition, the students were not being asked to write stories but to free-associate and write down the words, phrases, or images that came to mind. The students taped their slips into their notebooks knowing they could write from these responses if they chose to, and many did.

Jeanine, who had jotted in a rather helter-skelter fashion, was taken by the juxtaposition of surprising combinations of words. After she reread her jottings, she began a separate notebook page for "Chocolate happy, junk leaves, sleeping trees, raining books and yum-yummy summer." Her fanciful free-writing proved once again that where ideas come from is never as important as where ideas lead. (Jeanine's jottings are illustrated in Figure 26.)

Not Just Read Alouds

Students became comfortable reacting to a piece of literature when they heard it read aloud as well as when they read to themselves. And their written responses were no longer limited to personal narratives.

We continued to challenge them in order to understand the kinds of literature that have most meaning for young writers. Eventually, of course, we hoped students would internalize responding to literature as just one more strategy in finding their own writing topics. Their writer's notebooks now contained many entries that were sparked by literature, but alongside these were entries inspired by the view out the window, old photographs, random thoughts, walks through shopping malls, reactions to movies, and so on.

One Monday morning during reading time, the students found some specially prepared reading material on their desks. Over the weekend I had excerpted four scenes from some of their favorite writers' memoirs: Beverly Cleary in *A Girl from Yamhill* writes of staining the Thanksgiving tablecloth with ink fingerprints. Eloise Greenfield in *Childtimes* writes of how her mother sewed for her. Madeleine L'Engle in *A Circle of Quiet* writes of wetting her pants in school, and Jean Little in *Little by Little* writes about her fear of entering a new class. These

FIGURE 26

excerpts were reproduced on pages with very wide margins so students could write their responses next to particular scenes, since I was interested in collecting the responses for study. (Not only is it very hard to carry home thirty-five writer's notebooks, but most students don't want to part with them overnight.) Later, some students chose to paste their writing into their notebooks.

I told the students that they need not respond to all the excerpts, only those that "touched home" for them in some way. I was particularly interested in which issues, if any, were generative for students, and whether they connected closely with the topic or were able to follow unexpected threads.

Thanksgiving. Relatives are coming to dinner. The oak pedestal table is stretched to its limit and covered with a silence cloth and white damask. The sight of that smooth, faintly patterned cloth fills me with longing. I find a bottle of blue ink, pour it out at one end of the table, and dip my hands into it. Pat-a-pat, pat-a-pat, all around the table I go, inking handprints on that smooth white cloth. I do not recall what happened when aunts, uncles, and cousins arrived. All I recall is my satisfaction in marking with ink on that white surface.

Beverly Cleary
A Girl From Yamhill

I don't know why Mama ever sewed for me. She sewed for other people, made beautiful dresses and suits and blouses, and got paid for doing it. But I don't know why she sewed for me. I was so mean.

It was all right in the days when she had to make my dresses a little longer in the front than in the back to make up for the way I stood, with my legs pushed back and my stomach stuck out. I was little then, and I trusted Mama. But when I got older, I worried.

Mama would turn the dress on the wrong side and slide it over my head, being careful not to let the pins stick me. She'd kneel on the floor with her pin cushion, fitting the dress on me, and I'd look down at that dress, at that lopsided, raw-edged, half-basted, half-pinned thing—and know that it was never going to look like anything. So I'd pout while Mama frowned and sighed and kept on pinning.

Sometimes she would sew all night and in the morning I'd have a perfectly beautiful dress, just right for the school program or the party. I'd put it on, and I'd be so ashamed of the way I had acted. I'd be too ashamed to say I was sorry.

But Mama knew.

Eloise Greenfield
Childtimes

I was about eight, certainly old enough to have forgotten what it is like to wet one's pants. One day in French class I asked to be excused. The French teacher must have been having problems with children wanting to leave the room for other reasons, and using the bathroom as an excuse, because she forbade me to go. I asked her three times, and three times was told, No. When the bell for the end of class rang I bolted from my desk and ran, but I couldn't make it, and spent the rest of the afternoon sodden and shamed.

When my mother heard what had happened, she demanded to see the principal. I remember with awful clarity the scene in the principal's office, after the French teacher had been summoned. She said, "But Madeleine never asked to go to the bathroom. If she had only raised her hand, of course I would have excused her."

She was believed. I suppose the principal had to believe the teacher, rather than the child with wet clothes. I was reprimanded gently, told to ask the next time, and not to lie about it afterwards, it really wasn't anything dreadful to make that kind of mistake.

Madeleine L'Engle
A Circle of Quiet

I followed Mother through the girls' door of St. John's School. It was nine o'clock and the hall was empty. I stared at all the coats hanging on hooks outside the grade four classroom door. There were so many of them! I swallowed and hung back.

Mother, feeling my hand tug at hers, turned and saw the panic in my eyes. She smiled at me and paused long enough to murmur words meant to be comforting.

"Your teacher's name is Mr. Johnston. He knows we're coming. I'm sure you'll like him."

What she did not seem to understand was that it was not the thought of Mr. Johnston that was frightening me. I had not yet met a teacher who had not liked me.

The sound of children's voices came from behind the closed door. It was those children who worried me. How would they feel about a cross-eyed girl joining their class at the end of November?

Jean Little
Little by Little

Many students did connect with Madeleine L'Engle's experience. Their writing told almost exclusively of their own memories of pants-wetting, which seemed so overwhelming they didn't connect with any of the other issues L'Engle deals with—adults who lie, parents coming up to school, and so on. Pants-wetting stories elicit pants-wetting stories for ten-year-olds, much the same way stories about airline delays or lost wallets can become contagious in an adult conversation.

Beverly Cleary's recollection of the Thanksgiving tablecloth also had resonance for many students. Some told of similar moments of being naughty—finger painting on the walls or draping toilet paper around the house. Several students wrote about Thanksgiving celebrations in general. Holiday words clearly seemed to push a button in these young students.

Students responded least frequently to Eloise Greenfield's memory of not trusting her mother's sewing abilities and then feeling ashamed upon seeing a lovely finished dress. Several students wrote in the margin "My mother doesn't sew," meaning "therefore, I can't connect to this piece." Many young writers seemed to respond only to the particular events rather than to the feelings in the pieces.

Jean Little's description of her fear of entering a new classroom inspired the most response. This is clearly a subject that resonates for ten-year-olds. Here, they seemed to identify closely not only with the events but also with the overriding feeling of fear that is so closely interwoven. Little was afraid to enter the new class because of a physical difference—she was cross-eyed. Of course the fifth-grade students did not have the same problem, but they wrote of the differences that made it difficult for them to enter a new classroom (Figure 27).

At first glance, these student responses seem to resemble the traditional assignment, "Write about a first day at school." They differ, however, in several important ways.

The students had a choice. They had several pieces to respond to. And they had the option not to respond.

FIGURE 27

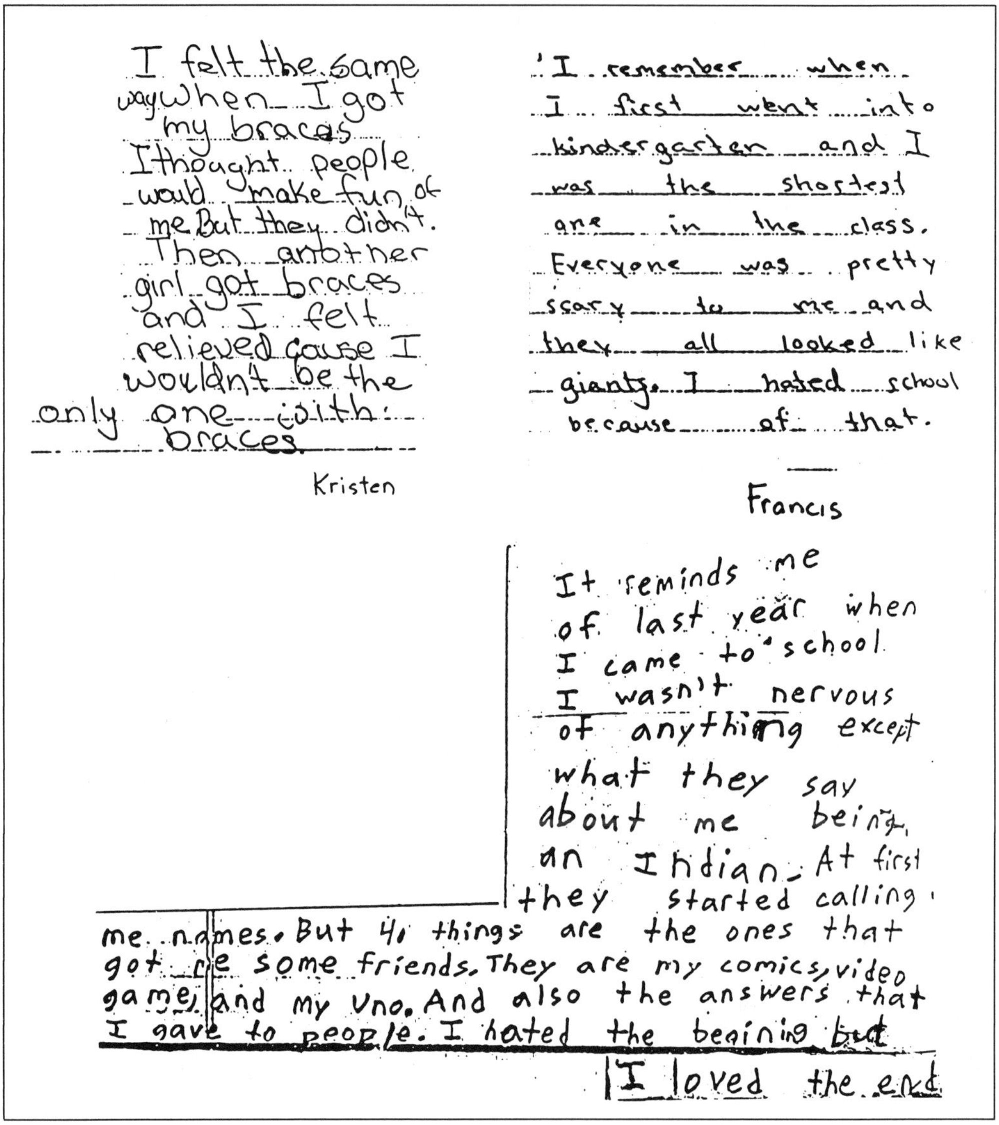

> I felt the same
> way when I got
> my braces
> I thought people
> would make fun of
> me But they didn't.
> Then another
> girl got braces
> and I felt
> relieved cause I
> wouldn't be the
> only one with
> braces.
>
> Kristen

> 'I remember when
> I first went into
> kindergarten and I
> was the shortest
> one in the class.
> Everyone was pretty
> ssary to me and
> they all looked like
> giants. I hated school
> because of that.
>
> Francis

> It reminds me
> of last year when
> I came to school.
> I wasn't nervous
> of anything except
> what they say
> about me being
> an Indian. At first
> they started calling
> me names. But 4 things are the ones that
> got me some friends. They are my comics, video
> games and my Uno. And also the answers that
> I gave to people. I hated the beginning but
> I loved the end

Their writing was added to their writer's notebook. There was no need to turn these responses into drafts or finished pieces. Their responses could also move totally away from the source ideas toward greater levels of abstraction. Danielle's response to both the Greenfield and Little excerpts indicates her ability to connect to emotions as well as to events (Figure 28). She has let the literature lead her to surprising new places. She did not interpret the assignment simply as writing about problems when your mother sews for you or your fear of entering a new class.

In addition, these response tasks involved several valuable lessons.

• The students were receiving practice in valuing literature as a well from which they could draw in choosing topics.

FIGURE 28

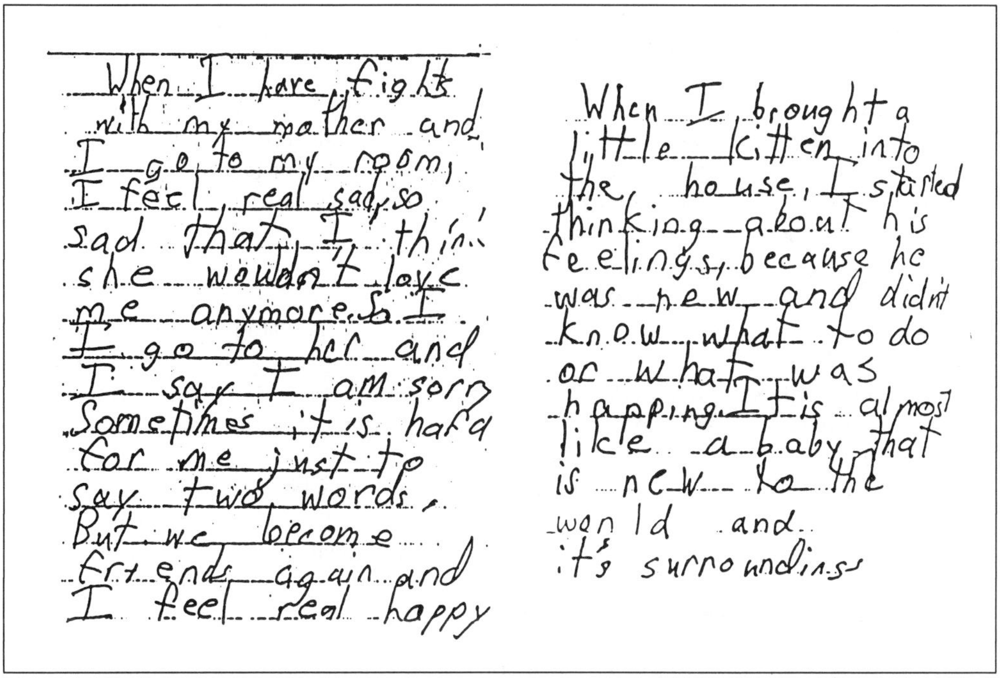
When I have fight with my mather and I go to my room, I feel real sad, so sad that I think she wouldn't love me anymore. So I I go to her and I say I am sorry. Sometimes it is hard for me just to say two words. But we become friends again and I feel real happy

When I brought a little kitten into the house, I started thinking about his feelings, because he was new and didn't know what to do or what was happing. It is almost like a baby that is new to the world and it's surroundings

- The students were being given full permission to respond to literature during writing time.
- The students were shifting from writing about literature to writing generative bits with the potential to become literature: not "I liked or I didn't like" but "I wonder, . . . I realize, . . . I think, . . . I notice."
- Literature helped recreate very powerful moments for students, those that they often forget when they sit down at their school desks for writing time.

During the first few weeks of school we prepared several packets of short reading materials and asked students to read them and respond if the texts sparked their thinking. We selected poetry as well as short stories and nonfiction articles from children's magazines.

We also invited students in on the fun. We left a stack of *Cricket* magazines atop the back bookcase so students could look for articles they thought would generate student response. They were to request three or four copies of a chosen article and select diverse readers in the class—those they thought might find it particularly inspiring or thought-provoking. They folded the copies, placed them in envelopes, and distributed them. The ceremony and surprise added to the drama of these "by-invitation-only" readings. Each student would then write in response to the text in their writer's notebook and meet with the others to share their ideas. Stacey, for example, chose a short story about preparing the home for the arrival of a new baby and invited three classmates to respond—a student expecting a new sibling, a student with no siblings, and another who was the youngest of four children. Stacey lives with her grandparents, apart from her own sisters and brothers.

Even the students' weekly current events assignment became grist for their literary mills. Instead of asking for the usual summary, ("This article is about . . .")

we encouraged students to treat this writing as yet another kind of literature. "Let it, too, lead you to new thinking," we suggested. We especially encouraged students to follow an intriguing story over several days in order to really follow their own thinking.

Jeanine stopped writing summaries and began reflecting on the content of her articles. Figure 29 shows her response to an article about trends in adoption.

Students began to understand how reading a poem, a picture book, a novel, a newspaper article, a magazine cartoon, or a letter from a friend could serve as a catalyst for their own important writing.

Responding on Their Own

During the first month of school Antoinette and I challenged students with more structured invitations to write in order to shake them free of their traditional modes of responding to literature. We wanted them to know that they need not retell entire plots or write book reviews. Instead we wanted them to use literature as a seedbed for their own fresh thoughts and ideas.

As I have already described in the early pages of this chapter, we began by inviting and celebrating lots of open discussion after we read aloud. Then we asked for written responses without giving much direction. Finally, we created specific invitations to respond so students could begin to broaden their ways of responding and deepen their responses. So far, these have included:

- Jotting a key word or issue, then writing to elaborate, "to get to the bottom of it".
- Two-column activity—what it is about, what it makes me think about.
- Free-associating lists of words, then writing from the lists.

FIGURE 29

9/26/90

I feel sorry for the babies that are put for adoption. It feels like the child's parents don't care for their very own child or children, and they don't care for any of the children at all. I think that it is really sad for the child to be a orphan.

Of course, we were hoping students would internalize many of these strategies. After each response task I would add, "What we did today together you could do on your own whenever you're reading." We were also hoping students would invent their own ways of using literature as a seedbed for their own writing and that entries sparked by literature would become commonplace in their writer's notebooks.

At first, students used several of our structured tasks as scaffolding. Figure 30 shows how Kareen used the two-column activity to help her identify several important issues. She had just read the Gilbreths' *Bells on Their Toes.* Later she would elaborate on the meaning of separation in her own life and imagine what it would be like to have such a large family. Eventually, the scaffolding disappeared and responding to literature in their writer's notebooks became as natural for students as responding to an argument, a party, or a family vacation.

We noticed that initially students tended to respond only to material that they had heard read aloud. Perhaps the adult voice or the brief class discussion or the expressions on their friends' faces helped the piece to linger in their minds and become more evocative when they returned to their desks.

Kareen chose to respond to Kathleen Fraser's poem about playing marbles, one the class had used in choral reading (Figure 31).

Students also chose to write on their own in response to picture books we had shared together. Zanvi responded to Florence Parry Heide and Judith Heide Gilliland's *The Day of Ahmed's Secret,* a book that motivated many students to tell stories about learning to write their names (see Chapter 2). Zanvi lets the setting of the story remind her of her homeland and then wanders off into her life today (Figure 32).

FIGURE 30

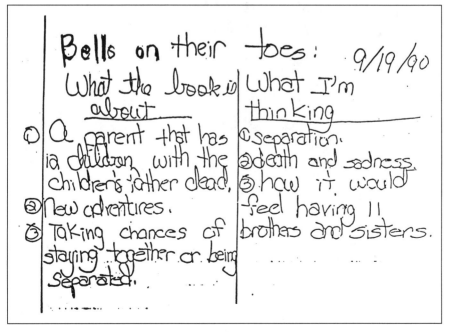

FIGURE 31

Marbles make me think about someone who is always being pushed around. For example when people like to push other people around. It makes me think about that because marbles are always being pushed or hit this way and that way.

FIGURE 32

The book some how reminds me of India because it has alot of old billings buildings and they have people on the streets and so many sounds. When I come home and I here the telivision on and I hear my brother playing so loudly that my homework is too hard for me to work on so I go upstairs and lock the door and sometimes thier is no sound at all and I feel like the house is missing some thing. It reminds me of my mom and my dads room the smell of thier clothes.

They noses are all over the cars are moving fast but I am like a statue standing all alone at last.

FIGURE 33

In half a moon inn. Aaron is
mute. I had a mute friend and
at was in camp, he was my
best friend. He was older than
I was. He's in his twenties.
There was a boy and he was
my age and he was mute too.
After that year of camp I
had to move and I hadn't
seen him since. Except one day
I was in the train and I saw
him. Now I'm in this school
and I've made so many friends
since last year. I miss my old
friends and all my other teachers.
I like the teachers in this
school there the same as the
teachers in my old school. I hope
I don't move again because I
don't want to leave my friends
again, like last year in fourth
          grade. I hope all my friends
go to the same school as me
because I will be lonely without
them. My is in the Junior high
school that I want to go to.

Many students chose *The Half-A-Moon Inn,* the book I had been reading aloud over several days. Emil allows each thought to push him further, as he continues toward the bottom of the page (Figure 33).

What began as a response to *The Half-A-Moon Inn* (Figure 34) turned into Francisco's first writing project: a collection of poems about leaving New York.

Fairly soon thereafter, students began writing spontaneously without scaffolding and without having heard the text read aloud. Danielle's wrote the entry in Figure 35 during writing workshop.

Other Occasions for Response

The high school my children attended was known for its incredible musicals—original plays as well as Broadway classics. It was also known for its incredible audiences. It was not surprising during any performance for good-natured, fun-loving hecklers to call out, "SING about it!" at just the right moments. In some ways, the students in our classroom could call out, "Write about it!" at just the

FIGURE 34

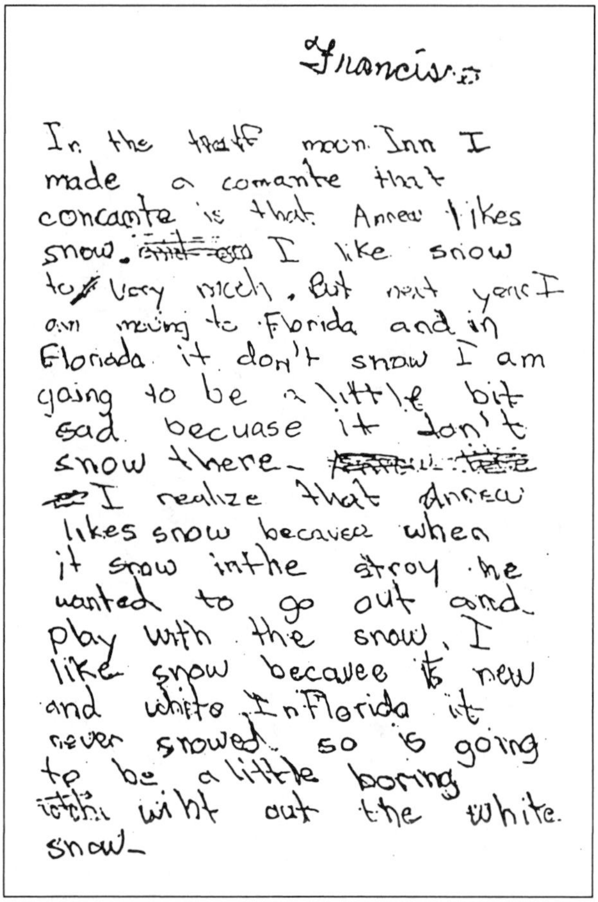

> Francisco
>
> In the half moon Inn I made a comante that concante is that Annew likes snow. And so I like snow to very much. But next year I am moing to Florida and in Florada it don't snow I am going to be a little bit sad becuase it don't snow there. I realize that Annew likes snow because when it snow in the stroy he wanted to go out and play with the snow, I like snow because is new and white In Florida it never snowed so is going to be a little boring with out the white. snow—

right moments. Throughout the year and throughout the city, teachers and students have come to value literature as an important way to generate writing.

As soon as students seemed comfortable responding on a regular basis to all the different kinds of reading they were doing, including the books teachers read aloud, the books they read at home in bed, the articles/excerpts they read with their response group, the poems they performed chorally, or the newspaper articles they skimmed, teachers added energy to the writing workshop by creating special occasions and new structures. As soon as students began to view reading as just another thing that happens, teachers extended some of the following invitations:

- Bring in three books that say a lot about you and write to explain your choices. (This task can be varied by requesting three fairy tales, three poems, or three non-fiction texts.)
- Rather than write new entries after your reading, find an old entry that you now see in a new way and write to explore these insights.
- Share a piece of literature with your family and write in response to your family's response.

FIGURE 35

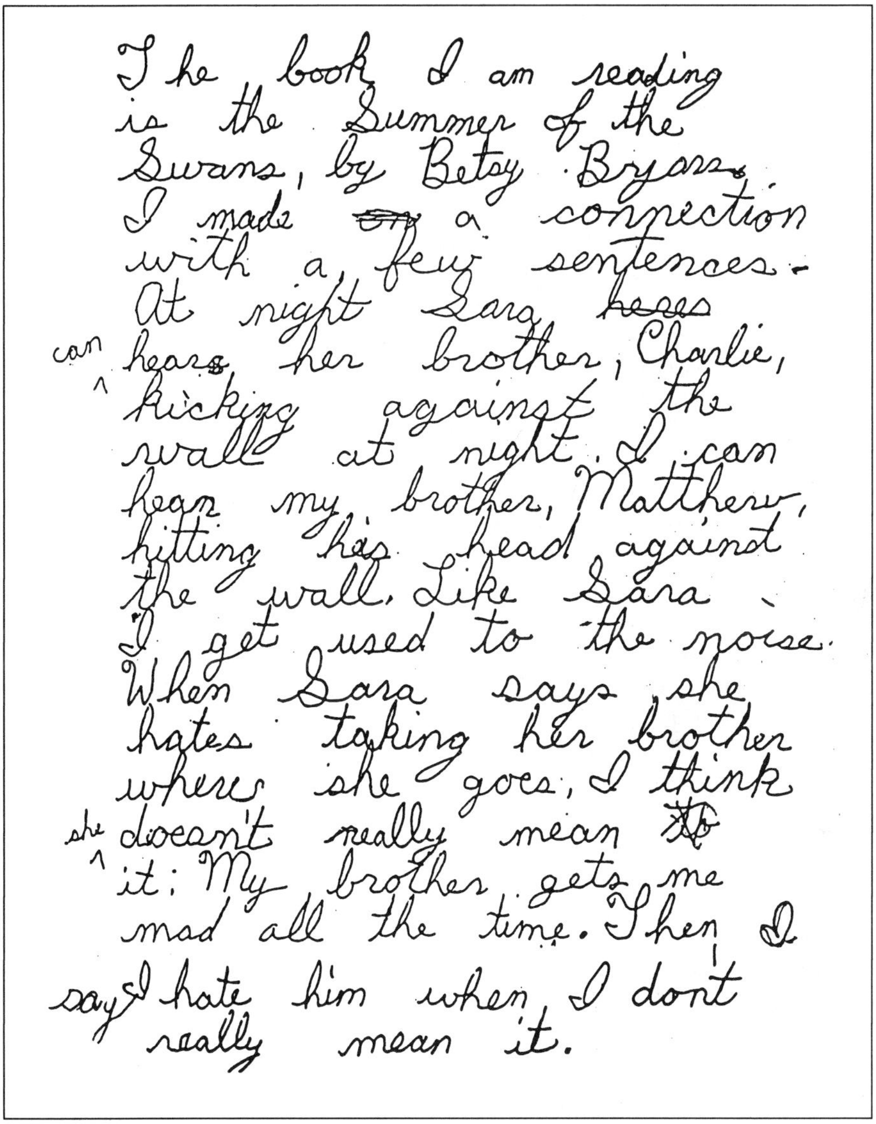

> The book I am reading
> is the Summer of the
> Swans, by Betsy Byars.
> I made ~~on~~ a connection
> with a few sentences.
> At night Sara ~~hears~~
> ^can hears her brother, Charlie,
> kicking against the
> wall at night. I can
> hear my brother, Matthew,
> hitting his head against
> the wall. Like Sara
> I get used to the noise.
> When Sara says she
> hates taking her brother
> where she goes, I think
> ^she doesn't really mean ~~to~~
> it. My brother gets me
> mad all the time. Then I
> say I hate him when I don't
> really mean it.

- In reading memoirs or autobiographies keep a special response log. Respond to each chapter, allowing someone else's life to touch yours.
- Read a text with a partner and write letters to one another to take your thinking further.

I've often been asked, "How do teachers think of these ideas?" Most teachers, I suspect, are following their students' leads. When they see a student inventing his or her own way of writing in response to literature, in a Johnny Appleseed spirit they spread the idea around. If, for instance, a student quite naturally writes about how his family responded to a poem he brought home, the teacher wonders if this would be a powerful strategy for other students and offers the idea to the entire class.

One of my favorite sources of inspiration for inventing new classroom techniques has its roots outside the classroom. I have always found it particularly helpful to pause and to hold in my hand those literacy events that have touched me deeply. Then I wonder if this experience would be accessible to students. Perhaps I'm following Jerry Harste's advice, "If language users don't do it in the real world, why should we do it in our schools?" A few examples would probably help.

On several occasions I've worked with the Public Education Coalition in Denver. Each time I do, a splendid teacher, Joetta Heiney, gives me a carefully selected book as a parting gift. But Joetta does more than that. Each year she has slipped in a piece of purple ribbon to mark the page that speaks to her of me and the ideas I've shared. Inevitably on the airplane ride home, I read those carefully selected pages first and then I have much to reflect on in my writer's notebook. Why did Joetta select Margaret Murdoch's story in Charlotte Painter's *Gifts of Age*? The Chinese proverb "The sound stops short, the sense flows on" in Sylvia Shaw Judson's *The Quiet Eye*? Joetta's gifts have meant a great deal to me and so I begin to wonder about the students I teach. Would it work for them? Can children select particular passages that somehow remind them of a classmate? Can that classmate write in response to those choices? Would the experience lead to new insights? Would the students take pleasure in giving and receiving? For me that's how new classroom rituals get started.

Last summer I was struck by how a really "good read" influences the way I look at the world. As I traveled around Sweden, I filled my notebook with second-language learning stories. I wrote about hearing so many new sounds in a crowded restaurant, my attempts to spot familiar words in the daily newspaper, the Swedish teachers' ease with English, my efforts to speak English at a slower pace, my delight at hearing American songs on the radio, and my frustrating attempts to learn some Swedish.

So many language stories, and it was no surprise. I had been traveling with Eva Hoffman's *Lost in Translation*. The power of her memoir influenced the way I looked at the world. Once again, I thought, "Is it true for our students?" Does a really strong text linger in their minds and get us to pay attention to new things or perhaps see old things in new ways? In Antoinette's class, I brought the issue up with the students. "Has this ever happened to you? If it does, will you share it with the class?" "When you read Lois Lowry's *Number the Stars,* did you pay more attention to anti-Semitism in your community? Did you have new questions to ask Stacey, the only Jewish child in the class? Did you read the daily newspaper differently?

Yet another class routine had its roots in the real world. In our adult reading groups at the college we challenged the old notion that "a good book is one you can't put down." Instead, we discovered that a good book is one you have to put down because the writer has pushed you to stop and think and reflect and question and remember. The dozens of little yellow stick-on notes marking pages in our copies of a novel bore witness to this. I wondered if this could be true with even very young students.

One day I gathered a group of first graders round and told them what happens when adults read really good books. "Their minds sometimes wander to their own lives." Then I wondered out loud if it were true for young readers. I left a pack of stick-on notes on each student's desk. "If your mind wanders, stick on a note and jot down where your thoughts traveled. We can share your ideas at the end of the hour."

Ilana had read *Caps for Sale* by Esther Slobodvinka and her book was filled with markers. She explained, "This page here, where the man is leaning against the tree, that made me think about *Little House on the Prairie,* not the book, the television show. The daddy gets tired and he always sits against the tree to take a rest. And this page here, where the man is sleeping, that's like my sister. We both take naps but she forgets to wake up. I have to wake her. She might sleep all day." And on it went. From that day on, the first graders used stick-on notes to jot down a word or two about their thoughts as they read. The words reminded them of stories to bring to share time.

Over the years I've tried many classroom activities that have not succeeded. Those moments are also part of the joy of teaching. The failures remind me that the work we do is not carved in stone, that each day brims with new possibilities. There are no yellowed planbook pages. To teach is to learn new things every day.

Looking Back

Antoinette and I had put responding to literature on the front burner during the early weeks of school. After a while we focused our attention on helping students complete their first writing projects. We became busy helping Jennifer work on a poem, Najib on a letter to the editor, Amaury on a picture book, and so on (see Chapter 12). Soon after that, the class used their writer's notebooks as a tool in a course of study in poetry, and following that, a course in nonfiction writing. Writing in response to literature was no longer our main area of interest. Of course we hoped that the attention we paid to it early on would encourage students to continue valuing literature as a catalyst for their own writing.

At midyear we read over students' notebooks looking for entries that were sparked by their reading. It was clear that many students had continued to respond to literature naturally and frequently. But a few rarely used literature to generate notebook entries—at least their writing didn't indicate that their response was inspired by their reading.

Some did respond to what they were reading but fell back on simply retelling plots. This was particularly true for those students who had kept separate reading logs for many years. It seemed hard for these students to break their habit of recording the date started, the date completed, a summary, and a comment. In fact, they often chose to keep these entries in a separate section of their writer's notebook. Because they did not view reading as just another thing that happens, they lost the opportunity to discover more from a juxtaposition of a response entry and a childhood memory or an overheard conversation, one enhancing the other. Antoinette and I kept close tabs on these students, watching for signs of more flexibility and risk taking in their writing.

Jeanine's midyear responses to literature are worth noting because of their frequency and variation. Jeanine felt obliged to respond to everything she read, not merely those books that touched her deeply. When confronted with formulaic series books, Jeanine resorts to retelling the plot (Figure 36). When she responds to stronger texts, like *The Secret Garden* and *One-Eyed Cat,* her writing changes (Figure 37). Jeanine's entries serve as testimonials to the power of fine literature.

Zanvi's responses to literature are also worth noting. They remind us that retelling a story is often a way into a more reflective stance and personal connections. Its interesting to note that Zanvi, who is one of the most sophisticated

FIGURE 36

I'm reading a novel called The fabulous five Super Edition number 1 The fabulous five in trouble. This novel is by the author Betsy Haynes. It is about five girls. And their names are: Jana Morgan, Katie Shanon, Melanie Edwards, Beth Barry and Christie Winchell. The 5 girls form a club called The fabulous 5. Then 1 day, they have a sleepover and everyone dreamed about the same thing. They dreamed that they were "someone else else's skin. Melanie dreamed that she was Christie and she almost flunked Christie on a ten test. And Christie was in a honors class, which is only for children who are really smart. And Melanie wasn't in the honors class. Katie turned into Melanie and nearly made her lose a good friend of hers.

I'm still reading The Browbird, but I just started another book called River Heights #2 Guilty secrets. It is about a girl named Nikki Masters. By Carolyn Keene. She just got a new car and she thinks she's lucky, but whenever she mentions the new car to her boyfriend Tim Cooper, he acts strange. Brittany Tate, Nikki Masters's enemy is playing tricks on her. To try to get Nikki's boyfriend + to get her to be a fool in front of the whole school.

writers in the class, is also the first to show signs of reading like a writer, commenting on the author's craft in her writer's notebook (Figure 38).
Antoinette asked Zanvi to share several of her notebook entries with the entire class. Commenting on the author's craft as she does became another avenue of response for students. (As I discuss further in Chapter 9, we were careful not to encourage response to craft without response to content.)

FIGURE 37

The novel I'm reading is called The secret Garden by Frances Hodgson Burnett. This book is terrific. When I was reading the book, I set my stuffed animals on my bed and read it aloud to them. I don't think its fair of the mother not to like this child or children. If I was Mary's mother, I'll treat her with respect. Not ignore her. I have a connection with Mary Lennox. My connection is when some kids teases Mary, she feels really bad. "Because she's not part of the family." Well when I went to Janir's brothers birthday party, Janir's uncle's brother dised me Danielle, Matthew and Vincent out by saying "What are all those white people doing here." I don't like white people coming to my Nephew's birthday." So far, that's all I read today in the secret garden.

U novel I am reading at this time is named One-Eyed cat. It is by Paula Fox. Sometimes when I read this book, I feel sorry for Ned that his mother is ill. If I had a choise who I want to be between me and Ned, I would choose me. But If I was Ned, I would tell my father about the riffle and get over it. I wondered alot of this book. I also wondered if I went into a cat shop, would I find a cat with only one eye. I might write a book called One-eyed fish becouse when I went in to a fish shop, I found two fishes with only one eye. Paula Fox may be a good writer to who thought she should get a Newbery honor in 1984, but I ~~agreed think she writes kind of boring. I think it is a little boring because she put in almost every little detail. Otherwise I would give her a thumbs up.~~

Paula Fox

FIGURE 38

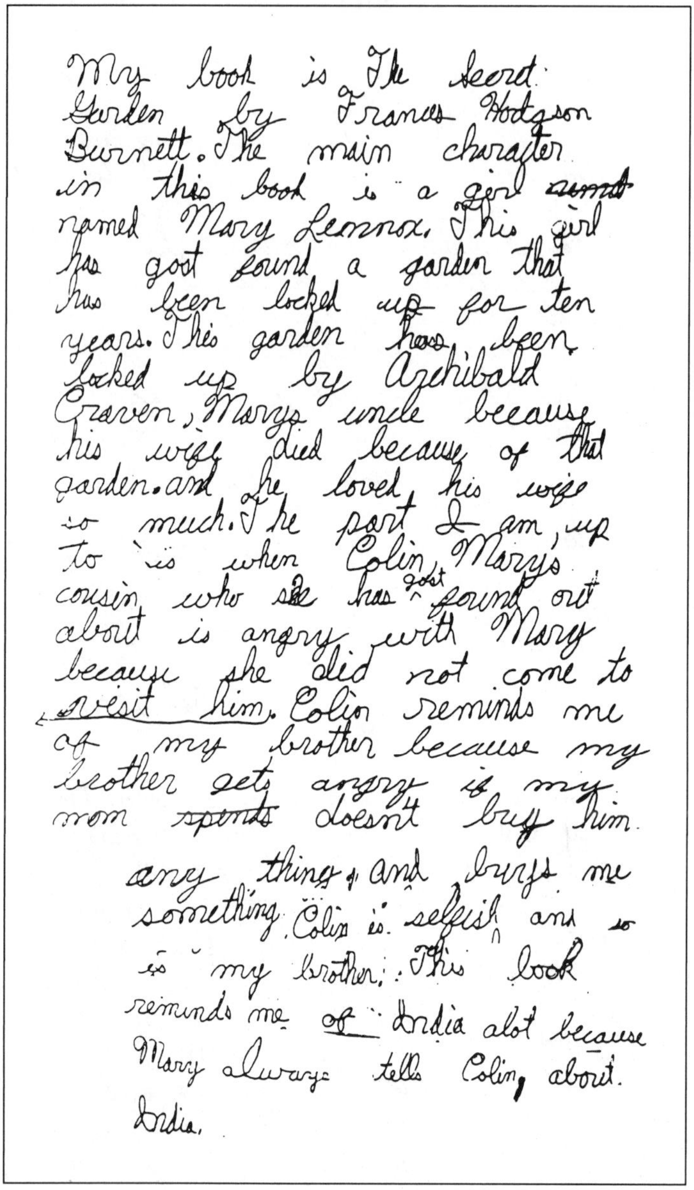

My book is The Secret Garden by Frances Hodgson Burnett. The main character in this book is a girl named Mary Lennox. This girl has got found a garden that has been locked up for ten years. This garden has been locked up by Archibald Craven, Mary's uncle because his wife died because of that garden. and he loved his wife so much. The part I am up to is when Colin Mary's cousin who she has got found out about is angry with Mary because she did not come to visit him. Colin reminds me of my brother because my brother gets angry if my mom doesn't buy him any thing and buys me something. Colin is selfish and so is my brother. This book reminds me of India alot because Mary always tells Colin about India.

Bigger Pay-Offs

Writing in response to literature became an important tool for students attempting to find their stride as writers. It helped them generate important entries in their writer's notebook, but it also taught them to respond to their own writing. One of the crucial components in making use of a writer's notebook is regular rereading of entries. By rereading their notebook pages looking for sparks to new thinking, students began to react to their own writing as they had to published poems and picture books.

FIGURE 38, continued

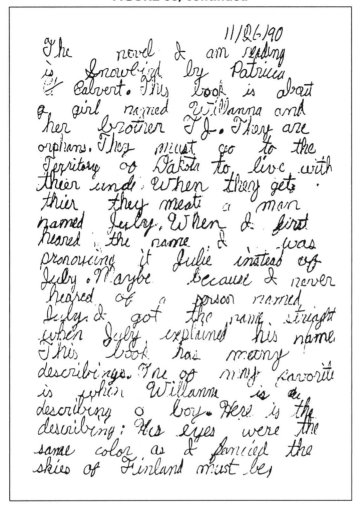

After rereading her response to "Marbles," Kareen might choose to spend time figuring out why being pushed around is significant in her life. She needs to ask herself, "Where is this idea coming from?"

When Rosa reread her entry on Jean Little's poem "Wars," she chose to probe her original thoughts even further. She began with one line from her original entry (Figure 39).

If responding to literature helped children generate notebook entries and learn to elaborate on those entries, it also helped them begin to take a more reflective stance. By learning to hold all kinds of literature in their minds long enough to think deeply about them, the students found it easier to hold a moment in the mall, a childhood memory, or a view from their bedroom window long enough in their minds to reflect upon it.

It was not surprising that Antoinette's students could respond deeply and diversely to shared experiences as well as to shared texts. Over one holiday

FIGURE 38, continued

My novel is Number the stars. By Lois Lowry. The reason I chose this book is because of its tittle and when I read the back. This line really caught my attention Annmarie is asked to do a dangerous mission. I wonder what the mission is. When the the girl says she her long legs I wonder if her long legs will help her in the mission. When I got to this sentence when the man reconized that the girl was Annmarie. They reconized her by her long legs and they called her the "Giraffe". I think this book took place long ago, it reminded me of when I was in little preschool

weekend the class gerbil had jumped out of its cage and into a nearby fish tank. On Monday morning the students found it standing stiffly at the bottom of the tank.

The children didn't pledge allegiance to the flag. They didn't pass in their lunch money. They didn't even swap their usual "What did you do this weekend?" stories. They couldn't. Instead, they huddled around the tank, whispering. They sat, shoulders drooping, in their own quiet places. They comforted Edwin, who had donated the gerbil to the class menagerie.

Antoinette set aside her Monday morning plans. "We're all so upset," she began, "so filled with strong emotions. Perhaps we need to take time to sort out our feelings. Let's begin by taking out our writer's notebooks. Do whatever kind of writing you need to do right now."

The class grew still. The children wrote. Some wrote about the event with all its gory details: who first found the gerbil and screamed, who scooped up the dead animal, how it was discarded. Others let the event lead them further, to remembering a pet that had died, wondering about how accidental deaths differ from those caused by illness, musing about days when everything seems to go wrong, asking questions about responsibility and guilt and blame.

FIGURE 39

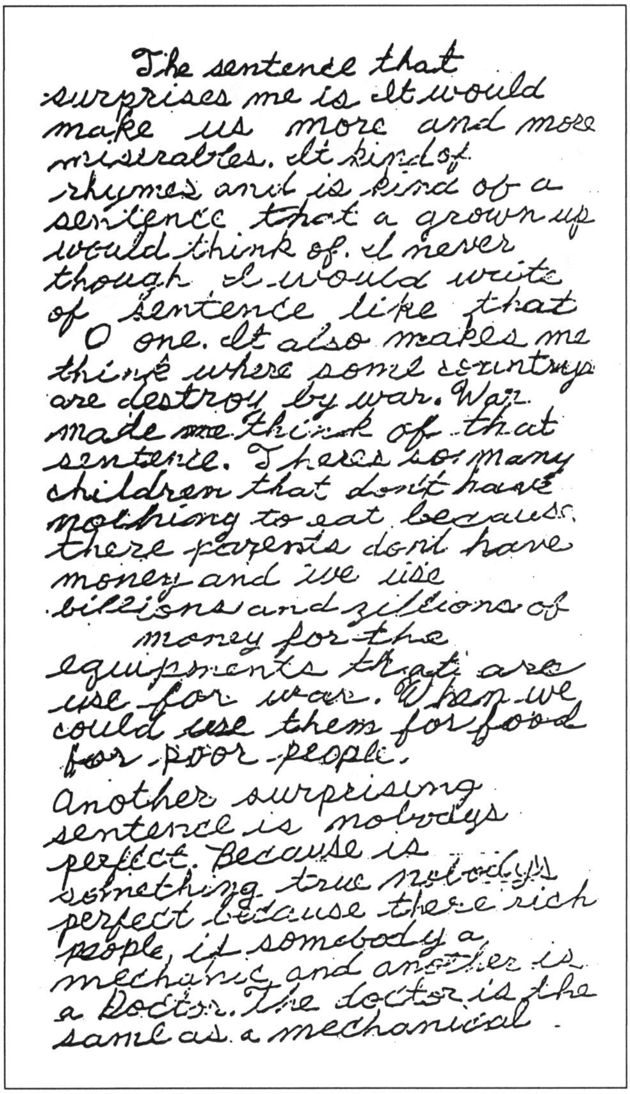

> The sentence that surprises me is It would make us more and more misserables. It kind of rhymes and is kind of a sentence that a grown up would think of. I never though I would write of sentence like that O one. It also makes me think where some countrys are destroy by war. War made me think of that sentence. There so many children that don't have nothing to eat becauss there parents don't have money and we use billions and zillions of money for the equipments that are use for war. When we could use them for food for poor people.
> Another surprising sentence is nobodys perfect. Because is something true nobodys perfect because there rich people, if somebody a mechanic and another is a Doctor. The doctor is the same as a mechanical.

Scenes like this one—students filled with emotion and writing—took place frequently throughout the year in Antoinette's classroom.

The groundwork had been laid early in September. Powerful literary moments gave students an urgent need to write, and they became comfortable responding deeply and personally. Their growing ease carried over into such shared emotional experiences as the gerbil's death, spotting a homeless man asleep on the school playground, or hearing that their teacher the year before had given birth to a baby girl. What the students learned to do in a community they learned to do on their own. They learned to pause, to let things in their lives matter, to hold their lives in their hands and reflect upon them.

5

Inviting Students in on the Search

*When I . . . discovered libraries, it was like having
Christmas every day.*

Jean Fritz

Stuyvesant High School in New York City has a publishing tradition. Seniors are invited to select an appropriate quotation to place under their photograph in the graduation yearbook. When my daughter came home with this challenge, the search was on. She began by rereading her brother's yearbook from three years earlier. She found lots of lines from Woody Allen routines and Billy Joel songs, but also quite a lot of quotes from literature, especially children's literature. Among her favorites were "I won't grow up. I don't want to wear a tie or a serious expression in the middle of July" from *Peter Pan,* and "Just up from the top of the hill, upping and upping until I am right on the top of the hill" from A. A. Milne's *Now We Are Six.* She also thought of borrowing E. B. White's lines: "The way seemed long but the sky was bright and he somehow felt he was headed in the right direction" from *Stuart Little,* or "This is our moment for setting forth . . . we are going out into the world to make webs for ourselves" from *Charlotte's Web.* Perhaps her favorite line was from Maurice Sendak's *Where the Wild Things Are,* " 'And now,' cried Max, 'let the Wild Rumpus begin.' "

None, however, was exactly right. They weren't quite beautiful enough or they just didn't have the right message. Her plan was to spend a Saturday afternoon reading, browsing, flipping through the pages of the childhood favorites that still line her bedroom walls. I envied the task before her. I would have loved to join her. In fact, I would have done it without her. I would have loved to create a long list of possible quotes for her to choose from. But I resisted, knowing it was her responsibility, her reward. I knew it was the experience of reading and rereading and searching that would last a lifetime and add to the other memories in that yearbook.

As parents, as teachers, we need to stop having all the fun. Instead, we need to invite students to become part of the process of finding good writing, not merely enjoying the good writing we put before them. It's true for sixteen-year-olds; it's also true for six-year-olds.

Several months ago I received a call from the head nurse at a public health facility. She had received an anonymous donation of $800 for her clinic on the Upper West Side of Manhattan. She and her colleagues thought about creating a library for the parents and children who spend countless hours waiting to see their physicians. "Could you help?" she asked. "Could you send me a bibliography of books appropriate for infants through six-year-olds?"

I had learned my lesson well. "How quickly do you need to spend the money?" I asked. When she told me she had no deadline, I asked, "Would you mind if I put this project into the hands of a wonderful teacher and her group of first graders? Who better to select books for young children who sit in waiting rooms than young children who sit in waiting rooms?"

Elizabeth Servidio and her first graders eagerly got to work. They researched the titles in their own doctors' and dentists' offices. They browsed through publishers' catalogues and classroom library shelves. They read, reread, and talked about their possible selections. Elizabeth didn't tell the students which books to order. She believes it's not enough for teachers to have criteria for what makes for good writing; young students need to be developing their own.

Throughout the grades teachers are challenging students to search for and explore quality literature. And they're initiating these activities early in the school year for several reasons. Students who become investigators of good writing become colleagues of their teachers, sharing the responsibility of discovering quality literature. They also become an invaluable resource as their classmates study new genres in their reading/writing workshops. Students in on the search for good writing offer their teachers ongoing insights into students' tastes, attitudes, and images of good writing. And students who roll up their sleeves and search the library stacks offer rich data to teachers interested in assessing student's growth throughout the year.

Perhaps most important of all, students who are invited in on the adventure of discovering literature also discover yet another reason to love reading. As Wallace Stegner suggests, "Throw open the library, the delight of discovery is a major pleasure of reading." Several years ago I watched a young student accidentally slip the book jacket off of Eve Bunting's *Jane Martin, Dog Detective,* whose cover looks like a black and white marble composition book. When he saw it, his face said it all. He had experienced the delight of discovery.

I've never known a student to turn down an authentic, rigorous challenge to search among the library stacks. Karen, a first grader who can whip through five or six picture books in any reading hour, needed a bigger challenge, one that would allow her to slow down, to reread, to research. When I approached her, she was eagerly reading Janet and Allan Ahlberg's *Each Peach Pear Plum*. When I asked, "Do you know who Baby Bunting is? Robin Hood? Cinderella?" I found that some were familiar to Karen but others were not. I left her with an important challenge: "Why not find out about these other famous literary characters? Visit the school library. Do some investigating. Then you can share what you've learned with the class." As I was leaving, Karen smiled broadly. "Thanks for the job," she said.

In the Library
The school library is, no doubt, the best equipped place for children to experience the delights of discovery. One afternoon Pat Nevins, the school librarian at P.S. 148, invited Antoinette's students to use their weekly library visit to help her take care of the forgotten treasures on the library shelves. She explained that many of the old books, the ones without beautiful, crisp book jackets, were rarely borrowed, even if they were written by top authors. "Help me find them." she asked.

The students began scanning the shelves and pulling out old volumes, the ones with faded book jackets or no jacket at all. The students admitted that never before had they even bothered to look inside those khaki or dark grey covers with the pebbly texture. They read a few pages to decide if any these books qualified as a "forgotten treasure." By the end of the afternoon they had rescued over twenty books, including *Amigo* by Byrd Baylor Schweitzer, *The Beach Before Breakfast* and *A Winter Friend* by Maxine W. Kumin, *When a Boy Goes to Bed at Night* by Faith McNulty, and *I Go Out* by Muriel Rukeyser.

The students brainstormed ways to make these texts more attractive to borrowers. They suggested

- Setting up a special shelf to announce "Forgotten Treasures."
- Preparing read-along tapes to accompany these texts.
- Designing new book jackets as an art project.
- Pairing these books with a newer companion text (reading Kumin's *Beach Before Breakfast* with *A Day at the Beach* by Mircea Vasilliu).
- Covering the faded jackets with new plastic covers.
- Highlighting these writers through author studies complete with time lines of their work over the last thirty years.

Pat's treasure hunt reminded me of Uri Shulovitz's 1978 Caldecott honor book, *The Treasure*. It is a retelling of the classic folktale about Isaac, a poor man who dreams of a treasure hidden under a bridge near the royal palace. Isaac travels to the royal city, and the palace guard tells him that there is no such treasure. The guard mockingly suggests that the treasure in fact is hidden in Isaac's very own kitchen. The sarcastic words turn out to be true and Isaac becomes rich forever; thereby proving that sometimes you have to leave home in order to appreciate the things you already have.

I often read this story aloud to remind teachers that we already have treasures in our school and class libraries, as well as in our attics. Each of us needs to take time out to reread the books we already own.

Pat's third-floor library has become home to several other literary investigations. For example, Pat has an ongoing "Drop and Swap." Students and faculty alike are invited to drop any book from home into a large plastic bin and receive a coupon that entitles them at any time to return and search for a book in exchange. She also hosts a schoolwide KISS program, "Kids Interested in Sharing Stories." Children select wonderful books to read and share with other interested students. Students have also been invited to become researchers in the school library, studying the tastes and reading habits of their peers. They've kept records of books sold at book fairs and those picked at Reading is Fundamental distributions. They've also studied the trends in everyday library borrowing. Their findings help Pat and Laurie decide how to spend their library funds.

The school library is also a perfect setting for compiling reading lists. Each year Judy Davis's sixth graders interview children from each grade about their favorite texts. The sixth graders then use their library visit to read the younger students' choices. They choose the best ones and prepare annotated lists of recommended readings for each grade level, which are distributed to the parents of the entire student body.

A "Help Wanted" section on a library bulletin board is another way to invite children in on the search for good writing. All members of the school community can ask for help in locating needed materials. Those of us in the Teachers College Writing Project family have long appreciated that New York City does have advantages for book lovers. An unbelievable number of public libraries, publishing houses, specialty bookshops, and famous writers are at our fingertips, as are so many experts in these areas. Bee Cullinan is one of our favorites. Several years ago when Hindy List was off to make a speech in Texas, she wondered about the possibility of weaving some Texas literature into her presentation. She called her friend Bee. That's all it took. Hindy began her speech with Tomie dePaola's *The Legend of the Blue Bonnet.*

In our schools, teachers are often wondering about how to find just the right story or poem to read aloud on a field trip, share at a celebration, or add to a thematic study. We can't all have the privilege of just calling Bee Cullinan, but we can seek out others for help.

Just recently my own children complained that my answering machine message was too monotonous, too ordinary, too boring. I wondered if there was a short poem that would serve as an appropriate greeting. So I posted a sign on the "Help Wanted" board: "I'm looking for an appropriate poem to record on my telephone answering machine. Any suggestions?" Pat allowed several interested fifth graders to pore through the poetry anthologies. A week later the students handed me "ELTELEPHONY," by Laura E. Richards.

> Once there was an elephant,
> Who tried to use the telephant—
> No! no! I mean an elephone
> Who tried to use the telephone—
> (Dear me! I am not certain quite
> That even now I've got it right.)
> Howe'er it was, he got his trunk
> Entangled in the telephunk;
> The more he tried to get it free,
> The louder buzzed the telephee—
> (I fear I'd better drop the song
> Of elephop and telephong!)

They suggested that I record the poem and then say, "And, Who's trying to use the telephone now?"

They also suggested that I record Felice Holman's "Who Am I?"

> The trees ask me
> And the sky,
> And the sea asks me
> *Who am I?*
>
> The grass asks me,
> And the sand,
> And the rocks ask me
> *Who I am?*
>
> The wind tells me
> At nightfall,
> And the rain tells me
> *Someone small.*
> Someone small
> Someone small
> *But a piece*
> *of*
> *it*
> *all.*

They wanted me to end the recording with " 'Who Am I?' by Felice Holman and 'Who are you?' "

Their last choice was one of Emily Dickinson's poems.

288

> I'm nobody! Who are You?
> Are you nobody too?
> Then there's a pair of us—don't tell!
> They'd banish us, you know.
>
> How dreary to be somebody!
> How public, like a frog
> To tell your name the livelong day
> To an admiring bog!

After recording this poem they suggested that I add, "But please tell your name right now; Emily Dickinson won't mind."

Throughout the year teachers use the library bulletin board as a central clearinghouse for schoolwide requests. They've asked for help in locating well-written nonfiction books on spiders to read alongside *Charlotte's Web*. They've asked for contributions to a lullabye collection in preparation for a new genre study. They've asked for endangered species literature appropriate for first graders. They've asked for texts with an Appalachian setting for a social studies course of study. They've asked for appropriate poems to share on their school's Career Day. Students have also posted "help wanted" requests. One asked for help in finding literature to display along with his science fair project. Another asked for help in finding a good poem to include on his new brother's birth announcement. And many students asked for help in locating literature that would support their move from notebook writing to a finished piece (see Chapter 12).

Of course, the bulletin board could also be used to put out a call for schoolwide literary events. I recently heard Georgia Heard talk about a school in which children and teachers were asked to collect and share poems that comforted them during the Persian Gulf crisis. Literary gatherings like these can become monthly rituals. The bulletin board can announce important issues—homelessness, endangered species, or water conservation—and children, teachers, and parents can take part in auditorium performances in response. What better way to raise our consciousness about such issues than to fill the air with beautiful words read aloud, read chorally, or dramatized.

In the Hallways

Susan Pliner, an administrator at the Teachers College Writing Project and a poet, always adorns the third floor women's restroom with her favorite poems. She hangs them strategically at eye level and next to the poems she has posted a little note: "Please do not remove. If you'd like a copy, see Susan in Room 331." Much to her surprise, a man entered the office one day asking for a copy of one of the poems, Adrienne Rich's "Living Memory." Sensing Susan's surprise, he explained, "I'm the window washer, and I couldn't help but notice. . . ."

Susan has encouraged many of us to read more poetry these last few years, as have students in several of the elementary schools we work in. A small group of students at P.S. 148 meets once a month to choose new poems to hang in the school's popular waiting areas. Poems hang above the bench in the general office, along the walls of the cafeteria, and even inside the restroom stalls. Students have also chosen appropriate poems to hang on the doors of the cafeteria, the general office, the computer room, the gym, the library, and the custodian's office.

Isabel Beaton, a kindergarten teacher from the Bronx, also values hanging poetry in surprising places and puts the poems to surprising use. The students' favorite nursery rhymes and chants hang low on the walls of the school building. As she escorts her group of twenty-five students through the hallways and up and down the stairwells, she often suggests, "Walk to the 'Eensy weensy spider,'" or "Stop when you get to 'I'm a little teapot.'" When they stop, of course, everyone takes part in a quick group reading.

Older children can also be invited in on the fun. They can help put Isabel out of a job by searching for and preparing enlarged rhymes to hang as landmarks around the school building.

In other school buildings around the city, students have been given the responsibility of filling the lobby and hallway showcases with important tributes to writers and their works. In one building, students select an author to highlight each month. They search for as many of the author's works as they can find. They stand these books on end across the display cabinet shelf, creating a time line of the author's work. In other buildings, children have been asked to search for works that pay tribute to the time of year. Early in September, students display end-of-summer poems, arranged with picture books about first days at school. Later on, they replace these with autumn poems and picture books about the harvest and Halloween season.

In Claire McEntee's school, the students post personal reading ads on a hallway bulletin board:

I'm interested in a person, male or female, who enjoys sports, sports books, and mysteries. P.O. Box 1303.

I want someone who like adventures. I want a very mature person who would really like to talk about a book and not fool around. I love books by Beverly Cleary. P.O. Box 909.

Looking for someone interested in Betsy Byars books. So far I have read *The Not-Just Anybody Family, The Cybil War,* and *Pinballs.* P.O. Box 206.

Reading *Tuck Everlasting,* desperately wanting to talk about it and ask questions. I love the book so far. P.O. Box 608.

Need a counterpart who would trade ideas with me in books about sports. P.O. Box 1301.

Looking for books about dogs, like *Summerdog Comes Home* by George Zabriskie. Any dog lovers out there? P.O. Box 101.

Students welcome talking about books with new-found friends from different classrooms and different grades.

How powerful it is when students, teachers, administrators, parents, and visitors walk through buildings in which in every corridor, office, stairwell, and classroom the message is loud and clear: "Literature is at the center of this school's life."

A Word of Warning

Our teachers have learned not to launch any of these literature investigations until they have done some long-range planning. First they ask themselves, "How can the students keep this going without me?" "What structures can I put in place so that the project succeeds without me?" "Who else might help the students?" Teachers don't want to give themselves tasks they don't have time to see through.

Some hold parent workshops asking for support from home. Others share student projects with other school personnel—music, art, and drama instructors or the reading or English-as-a-second-language teachers. Older students are also scheduled to work regularly with younger ones, parenting projects in place of the classroom teachers.

When the students at P.S. 148 formed their small poetry selection committee, the teachers recommended that it be made up of children from six different classrooms across the grades. This across-grade grouping of students is significant not only because it results in a varied selection of poems, but also because it prevents the project from becoming a burden to any one busy classroom teacher. The students assumed the major responsibility, and this time the librarian served as the faculty advisor.

In their long-range planning, the teachers also ask themselves, "How can we extend the activities once they've begun?" Can the fifth graders sit alongside the first graders who have borrowed the "forgotten treasure" read-along tapes? Can they watch how they're used and think through ways to improve them?

Can the sixth graders write a cover letter to parents about the recommended reading lists or compare their lists with professional bibliographies? Can these older students arrange to have the books easily available at local libraries and bookstores?

Should paper be hung next to the poems on the wall so readers can respond? Should students think about places outside of school where poems could be displayed—on bedroom mirrors, on refrigerator doors, in frames atop their desks?

In Classrooms

Many literature investigations begin as a natural part of regular classroom instruction. These literature searches should not be thought of as extras but as ways to enrich the ongoing reading and writing work in that community. Inviting students to search for and linger with fine writing is not busywork, it is informing work.

Atop the bookcase in Kathy's sixth-grade classroom sits a large leatherbound photo album with clear acetate pages into which the teacher and her students feel free to slip favorite excerpts from novels, poems, and stories—duplicated, handcopied, or clipped from newspapers and magazines.

This literature collection is not all that different from the one Alberto Manguel recently described in *The New York Times Book Review* in an article entitled "Sweet Are the Uses of Anthology." He writes: "When I was ten or eleven, and living in Buenos Aires, my eldest aunt . . . gave me her commonplace book. It was a scrapbook with fake white marble covers, and on the gray pages my aunt had copied out favorite passages from a long life of reading."

The anthology in Kathy's classroom has become a valuable tool; both teacher and students have discovered ways and reasons to return to it often. Kathy reads aloud from it during mini-lessons and often refers to its pages when she confers. Students copy out examples of writing techniques they admire and refer to them in their peer conferences. They also slip bookmarks into their favorite pages and add yellow stick-on notes with their comments in the margins. They reread their anthology looking for gems in the same way they search through their writer's notebooks.

Students who find the anthology especially useful often decide to begin one of their own. The life of these individual anthologies can also be extended. Students can swap anthologies during reading time. They can do research on their own choices and those of others. They can study how anthologies are assembled and organized and arrange their selections with the same deliberateness. Individual collections can also be reproduced and added to the permanent classroom library. Students who are familiar with literature anthologies find it easy to create genre-based ones when a course of study begins in their classroom. Their collections are similar to the manila folders I keep in my file cabinet marked, "Favorite Poems," "Nonfiction Writing," and "Excerpts from Memoirs."

Carol's second-grade literature investigation takes its cues from Beatrice Schenk de Regniers poem, "Keep a Poem in Your Pocket." Each of her students keeps a handcopied poem in a jeans pocket at all times. Every month new poems replace old. Throughout the day the children put the little slips of paper to good use. Some are read aloud, recited, or read chorally as part of the daily opening exercise. Others are shared when the need arises. After a rigorous visit to the gym, Carol might suggest, "Who has a poem that might calm us all down?" After the class has shared a sad book, Carol might ask, "Who has a poem that might lift our spirits?" At the end of a mini-lesson on the importance of surprising your reader, Carol might ask, "Who has a poem in which the poet either made a surprising connection, wrote about a surprising topic, or used old words in surprising ways?"

Carol's colleagues have learned from her teaching techniques. It's not unusual to find poem requests posted on the "Help Wanted" board in the school library. "I'm looking for a poem to read aloud at my parents' fiftieth wedding anniversary. Any suggestions?" or "I'm searching for a poem to include in a welcome back letter to a student who has been in the hospital."

Yvonne began a new classroom practice after she took part in a special celebration with members of her adult reading circle. For the final meeting of the year, members of her group were asked to bring in a piece of writing that resonated with one that had touched them deeply during the year. Yvonne read Rachel Field's "If Once You Have Slept on an Island" and explained why it connected with her reading of Pat Conroy's *Prince of Tides*. Other members of her group explained connections between Betty Bao Lord's *In the Year of the Boar and Jackie Robinson,* and Maxine Hong Kingston's *Woman Warrior,* Montzalee Miller's *My Grandmother's Cookie Jar* and Louise Erdrich's *Tracks,* Brock Cole's *Goats,* and Tom Wolfe's *Bonfire of the Vanities,* and Beverly Naidoos's *Journey to Jo'Burg* and Alan Paton's *Cry, the Beloved Country.*

Now her students do likewise. After Yvonne read Ann Turner's *Nettie's Trip Down South,* she gave the children a week to find another text that in some way connected with this one. Children not only shared and explained their selections but often grouped several of these pieces together to form a new text-set for their reading workshop.

The books in Adrianne's third-grade classroom have envelopes pasted onto the back covers. Students not only tuck into these envelopes pieces of literature they think should be read alongside the key text, they also collect book reviews, lists of related titles, and related newspaper articles. Inside the back cover of Satoshi Kitamura's *UFO Diary* a student neatly folded a newspaper article entitled, "The Search for Extraterrestrial Intelligence." Several pieces were slipped into Nicholas Heller's *The Front Hall Carpet,* a picture book in which a young child's play is inspired by the shape, color and design of the rugs in her home. The children chose three poems about pretend play, a piece of student writing about having a special hiding place to pretend, and this excerpt from Phyllis Reynolds Naylor's *How I Came to Be a Writer:*

> These were not just books to read, I'm afraid, but they were also our toys. The volumes of the *Collier's Encyclopedia,* stood on end, formed the walls of the first floor of a dollhouse; the Mark Twains became the upstairs; and the Sherlock Holmes books formed the attic. Whenever we stretched bedsheets across the backs of chairs to play train, a good heavy encyclopedia volume held the sheet in place, and books were the tunnels through which my little brother sent his cars spinning. When evening came and it was time for my father to read another chapter from *The Prince and the Pauper,* no one complained that the dollhouse or tunnel had to be dismantled. Even now it bothers me to see, in someone's study, rows of pristine books that look as though they have never been opened, much less read and treasured—and certainly never used for holding a bedsheet in place.

Another classroom literature investigation began in Antoinette's fifth-grade classroom when we realized that the share meetings lacked energy. Students' responses seemed routine, and the children no longer looked forward to what we considered a precious ritual. I asked the students to choose any piece of published literature, student or professional, that somehow connected with the piece of writing they were about to share. The student in the author's chair began by explaining his or her choice. Most children selected a topic-related text. Alejandro brought *Homesick* by Jean Fritz when he read his own collection of vignettes about missing his country, Colombia. His work was a finished draft, so at the share meeting the members of the audience began by celebrating what they appreciated in his work and then got him talking about whether or not these same qualities appear in Fritz's book.

Jennifer brought a rough draft of a new best-friend poem along with Langston Hughes's poem about a friendship. Since her work was still in progress, her audience probed how Hughes's way of writing might help her solve any problems she faced in her own text.

In order to help students realize that connections to literature can extend beyond topics, I demonstrated some of my own. One day I sat in the author's chair and shared a notebook entry about Sunday mornings in my house and then a published poem about a spring rainfall that, I explained, "had a similar quiet tone." On another day I shared an example of a professional writer's use of flashback and a piece in which I had tried this technique myself.

Students eventually expanded on their reasons for bringing published pieces to share. One day Emil brought a draft about his grandmother getting older along with Ezra Jack Keats's *Snowy Day*. He explained that the whiteness of the snow got him thinking about how his grandmother's black hair is quickly turning silvery white. Emil's choice reminded the students that such surprising connections can get our own thoughts going.

In the days that followed students brought along companion pieces that were of the same genre, began with the same literary device, or put the reader in the same mood. Students also shared pieces that had similar main characters, a similar reliance on dialogue, or similar settings. Bringing literature to share meetings often led group talk into avenues that had otherwise gone unexplored.

Another classroom-based literature investigation had its roots in a staff development workshop on multicultural literature led by Hindy List. Hindy began her workshop by flipping through a copy of *The New York Times* and stopping to read some of the important headlines aloud: "Scraping By, Illegally Mining Kentucky Coal," "Anti-Apartheid Alliance Disbands in South Africa," "Census Finds Many Claiming New Identity, Indian." Then Hindy spoke of the adult books she has read that have deepened her understanding of these issues. She spoke of James Agee's *Let Us Now Praise Famous Men*, Alan Paton's *Cry, the Beloved Country*, and Louise Erdrich's *Tracks*. She then invited the audience to do likewise, to search the newspaper and think about their own reading and about their students. When the teachers spotted an article entitled "Zoo Animals in Kuwait City Also Suffered Iraqi's Torment," many of the teachers suggested reading Yukio Tsuchiya's *Faithful Elephants* at the same time.

Zoo Animals in Kuwait City Also Suffered Iraqi Torment

KUWAIT CITY, March 2 (Reuters)

The captives of the Kuwait City zoo did not escape the ravages of Iraq's occupation.

The charred remains of a large horned animal lie at the gateway to the zoological gardens, where humans ate exotic creatures and beast ate beast to survive the Persian Gulf war.

Inside, a pair of hippopotamuses lie together on the grass, barely breathing as they slowly die of starvation. A great Indian elephant whimpers for attention, reaching out with its trunk, in a compound bare of food or water.

The cages of five lions and two tigers are strewn with the skin, fur and bones of large beasts they have clearly eaten.

When and how the animals' torment began is difficult to ascertain. There is no one around to speak for the few who remain.

Following Hindy's workshop, I added a new twist to the fifth graders' weekly current events assignment. Rather than clip weekly articles, I asked students to select an article of interest each month. In addition to following the news story over time, I asked them to look for literature that would deepen and enrich their reading. At the end of each month, students would meet in small response groups to talk about their news stories and to "show-off" their related literature finds.

So far, the classroom literature investigations I've discussed have been deliberate invitations. The most exciting ones I've seen students take part in, however, are ones they were never asked to do. Just as students began tucking poems into their photo albums and carrying around "secret books" of poetry, so too they began borrowing some of the ways and reasons I search for literature outside of school. I told the fifth graders that every three or four weeks I mail a batch of clippings to my son at college on topics I know he'd hate to miss—the New York Yankees, the television industry, newspaper publishing. So too, I've sent articles on antique salt shakers to my colleague Susan Radley and poems on environmental issues to Georgia Heard. The students also heard about Phoebe Sophocles, a friend from Denver, Colorado, who has become my "bits and pieces" pen pal. We stuff envelopes periodically with batches of clippings, quotes, and articles we know the other will appreciate and then mail them across the country. We don't even include a letter but only a little stick-on note atop the very first sheet. Her last packet to me included several wonderful poems and articles from the *Christian Science Monitor* and *Smithsonian* magazine. How joyous it is to feel as if you have a subscription to magazines you don't subscribe to and to have articles hand-picked with your interests in mind.

Several students, especially those with best friends who've moved away, began swapping bits and pieces of literature through the mail. They clipped magazine articles, handcopied poems, and duplicated short stories.

I also told students about Mr. McPherson, a doorman who guards the apartment house next to my office. I frequently circle the block searching for a parking spot on this busy Manhattan street. "I can't help but notice," I told the children, "that Mr. McPherson has a kind word for everyone who passes by." I shouldn't have been surprised one day when he handed me an original poem (Figure 40).

Mr. McPherson's gift inspired me to return the favor. Since I didn't have any original poems to give him, I began searching for ones I thought he'd enjoy. I set out to find as many uplifting, neighborly New York poems as I could find. I began by handing him copies of the city poems I had shared with the fifth graders and continue to be on the lookout for more poems to share in this most natural of poetry exchanges. Several children in this fifth-grade class also decided to swap poems with neighborhood friends, including a crossing guard, a pastor, and a babysitter.

During Art

Antoinette places great value on the arts and never hesitates to carve out weekly time for students to mess around with paints and papier-mâché, clay and construc-

FIGURE 40

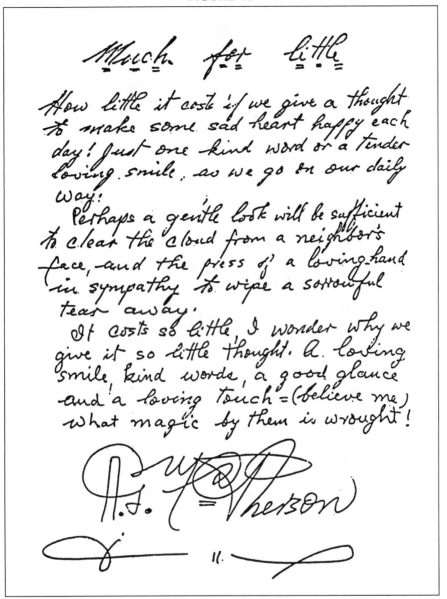

tion paper. She eagerly invited students to participate in several art-related literature investigations during their regularly scheduled art periods.

During one of our summer institutes, Mary Quinn, a primary teacher from Long
Island, shared a beautiful big book she had created with her first graders. When I
showed the book, a student-illustrated presentation of the Louis Armstrong song
"What a Wonderful World," to the ten-year-olds, they had the clear feeling that
"We could do that!" and the search was on.

One week I brought in my piano "fake-book" filled with words of popular songs
and stacks of sheet music. Students pored over these looking for those that could

FIGURE 41

be concretely illustrated and those that were popular enough for most parents or grandparents to recognize.

I explained to the children that Mary sends the completed big book home each evening with a different student. She slips it into a large red rope envelope complete with a tape recording of the children singing and a journal in which parents can write their responses to the book, the singing, and the sharing experience. In the following days, the ten-year-olds chose "Over the Rainbow," "On the Sunny Side of the Street," "School Days," "When You're Smiling," "Side by Side," "Singing in the Rain," "What the World Needs Now," and even the old Oscar Hammerstein classic, "The Surrey with the Fringe on Top." When the books were completed, they were to be donated to first-grade classrooms.

Another week I brought to class several framed poems and passages that an old friend had illustrated and bordered with wallpaper.

The rhyme in Figure 41 from *Father Foxes Penny Rhymes* by Clyde Watson used to hang on the kitchen wall next to my children's high chairs when they were toddlers.

Mark Twain's words have hung near my desk for over twenty years (Figure 42); a Francis Bacon quote has graced my side porch for as many years (Figure 43).

FIGURE 42

FIGURE 43

FIGURE 44

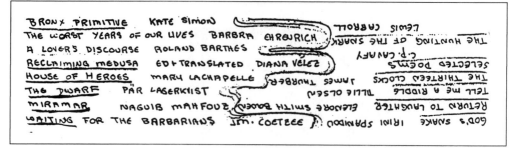

Antoinette then asked the students to find and illustrate poems they thought would be appropriate for hanging in various corners of their homes. Sylvia Cassedy's *Roomrimes,* Rose Agee's *How to Eat a Poem and Other Morsels,* Lee Bennett Hopkins's *Morning Noon and Nightime, Too* and Richard Margolis's *Secrets of a Small Brother* became hot anthologies.

Another art-related project was inspired by Andrea Lowenkopf, a senior member of the Teachers College Writing Project. She is always reading the books I wish I were reading. I've always been envious of her taste in literature and wish I could keep up with her. I'm forever copying down titles on little scraps of paper and then losing them. One day I asked Andrea to make a long list of titles she thought I'd enjoy. Andrea wrote them on the back of a lovely bookmark to be sure I'd hold on to them (Figure 44).

When the fifth graders saw my bookmark, they asked if they could make one like it. They drew one another's names out of a hat and then designed bookmark recommendations with that particular classmate in mind. On one side they wrote a list of titles, on the other their own inspirational words (Figure 45).

Students shared their bookmark lists with their parents as suggestions for holiday or birthday gifts or at least as good books to check out on their next visit to the public library. Some children even began swapping bookmarks much the way the children in Astrid Lindgren's *The Children of Noisy Village* did.

In yet another art-related literature investigation, Joanne Hindley invited students to study poems that had been published in picture book format. These included Robert Louis Stevenson's *The Moon,* Robert Frost's *Stopping by Woods on a Snowy Evening,* and Rachel Field's *General Store.* Joanne encouraged students to pay attention to layout and illustrations.

She then asked students to choose poems they thought would be appropriate in a picture book format. Most selected the work of published poets. One student chose Beatrice Schenk de Regniers, "I Looked in the Mirror," another John Ciardi's "Questions! Questions! Questions!" and still another A. A. Milne's "Disobedience." A few students chose to turn their own original poems into picture books. Jade published her poem "The Forest."

> I feel the thick, deep earth
> rise between my toes
> The whispering winds surround
> my ears and form a melody

The apple trees . . . The oak and
maple ones all guard me from
any danger lurking about.
The luscious grove of
stones and dust provides a
path for me to wonder
And most of all, I feel the
love . . .
That has brought the daisies
to bloom . . .
the apples to ripen . . .
the walnut trees to stretch across
the land.
The same love that has driven me
out here . . . to this new place

Jade Mondrake

FIGURE 45

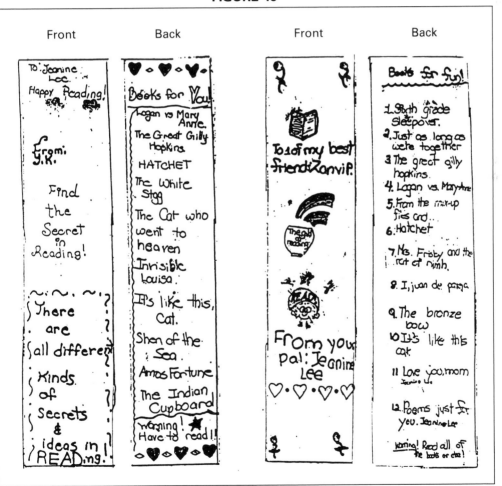

FIGURE 46

The walnut trees to stretch across the land.

On her book jacket Jade even included an explanation of her choice of medium: "I chose the medium of colored pencils because my poem is based on the wilderness and natural beings and it needs a soft tone of perpetual color. Something that would seem everlasting, yet silent." (Figure 46 shows a page from Jade's picture book.)

Joanne also asked students to create picture books based on works of art. She showed them Frané Lessac's *Caribbean Canvas,* the Metropolitan Museum of Art publications *Go in and out the Window* and *Talking to the Sun,* and Eloise Greenfield and Amos Ferguson's *Under the Sunday Tree.* In all these books, the texts have been chosen or written to accompany drawings and paintings. The students began their picture books with museum postcards and then searched for appropriate poems, songs, or proverbs to accompany each work of art. The student-compiled anthologies now share a shelf with their favorite published collections in the school library.

In Paula Fox's *One-Eyed Cat,* a teacher honors a student on his birthday by reading aloud a chapter from Jack London's *Call of the Wild.* How appropriate to think of sharing literature as gift-giving. In Antoinette's fifth-grade class we created a final art-related literature project that was part of year-long gift-giving by setting up a permanent "make-your-own" greeting card center. Stacks of poetry anthologies filled a corner table along with blank construction paper folders and beautiful bookmarks. Children were encouraged to select and illustrate just the right poem to honor their friends and family on birthdays, anniversaries, and holidays.

Life-Long Implications

Over the past few years we've discovered that inviting students to keep a writer's notebook has life-long implications. So too, investigating good writing is part of what it means to be a literate adult. As my colleague Lydia Bellino suggests, "By inviting students in on this process, we allow their voices to be heard in the school community and we invite them into the world of literate people."

Although many of these activities began with ten-year-olds, they have the potential to become part of our students' lives as they become twenty-year-olds, forty-year-olds, and sixty-year-olds.

The students who discover old treasures on library shelves might grow up to be adult readers who delight in secondhand book stores. The students who compile reading lists might become adult readers who always recommend books to their friends. The students who keep poems in their pockets might grow up to be adult readers who continue to look to poetry for nourishment.

Several years ago Mem Fox's daughter, Chloë, came to spend a few days with my family. She arrived at the airport late at night, but we were determined not to waste a minute of her first visit to New York City. We took her on a quick tour before heading home.

The first stop was the Metropolitan Museum of Art. From the backseat, Chloë said, "Oh, *From the Mixed-Up Files of Mrs. Basil E. Frankweiler.*" Then we drove through Times Square. "Oh, *Cricket in Times Square,* I loved that book." Our next stop was Washington Square, and Chloë added, "Henry James, right?" Then it was on to Brooklyn Heights to view the city from the promenade, and Chloë asked, *"Dinky Hocker Shoots Smack* takes place in Brooklyn Heights, doesn't it?" Needless to say, I was in awe of this teenager who clearly lived in a literary world.

If not enough of our students grow up in homes in which reading aloud, storytelling, poetry, and drama are woven into the fabric of everyday lives, we must extend generous invitations to students to enter these literary worlds in school.

Rachmaninoff once said, "Music is enough for a lifetime, but a lifetime is not enough for music." Don't we want our students to feel the same way about literature?

6

Listening at the Core

Listening to stories when you are really young and then reading them as you get older are really the best ways to becoming a writer.

Jane Yolen

There was something in the air at last fall's New York State reading conference. People were so collegial, so energized, so happy—and it was no surprise. Three thousand teachers listened together as local high school students performed Mussorgsky's *Night on Bald Mountain*. Three thousand teachers heard David Booth close his keynote by singing Judy Collins's classic song, "My Father." A workshop was even offered at 11:30 at night in a dark, dark room—a workshop on lullabies.

The Concord Hotel was filled with music and song that early November weekend. And the teachers were happy. Music and song can do that. We build communities when we lift our voices together, when we come together to appreciate the music and songs of others.

Early on I talked of building classroom communities by chanting, choral reading, and singing birthday songs in many languages. But music and song can do much more than create the right climate for writing; they can also improve the quality of the writing.

A year ago I led writing workshops in several black townships of South Africa. In both an elementary school in Soweto and a high school in rural Natal, I was surprised by the quality of students' writing. I didn't expect such high quality work in classrooms with very little literature.

In part, students were successful because they had such important stories to tell and they had an urgent need to share them with the world. But the writing itself, the words, were so beautiful, so lyrical, so literary. And yet there were very few books on those classroom shelves, if indeed there were classroom shelves. (Thanks to the READ Organization, classroom libraries are beginning to appear in the townships.) After several weeks of traveling and working with teachers and students, I realized that one of the rich wells the students were drawing from was the music in their lives.

I'll never forget hearing the teachers sing the African national anthem in six-part harmony to thank me for visiting. I'll never forget the Sunday morning service in Bishop Tutu's former church in Soweto. I watched as the congregants clapped out the rhythm of their prayers and hymns. They held their closed Bibles high in their left hands and with their right hands they made a rich resounding beat by tapping on their books at just the right moment, followed by a sweeping circular motion of their hands. I'll never forget the high school students paying tribute to my daughter's visit with gospel singing on our last day in class.

Music is part of African students' lives. They listen to street performers sing their songs. They hear people singing as they work, protest, or walk long distances. It was no surprise, then, that their stories and poems were so beautiful, so lyrical.

My visit to Soweto was a turning point for me. I began to think about our New York City kids. Is there enough music in their lives? Is music another resource students can rely on when they write their own wonderful texts?

Kathy Beardon, a staff member of the Teachers College Writing Project, also wondered about the role of music in our students' writing lives. Kathy's interest is easy to explain. In addition to being a gifted teacher and writer, Kathy is also a member of a choral society and has worked professionally as a singer in a rock band. I marveled at the way she began to weave music into her writing workshops. Her students not only wrote as the music of Vivaldi, Mozart, and Bach played softly in the background, they also learned to write original lullabies, jazz chants, and blues songs. They were then able to bring rhythm, repetition, and cadence to their poetry and prose. I watched Kathy teach and I watched her students fall in love with music and song and writing. I wondered if I could do what she had done.

I live with a daughter who is a jazz clarinetist, a son who plays a fine piano, and a husband who doesn't let me forget that he was a member of the Columbia University Marching Band. And I've always found it rather disheartening to watch their eyes roll when I sing, and even when I hum or tap to the music on the car radio. I've never had any formal music training. I play no instruments. I carry few tunes.

I began to wonder if I could ever bring music into students' lives, much less help students connect that music to their writing. Yes, I could press a button on a tape recorder and have students write as Vivaldi, Mozart, and Bach filled the classroom. I could invite children to research and write biographies of their favorite musicians. I could surround students with songs that have been published in picture book format and invite them to do the same. I could help students select music to accompany a read-aloud. I could invite students to realize that there are stories attached to the songs that have been important in their lives.

But, I was not confident enough to sing many songs or clap out rhythms or explore pitch and tone and melody. How then would I be able to help students bring a lyrical quality to their writing as the African students had so ably done?

And then I remembered an old saying, "If only the birds with the sweetest voices sang, the forest would be silent." If singing has taken a backseat in our school day, perhaps curriculum pressures aren't the only place to point a finger of blame. It's probably teachers like me, who are hesitant to sing in public, that are also at fault. I realized that I didn't need to have a great voice or carry a tune especially well in order to sing with students. The children deserved an opportunity to tap into the music of their lives. The children had a right to sing. And they had a right to sing more than just, "Happy Birthday to You."

And so we carved out time and with a little help from the students' favorite singers, we began to listen to tapes and records and sing along joyfully, regularly, and with gusto in our classroom.

Then too, and more important, I began to realize, perhaps out of my own insecurities, that there is another kind of music that writers need.

In Helen Griffith's picture book, *Georgia Music,* a little girl spends her summer visiting her grandpa who lives by himself in a cabin near the railroad tracks. Griffith writes, "In the evenings, the two of them sat out on the rickety porch steps and the old man played tunes on his mouth organ. He knew a lot of songs and he taught the words to the girl so she could sing with the music."

As the year rolled on the grandpa grew old and ill. He had to leave his country cabin and join his granddaughter at her home in Baltimore. He's very sad, missing his home in Georgia. The little girl realizes that she can cheer him up by playing the songs he had taught her to play on a mouth organ. She plays the songs again and again until she realizes that it's not just the songs that can cheer up her grandfather, but simply the sounds of a Georgia summer.

The little girl discovered a different kind of music—not the music of song, but the music of sounds. It was listening to the familiar sounds of animals large and small that comforted the grandfather. Simply the sounds.

In my work in New York City classrooms, I've broadened my definition of music to include listening to the sounds of beautiful language. There's music in songs, but also in sonnets. There's music in chants, but also in chapters. It's listening to wonderful language and the performance of wonderful texts that can make a difference in our reading-writing workshop.

Why Listening and Why Performing

Verah Darby teaches in an overcrowded elementary school in the North Bronx. When the school's register rose to more than six hundred students, Verah's reading-writing workshop had to be held in the auditorium. "What will I do?" she asked. "How can I teach reading and writing in that setting?"

Today, Verah thinks of the auditorium as an ideal place to teach reading and writing. "Just as the school library could have offered me some unique advantages," she says, "I discovered that the auditorium has its own pluses." Verah made good use of the auditorium. Now she can't imagine teaching reading and writing without a stage, a microphone, a podium, and comfortable seats arranged just right for an audience.

Verah and her New York City colleagues have carved out ample classroom time for students to read wonderful literature. They don't think of listening to and performing wonderful texts as a substitute for reading but as a complement to reading. They have come to value choral reading, storytelling, retelling and reading aloud in their students' writing lives because they have begun to value it in their own.

New York City teachers regularly meet at the 42nd Street library and the 92nd Street YMCA to hear their favorite writers read aloud. Eudora Welty, Annie Dillard, and Jamaica Kincaid were the hits of this past season. Our teachers tape-record poetry readings from the public radio stations and swap tapes with colleagues. When the Writing Project calendar announces presenters who share their love of literature, we shift venues from the small chapel to the huge auditorium, and with good reason.

There's been magic in the air on conference days when Marni Schwartz, Marcia Lane, and Tom Lee have told their stories. There's been magic in the air when writer and storyteller Mem Fox, poet lindamichellebaron, and local teacher Gloria Waller have orchestrated and participated in auditorium-size choral readings. There's been magic in the air on the days when David Booth, Larry Swartz, Don Holdaway, John Poeton, Gail Haley, Karla Kuskin, and Yetta Goodman have read their favorite texts to five hundred teachers gathered in the Horace Mann Auditorium.

At the end of these six-hour conference days, teachers spill out onto Broadway filled with the joy of being literate, filled with the rhythms and cadences of stories and poems. If teachers had worked on their own writing at the end of those days, they would have found it hard not to be influenced by those powerful presentations.

What Experienced Writers Say

Many accomplished writers, like our teachers, readily and graciously acknowledge how they too have been influenced by an immersion in powerful presentations. The entire text of Robert MacNeil's perfectly titled memoir *Wordstruck* is a tribute to the importance of listening to language. In the short preface he explains, "*Wordstruck* is exactly what I was—and still am: crazy about the sound of words, the look of words, the taste of words, the feeling for words on the tongue and in the mind." He credits "a childhood which made words important" and a mother who "read with enthusiasm and delight."

MacNeil is not alone. Many writers have written eloquently about the importance of having been read aloud to. Mem Fox in her powerful memoir *Dear Mem Fox* explains how she relies on her rich storehouse of language to improve the quality of her writing.

All my childhood I was exposed to the music of the Bible. The sound of the often-repeated words in all the church services I attended affected me forever, as a speaker and a writer. The sonorousness, the position of words, the number of words per phrase, the rhythms of those phrases and the placement of the pauses have been collected in a storehouse from which I draw constantly, particularly for opening and closing sentences. Listening to the Bible developed my need to read aloud every sentence I write in order to check its balance and meaning. When I read or write, I hear. The words I've read ring in my ears and reverberate against the ceilings of my storehouse, echoing their way into my own writing.

Mem goes on to explain how she spends hours revising her own writing, aiming for the wonderful sounds that have become part of her oral memory bank. "I spent whole days working on single sentences, reading them aloud, rewriting them and reading them aloud again. To use another musical analogy, I could hear the tunes in my head, but I couldn't sing them on to the paper. It drove me mad."

Many of us have attempted to do as Mem does. We write, read aloud, rewrite, and read aloud again. We are following Don Murray's advice: "Read aloud, for your ear is a better editor than your eye, and if you listen to how the piece reads it will tell you when it needs a definition woven in, some description, more evidence, a change of pace. A writer who listens well to the evolving text will find out that the text is teaching the writer how it should be written."

We are following Sven Birkerts's advice: "Writing—effective, memorable writing—depends upon hearing the language. One balances sounds, their values and meanings; one holds in readiness clauses and word chains; one speeds up and slows down according to the needs of the expression. The ear does the brain's fingertip work—it joins and adjusts, adds and subtracts. It hears the rightness of a phrase, rejects a dissonance. If you can't hear words and their arrangements—the music that accompanies and enforces meaning—then you can't write. Certainly not well."

Often, at summer writing institutes when I ask teachers how they are doing, they say, "It just doesn't sound right!" They've learned to let their ears do the brain's fingertip work.

Well, what about our students? Is it true for them? Do they hear tunes in their heads? Do they struggle to sing them on paper? Can any of this be taught? Is it wholly instinctive?

Several years ago in an article in *The Horn Book Magazine,* Paul Fleischman explained that he "never consciously set out to write metrical prose." It didn't even dawn on him that that's what he had been doing until he had finished five or six books. "It was simply instinctive," he said. It was probably instinctive for Paul Fleischman because his father is Sid Fleischman and he grew up listening to the sagas of Billy Bombay, Gentlemen Jack, Colonel Phigg, and Mr. Peacock-Hemlock Jones.

Our students don't have Sid Fleischman for a father and they don't have Annie Dillard's language-loving mother. Dillard tells about how her mother stopped dead in her tracks when she heard the baseball announcer on the radio say, "Terwilliger bunts one."

"What was that?" her mom asked, "Was that English?"

She loved the sounds of the "surprising string of syllables." And for the next ten or twelve years, Dillard writes, "If she was testing a microphone, or if she was pretending to whisper a secret . . . she said, 'Terwilliger bunts one.' "

As teachers we must refuse to believe that our students have to be born into the right family in order to have an ear for language. There are things we can do to nurture this sensibility.

Working with Our Students

Perhaps the most surprising and personal way for us to help students build a rich storehouse of language to draw upon when they write is to care about the words that come out of our mouths.

When librarian Pat Nevins invites children to have "Library on the Lawn" or "Poetry in the Park," she is demonstrating her love for a well-turned phrase. Her students know she cares about language. But, our concern for language doesn't end with catchy labels. We need to tend to our classroom conversations, lessons, and directions.

If we wouldn't be proud to have the books in our classroom library in our bookcases at home, the books probably aren't fine enough. So too, we need to talk in ways that wouldn't embarrass us if our words were somehow broadcast throughout the building. Children learn what we demonstrate. Our own talk, though, is only a beginning.

Students develop a rich storehouse of language when they are both the audience and the participants in the performing arts, in storytelling, drama, readers' theater, recitation, and the like. In order to begin placing listening at the core of students' writing process, I found myself relying on noted experts in these fields. I read and reread books by David Booth, Bob Barton, Sonja Dunn, Larry Swartz, Ellen Greene, and Mem Fox.

These experts informed my teaching. They not only offered specific classroom techniques, they also reminded me how crucial it was to set aside regular classroom time for students to tell stories, do choral reading, and perform dramatic interpretations of texts. Early in the year we had set aside big blocks of time for performing texts. We soon realized, however, that these were not just beginning-of-the-year activities. Students needed to continue to interact with wonderful words and stories throughout the year. We had also set aside big blocks of time for reading aloud to students. But this was not just a beginning-of-the-year activity either.

Above All, Read Aloud

In Chapter 1, I described a classroom filled with students who memorized poems, shared words in other languages, and swapped street songs and prepared choral readings. Above all, they were read aloud to. Reading aloud was so central to the life in our classroom that it deserves additional attention.

I read aloud as often as I could, and I was fussy about the material I chose. I searched for writers who care, who are meticulous about the sounds of words and their arrangement. I read and reread their wonderful pages aloud.

Not too long ago, my good friend and colleague Hindy List told me she had finally come to appreciate the beautiful sounds of Shakespeare's *Henry V.* Hindy had seen a recent movie version of *Henry V* and then happened upon the 1940s version. "I knew the story so well," she said, "I could finally linger in the sound." As she went on to say, she thinks the same thing happens to our kids. "If they hear *Sarah, Plain and Tall* only once they can only worry about how things will turn out. There isn't the mental time and space to appreciate the language. We have to reread," she says,"many times."

Selecting fine texts and immersing our students in them is only valuable if we attend to the quality of our reading. Because I now know how crucial reading aloud is for the child who is learning to read and for the child who is learning to write, it surprises me how little time I spent learning to do it well during my undergraduate and graduate studies. Reading aloud was something you simply did. It was rather easy, I thought, like teaching writing. You just assigned a topic. You just read aloud.

Today it doesn't surprise me to hear David Booth and Bob Barton say that reading aloud has been the lifeblood of their work for over thirty years. It doesn't surprise me because I've seen, we've all seen, the power of the person who reads aloud well.

Philip Lopate describes the master teacher as one who casts a spell through timber of voice, choice of words, and quality of concentration. The teacher or parent or librarian or next-door neighbor who reads aloud well also casts that magic spell. In Chapter 9, I talk about mentors and suggest that Don Holdaway, Bee Cullinan, and Mem Fox have been my "read-aloud" mentors. We need to pay attention to people who read aloud well.

When teachers do read aloud well, their reading is marked less by attention to words than by attention to meaning. The question is not "How can I read these words expressively?" but "How can I enter the meaning of these words?" Recently at Teachers College, Lucy Calkins read aloud *The Wall,* Eve Bunting's powerful story about a child searching for his grandfather's name on the Vietnam memorial. First she demonstrated how every word could be read with a somber, tragic tone. Then she reread the text, losing herself in the meaning of the story. True to the spirit of the six-year-old child, not every line was laden with sorrow. It was, of course, a remarkably better performance.

Maxim Gorky, in *My Childhood,* writes about his grandmother. "She told her tales in a quiet, mysterious voice, her face close to mine, gazing into my eyes with dilated pupils as she was pouring into my heart a stream of support. She sang rather than spoke, and the further she went the more rhythmic her style. It was an inexpressible joy to listen to her, and when she had finished a tale I would cry: 'Go on.'"

When teachers read aloud well, their students want to cry, "Go on!" Their readings are marked by an individual voice. We all know teachers who can take the lunchroom menu and make it sound like a feast. They're able to get children's mouths watering by the way they announce, "Today, girls and boys, we're going to have fried fish sticks on a whole wheat bun with a little cup of peaches on the side." They use just the right lilt, pause, and gesture to invite children to listen well. If they can do it with the lunchroom menu, think what they can do with Eloise Greenfield, Patricia MacLachlan, or Paul Fleischman.

When teachers read aloud well, their words have an intimate quality. The poet Suzanne Gardinier describes the intimacy in her favorite poets: "It's as if they're saying, 'Come here, I have something important to tell you.'" People who read aloud well are also saying, "Come here, I have something important to tell you." Sarah Lawrence Lightfoot describes a great teacher as one who weaves a web of intimacy. Teachers who read aloud well also seem to create and respect the aura that surrounds a powerful reading. Several years ago, Nancy Henderson, a participant at our summer institute, wrote in her log:

> I bought *The Bat-Poet* and as I was reading, I couldn't read it silently. I kept reading aloud because I just liked the way the words rolled over each other off my tongue. As I finished reading one of the full page poems, I realized that a good reader has to know something that a good symphony conductor knows. After the piece is finished, he continues to hold his baton up and the audience, because of tradition, knows not to respond, and the performers know they dare not move until the conductor signals the end of the silence by lowering his arms. We need that silence after something read well to let the listener reflect or just enjoy the piece a moment longer.

Nancy discovered a way to elevate her readings by allowing a moment of silence at the end. Several of my New York City colleagues have chosen to demonstrate the importance of read-aloud time by creating rituals as they begin. One teacher washes her hands ceremoniously before lifting the book from the shelf. Others light candles. Another precedes her reading by echoing the words of the Bushman prisoner in Laurens Van Der Post's *A Story Like the Wind*. " 'The story . . . is like the wind. It comes from a far off place and we feel it.' "

These teachers have learned to give reading aloud top priority. It's not something they squeeze into a few minutes before lunch break, nor is it a filler activity they use when half the class is pulled out for chorus. Instead, they consider it one of the most important components of their school day—every day. They won't create auras, weave webs of intimacy, or hear children cry, "Go on!" however, if the pieces they select are not wonderful texts. It's hard to read poorly crafted words aloud and it's hard to give an inspired reading if you don't love the text yourself. Again, we need to search for the writers who care about their writing—about the sounds of words and how they are arranged.

Inviting Children to Read Aloud

Teachers who select fine literature and study ways to read aloud effectively also know the joy of inviting students to do the same. Teaching children to read aloud well, like keeping a writer's notebook and investigating good writing, is another one of those lifetime gifts we need to give our students.

Each year at my family's Passover seder, as I look around my crowded dining room table, I'm reminded and saddened by young people's distaste for reading aloud. I often spot children and even young adults counting the people around the table and then counting the paragraphs in the Haggadah, anticipating which will be theirs as we take turns reading aloud. I know they're hoping not to get the long passages, or the ones with the impossible pronunciations. How do you pronounce "paschal lamb?" I realize, of course, that they're probably out of practice. They probably haven't read aloud in front of an audience for a long time, and perhaps their schoolhouse memories are of round robin readings of basal passages. No wonder they find it distasteful. They need joyful read-aloud experiences and they need them regularly.

Karla Kuskin writes, "Remember the days when sesame was a seed, channel was a deep waterway, and people read aloud for entertainment." In our classrooms, we need to recreate those days and allow children to be active participants in reading aloud for entertainment. How can students notice a jarring sound, an incomplete parallel structure, or an alliteration that has gone overboard in their own writing if they don't read aloud enough to begin to hear the words and their cadences?

In Antoinette's fifth-grade class I began a two-week course of study on reading aloud. We devoted our regularly scheduled reading time to this important work. I began by asking the children to talk about the people in their lives they considered good readers. "What do those people do?" I asked. "What can you learn from them?"

Our fifth graders had obviously been paying close attention to the people who had been reading aloud to them. They shared stories about grandmas who read in whispery voices, babysitters who made up their own words to stories, and parents who sometimes dozed off as they read. They appreciated people who stopped to explain complicated parts, who laughed along at the funny parts, who let them look at the pictures for a long while.

Students listened to tape recordings of three different people each reading the same story. We had asked parents, teachers, and upper-grade students to read familiar picture books into a tape recorder. They talked about the variations in these presentations as well as the qualities they admired.

Finally, the children selected a book they loved and would be willing to read aloud to a first grader at the end of two weeks. Jonathan chose *The Little Red Lighthouse and the Great Grey Bridge* by Hildegard H. Swift and Lynd Ward. During the two weeks, he practiced reading it aloud. He taped his read-aloud and critiqued himself. He retaped his readings. He listened to read-alouds done by professional readers. He read aloud to different audiences of classmates and family members. He asked for feedback. He tried again and again and again. During class reading time when his teacher stopped to confer with him, they talked about how to read the bold print: "the VERY, VERY PROUD and the MASTER OF THE RIVER!" They talked about how to read the special sounds of "SSSSSSSSalute!" and "Chug, chug, chug, ch-ch-ch-cheerio!" They talked about which parts require a soft voice and which a booming one. They talked about how long to let the young listener linger on the illustrations and how to read passages filled with exclamation marks without sounding too dramatic. They talked about how to read the first page to guarantee that the listener will really listen and how to make the ending sound like an ending.

Not only did Jonathan learn to read Swift and Ward's words well; he learned lessons that carried over when he read his own finished pieces aloud. In preparing for author's night at his school, he considered almost the same issues in his own writing. He knew that he should select a piece he really loved, and he again thought about volume and pace, beginnings and endings.

Elizabeth Henley, a poet and former member of the Teachers College Writing Project, often coaches her students as they prepare for a poetry reading. She suggests that they practice in front of the bathroom mirror so that they don't stumble and that they read aloud to their dog or cat to get rid of their nervousness. She reminds her students to make their faces match the emotional content of their poem and to hold the paper down so their voices sail out. Above all, Elizabeth advises, "Say it as if you love it and hear the meaning of the words as you read."

Developing a Critical Ear

We began placing listening at the center of our students' writing when we invited them to take part in the performance of literature. We read aloud and invited them to read aloud. Because these activities required significant stretches of time, we also designed several other fun ways for students to listen critically to other people's words, so they would come to feel at home listening to their own emerging texts. These activities were tucked into odd moments of the school day—transitions between activities, time spent waiting, opening and closing rituals, free time or center activities, or homework assignments.

Noticing Language Everywhere. Hart Crane said, "One must be drenched in words, literally soaked in them, to have the right ones form themselves into the proper pattern at the right moment."

We wanted students to delight in the sounds of words and how words go together, so we spent time flipping through the pages of what might be considered unorthodox literature. We searched atlases for wonderful sounding cities, rivers, and mountain ranges. We laughed at the names of colors on fancy paint charts (bohemian blue, frothy orange, and fire engine red). We read out enticing names from What to Name the Baby books. We looked through the card catalogue in the school library selecting names and titles that appealed to us. The children loved alliterative names: Lois Lowry, Milton Meltzer, Karla Kuskin. They loved the sound of *Magic Michael, Danny and the Dinosaurs, The Mouse and the Motorcycle, The Great Gilly Hopkins, Yertle the Turtle,* and *Little Red Robin Hood.* Students also offered lines from texts they were reading. Zanvi loved saying "snapdragon patch." Paul added "a cream colored calf" and "a seemingly endless hill" to our growing list of lines that felt good to say. All this helped to prepare students for the time later in the year when they would need to appreciate the language gems in their own notebook writing.

We wanted students to be on the lookout for intriguing language outside of school as well. I told them that I loved shopping for cloudberries, lingonberries, and gooseberries in Sweden. I told them I loved eating with my colleagues at the Cafe Avenue where you could order "fromage from afar" and "penne putanesco."

The children suggested that they should look for wonderful-sounding language when they read the flavor lists on ice cream parlor walls or the brand names of cereals on supermarket shelves. And it wasn't just food names the children suggested. They also planned to pay attention to newspaper headlines, movie titles, and magazine ads.

We wanted students to pay attention to spoken as well as written language. One day we sent a small cluster of students around the building to hang out, eavesdrop, and find potential poems. They jotted down phrases spoken by the custodians, the school secretary, the kitchen workers, and the school crossing guard. We also talked about places outside of school that are language-rich: laundromats, hair salons, subways, and restaurants.

Children enjoy doing word search puzzles, and we wanted them to find the same delight in language searches. We made sure to recognize and honor all their attempts to hear the language in their environment. Some students recorded their favorite phrases in a special section of their notebooks. Others posted them on a special class bulletin board. Still others made deliberate attempts to weave them into their talk and into their writing.

Listening to Other Languages. On my last birthday, my children gave me a bilingual English-Spanish edition of P. D. Eastman's *Are You My Mother?* After I had decided that there was no deep psychological meaning attached to their choice, I brought the book to school. I read it aloud in both languages, and then invited comments about the sounds of the two languages. The students' opinions were almost unanimous: many Spanish words have a lovelier sound than their English counterparts. They preferred *pájaro* to bird, *arbol* to tree, and *abajo* to down. We talked about the sounds that were particularly pleasing to our ears.

I also read aloud several books that easily lend themselves to the comparison of sounds. Ruth Brown's beautifully illustrated *Alphabet Times Four: An International ABC* contains words in English, Spanish, French, and German. Brown has chosen words with similar roots, which thus have only slight variations in pronunciation: "ball, bola, boule"

Meredith Dunham's *Picnic: How Do you Say it?* allows children to compare the names of foods in four languages, and Esther Hautzig's *In School* adds the sound of Russian words to the more usual French, English, and Spanish.

On other occasions, we invited students and parents to read aloud poems in languages for which we had no English translation. Our talk then was exclusively about the sound of the words and not their meanings.

Arranging Sounds. Students not only had opportunities to discover wonderful sounding words and phrases, we also invited them to arrange, juggle, and rearrange those phrases into pleasing combinations.

One day I gave each fifth grader a copy of the school's organization sheet listing all school personnel. I asked them to work in pairs and create chants by using teachers' surnames. "Arrange them in pleasing ways. Listen to their sounds. Work at it until it sounds right." Children chanted "Fabilli, Fazzini, Salerno, Spinelli" over and over again as if it were a tongue twister. They clapped a beat to "Epstein, Torres, Tittle, and Vitolo." They snapped their fingers to "Cohen and Fernandez, Gonzalves and Rosen."

On another day, students recorded a long list of their classmates' native countries. Then they arranged the country names into rhythmic chants. Students jumped rope to the beat of "Poland, Peru, Puerto Rico, Malaysia" and "Hong Kong, Ecuador, Mexico, Romania." We asked the students to listen to the difference when the chant was read from bottom to top. "Does 'Malaysia, Puerto Rico, Peru, Poland' sound as lyrical as 'Poland, Peru, Puerto Rico, Malaysia?' Is 'Romania, Mexico, Ecuador, Hong Kong' as satisfying as 'Hong Kong, Ecuador, Mexico, Romania'?"

Students also made long lists of precise words chosen from areas of individual interest or expertise. One child named twenty different kinds of bread and then selected a few to turn into a chant. The room filled with "biscuits, bagels, muffins, and croissants." Another went from a whisper to a roar as he repeated "loafers, galoshes, moccasins, and saddle shoes." Yet another used a pencil to tap out the rhythm on his desktop for "We play piano, tambourine, and oboe." A group of children created a hand-clapping round from the names of clouds: "Cirrus, Cirrus, Cirrus and Cumulus, / Cumulus, Cumulus, Cumulus and Stratus, / Stratus, Stratus, Stratus and Cirrus."

David Shookoff, our friend from the Manhattan Theatre Club, taught us another sound-arranging activity. At one of our yearly principal conferences, David invited administrators to do some of their own critical listening. First he read aloud a passage from C. S. Lewis's *The Lion, the Witch and the Wardrobe.* Then he reread the passage, asking members of the audience to jot down a line or two that caught their ears. He suggested that they choose lines that were particularly vivid, dynamic, or emotional. Participants called out their chosen lines and David asked several of them to join him in the front of the room where he conducted them in a performance of their favorite lines as if he were the leader of a full orchestra.

Of course, David had selected the performers deliberately, listening for lines he thought he could more easily turn into a performance rich in consonance and contrast. "The hardest part," he suggests, "is remembering the words that are up there." When David points in their direction, the performers repeat their lines. He reminds the performers to let their way of saying the words reflect the feelings they attach to them. David says a bit of musical instinct informs his orchestration, but quite simply he's just playing and improvising with the sounds of words. He tries to couple lines that reinforce one another or those that create a tension. He also listens for lines that would make a satisfying beginning and ending. With that, his musical piece is complete.

Children too can take the role of orchestra leader and performers. A student can select a read-aloud passage and invite classmates to choose their favorite lines. The student leader can then conduct his classmates in this literary musical composition.

Trading Places. One morning I filled the the chalkboard with some rearranged titles. They included *Ham and Green Eggs, Ramona and Beezus, Toad and Frog are Friends, Sarah, Tall and Plain,* and *Gretel and Hansel.* The students all sensed the awkwardness of the wording. I opened up the discussion by asking, "Do you think we find these titles uncomfortable because we're so used to the correct wording or do you think it's because this ordering really doesn't sound as beautiful as the original?"

I suggested to the students that the authors probably worked long and hard deciding on the most pleasing arrangement. "Have you ever overheard parents discussing what to name a new baby?" I asked. "They select names that sound right with the family's last name. They juggle middle and first names. They say names out loud, checking for any awkwardness. Some sounds easily flow together, others are jarring and abrupt."

Students took to rearranging familiar phrases on their own. Over the next week they challenged their classmates to evaluate the sound of Jerry and Ben's, Treat or Trick, down and up, Hardy and Laurel, Vanilli, Milli.

Poems Too Good to Resist. I once heard poet Suzanne Gardinier say that when she reads a poem aloud, she asks herself, "Did it feel good to wrap my mouth around it?" Students too can think about the quality of texts by judging the feel of words in their mouths.

After sharing the following two poems with students, I invited them in on the search for poems they couldn't resist reading aloud because it felt so good "to wrap their mouths" around the words.

I Am Growing a Glorious Garden

I am growing a glorious garden,
resplendent with trumpets and flutes,
I am pruning euphonium bushes,
I am watering piccolo shoots,
my tubas and tambourines flourish,
surrounded by saxophone reeds,
I am planting trombones and pianos,
and sowing sweet sousaphone seeds.

I have cymbals galore in my garden,
staid oboes in orderly row,
there are flowering fifes and violas
in the glade where the glockenspiel grows,
there are gongs and guitars in abundance,

there are violins high on the vine,
and an arbor of harps by the bower
where the cellos and clarinets twine.

My bassoons are beginning to blossom,
as my zithers and mandolins bloom,
my castanets happily chatter,
my kettledrums merrily boom,
the banjos that branch by the bugles
play counterpoint with a kazoo,
come visit my glorious garden
and hear it play music for you.

Jack Prelutsky

The Peaceable Kingdom

Alligator, Beetle, Porcupine, Whale,
Bobolink, Panther, Dragonfly, Snail,
Crocodile, Monkey, Buffalo, Hare,
Dromedary, Leopard, Mud Turtle, Bear,
Elephant, Badger, Pelican, Ox,
Flying Fish, Reindeer, Anaconda, Fox,
Guinea Pig, Dolphin, Antelope, Goose,
Hummingbird, Weasel, Pickerel, Moose.
Ibex, Rhinoceros, Owl, Kangaroo,
Jackal, Opossum, Toad, Cockatoo,
Kingfisher, Peacock, Anteater, Bat,
Lizard, Ichneumon, Honeybee, Rat.
Mockingbird, Camel, Grasshopper, Mouse,
Nightingale, Spider, Octopus, Grouse,
Ocelot, Pheasant, Wolverine, Auk,
Periwinkle, Ermine, Katydid, Hawk.
Quail, Hippopotamus, Armadillo, Moth,
Rattlesnake, Lion, Woodpecker, Sloth,
Salamander, Goldfinch, Angleworm, Dog,
Tiger, Flamingo, Scorpion, Frog.
Unicorn, Ostrich, Nautilus, Mole,
Viper, Gorilla, Basilisk, Sole,
Whippoorwill, Beaver, Centipede, Fawn,
Xanthos, Canary, Polliwog, Swan.
Yellowhammer, Eagle, Hyena, Lark,
Zebra, Chameleon, Butterfly, Shark.

Traditional Shaker abecedarious

Children's suggestions for reading aloud included Eve Merriam's "Mean Song" from *Potato Chips and a Slice of Moon* and her "What in the World?" from *Poems Children Will Sit Still For.* From the *Random House Book of Poetry for Children* they chose Pauline Clarke's "My Name is . . ." and Mary Ann Hoberman's "Click-beetle." They also loved Philip Booth's "The Round" from *New Coasts and Strange Harbors.*

Writing to the Rhythm. When I told the students that Dr. Seuss's *And to Think That I Saw It on Mulberry Street,* was written to the rhythm of a ship's engine as he crossed the Atlantic Ocean, they wanted to hear the sound of a ship's engine. They probably would have appreciated hearing the book read aloud with a ship's engine in the background. Perhaps then they would have really understood what it means to put words to a rhythm.

Of course we didn't have any ship's engine, but we did have steam pipes that knocked, clocks that ticked too loudly, and rain that beat down on the windowsills. One morning I shared with the students four lines I had written as I sat listening to a mantle clock ticking in my living room.

> "The cat is watching me right now.
> She sits upon the windowsill.
> I wonder what she's thinking now
> Perhaps she needs to eat or drink."

I read it aloud to the beat of a clock, chunking my phrasing into groups of two syllables, each line matching the steady sound of tick-tock/tick-tock/tick-tock/tick-tock. I invited students to attempt to write to the rhythms they heard at school or at home. None accepted the challenge, but they did become more sensitive to the rhythms inherent in the texts they read. They began naming those poems and picture books that to them had the beat of rock, jazz, or classical music.

Comparing Versions. Another way we invited children to listen carefully in order to learn to judge the quality of a text was to read aloud several versions of the same story. I read for example, five versions of the Aesop's fable "The Town Mouse and the Country Mouse," which I prepared on tape so students could hear the texts several times. The various translations and retellings differed greatly: Some sounded old-fashioned; others felt contemporary. Most were in prose, but one was in verse. Some were filled with fancy vocabulary; most with rather simple words. Many had long, winding sentences; some had short, crisp ones. Children chose their favorite and explained their reasons. They explored other fables in a similar way and wondered about the possibility of retelling their own stories in different styles.

Bringing It All to Yourself as a Writer

Of course the major reason for providing students with many different opportunities to listen to the sounds of words is to fine-tune their ability to listen to their own drafts so that their ears become part of the revision process. Reading their own work-in-progress aloud can serve as an impetus toward revision.

In many classrooms, tape recorders and blank cassettes have been added to the writing centers. Children record their drafts and then listen for places that are working well and weaker places that need tightening. They're also listening to the language they have used, noting which parts are awkward to say and which sound just right.

In other classrooms, read-aloud circles serve a similar function. Young writers read their writing-in-progress to a cluster of friends, keeping one eye on the audience for moments of boredom and moments of rapt attention. Auditorium appointments have also become popular. Students sign up for a ten-minute visit to the auditorium to practice reading their drafts aloud into a microphone. All the while, they're asking themselves, "Is it my best? Can I imagine reading this to a standing-room only crowd?"

7

Literature and the Writer's Notebook

Writers generally enjoy reading, just as readers feel they might have been writers.

Holbrook Jackson

Several years ago, I read a short story called, "Knives on the Right, Forks on the Left" by Betty Vander Els. It begins, "My great-grandmother taught my mother and my mother taught me—'When you set the table you put knives on the right, forks on the left, except for the father of the house'—and that's the way I'd always done it."

It isn't until a friend asked, "Why?" that the author traced the roots of this unusual family tradition. She discovered that her great-grandfather had been left-handed. Things get started and then they're hard to change. This is particularly true in education.

When I attended elementary school in New York City, I remember with great clarity our weekly spelling assignments. On Monday mornings we took a pretest. On Monday evenings, we wrote those words in alphabetical order. On Tuesday evenings we wrote them three times each. On Wednesdays we used each word in a sentence. On Thursday evenings we had to write a story using all ten words. On Friday, we took a retest.

Today, more than thirty-five years later, I see my nieces and nephews, who attend public schools in different boroughs of the city, still doing the same weekly spelling assignments. Things get started and then they're so hard to change, except of course, if we've become what Donald Schön has termed, "reflective practitioners."

We all need to be the kind of teacher who stops to ask, "Why are we doing what we're doing?" Sometimes we become that kind of teacher when we have a friend who takes a reflective stance and has the courage to ask us, "Why?"

To the Teachers College Writing Project family, Dorothy Barnhouse has been such a friend.

Several years ago Dorothy asked, "Why are you rushing the children to write? Why is everything they put down labeled draft one? Why are details and a sharp lead added to everything the they write?"

Dorothy challenged us to take a good, hard look at the way we had invited young children to participate in writing workshops. She wondered why our students didn't have a place to do imperfect writing, to gather seeds for writing, to collect the bits and pieces of their lives. Dorothy wondered aloud why our students weren't keeping writer's notebooks.

We knew that Don Murray honored his notebook and that Madeleine L'Engle kept a journal. We realized that dozens of the writers we read and admired valued keeping a writer's notebook. Many of our teachers too, had been doing so, and yet, we had never invited children in on the fun. Dorothy inspired us to take a chance.

When the teachers in the Writing Project tried to change the way they had involved children in a writing workshop, they found themselves groping and stumbling around, not quite sure where to turn next. Teachers were uncomfortable, but their uneasiness brought out the pioneer spirit once again. They found new ways to support one another and the work at hand.

At district in-service courses, at summer institutes at the college, and at network meetings at key project schools, teachers re-discovered literature as a good friend in the writing workshop. The teachers realized that literature can help to introduce the entire notion of keeping a writer's notebook, but it can also be used throughout the year to enrich students' notebook jottings.

Using Literature to Launch the Writer's Notebook

The most effective way I've discovered to launch the idea of the writer's notebook is to convince children that they have unique, worthwhile, and important ideas that deserve to be recorded. We begin by filling classrooms with children's voices. And nothing serves as a better catalyst than fine literature.

I often introduce the writer's notebook with three stacks of carefully selected texts. The first stack contains *Knots on a Counting Rope* by Bill Martin and John Archambault, *The Chalk Doll* by Charlotte Pomerantz, and Montzalee Miller's *My Grandmother's Cookie Jar*. With older students I include Mel Glenn's poem, "Jonathan Sobel, Pd-5, Room 206". ˙

All these works are about family stories. I share the gist of them with my students, and remind them that we all have family stories. I tell a few myself and then invite students to do the same. Some of the children can't help but respond to the blindness in *Knots on a Counting Rope* or ask questions about Jamaica after hearing the *Chalk Doll,* but most share a story that's been told and retold in their own families.

The second stack contains Patricia Polacco's *The Keeping Quilt,* Dayal Khalsa's *Tales of a Gambling Grandma,* Faith Ringgold's *Tar Beach,* Lauren Mills's *The Rag Coat,* and Eloise Greenfield's poem "Keepsake" (see p. 69). "All of these stories and poems," I tell the children, "remind us of how certain objects in our lives can become very important to us."

I then tell the students about a wooden ashtray from Cuba that reminds me of my father, an old oak time-clock that holds stories about my mother, and old photographs that make me daydream, wonder, and ask questions about relatives I hardly knew. Students then begin to tell the stories attached to the important objects in their lives.

The final stack of texts includes Cynthia Rylant's *When I Was Young in the Mountains,* James Stevenson's *When I Was Nine,* and Charlotte Zolotow's poem "So Will I" (see p. 69). With older students I also include Alden Rowlan's poem, "Great Things Have Happened."

All these prompt talks about memories that haunt us, those moments and images we'll never forget. "Thirty, forty, fifty, years from now," I ask the children, "what are the scenes that will linger in your mind's eye?"

When the classroom is brimming with talk I say to the students, "Your lives are so interesting. You each have so many incredible things to say, you must have a place to record your ideas. A friend once told me," I continue, "that objects give her the itch to write. Well, family stories and memories can do that too. This year we're each going to carry a writer's notebook, so that whenever we have the itch to write we'll have this handy place to record our thoughts."

Books and poems that evoke family stories, personal treasures, and vivid memories are not the only categories of texts which can invite students to talk and then feel the need to write.

There are several other literature stacks I can imagine creating that would convince students they need to keep a writer's notebook. Perhaps I'd put together a collection of texts on dreams, another on good friends, or others on feeling alone, or scared, or jealous. I'd deliberately choose issues that easily resonate with students. I'd create stacks that lead to 'on-the-spot' talk. Children would not have to research, observe, or interview to get their voices going; these strategies will come later. At this early stage I simply want students to get the feeling, "I have so much to say, I need to have a place to record these important thoughts."

Using Literature to Enrich Notebook Keeping Throughout the Year

There are myriad ways that literature supports the writer's notebook. We can use literature to launch the writer's notebook and we can use literature to inspire notebook writing. All the information in Chapter 4 in fact, demonstrates how literature supports keeping a writer's notebook. There I shared ways to help students value literature as a generative seedbed for their own writing. Anytime students read and are inspired to write, literature has supported their writer's notebook.

Literature can even strengthen a student's commitment to this kind of writing. There's a wonderful scene in Lynn Joseph's *A Wave in Her Pocket—Stories from Trinidad.* A group of young children are eating a special coconut currant cake.

Their Tantie has baked a surprise into every slice. When Amber bites into her piece the author writes, "I felt something hard in my mouth. I reached in and pulled out a tiny notebook covered in coconut and currants. I wiped off the cake and opened it. Inside were tiny blank pages. I looked over at Tantie, and she smiled. "Must mean you go be a writer someday," she said. I smiled back. I liked that idea." Whenever I share this scene, students are reminded once again that writers the world over value keeping a writer's notebook.

At one summer institute, I asked participants to bring in a piece of literature that in some way informed notebook keeping in their classroom. We filled the chalkboard ledges with our finds and then tried to categorize them. In the following pages I list the categories that have proven useful to teachers in making the writer's notebook an important part of their students' writing lives. All these categories can be resources for mini-lessons and conferences as well as small and whole-group discussions. Each heading includes a few titles and examples that invite readers to add more.

When the Main Character Keeps a Notebook

For many years I've been collecting children's literature in which the main character is a writer. I read excerpts from these books to teachers as well as to students in order to encourage talk about the place of writing in other people's lives and to share other writers' composing strategies. I love reading about the child who is obsessed with keeping lists of Ten-Best in Bernard Waber's *Nobody is Perfick*, the child who is fulfilling a school composition assignment in Robert Kimmel Smith's *The War with Grandpa*, and the one writing a research report in Kathryn Lasky's *Pageant*. I love reading about how important keeping a diary became to a blind child in Marguerite Vance's *A Rainbow for Robin*.

Friends and colleagues are always adding titles to this collection, and as I read through professional journals, I'm always delighted to find articles by other educators with a similar obsession; for example, Louisa Smith's "Child Writers in Children's Literature" (*Language Arts*, May 1980), Eileen Tway's "Come Write With Me" (*Language Arts*, October 1981), Carl A. Anderson's "Young Writers in Adolescent Literature: Models for Student Writers" (*ALAN Review*, Spring 1990), and Karla Hawkins Wendelin and Kathy Everts Danielson's "Fictional Writers as Models of Writing" (*The Dragon Lode*, Winter 1990). All these articles have valuable bibliographies.

In the last several years I've been shelving together those books in which the main characters are not just writers but writers who've made notebook keeping a regular part of their writing lives. The following titles are among my favorites:

- *Hey World, Here I Am* by Jean Little
- *Arthur, for the Very First Time* by Patricia MacLachlan
- *I'm in Charge of Celebrations* by Byrd Baylor
- *Mr. and Mrs. Thief* by Naomi Kojima
- *Sister* by Eloise Greenfield
- *Summer Rules* by Robert Lipsyte
- *Harriet the Spy* by Louise Fitzhugh
- *Anastasia Krupnik* by Lois Lowry
- *Poor Jenny, Bright as a Penny* by Shirley Rousseau Murphy
- *My Stories by Hildy Calpurnia Rose* by Dale Gottleib

FIGURE 47

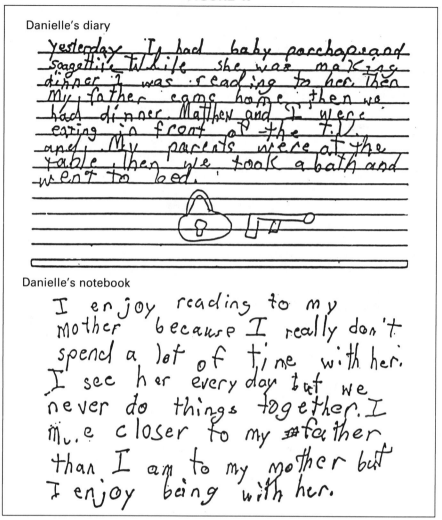

Danielle's diary

Danielle's notebook

These books can be used in various ways in the writing workshop. I can read aloud a selection of excerpts and point out how each character leads what Don Murray has described as "the examined life." I can then invite students to do the same.

I can read aloud any one text in order to highlight the fictional writer's strategies for using the notebook. One day, for example, I read the simple, humorous picture book *Mr. and Mrs. Thief* to Antoinette's fifth graders. I was able to remind the students that the main character not only closely observed and recorded his neighbor's comings and goings but also tried to make his observations add up. The young notebook keeper paid attention to the details of his world and tried to understand their significance.

I can also share such texts in order to improve the quality of students' notebook jottings. At one point early in the school year, we discovered that several fifth graders were using their notebooks as diaries, filling in page after page with

FIGURE 47, continued

Jeanine's diary

> Diary,
> Got up, walked to school, sheley came, ate lu
> After school went home did homework read
> write TV. ate rice rest alittle to brush
> teeth, went to bed

Jeanine's notebook

> Notebook
>
> Why rice?! Sometimes I just hate
> rice. Why does mom always waste
> time cooking rice. Why not Pizza or
> Fried chicken? I mean rice nearly
> everyday makes me very sick. My
> Stomach is full of rice and it
> has no taste, So mom has
> to make or Cook vetables and
> we have to have Soup and all that
> Dishes. Sometimes we have to eat
> that vegables or Dishes for a
> week. o.k. So were Chinese. But
> why can't we have Pizza or Friled chidce
> once a week.

bed-to-bed recordings of daily happenings. Because their notebook jottings were so limited, these students were struggling to find any generative seeds.

I invited this small group of students to meet me at the round table in the back of the room where I had stacked multiple copies of a surprising text, Ann Martin's *Babysitter Club #29—Malary and the Mystery Diary,* and some index cards. The students seemed stunned that they were being asked to read a book they considered underground literature. In some ways, I was a little surprised myself. But in the opening pages of the book, Malary talks about the difference between a diary and a journal. (Her "journal" writing resembled the kind of notebook writing we were hoping for.) Her diary entries begin, "Got up. Went to school. Made gum chains with Jerri during recess." Her journal entries were much more reflective. One began, "I feel as if I'm going to be eleven forever."

FIGURE 47, continued

Francis's diary

> I woke up, ran downstairs patted the hamster, said hello to the gerbils packed my bookbag got dressed ate Corn Flakes and ran out the door to school.

Francis's notebook

> I feel sorry for hamsters. They try and get warm so they roll up into puff balls but the gerbils they shred everything up build a cave and sleep in their they sleep together. One is awake to watch for intruders and the other sleeps. They are very alert.

I asked the students to read the first three pages, and we chatted briefly about their content. I then asked them to demonstrate the difference between diary writing and notebook writing on the index cards.

On one side they were to record the day's happenings. On the other side they were to select something significant from that day and do some notebook writing.

Figure 47 shows three student samples.

The task proved to be a particularly effective way of shifting students to a new way of using their writer's notebook. They appreciated having concrete models that clearly demonstrated what had previously remained an abstract distinction to them. They benefited from being asked to do both kinds of writing side by side. They were now able to hold these two kinds of writing in their hands at the same time, naming them in almost a point-counterpoint way. They were now able to see the difference between logging a day's events and reflecting on those events.

I asked students to read through their notebooks, searching for other examples of "diarylike" entries or "notebooklike" entries, or a combination of the two, and to bring them to the share meeting.

When the Main Character Leads a Wide-Awake Life

Vladimir Nabakov said, "Think how boring it would be if you didn't look at the world with a writer's eye—making up stories, guessing reasons, finishing conversations, making blurred visions come clear."

There are many children's books in which characters do look at the world with a writer's eye. In Joan Lowery Nixon's *If You Were a Writer,* the main character, Melia, learns to care about words, to see ideas everywhere, and to take a "What if?" stance. But it's not necessary for main characters to be writers in order to demonstrate wide-awakeness. Aspiring writers can learn from anyone who finds the world a fascinating place.

During one mini-lesson, I read aloud Catherine Brighton's *Five Secrets in a Box,* the story of Galileo's curious little daughter Virginia who investigates the instruments on her father's desk. I then said to the students, "If only Virginia were around today and in our class, I think she'd be such a wonderful writer, because she is so curious about everything."

I went on to talk about the young boy who's a night-watcher in Kathryn Lasky's *Tugboats Never Sleep.* When everyone thinks he's asleep he's listening to the sounds and marveling at the sights in Boston Harbor. "What a fine writer he'd probably be."

I also talked about *Josephina the Great Collector* in Diana Engels's book by the same name. "For her, the world was full of treasures just waiting to be seen and held and kept," even though her family thinks her collections are worthless junk. "What a fine writer she would be."

I ended my mini-lesson by suggesting, "If I were Virginia's writing teacher, or Josephina's writing teacher, or the teacher of that night-watcher, the most important thing I could do for them would be to encourage them to record their observations and questions and passions in a writer's notebook."

Over the years I've shared many other picture books that challenge youngsters to live their lives in active and alert ways in and out of the classroom. Some of my favorites are listed in Table 1.

Literature as a Metaphor for Keeping a Writer's Notebook

Although I have always loved Eloise Greenfield's poem "Daydreamers," just recently I've realized that this poem offers an important challenge to teachers of writing. If students are to write well, we need to create occasions for their dreams to "hopscotch, double dutch, dance" and their thoughts to "roller skate, crisscross, bump into hopes and wishes." We need to give students opportunities to be "thinking up new ways, looking toward new days, planning new tries, asking new whys." The daydreaming pastimes Greenfield describes can all take place between the covers of a writer's notebook. Her poem serves as a metaphor for all that we hope will happen when children pause to reflect on their world.

Similarly, in Norton Jester's *Phantom Tollbooth,* Alec speaks to Milo in the land of Discord and Dynne. He is describing a telescope, but he might be referring to a writer's notebook.

"Carry this with you on your journey," he said softly, "for there is much worth noticing that often escapes the eye. Through it you can see everything from the tender moss in a sidewalk crack to the glow of the farthest star—and most important of all, you can see things as they really are, not just as they seem to be. It's my gift to you."

When we hand a student a writer's notebook we are also hoping that this portable writing tool will help them see things as they really are. We're hoping not

Table 1

Title	Author	The main character would probably be a fine writer because:
The Chalk Doll	Charlotte Pomerantz	Writers nudge their family and friends to tell stories.
The Listening Walk	Paul Showers	Writers pay close attention to sounds.
Home Place	Crescent Dragonwagon	Writers discovers clues and follow trails of thinking.
One World	Michael Forman	Writers pay attention to their world and take responsibility for it.
Miss Maggie	Cynthia Rylant	Writers pay attention to other peoples' lives.
Roxaboxen	Alice McLerran	Writers can imagine their own new worlds.
A Visit to Oma	Marisabina Russo	Writers love to make up stories in their minds.
Our Home is the Sea	Riki Levinson	Writers reflect on the sights around them.
Hello, Tree!	Joanne Ryder	Writers use all their senses to learn about the world.
That's What I Thought	Alice Schertle	Writers delight in asking questions.

only that they'll see more, but also that they'll hear, think, feel, learn, comment, reflect, reminisce, and imagine more.

As I read, I'm always on the lookout for words and passages that might help young students better understand what it means to live a wide awake, self-conscious life.

I've shared the title of Paul Fleischman's young adolescent novel, *Rear-View Mirrors.* I explained that Olivia, the main character, uses the ordinary objects around her—a tavern jukebox, a birdcall, an epitaph—as rearview mirrors to help her to look back at her memories. The fifth graders began talking about the rearview mirrors in their own lives—a painting in their grandmother's kitchen, their father's passport, a stuffed animal won at a carnival. I suggested that they record the memories attached to those objects in their writer's notebook.

I've also shared lines from Diana Engel's *Josephina the Great Collector.* These not only remind children to pay attention to the treasures that surround them, they serve as a metaphor for keeping a writer's notebook. On the very last page, Josephina's sister has to admit that all that collecting was worth it. "Out of all that junk," she says, "you've made a masterpiece." Writers too need to know that all their collecting will be worth it. They too can attempt to create masterpieces.

Published Notebooks

There's a popular soft drink jingle with the refrain, "There ain't nothing like the real thing." For teachers who want their students to keep a writer's notebook, "there ain't nothing like the real thing." Teachers can share with children their own writer's notebook and those of other students, but the published notebooks of professional writers are also a resource they can draw upon.

Many published notebooks, journals, and diaries are written by authors of adult material and not all can be shared with very young writers. I find myself carefully selecting excerpts from such books as *Our Private Lives,* a collection of journals, notebooks, and diaries written by famous writers. "One thing I noticed about Annie Dillard's notebook," I tell the children, "is that she truly cares about unusual words. Listen to these entries, 'Glabella: the space between the eyebrows. CAVU: pilot acronym: ceiling and visibility unlimited'." "It's no surprise that Annie Dillard records curious words," I continued, "she has said that a deep love and respect for language is what keeps her writing. Some of you might want to do what Annie Dillard does and record the words you fall in love with."

On another day I read a few of Edward Hoagland's notebook entries. "He seems particularly interested in folklore. Listen to these: 'You butter a cat's paw when moving it to a new home, so it can find its way back after going out exploring for the first time.' He also wrote, 'Learning to eat soup: Like little boats that go out to sea, I push my spoon away from me.' Some of you may want to do what Edward Hoagland does and record the family sayings and customs that interest you."

If excerpts from writers' notebooks are a rich resource, so are commentaries by writers about their colleagues notebooks. In her collection of essays *Granite and Rainbow,* Virginia Woolf has written about the diaries of Katherine Mansfield. I told students that in her notebook this famous English writer "noted facts—the weather, an engagement; she sketched scenes; she analyzed her character; she described a pigeon or a dream or a conversation." Mansfield really used her notebook as a tool for her writing. She made purposeful and planful notes to herself. One time she wrote, "Let me remember when I write about that fiddle how it runs up lightly and swings down sorrowful. Or, 'Lumbago. This is a very queer thing. So sudden, so painful, I must remember it when I write about an old man.' "

In writing about *The Journals of John Cheever,* Mary Gordon also offers helpful information to share with students. She explains that a journal is a place where a writer "is not performing, not showing off. In his or her journals, the writer is unprofessional, unbuttoned, unguarded. A writer uses a journal to try out the new step in front of the mirror."

Recently, the New York Public Library held an exhibition entitled "Self-Explorations: Diarists in England and America." On display were the works of fifty authors, including Virginia Woolf, Charles Dickens, Mark Twain, Louisa May Alcott, e. e. cummings, Nathaniel Hawthorne, and Herman Melville. A *New York Times* journalist describing the event commented, "For a number of the authors, their diaries served as more than sentimental keepsakes. Private notes formed the ideas and language that later appeared in their books and plays." It's these kinds of diary entries that are most helpful to young notebook keepers. Students can appreciate the fact that Hawthorne's notes about Rome later appear in his novel *The Marble Faun* and Washington Irving's jottings about Spain later become part of *The Alhambra.*

How helpful it would be if more of today's popular writers for children would share some of their notebooks, diaries, or journals. Writers often add their drafts, galleys, and dummies to special library collections and some have published the notebooks they kept when working on a particular book. In the Author's Eye series published by Random House, for example, children can see the notebook Katherine Paterson kept as she wrote *Bridge to Terabithia.* It's next to impossible, however, to let children see notebooks kept by their favorite writers on an everyday basis. An anthology of those would be a wonderful addition to our classroom libraries.

The Memoirs and Biographies of Professional Writers

Ann Morrow Lindberg has said, "Writing isn't living, writing is being conscious of living." I often give students selections from literature demonstrating that writers are particularly conscious of living. They live their lives a little bit differently than people who don't write. They have discovered important ways to pay attention to the world, and these discoveries can become strategies for young notebook keepers.

A major source of such selections is memoirs by professional writers. Several of my most dog-earred were written by writers of adult literature. They include, Russell Baker's *Growing Up,* Eudora Welty's *One Writer's Beginnings,* Annie Dillard's *An American Childhood,* and Robert MacNeil's *Wordstruck.* Throughout the pages of these texts I've found excerpts to share with fifth-grade notebook keepers.

They know that Robert MacNeil was a "collector of expressions and pronunciations that tickled [him] whenever [he] travelled." They know that Russell Baker valued listening to "long kitchen nights of talk." They know that Annie Dillard appreciated that the "world is full of fascinating information" to "collect and enjoy." They know that Eudora Welty credits her family's summer trips by train and car with giving her a sense of story, complete with form, "direction, movement, development, change."

The memoirs of writers who write primarily for children are perhaps an even more powerful resource. Some were written for children to read, like Jean Little's *Little by Little: A Writer's Education,* Beverly Cleary's *A Girl From Yamhill,* and Phyllis Reynolds Naylor's *How I Came to Be a Writer.* Some were intended for more adult audiences: Mem Fox's *Dear Mem Fox* and Madeleine L'Engle's *Crosswicks Journals* (including *A Circle of Quiet, The Summer of the Great-Grandmother,* and *The Irrational Season*). All contain excerpts worth sharing with young students who carry notebooks in their backpacks.

Can students do as Jean Little has done? She became the characters in the books she read. She made a vow to remember more, "to hold onto special moments and ordinary, everyday ones, too."

Can they do as Beverly Cleary has done? She allowed newspaper articles to inspire her writing. She became fascinated by the people behind the institutions on class trips.

Can they do as Phyllis Reynolds Naylor has done? She put little incidents "together one by one until eventually they fit together like pieces of a puzzle." She created a story by combining an old Scottish lullaby with a superstition about a ghost-horse and her memories of a year spent on her grandmother's farm.

Can they do as Madeleine L'Engle has done? She recalled an important moment when she was seven or eight years old: "That afternoon when I went to the park I looked at everybody I passed on the street, full of the wonders of their realness." She learned to write everywhere, "with all kinds of commotion going on . . . records, arguments, noisy games."

Can they do as Mem Fox has done? She decided to write in her journal every day for an entire year, "no matter how tired or pressed for time" she was. She gains insight about particular subjects "simply by reflecting on the page or paragraph just written."

Biographies of well-known writers are also filled with glimpses of how writers look at the world and insights into their composing processes. After listening to readings from Alice Walker's biography of Langston Hughes, our fifth graders talked about the attitudes and activities that nurtured Hughes's writing talent. They listed his love of books, beautiful language, and his grandmother's stories. They spoke of his need to write when he was sad, his determination to write poems people would remember, and his decision to write in honor of people who touched him. Although no mention is made in this biography of whether Langston Hughes kept a writer's notebook, I asked the children to speculate, "If he were a notebook keeper, when are the times you could imagine him writing?" They suggested: on his long train rides, aboard ships, and at breaks from all his service jobs. The students also imagined what kind of jottings he might make.

I can easily imagine a month-long project inviting every student to read either a biography or an autobiography of a writer and then report back on what they learned about leading a wide-awake writerly life. Students could list the notebook-keeping insights they gathered in reading such diverse autobiographies as *Childtimes* by Eloise Greenfield and Lessie Jones Little; *A Grain of Wheat: A Writer Begins* by Clyde Robert Bulla; *Boy: Tales of Childhood* by Roald Dahl; *Starting from Home: A Writer's Beginnings* by Milton Meltzer; *How I Came to Be a Writer* by Phyllis Reynolds Naylor; and *Self-Portrait: Trina Schart Hyman.*

They can do likewise when they read biographies. Imagine the range of insights they would gather from such titles as *Henry David Thoreau: Writer and Rebel* by Philip Van Doren Stern; *Edward Lear: King of Nonsense* by Gloria Kamen; *Invincible Louisa*, the story of the author of *Little Women* by Cornelia Meigs; or *Land of Narnia* by Brian Sibley.

Speeches, Profiles, and Interviews

Professional journals and children's literature textbooks are filled with author profiles, interviews, and transcribed speeches. They often yield a gem of an anecdote or a comment that would help young notebook keepers. The following are among my favorites for sharing with students.

- Audrey Woods keeps a cardboard box filled with "snatches of childhood memories, life experiences, titles, names, proverbs, poems, single words, maps, magazine articles, and written and drawn character sketches."
  The Horn Book Magazine (September/October 1986)
- Marc Brown keeps "an idea drawer full of scraps of stories, bits of dialogue, quick drawings, titles, concepts. At any one time there are probably one hundred ideas in the drawer, not all of them good."
  The Dragon Lode 8, no. 1 (Winter 1990)
- Patricia MacLachlan describes her writing process this way: "I now believe that writing is for me like tending a garden. There are plants that come up every year, perennial plots and themes and characters, that grow and bush until you must trim them back. There are the seeds you plant that never flourish, that become bits and pieces of people or places you set aside for later. Then there are what my father has always referred to as volunteers, which come from somewhere unknown, from someone else's garden, or by wind or birds. 'Look, right there in the compost heap. A volunteer!' And we would smile."
  The Horn Book Magazine (January/February 1986)
- Patricia MacLachlan has also said, "I'm reading E. B. White essays and they make me breathless. sometimes because they say something and I have to go write it down right away and keep it and save it and think about it."
  Language Arts 62, no. 7 (November 1985)
- Paul Fleischman says that when he's looking for an idea for a book he often goes to "used book stores" and looks "through books people have 'thrown out.'" He says the old books sometimes give him ideas for new ones.
  Cricket 18, no. 8 (April 1991)
- When asked if she uses a notebook Eve Merriam responded, "Yes and no. I always have a notebook, always. I have a notebook by my bed. I never travel, even to the post office, without a notebook in my purse or in my pocket, but I don't always go back to it. Sometimes I'm very surprised when I go back to those old notebooks, and I think, 'Ah, that's interesting. That's a phrase that I used, and I didn't even know that I had put it down then.' But the good thing about a notebook, of putting it [a word or phrase] down is that it's fixed there—you don't have to carry it around in your head."
  The New Advocate 2, no. 3 (Summer 1989)

Publishers' Pamphlets and Promotional Materials

When I first attended state and national conferences, I used to return home with countless shopping bags filled with "stuff." The catalogues weighed a ton, the posters were usually crumpled, and I never had quite enough free buttons, pens, or bookmarks to please an entire class. I've since learned to be more selective. Today my favorite conference souvenirs are the promotional pamphlets and fliers offered by the publishers of children's literature. They usually have a photograph of the author along with a detailed close-up of the author's life and comments on his or her composing process. Much of this information can inspire children to lead wide-awake lives.

How helpful it would be for young writers to know that Cynthia Voigt's idea for *Homecoming* had its roots in a supermarket parking lot scene. She saw children waiting and began to wonder "what would happen if the person for whom they were waiting just never came back."

Similarly, Robert McCloskey's *Make Way for Ducklings* has its roots in a street scene. The author noticed the traffic problem as ducks walked through the Boston Public Garden.

Jean Craighead George's *Julie of the Wolves* also had it's roots in two strong images. "One was a small girl walking the vast and lonesome tundra, the other was a magnificent alpha male wolf leader of a pack in Mt. McKinley National Park." The author notes that these scenes haunted her for more than a year, as did the words of a fellow scientist: "If there ever was any doubt in my mind that a man could live with the wolves, it is gone now. The wolves are truly gentlemen, highly social and affectionate."

Publishers' newsletters are also premium conference souvenirs, since they contain noteworthy items about writers and illustrators, In a news bulletin from Viking Penguin Children's Books, author illustrator Maira Kalman offers a way of working that closely resembles the way some students may choose to enrich their notebook writing.

> She always carries a sketchbook and usually keeps a camera with her. "I thrive on the visual and emotional parade in New York. People walking by are always sparking images and stories," she says. Maira cuts out innumerable images from magazines. Clippings about architecture, fashion, cinema, and food are all stored for reference. She often browses through the collection, pulls out materials related to her current project, and displays them on the walls around her work space. Maira also collects postcards, labels, leaves, and pieces of fabric. "Somehow," she says, "they combine with my personal fantasy and history and are woven into a story." A large collection of art, photography, and children's books completes Maira's reference library.

In a newsletter from Dell Publishing Company, Gloria Miklowitz began an article entitled "How I turn Curiosity Into Young Adult Novels" with the words:

> As a child growing up in Brooklyn, I used to travel the elevated trains a lot. Often I'd daydream. Learning an elbow on the windowsill, I'd stare out at the people and houses as the train thundered on to the city. What were those people like? Who lived in those homes? What went on behind those walls? I'd stare at the men and women seated or standing around me and try to imagine what was happening in their heads, and in their lives.

Children need to know that their daydreams and questions count, that their own curiosity can inspire their writing.

Texts with Process Notes

Writers sometimes publish their work with accompanying notes, often in italics, to explain the seeds from which their writing grew.

In his *Collected Stories,* Richard Kennedy prefaces each story with a short explanation. For "The Wreck of the Linda Dear" he writes:

> I was living in a coastal town in Oregon. For a while I worked on a fishing boat, and then did odd jobs in the winters. One day I was roofing an old lady's house and had occasion to be in her basement, and in a chalked heart in a small hand was written, "I love you grandpa. Linda dear." So I made up an old man, and occupied my mind as I chopped wood, dug ditches, picked moss, and waited for clear skies and calm waters.

For "The Rise and Fall of Ben Gizzard" he writes:

> I was on my hands and knees, never mind why, looking through my legs, and the "V" of my crotch looked like a mountain upside down, and I remembered an old Indian at a watering hole telling me that he was looking for a man he was going to kill for doing him wrong, but he hadn't found the man yet, but he would, and he'd cross more mountains to find him, and he assured me that I wasn't him. Some stories are just given to you.

Each of Kennedy's notes demonstrates that writers pay attention to things other people don't pay attention to, that writers see connections between things that other people don't see.

Karla Kuskin's poetry collection *Near the Window Tree* also has accompanying notes. I bring these in whenever I want children to understand how a small detail or thought or even an object in the environment can lead to surprising new insights if you follow them. For example, I read Kuskin's explanation of how she came to write a poem about being inside a paperweight: "There is a paperweight on the shelf. I bought it for Julia two Christmases ago. It is a round glass ball and inside it there are an evergreen tree, a house and a tiny snowman. When you pick up the paperweight and turn it upside down, snow rushes all around, making a small storm. Imagine being in there."

I also shared her explanation of a poem that begins "Moon have you met my mother?" Kuskin explains, "Daydreaming. Try some. Sit very still in a quiet spot and let your mind go anywhere. Let your thoughts jump from place to place and follow them. Write them down.

I was coming home from Philadelphia on the train very late one night. As the train crossed over a river I looked down and saw the moon's reflection. I was very tired, almost asleep, and some sleepy rhymes went through my head. They woke me up a little and I wrote them down."

Students need to know that their notebooks are a perfect container for day-dreaming notes.

In Gary Soto's poetry anthology, *A Fire in My Hands,* every poem is preceded by an anecdote and each one reveals a different source of inspiration. Students will appreciate why writers value strong images, memorable outings, close observations, retold stories, and powerful conversations.

Authors of short stories, poems, and picture books often add process notes to their published texts. In the back of her picture book *Henry's Wrong Turn* Harriet Ziefert includes the newspaper article that first inspired her to think about a humpback whale swimming into the New York City harbor. I've shared this note with young writers to encourage newspaper reading as a catalyst for writing.

Notebooks, Diaries, and Journals

Children's literature in the form of a notebook, a diary, or journal entries seldom reflects the potpourri of disparate thoughts, questions, and musings we find in student writers' notebooks. The authors have chosen instead to tell a particular story using the "entry" format. Even if their uses are more limited, these texts are still a resource for teachers wishing to inspire notebook keeping.

Some entry format texts that follow a chronological story line are Joan Blos's *A Gathering of Days: a New England Girl's Journal, 1830–32,* Diane Johnston Hamm's *Bunkhouse Journal,* Robin Klein's *Penny Pollard's Diary,* and Robert Kimmel Smith's *Mostly Michael.* Although in their entirety none resembles the messiness of most writer's notebooks, selections can be used to enrich students' notebook keeping.

When I share excerpts from *Bunkhouse Journal,* I talk about how some entries can go on for several pages, while others remain one-liners. When I share pages from A *Gathering of Days,* I highlight the variety in Catherine's journal entries, which include recipes, quotations, letters, and poems as well as many reflective pieces.

When students read *Penny Pollard's Diary,* I stress the reflective stance the diary keeper has taken. I invite students to study the quality of the writing. I challenge them to think through the "outside" information (what happened to Penny), and the "inside" information (what Penny thinks about what happened). I then ask them to consider the balance between outside and inside information in their own notebooks.

After reading *Mostly Michael,* students come to appreciate how writing can help people handle strong feelings that change over time.

Several related books fall under the heading of nature diaries. These include Barbara Brenner's *A Snake Lover's Diary* and Bernd Heinrich's *An Owl in the House: A Naturalist's Diary.* When I share books like these, I compare them to what might happen when students become obsessed with a topic in their writer's notebook and devote many pages to one particular issue. I point out that both Brenner and Heinrich have learned to observe closely and write with rich sensory detail. I also call students' attention to Brenner's note-taking style, which uses fragmentary sentences, and Heinrich's use of the present tense, as if he's writing while he sits observing.

Some published notebooks, diaries, or journals don't seem to follow one partic-ular story line or examine any one topic. Instead, they more closely resemble a writer's notebook in that the entries are on scattered topics written in a variety of ways. Kendall Hailey's *The Day I Became an Autodidact* or Sue Townsend's *Diaries of Adrian Mole* are filled with observations and reflections. Since they are intended for older audiences, I found myself sifting through them for entries that would be appropriate for fifth graders. I shared this one from Kendall Hailey in order to help children take a reflective stance.

It is Halloween and I am a wreck. I have never been the most skilled dispenser of Halloween candy, but tonight I have failed more hopelessly than usual. Having had years of experience as a trick-or-treater, I remember how I hated to make the trip up to a house, ring a strange doorbell, and avoid a snarling dog, only to be rewarded with a single Tootsie Roll. So I'm an over-generous dispenser, yelling at little children to come back and let me give them more candy.

The Diaries of Adrian Mole are a bit too outrageous for elementary school students, although teenagers enjoy them. More helpful for the elementary school crowd are Opal Whitely's *Opal, the Journal of an Understanding Heart* adapted by Jane Boulton, *Jenny* by Beth P. Wilson, and Graham Oakley's *The Diary of a Church Mouse.* Opal's story is an actual journal written by a young child in an Oregon lumber camp at the turn of the century. In addition to the entries, I read aloud Jane Boulton's explanation of this unusual work. After a foster sister tore up her precious pages, the young writer stored the scraps in a secret box. Years later, her editor writes,

> After urging her to send for the pieces they came. There were hundreds, thousands, one might say millions of them. Some few were as large as a half sheet of notepaper, more, scarce big enough to hold a letter of the alphabet. The paper was of all shades, sorts and sizes: butcher's bags pressed and sliced in two, wrapping paper, the backs of envelopes—anything and everything that could hold writing.

This passage can lead to a lively discussion of how important writing can be in our lives and how we need to value and honor our writer's notebook.

Wilson's *Jenny* contains very short entries that in their honesty and simplicity sound true to the spirit of a young child's observations of the world. The author includes thoughts on the very small pleasures in life—bringing flowers to school, taking bubble baths, and wishing for a new baby in the family.

When I read students entries like these, they realize that they too have a place to record the surprising thoughts that cross their minds and that not everything they write need be a full-fledged "story."

In Oakley's *The Diary of a Church Mouse* Humphrey records his observations on a church mouse's life. I asked our fifth graders, "If Humphrey used his diary as we do our notebooks, what important issues might he discover? What might he turn into an important piece of writing?" These questions can be asked of any diary.

Speculating on Any Well-Written Text

Teachers can connect notebook keeping with any well-written text simply by asking, "If this author had kept a writer's notebook, what kinds of jottings might you find? What kinds of things do you imagine this writer really pays attention to? In what ways do you think this writer lives that are different from people who don't write?" Children can speculate on an author's writing process.

The staff of The Five Owls magazine recently (February 1991) published a list of fictional works that were based on the actual childhood experiences of the authors. These included Dayal Kaur Khalsa's *My Family Vacation*, Robert Mc-Closkey's *Lentil*, Tomie de Paola's *Nana Upstairs and Nana Downstairs,* Bette Bao Lord's *In The Year of the Boar and Jackie Robinson*, Robert Newton Peck's *Soup,* and Lois Lowry's *Autumn Street.* The works of these writers are a good place to start asking the questions, "If this author had kept a writer's notebook, what kind of jottings might you find?" Students know that the events recorded in these books really occurred, and they find it easy to imagine how the writers might have used a notebook. They can imagine Dayal Khalsa recording scenes from her car window and Robert McCloskey keeping tabs on his harmonica playing.

But we needn't stop with texts grounded in real experiences. Students can speculate on how any of their favorite writers might have used a notebook as they composed a text. Students and teachers alike admire Cynthia Rylant's picture books. We can talk about her strong imagery, her sensory detail, and her beautiful language. But students need Rylant's roots, not just her flowers. It's not enough for students to say, "Mr. and Mrs. Crawford looked alike and always smelled of sweet milk," is a beautiful line from *When I Was Young in the Mountains*. They also need to wonder how it is possible for her to craft such powerful words.

"Does Cynthia Rylant lead a writerly life? Does she eavesdrop a lot? Does she stare at people? Does she have a place to record sights, sounds, smells, tastes, and textures?" Children can talk about imagery and detail and language, but if they are to bring these qualities to their own writing, they need to think about how they live their lives. Speculating on their favorite author's wide-awakeness is one way to begin.

One day I shared these two poems with our fifth graders.

Dog

Under a maple tree
The dog lies down,
Lolls his limp
Tongue, yawns,
Rests his long chin
Carefully between
Front paws;
Looks up, alert;
Chops, with heavy
Jaws, at a slow fly,
Blinks, rolls
On his side,
Sighs, closes
His eyes; sleeps
All afternoon
In his loose skin.

Valerie Worth

Day at the Beach

a little girl
not more than two or three
years old
standing in water
up to her ankles
in a brand new swimsuit
looking out at the seagulls,
squinting, her face scrunched-up
because of the sun

abandoned pail
and shovel
in a trampled sand-castle.
once in a while stooping
squatting
to touch the water
palms and fingers spread out
the way little kids do.
easily distracted
by each new sound looking all around
. . . happiness is . . .

and off in the distance
mother can be heard
softly screaming
"Don't go near the water!"

Gary Toushek

After reading the poems aloud so students could respond to them, I asked, "How do you think the poets were able to do such a fine job?" The students agreed, "The poets are good watchers. They probably observe closely and take careful notes."

"I think you're right," I told the children. I then told them my favorite quote from Leon Garfield. "While it is the business of the scientist to make the marvelous commonplace, it is the business of the artist to make the commonplace marvelous." Before they left the meeting area, I asked, "Do you think you could use your notebooks to make the commonplace seem marvelous? Perhaps you'll find a scene that really intrigues you and you'll try to do what these poets have done."

On another day, I brought in an October 1990 *Life* magazine article written by John Updike as part of the feature column, "Snapshot." Updike wrote an entire page based on one family photograph. We speculated on how he was able to say so much about one snapshot of himself as a young boy sitting on his front porch reading a book.

The children's list of probable writing strategies included:

• He asked himself questions about the snapshot.
• He spoke to other family members.
• He studied the photo under a magnifying glass.
• He figured out the exact date.
• He added thoughts about the rest of the day.
• He gave information about the setting.
• He tied the scene to his life today.
• He let his mind wander and connect to other memories.
• He thought about his feelings in the photograph.
• He probably invented some information.

I then suggested that children who had taped family photographs onto the pages of their writer's notebooks could attempt to use some of these strategies in order to say more about them.

Jennifer originally wrote the caption in Figure 48 under a photograph of herself as an infant and of her godfather.

FIGURE 48

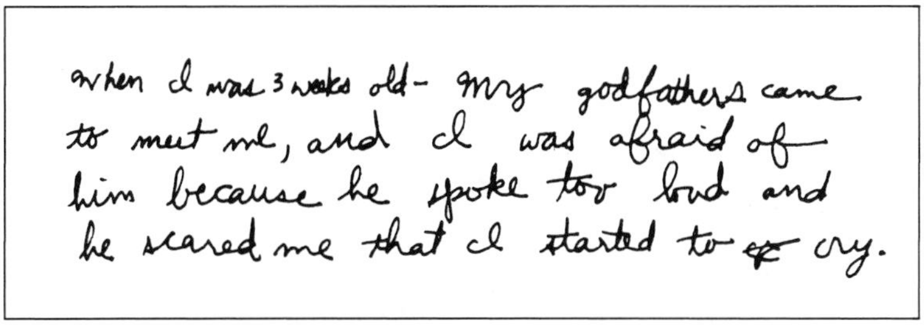

> When I was 3 weeks old – my godfathers came to meet me, and I was afraid of him because he spoke too loud and he scared me that I started to cry.

After speculating on Updike's writing strategies, Jennifer wrote the version in Figure 49.

Yoorak was also able to learn from Updike's writing. She first wrote the description in Figure 50. Later she wrote the version in Figure 51.

Texts for Teachers

When teachers in the Writing Project first began thinking through the notion of asking young students to keep a writer's notebook, they began reading as much professional literature as they could find. They pored over Don Murray's articles on his daybook in *Write to Learn* and *A Writer Teaches Writing*. They read and reread Joan Didion's chapter "On Keeping a Notebook" in *Slouching Toward Bethlehem*. They shared excerpts from "Portrait of the Artist as a Young Scrap Heap" by Jane Yolen in *Writing Books for Children* and thoughts on how to get writing ideas from Joan Aiken's *The Way to Write for Children*.

They read related works about leading a writerly life, including Annie Dillard's *The Writing Life* and Natalie Goldberg's *Wild Mind: Living the Writer's Life*. More recently, they've been reading Pamela Lloyd's *How Writers Write* and Don Murray's *Shoptalk*. These texts helped teachers get started on their own notebook keeping, but as they also realized, these texts contained important lessons to share with their students.

They often talked about the list Don Murray keeps taped to the inside cover of his own notebook. Young students found it helpful to know that one professional writer's notebook includes, among others things, "observations of people and places . . . questions that need answers . . . lines that may become poems or stories or articles or books, quotations from writers about writing, pasted in or written down, postcards or pictures . . . , titles of books, books to read . . . , paragraphs from newspapers or magazines."

Teachers also read aloud from Goldberg's *Wild Minds:* "When you reread a notebook and it has all of your writing, then you have a better chance to study your mind, to observe its ups and downs, as if the notebook were a graph."

They shared suggestions from Lloyd's *How Writers Write*. Michael Foreman carries a sketchbook as he travels, recording story ideas. Victor Kelleher has a file marked "Ideas" filled with "bits torn off the edges of newspapers," where he "had an idea and scribbled it down on the unprinted edge." Cynthia Voigt "travels with pieces of paper" and "an ideas notebook."

FIGURE 49

3 weeks old

It was the year 1980. I was born January 11, 1980. My godfather came to my house and in this picture they were in my mother's bedroom, and the couch is a bed that you pull out. The wall is still the same wooden lined walls. I used to cry because my godfather was so big and he scared me that I always cryed when he came. because its all started when my godfather dressed as santa claus and he said ho, ho ho! and he made me so scared. My mother is in the picture too. Ever since he came after he dressed as santa clus I was scared of him until I got bigger. When my father knew him he dicided that he was good to be my godfather and he worked with him and was friends with him. In the backround that blanket was my favotite blankt because it felt so snuggley and warm and cuddly and I still have it and it brings back alot of memories. That couch too brings alot of memories back because of my and my family siting on it and when I was scared I would sleep with them and then I would feel secure. I remember the rough wall.

FIGURE 50

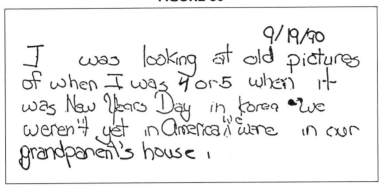

They let their students know that Jack Prelutsky trained himself to be aware: "I never know ahead of time which idea coming into my mind is going to be the most valuable, so I always carry a notebook with me and I write down everything. . . . They're all just grab shots," he says, "like the photographs I'm always taking."

Teachers also looked to books on writing intended for student audiences. They shared suggestions on journal and diary keeping from James Moffett's *Active Voices II* and ideas on "Taking Notice" from Sylvia Cassedy's *In Your Own Words: A Beginner's Guide to Writing.*

Perhaps the book that proved most valuable in helping students lead a writerly life was Jacqueline Jackson's *Turn Not Pale, Beloved Snail: A Book About Writing Among Other Things.* As Jackson explains, she wrote this text "because it's the sort of book I wish someone had written for me. From third grade to seventh I filled dozens of notebooks and a fat briefcase with an assortment of stories and poems, but I never saw a book for kids about writing except textbooks." Her book is not only filled with suggestions on how young writers can pay more attention to their world, it is also studded with excerpts from literary works.

The Most Important Connection of All

Throughout this chapter I've highlighted some of the ways literature can support students' efforts to keep a writer's notebook. There are, however, more global, more important, if more abstract connections between literature and keeping a writer's notebook. Students who are used to living with literature in a "whole language" way seem to have a distinct advantage when it comes to keeping a writer's notebook: because they know what it means to honor literature, they seem to find it easier to honor these blank books. Students who never leave home without books tucked into their backpacks, overnight bags, or camp trunks seem to understand the value of keeping a writer's notebook handy. Those who reread their favorite texts seem to understand the importance of rereading their own words. Those who've learned to be touched by passages from literature seem to find it easier to be moved by the entries in their own notebooks. Students who've learned to probe the significance of what they read seem more comfortable finding the significance in the words they've written. Those who've learned to follow their

FIGURE 51

It was a special day
in winter in Korea
in the year 1985.
They took this picture
with Fuji color film.
March was March, 1985
was the date. It was a
special day. The curtains,
the masks the couch is
still there but the the table,
the balloon and the dresser
on the right is not there.
It was a night it was
dark out. The E.T.
balloon was a special
gift my grand-father bought
for me. My parents were
in America and I was
staying at my grand parents.
When my
parents went I didn't
understand what was going
on. I could still hear
my mother saying "Be
a good girl now, listen
to your grandparents
and I love you." I didn't
know where she was or
when she was coming back
but I did know that
I was going to stay
with my grandparents.
I felt sad without my parents
so my grandfather bought me
the E.T. Balloon. me
and my sister kept
playing with it until
it suddenly popped.
my sister and I
fell on the floor and
we giggled so much
we had a stomach ache.

obsessions when they read seem to find it easier to dwell within a topic when they write. And, of course, students who have been immersed in a wide range of literature continue to have an advantage as they begin to shape their notebook material into stories and songs, poems and picture books. These connections will be closely explored in the second half of this text.

Becoming Passionate About Literary Technique

Moving Toward Closer Study

*I read as much as I can. I read books, not to pinch
ideas, but to see how other authors write. I read
to see how stories are put together, and to see
which sort of story appeals to me, and to
others—and why.*

Simon French

y daughter J.J. recently got her driver's license. "How do I get to Manhattan?"
she asks. "How could you not know?" I answer. "We've driven to school there
five days a week for the last four years." "But I wasn't paying attention," she
admits.

She's right. She wasn't paying attention. But now she is, because she needs to
know. Now she jots down the names of highways. She notices that there's an
exact fare lane for tolls. She realizes that you can take the Brooklyn Bridge or the
Battery Tunnel to get into Manhattan.

Like my daughter, the students in our writing workshops are paying attention
to the literature that surrounds them because they have a need to know. And
that's cause for celebration.

Students too are jotting down not the names of highways but the qualities of
good writing. They too are noticing not toll lanes but beautiful language and telling
detail. They too are recording options, not in driving routes but in genres—
poems, picture books, and research reports. But like my daughter, they need

more than this. It's now the perfect time for her to take the wheel, to sit in the driver's seat. She'll learn most when the journey is really hers, when she's making all the decisions.

So too, young writers need more than a list of the qualities of good writing. Teachers know that deep, important connections don't take place from the outside in, by merely mentioning someone else's use of beautiful language in a mini-lesson or because of elaborate bulletin board decorations. They would agree with Milton Meltzer that literary quality cannot be applied like a coat of paint. These teachers are no longer engaging in what Janet Emig has so perfectly described as "magical thinking."

They now know that deep and important connections take place from the inside out. Students who write from the rich abundance of their own thoughts and ideas discover that they have important things to say, and they make a deliberate decision to say them well. Lucy Calkins describes this crucial shift— from recounting information to spinning a story—as the essential and ground-breaking reading-writing connection. She goes on to describe this shift as a stance writers take.

My young nephew David recently went to sleep wearing one of his father's silk ties on top of his pajamas. In the morning, when my sister asked him why, he answered, "I wanted to dream about being an important businessman." David has every intention of becoming a successful businessman one day. He's purposeful and he's planning ahead. He's taken a very early yet deliberate stance: "I want to do well in the business world." Of course, the dream is only the beginning. Later he'll need lots of tools and techniques to help him do well.

When we make the conscious decision not to run just a writing workshop but to run the best possible writing workshop, we become magnets, gathering ideas and information everywhere. We attend summer institutes, we participate in conferences, we read professional texts, we subscribe to journals, we visit our colleagues' workshops. In the same way, our students need to begin with the intention of writing well and to live with the consciousness of a craftsperson who understands the need for tools and techniques.

Information conveyed in mini-lessons becomes more urgent, conferences become more task-oriented, share meetings become more valuable, and students begin to value what they read and to dig deeply into their own literary resources.

They need to call upon their own internalized sense of what good writing is and to recall those works that have affected them as readers. They need to form mentor relationships with the writers they admire, trying to do what these writers have done.

They also need to recall pieces of their own writing that have affected other readers, to become in effect their own mentors, keeping this successful writer image in mind as they write.

I recall meeting Tien Tien, a fourth grader. When I stopped by his desk, he was rereading a draft of a short story about his recent immigration. He looked unhappy and simply explained, "It doesn't have enough literature in it."

Angelica, a sixth grader, also longs to create a work of art. Here, she reveals her intention to write well as she tells the story behind her latest picture book.

"I said, think, what would make a good topic? I knew it was the homeless so I kept my mind on the homeless. Think what would make a good topic about the homeless.

And I put down "children," "shelters," "the mentally ill," "the aged." At first I thought I'd do something about a mentally ill man. I wrote "Henry the Homeless Guy." But in my story, Henry turned out to be really mentally ill and after a while he wasn't getting too appealing. The reader knew he was mentally ill already and of course Henry didn't know that. I didn't know how to keep the reader in suspense after I gave off the mentally ill part, and I gave that off just a little after the start of the story. So I said to myself, "Henry is not working; he's got to go." So I said, "Children, children are okay." I had to think, "Okay. Kids. A little girl or a little boy?" I weighed the options. A little girl would mean I had to write about dresses . . . I realized that whatever this book was, it needed a little boy, one that was afraid and didn't show it too much. Remember when she was on the train and she thought of him and his dirty hands? If it had been a little girl, she'd have to think about a little girl's dress with ruffles, and it just didn't sound right.

The other thing is, when I was thinking about my topic, I knew I didn't want to dwell on abuse because I don't know about abuse. I didn't want to dwell on it. I wanted it to be about the relationship between the little boy and Catherine. So the next thing I had to make up was Catherine. So, I said a middle aged lady that wants children. And I started accumulating from that. Where would she live? A home or an apartment, a brownstone? A brownstone sounded perfect. So I put a brownstone on 76th and Broadway. I don't even know if there are brownstones there, but it sounded right, and the characters kept on developing. Like I said, it can't be that easy for her. There has to be a catch, because everything in life has a catch. The other thing I kept saying is that I wanted this book to be powerful.

I wanted to write it higher up than for little kids, like something an eighth grader could get into, so they would say, "Wow," at the end, just like little kids who say, "Read more, read more!"

Angelica has made deliberate decisions about her writing. When Lucy Calkins interviewed this young writer, she was struck by her internalized sense of story. "Angelica has an image of an effective text that allows her to say that this draft isn't working, it's got to go. Angelica is after a response—she wants to see the effect her words have on readers."

Children like Tien Tien and Angelica are lucky. They have images of effective texts in their minds. They are reaching for an ideal. They seem to have discovered important ways to allow the reading they do to inform the writing they do. Unfortunately, these deep and important inside-out connections seem to happen instinctively and effortlessly for only a small number of our young writers. In working with the fifth graders in Antoinette Ciano's class, I discovered that if students are to make these deep reading-writing connections, they need to be more active. They need to be in the driver's seat doing things with the literature they love. As Don Murray suggests, "If we really want to understand why a good writer is effective, we need to attempt what that writer has attempted."

Charles Moran suggests that when young writers study a treasured text they need to "understand the writing, the making of the work, at a level so deep that [they] vicariously participate in its performance . . . see the choices the writer has made, and see how the writer has coped with the consequences of those choices."

In the introduction to her cookbook, Uta Hagen writes, "When you do something with nature, you become a hundred times more aware of it. And so it is with food." Our teachers would add, "And so it is with literature." Over the last several years, writing teachers have become a hundred times more aware of literature because we've been doing things with the literature we love. We've rolled up our sleeves and searched the stacks for writing that made our hearts beat just a little bit differently. We've rehearsed those works aloud with just the right intonation. We've decided that we could learn about telling detail by studying Cynthia Rylant or about character development by reading Anthony Browne. We've stood in front of our classrooms and given ourselves time to talk about good writing. We've met the challenge of finding just the right words to convey what we love about Mem Fox, James Howe, Katherine Paterson. If more of us had been trying to write ourselves, no doubt we would have written some fine pieces.

Many years ago, Lucy Calkins said that the job of a writing teacher is to put yourself out of a job. This same idea holds true in the world of reading-writing connections. If our students are to take lessons from literature, they need to be doing more of the legwork, having more of the fun, reaping more of the rewards.

In Chapter 5, I suggested that children roll-up their sleeves and search the stacks. But their active involvement needn't stop there. Students too need to practice reading their favorite texts aloud with just the right intonation. They need to choose mentors who can teach them about detail and character development. They need to stand in the front of the classroom and have time to share their images of good writing. They need to meet the challenge of finding just the right words to convey what they love about their favorite writers.

In this half of the book we move from considering how to immerse children in fine literature to zooming in on the work of particular writers. Our colleague Vicki Vinton often reminds the staff that "we not only have to be good at embracing literature and feeling enthusiastic about literature, we also need to be able to carry that passion over into thinking about literature more formally. Teachers and students need to talk as easily about structure, voice, language, and point of view."

In *Weaving Charlotte's Web*, C. Ann Terry quotes Joan Aiken's description of her parents as writing teachers. Of her mother, Jessie McDonald, she writes:

> My mother was pragmatic in her approach to my writing. When giving me dictation, she nearly always chose poetry; I have reams from *The Oxford Book of English Verse*, written down in careful copperplate, which got poetic language and verse forms very thoroughly in my head. And many of her casual remarks were pungent and memorable in themselves. "Look at the squirrel, how he suddenly stops and strikes an attitude," she would say, and I would write a poem about a squirrel. Or my mother, coming into the kitchen, would exclaim, "I dropped a pea in the larder—that sounds like the first line of a poem" and I would scoot upstairs to the fine writing desk that I shared with my sister and write. . . . My mother was a direct teacher and believed in learning by imitation. "Write a poem like Wordsworth, like Chaucer . . ." and I would produce accordingly.

Then Terry describes Aiken's father. "Conrad Aiken made no such suggestions to his daughter, but he gave her *The Oxford Book of French Verse*, Keats' letters, Webster's plays, and volumes of poetry. He opened his extensive library to his children and made suggestions about what books to read."

In some ways, the first half of this book has represented the Conrad Aiken school of teaching writing—fill them up, let them revel in literature. Now we enter Jessie McDonald's school in which the teachers are more interested in deepening students' stylistic and structural awareness and in sharing the specific tools and techniques that enable young writers to raise the quality of their work.

In the chapters that follow, I explore ways to use the more traditional workshop structures—author studies, mini-lessons, conferences, and reading response groups—to help students become more actively involved in the literature they love. Such interactions should give them the resources they will need when they decide to take the time to write well.

9

When Mentors Really Matter

*Read, read, read. Read everything—trash, classics,
good and bad, and see how they do it. Just like a
carpenter who works as an apprentice and studies
the master. Read! You'll absorb it. Then write. If
it is good, you'll find out. If it's not, throw it out
the window.*

William Faulkner

The New York Public Library asks the writers in its lecture series to accompany
their presentations with a list of books that have been useful to them as they write.
These lists have become a precious resource in my own filing cabinet. I treasure
them not just for the names of the individual titles but for the subheadings the
writers use to categorize their resources. Katherine Paterson clumps one group
of titles under "Theologians to Whom I'm Indebted" and another under "Other
Helpful Thinkers." Jean Fritz lists some of her favorites under "Commentaries on
the Human Condition." Jill Krementz has a section marked "Here are some other
books that have shaped the way I look at the world." These subheadings serve to
remind me time and again that writers have mentors who influence their writing
style and, just as important, that they read and reread the works of people who
shape their beliefs, attitudes, and values.

This reminder is an important one. When we talk about learning from other
writers, we need to remember the full range of possible areas of influence,
everything from what inspired them to become a writer and how they choose

topics to the experiences that have shaped how they see the world and specific writing techniques.

In many classrooms, teachers are continually reminding their students that writers value their reading and sharing anecdotes about writers' tastes in reading. When Patricia MacLachlan is beginning to write she starts reading what she thinks of as good literature, works by Natalie Babbitt and William Steig. She says that she can always tell when she's about to start writing because she goes through these cycles in reading. Cynthia Rylant says she protects the books she loves best like a mother lioness, and she credits James Agee for how she writes and what she writes about. According to Bill Zinsser, when S. J. Perelman was starting out, he could have been arrested for imitating Ring Lardner, and Woody Allen could have been arrested for imitating S. J. Perelman. When Herman Melville wrote he imagined himself writing for Hawthorne; Allen Ginsberg imagined himself writing for Jack Kerouac, calling him his "listening angel."

These stories pushed the teachers in our project to reflect on their own student writers. Do they go through reading cycles before they start a new piece? Do they imagine themselves writing with a favorite author peeking over their shoulders? Are there writers who influence what they write about and how they write?

In her bibliography for the New York Public Library, Rosemary Wells labels one part of her list "These books I read for style." She explained, "That's the same thing as going to a museum and staring at certain paintings or drawings before you begin to draw. It's like practicing tennis with a backboard after watching Martina Navratilova play for an hour. What you see or hear gets into the brain some- how, and what comes out is not imitation but tempered prose." In the world of children's literature, Wells says she admires Robert Lawson, William Steig, and Tomi Ungerer, whose work she reads for style. In our classrooms perhaps we need to be asking, "Do our students read particular authors for style?" And if so, "How can we help students make the most of these mentor relationships?" In *The Writing Life,* Annie Dillard says she is careful of what she reads for that is what she will write. Would this make sense to our students?

Author Studies

A common classroom technique for helping students get to know a writer well is often called the "author study." In many classrooms, students engage in such studies frequently. Whether individually, in small groups, or as a whole class, students often read a large body of work by a favorite author. In some rooms an author is chosen weekly, in others monthly, and in still others whenever "author fever" sweeps students' reading. The latter seems closer to what happens in the real world. In my adult reading circle, we devoted almost six months to the novels of Anne Tyler and another long period to the novels of Philip Roth.

After reading several books by the chosen author, the class tries to identify what it is that author does in most of his or her works. They compile a list of the writer's stylistic devices and literary techniques. Hallways and classroom walls are often decorated with the author's book jackets accompanied by the students' findings.

It's not surprising, for example, to see the following words in a chart in a primary room: Eric Hill: He writes about Spot. He makes pop-up books. His characters are animals. He uses bright colors. He uses speech bubbles.

Older students might do the same: Charlotte Zolotow: She writes a lot about relationships. Her books usually have a happy, comforting tone. Her language is poetic. There is a feeling of life cycles in her books.

Recently, however, the teachers in our staff development project began wondering if all these intense studies have had any impact on students' writing. "Yes, they're fun to do," the teachers admitted. "The kids are eager participants and they end up wanting to read everything by the author of the month. But," the teachers asked, "does all this study really make a difference in students' writing?" Although Rosemary Wells finds that what she sees or hears gets into her brain, teachers were finding that this just wasn't true for the majority of their students.

This comes as a surprise. After all, children are great imitators. They can reproduce television commercials, mock their substitute teacher's speech patterns, and sound just like the principal on the public address system. We know they're capable of learning from the masters, so why are they choosing not to apprentice themselves to the pros?

Perhaps they don't feel comfortable in doing so. In the *Primary Language Record,* an assessment handbook for teachers, the authors suggest that, "Often a child who has been reading a great deal of a particular author will take on their style and write in it for some time, like someone trying on another person's shoes." For me, trying on someone else's shoes never feels quite right. It's always an uncomfortable experience. Perhaps we need to be asking, "What kinds of additional classroom techniques can offer students a welcoming invitation to learn from the masters? What techniques are natural, comfortable, and easily accessible?" Are there additional strategies that could allow author studies to make a lasting impression on students and their writing?"

Stealing from Other Writers?

Maurice Sendak describes how picture book creators influence each other: "It's like a big soup." The ingredients, he suggests, are "the pictures you loved when you were a kid, what you borrowed from—lots of influences. Then, if the soup tastes good and original, that means you converted everything into yourself." Children too need lots of influences. They need to feel free to take the bits and pieces they've learned from others and integrate them into their own unique ways of writing.

Over the years I've paid close attention to people who read aloud well, folks like Don Holdaway, Mem Fox, and Bee Cullinan. I listen carefully, hoping to borrow some of their techniques. My intention is not to parrot them, but rather to recast what I learn in my own voice, to find my own style of reading aloud.

When Wallace Stegner was asked whether he considered reading "to be an important part of the preparation for writing" he responded, "Hemingway said you can steal from anybody you're better than. But you can steal—in the teaching of creative writing in the sense of being influenced by and, even, improving upon—those who are better than you, too. People do it all the time." And he continued, "You can hear Joyce in Dos Passos' *U.S.A.* and Dos Passos' *U.S.A.* in Mailer's *The Naked and the Dead.* Writers teach each other how to see and hear."

In her wonderful memoir *Dear Mem Fox,* Mem Fox shares a funny scene in which she enters her college lecture hall handcuffed to a police officer, who informs her students that she has been arrested on a charge of larceny for stealing from other writers. Mem goes on to talk about the ways in which other writers have helped her with the phrases, themes, rhyme schemes, and settings in her award-winning children's books.

It's true that we often do "steal" in one way or another from the writers we admire. I shouldn't have been surprised by a colleague's advice when I was about to write about conferring. I complained that it was hard to capture a writing conference on paper because there's so much more than the words that are spoken. "Why not reread Georgia's chapter on conferring in *For the Good of the Earth and Sun*?" she suggested. It's a book she knew I admired. I did and then I knew where I was headed. I had an image in mind of the kind of writing to work toward.

What happened when I apprenticed myself to Georgia is no different from what happened to me the first time I saw Hindy List's beautiful Manhattan bedroom. It has an incredible romantic, Victorian feel, and I left thinking how I'd love to have a bedroom like that. The next time I visited I lingered a little longer, making mental notes. If I were to attempt to create my own romantic Victorian bedroom, what would I need? Dark floral wallpaper, layers of drapery, tabletops covered with family photos in intricate unmatched frames, and so on.

When I first read Georgia's chapter I thought: "I'd like to have a conference chapter as effective as that one." Some of the connections I made were broad-based. I connected of course to the genre: I too was trying to write a chapter in a nonfiction text for teachers. I admired her honest, direct tone. As I reread, I asked myself, "What would I need to do?" I studied her text closely. What was it about the actual writing that I admired? What elements could I borrow? Her classroom scenes felt urgent, immediate. How did she do it? I guessed that it was her use of the present tense and her decision to lead the reader on a walking tour of the classroom, moving from desk to desk. I also guessed that it was her way of almost freeze-framing conferences in order to tell the reader what she was thinking.

How did she pack this seamless writing with so much information? Perhaps it was her use of subheadings, bulletlike lists, words in italics, samples of student writing, transcripts of conferences, and the like. I decided to apprentice myself to my good friend Georgia. She had become, in Frank Smith's words, "my unwitting collaborator."

Can the same thing happen with young students? When I visit reading and writing workshops I carry a clipboard. On the back of it is a line I lifted from a magazine. It reads, "I wonder if I can do that." As I've told countless young writers, those words remind me that it's okay to be jealous of the books I read. It's okay to fall in love with a writer and try to do what that writer has done. But inspirational words like these are not enough for many of the young writers I work with. For them, the old saying rings true, "Actions speak louder than words." Students often need a gentle push in new directions.

A Case Study

Mauricio is eleven and he loves football. It was no surprise to his teacher, Antoinette, that he chose to read Karla Kuskin's *The Dallas Titans Get Ready for Bed* to a group of second graders in their school's READ TO ME program. But Antoinette was surprised to find him rereading the same book two weeks later. "I love it," he explained. "I just love it."

"Do you love it because it is about football or is there more to it?" Antoinette asked. "It's a good book, and she's a good writer," Mauricio answered.

"Well, when you love a book, when you love a writer, you should learn from that writer. There are several more books by Karla Kuskin on the back shelf and also lots of her poetry. Why not read them all and figure out what you love about her writing style?"

Mauricio began with Kuskin's prose. He read and reread *The Dallas Titans Get Ready for Bed, The Philharmonic Gets Dressed,* and *Jerusalem Shining Still.* Antoinette had asked him to jot down some of the things he was noticing about Kuskin's writing. Not quite sure what to do, he returned to his teacher's desk. His teacher opened to the first pages of all three books and spread them across her desk.

> The big game is over. Under the lights the football field shines green. Above the green field the big night sky is full of yells and screams, cheers and stars. It is twenty-seven minutes after ten o'clock on Monday night, and the Dallas Titans have just won a big game. The cheerleaders do double-reverse banana splits and we-are-roaring, we-are-scoring slips and slides. The crowd keeps going crazy.
> (*The Dallas Titans Get Ready for Bed*)

> It is almost Friday night. Outside, the dark is getting darker and the cold is getting colder. Inside, lights are coming on in houses and apartment buildings. And here and there, uptown and downtown and across the bridges of the city, one hundred and five people are getting dressed to go to work.
> (*The Philharmonic Gets Dressed*)

> The bread is baked before sunrise. I have seen a loaf that looks like a pair of eyeglasses. And another in the shape of a ladder. Every morning sixty-four kinds of bread are baked here. Every day in these narrow old streets seventy languages are spoken. This is not a very large city. It is far, far away from many that are much larger and newer. Then why should so many people come from everywhere to here? And why should they have been coming here for more than three thousand years?
>   Sit beside me. The sky is getting lighter. The sun comes up behind that ridge. It puts gold on the crescents and stars of the mosques, gold on the crosses of the churches. It touches the Western Wall and turns the old, enormous stones pure white. This is a city made of stone sitting along the tops of stony hills.
> (*Jerusalem Shining Still*)

"Read all three pages," she suggested, "and try to figure out what makes a Kuskin text a Kuskin text." Mauricio still looked confused. "Well, the first thing I notice," Antoinette continued, "is that she talks a lot about the sky. You see it in this one and in this one and again in this one." Mauricio caught on. "I think I know what you mean, now." Antoinette asked him to return to his desk and jot down any other aspects of Kuskin's craft he noticed.

Mauricio began by noting Antoinette's point about the sky. Then he added his own observations.

1. She writes a lot about the sky.
2. She has numbers in her books.
3. Nobody talks.
4. She writes like it's today.
5. She makes pairs.

His teacher congratulated him on making such important discoveries. At lunch, Antoinette and I chatted about Mauricio, impressed with what he had done. Yet

Mauricio notices very different things than an adult reader might. When I study Kuskin's opening passages, for example, I'm impressed by her short, clear sentences and I admire the beautiful sounds of her words.

There is no reason to expect that Mauricio would see the same things I see. After all, I have different tastes as a reader and a different experience with this writer. I've read interviews and author profiles of her. I've collected her poems for years and heard her speak at national conferences. I even have several quotes taped into my notebook (my favorites: "How satisfying to say something heartfelt and true in the most streamlined way possible" and "I love words so much, I can't even throw out the fortune in a fortune cookie").

Of course Mauricio wouldn't see the same things I see, nor would he see the same things as his teacher or the child sitting next to him. All the same, Kuskin had become one of Mauricio's favorite writers and he'd noticed a lot. He was absolutely right. She does use a lot of precise numbers, but she doesn't use dialogue and she writes in the present tense. She also "makes pairs"—"here and there, uptown and downtown," yells and screams, cheers and stars."

"Do you think he's ready for a bigger challenge?" I asked Antoinette. "Let's see if we can encourage him to try some new things in his own writing."

"Mauricio," I began, "I'm wondering if Karla Kuskin can become your writing teacher." His response matched his sweet, open face. "Sure, but what are you talking about?"

"Well, one thing you might do, just for fun, just to stretch yourself as a writer, is to experiment with Kuskin's style. See if some of the things she does can work for you."

The following day Mauricio led the class mini-lesson. He read aloud the entry in Figure 52 and explained what he had learned from Karla Kuskin.

FIGURE 52

Could someone guess that Mauricio was studying Kuskin? Probably not, but that in some way makes his writing even more powerful. He dipped into Kuskin's writing toolbox, trying the tools that appealed to him on for size. He had rarely used the present tense before, and when he had it was all "I," never "they." He also made a deliberate attempt to "use pairs"—"colder and colder," "faster and faster," "back and forth," "hugged and kissed," "friend and relatives."

Mauricio had never intended to apprentice himself to Karla Kuskin. He had never said, "I want to write like her." And yet because he liked her writing, he was willing to accept the challenge and try new things.

When author Tom Romano asked his secondary school students to experiment with Winston Weathers's *An Alternate Style,* he set up a unit of study inviting them to break the rules they had learned, to fill their pages with lists, labyrinth sentences, and orthographic variations.

Mauricio, too, has learned the rules and they've limited him. His cumulative writing folders from past years are filled with brief personal narratives, opening with catchy leads and closing with endings that sound like endings. This year Mauricio has a writer's notebook. He no longer feels obligated to write "stories" every time he writes. Now he has a place to experiment with his writing. As staff developer Randy Bomer describes it, "a notebook is a workbench for your writing."

Antoinette Ciano believes in using writing to learn. I suppose that's why she asked Mauricio to jot down the techniques he noticed during his reading. I found myself following her lead. When I asked Mauricio to experiment with Kuskin's techniques I was also encouraging him to use writing as a tool for learning. We use writing-to-learn strategies in so many content areas—learning logs in math, double-entry ledgers in social studies, dialogue journals in reading. Why not use writing as a tool for learning when we help students connect their reading to their writing?

Although Frank Smith has said that if we learn at all, "we learn at the first encounter, vicariously and concurrently," some teachers have discovered that for many students, simply reading wonderful literature doesn't seem to be enough. In fact, in *Living Between the Lines* Lucy Calkins points out that to learn from reading we, as readers, must do a great deal more than float down the stream of someone else's words.

Children's literature expert Linda Lamme has recently described a project on illustration. Young children who were trying to get to know Trina Schart Hyman used calligraphy pens to letter as she does, wallpaper to make borders like hers, and refrigerator boxes and lumps of clay to create castles à la Trina. The children didn't just look at Trina's illustrations; they participated. Similarly, when I challenged Mauricio to mimic Kuskin, I was inviting him to participate in the performance of her texts.

As Don Murray suggests, we learn what makes a writer effective when we attempt to do what that writer has done.

Why Did It Work?

Mauricio was proud of what he had written. He read it aloud to his classmates with the same lilt and intonation that had captivated a group of second graders when he read them *The Dallas Titans Get Ready for Bed.* One wonders why Kuskin seemed to be so accessible to this fifth grader. Why was he able to abstract her techniques and apply them to his own writing with such apparent ease? Many beginning writers are only able to lift stylistic devices from pieces on topics similar to their own (see Chapter 11). Something special was happening here.

Perhaps Mauricio was successful because he had teachers nudging him along. Or perhaps he was successful because the three Kuskin excerpts clearly illustrate that there is such a thing as a "Kuskin" prose style. If Mauricio had decided to read her poems along with her prose, perhaps he would not have been as successful. Or if he had read another set of prose selections by Kuskin, perhaps he would not have found elements that cut across all of them. Many writers, many wonderful writers like Molly Bang and John Steptoe, show such diversity and variation in their style that trying to learn from more than one of their works at a time might be impossible for a beginning writer. Paul O. Zelinsky says, for example, that "rather than a style he has a chain, a continuous chain of ways" in which he works. Would Mauricio have done as well in a mentor relationship with Zelinsky?

Perhaps Mauricio was also able to learn from Kuskin because to him the elements of her style are so distinctive. Renee Apley, a New York City teacher, talked to me one day about learning to draw caricatures. "People with very distinctive features," she explained, "are, of course, the easiest to capture." It may be that Mauricio was able to capture a bit of Kuskin's technique because her style seemed so different from what he usually writes, from what he usually reads.

I can't read *Louis the Fish* or other books by Arthur Yorinks and Richard Egielski without paying attention to the clipped ethnic tones of the narrator ("Silvery scales. Big lips. A tail. A salmon") or Louis's mother ("What's the matter? You can't give him a little job in the store?"). My own upbringing compels me to see the New York speech patterns as a distinctive feature. Others will no doubt notice other attributes, but that's the one I'd enjoy trying to imitate. In listing writers who have influenced him, Paul Fleischman includes Isaac Bashevis Singer, Leon Garfield, Julia Cunningham, and of course his father, Sid Fleischman. He calls these mentors "stylists . . . who pay attention to sound and have distinctive voices."

How to Choose Subjects for an Author Study

I feel a bit like a Talmudic scholar: "On the one hand . . . but on the other hand." On the one hand, I believe that teachers do not need to choose the author for study (the "let the children be moved by a writer and follow their lead" school of thinking). When we really care about a writer, there are probably no limits on those from whom we can learn. We need to trust that when children fall in love with Tomie dePaola or Vera B. Williams or Virginia Hamilton, they are in good hands. Although the literary techniques of these writers may not be so obvious to us—in fact, their styles might be so diverse that we may not be able to name them in a mini-lesson or post them on a chart—the children will discover their own ways of learning from them.

On the other hand, I also believe that it's okay for teachers to surround students with wonderful writers who happen to be more accessible or more easily imitated. This is particularly true early on, when children have little experience of mentor relationships. We want our students to value these experiences so they'll keep on apprenticing themselves to the masters.

Several months ago, Paul McCartney received a special Grammy Award for Lifetime Achievement. In his acceptance speech he acknowledged Ray Charles,

Elvis Presley, Little Richard, and Chuck Berry, but above all he thanked his mentor, Buddy Holly. "You see," he explained, "all of Buddy's songs were in three chords only—A, D, and E. I was just learning the guitar then, so I could learn a lot from him." Paul McCartney was not afraid of apprenticeship. He celebrated it. He knew which musicians he could learn from at different stages of his composing life.

The question all of us need to ask is "Who are the Buddy Hollys for young writers? Which authors might be most easily accessible for writers just learning how to learn from someone else's work?"

Teachers have discovered quite a few whose voices are so distinct, so unique, that students can't help but notice, appreciate, and imitate. These writers include Byrd Baylor, whose long poetic sentences fall into narrow columns (see Luis, p. 000). Students have also noticed and played around with Joanne Ryder's "You are . . ." stance in her Just for a Day Books. (see p. 169). They have marveled at and attempted to imitate Judith Viorst's long rambling sentences, which, according to one second grader, "sound just like my little brother, who talks without taking a breath." They have even attempted the rhythmic rap beat in Leah Komaiko's *Annie Bananie* and *I Like the Music* (see p. 169).

I find it interesting that many of the writers whose styles are so instantly recognizable either write in a poetic style or compose both poetry and prose. I've recently discovered, in fact, in looking back over many years of author studies, that my most successful ones have been those in which I've shared the prose of people who also write poetry: Donald Hall, Judith Viorst, Paul Fleischman, Charlotte Zolotow, Cynthia Rylant, Nancy Willard, and of course Karla Kuskin. Grace Paley has said that "poetry is the school I went to, to learn to write prose." Perhaps this is true for many writers with distinctive voices.

Mauricio's Reading-Writing Connection

In Living Between the Lines we suggest matching students' reading to their writing. If children are writing their memoirs they need to be reading memoirs and reading widely enough to see options and develop a sense of taste. From Beverly Cleary's *A Girl from Yamhill* they can learn to use imaginary drama. From Eloise Greenfield's *Childtimes* they can learn to divide their writing into parts. From Sandra Cisneros's *The House on Mango Street* they can see how they might write about the significance of their own name.

These kinds of essential reading-writing connections are not the kind that happened in Mauricio's notebook when he studied Kuskin's writing. One reason, of course, is that Mauricio was not reading to get at the essence of any particular genre. He was not studying Kuskin to learn the art of picture book writing. Neither was he making the kind of topic choice connections described in Chapter 3: he was not inspired to write about football, music, or historic cities.

Nor was he selecting strategies to use in revising a current piece in his writing folder. He was not thinking, "Maybe if I switch to the present tense in my story about visiting Ecuador it will feel more alive."

No, he simply fell in love with a writer and was challenged to learn from her.

The connection between his reading and his writing, or rather, the challenge I suggested, was closer to the experiments Georgia Heard describes in *For the Good of the Earth and Sun*. She talks about how the poetic voice is often forced into hiding, "but having a pattern to follow, a puzzle to solve, often coaxes it back into the open." Although Georgia is talking about trying out another form, not necessarily studying any poet in particular, it seems that trying to imitate another writer's literary technique may serve the same purpose.

Kathy Bearden, a poet and a member of the Teachers College staff, recalls a graduate school assignment in which she was asked to imitate another poet in tone, language, or form. Kathy chose W. S. Merwin and set out to echo him; in turn, she says the assignment opened up her own voice. "I was in a rut," she explains, "in a set pattern of my own, and I couldn't get out. I couldn't just will myself out, but the assignment did it for me."

Mauricio's voice has also opened up. Now it will be important to watch and see if these new tools influence his future writing. Will he write in the present tense again or "use lots of pairs," and will he deliberately choose to use these tools because they create the effect he's looking for? These are the really important questions.

But there is a word of warning in all this: timing is everything. In asking students to write a sestina, a villanelle, or a ballad, Georgia reminds us that "writing in form is a challenge. I usually don't introduce it until the workshop is well under way. Even then I present it mostly as an option." Mauricio cared about Kuskin's writing. At the same time his participation in writing workshop was well under way and he seemed ready for a challenge. This particular challenge was one more option.

Exercises and Mentor Relationships

It's easy to believe that some kinds of reading-writing connections are more important than others. The ones that get you started on a trail of thinking, that push you to revise an already existing draft, that give you an image or a sense of options seem to be members of an elite group, the most sought after connections. But I have been hinting at a very different kind of reading-writing connection that has not been quite so popular. In fact, the first line in the last chapter of John Gardner's *The Art of Fiction* startles most elementary school writing process teachers. It reads: "One of the best ways to learn to write is by doing exercises." Of course, Gardner is *not* recommending fill-in-the-blank workbook exercises, story starters, or laborious and formulaic whole-class writing assignments. He is referring instead to individual exercises, "ones that belong in a writer's notebook," he says, "with other things useful to the writer—story ideas, impressions, snatches of dialogue, newspaper clippings." (Mauricio was doing an exercise when he imitated Kuskin's prose.)

Many experts who work with adults do suggest *exercises*. For older writers they can be as diverse as Gardner's individual exercises for the development of technique: "Describe a landscape as seen by a bird. Do not mention the bird," or "Write three effective long sentences: each at least one full typed page . . . each involving a different emotion." They can be like those Roy Peter Clark challenged our project teachers to do: "Take 3 minutes and write about a special place from your childhood."

They can be like those Don Murray includes in *Read to Write: A Writing Process Reader:* "Take an ordinary subject, such as tomatoes, and reveal, in a draft, how extraordinary it is," or "Imagine the last paragraph as the lead and outline the piece that would be rewritten as the result."

In her journal Madeleine L'Engle describes the "writing practices" she offers her students. She says they are "like finger exercises on the piano." Through them, "one can share the tools of the trade, and what one has gleaned from the great writers."

I'm not advocating just any kind of writing exercise with our youngest writers. But after working with Mauricio and hundreds of other New York City youngsters I have come to value the role of one particular kind of exercise—the kind that resembles the "imitative assignments" that Tom Romano speaks of. These mentoring exercises serve as an appropriate "culminating activity," so to speak, when students engage in an author study. Aspiring writers can be gently nudged to try to do what other writers have done. These exercises are close to Murray's challenge: "Take a draft of your own and rewrite it as Ellison might have, if he were to use it in an essay."

Many of the "mentoring exercises" I use with our youngest writers don't even require taking pen to paper. They're oral.

Oral Exercises Just for the Fun of It

Several years ago, Linda Wason-Ellan wrote an article in *Language Arts* warning of the excesses of literary patterning activities, particularly in the primary grades. She suggested that children whose steady diet is writing parodies of popular, predictable texts can get the idea that writing involves manipulating sentences rather than communicating ideas. She went on to suggest that "Literary patterning is better adapted to oral language activities."

There are also many oral activities that can help young students enter mentor relationships joyfully, without constraining them or taking away their ownership. These exercises are done in the spirit of fun and play and sheer delight. At the same time they can be thought of as a way to fine tune students' ability to borrow techniques from other writers.

When I visited Julie Liebersohn's early childhood classroom, where posters announced that the children had recently done author studies of Dr. Seuss and Eric Carle, I also noticed a huge papier-mâché dinosaur and an incubator filled with hatching eggs. I joined a small cluster of children sitting in the meeting area and asked, "If Dr. Seuss were to visit this classroom and he decided to write about that dinosaur, how might his writing go?" "Dinosaur-Finosaur, silly old Shminosaur," one child began, and they all pitched in with rhyming nonsense words. The children had the essence of Dr. Seuss down. To make Eric Carle's version of the incubator scene, one child suggested, "First, you have to get paper and cut funny holes." They knew Carle's work well. When I asked Julie's young students to "use" orally what they had learned from their author study, she was able to appreciate how much her students had learned from these deep studies.

After sharing several poems by Walt Whitman with a group of fourth graders, I read them Frank Jacobs's "If Walt Whitman Had Written Humpty Dumpty."

> O Humpty! O Dumpty! You've had a fearful spill,
> You've tumbled from the stony height,
>   you're lying cold and still;

> Your shell is cracked, your yolk runs out,
> your breath is faint and wheezy;
> You landed as a scrambled egg, instead of over easy;
> The king has sent his steeds and men
> To mend you if they can;
> I pray that they did not forget
> To bring a frying pan.

We talked a bit about how Jacobs captured the essence of Whitman. Then I invited the children in on the fun. "Who are the writers you know so well you could imagine their version of Humpty Dumpty?" The students did not choose a poet, as Frank Jacobs had, but rather picture book authors they had studied in class. It came as no surprise that the writers with very distinctive styles were the easiest to imitate.

Carlos, who had just finished reading several of Joanne Ryder's Just for a Day Books, was the first to have a go. He said,

> "One rainy morning
> You're in bed, your arm touches your face.
> Suddenly you wake up.
> Your skin feels thin, hard, brittle
> You try to get out of bed.
> You realize you have no legs
> You begin to roll
> You crash on the floor"

Then Richard fiddled around with one of his favorite picture book writers, Leah Komaiko. He tried to turn the egg's adventure into a text with a rap beat. He began with just the first two lines and then the other students pitched in. They couldn't resist snapping their fingers and singing,

> Humpty Dumpty had a fall,
> Humpty Dumpty is no fun at all
> He's too mean for me.

(The last line is inspired by Komaiko's "Earl's too cool for me.")

> Humpty Dumpty is yellow and white
> Humpty Dumpty is a terrible sight—
> He's too messy for me.

Although the students didn't attempt to compose versions of Humpty Dumpty in the styles of the poets they knew best, their comments suggested that they understood these writers' interests and techniques.

"What if Langston Hughes were to try it?" I asked. "He wouldn't write about anything like this," one child offered. "What if X. J. Kennedy tried?" I asked. "He'd probably have someone named Angry Andy push Humpty off the wall," answered one Kennedy fan.

Several years ago a teacher from Denver sent me a clipping from the *Rocky Mountain News Sunday Magazine* of Elliott Krieger's imagined sequels to *Gone With the Wind* by various writers.

Ernest Hemingway's read:

It was a short ride from Atlanta to Tara, but the ride was good. Looking out from the carriage, Scarlett watched the trees go past. There was a glow from the trees. The wind blew on them. She felt swell. "She's blowing," Scarlett said. "She'll blow like that for three days," Mammy said. She poured a whiskey-soda. It was a good whiskey. "How do you feel?" she asked. "All right," Scarlett said. "Swell."

Gabriel García Márquez's read:

On the day before she was to meet the man who was to tell her of the fate of Rhett Butler, the third of her three husbands, Scarlett O'Hara remembered the War Between the States. Scarlett O'Hara had sat at the mansion for 33 years, 11 months and 14 days and she had waited for the return of Rhett Butler, the third of her three husbands. She had survived five fatal diseases, including the influenza, typhus, salmonella poisoning, tuberculosis, and the mumps. She had hired 311 workers for her plantation and had fired all but 23 of them. One she killed with her father's shotgun. This was the one she was to remember until three weeks before she died of old age and forgot everything.

Stephen King's read:

Something or someone out there wanted Scarlett. Badly. She could only see it dimly. Its eyes were huge. Its mouth was turned down into a jagged line like a dark, hideous scar. From its throat gurgled a low moaning sound. Its malignant breath smelled like the rancid oil left over after frying several thousand shoestring potatoes. My God! she thought. Get this thing away from me! Then she knew who or what it was. She thought she was going crazy. He'd been dead for 30 years. But here he was, rapping at her window with his bony, skeletal hand, calling to her with his impenetrable voice. Rhett?

Whenever I read these aloud at workshops only teachers who are very familiar with these writers are able to guess which ones Krieger is imitating. They're also the only ones who really appreciate the columnist's talent.

With our fifth graders, almost as a parlor game, we imagined sequels to well-known stories. "What if Lloyd Alexander wrote a sequel to Katherine Paterson's *Bridge to Terabithia?* Judy Blume? Walter Dean Myers?" No one, of course, was asked to write them, but the lively discussion offered us insights into students' understanding of voice and techniques. It also heightened their awareness that such things existed.

Another parlor-type game has its roots in a story that staff developer Sue Smith tells about a first grader. One day Laura came to school very excited. As she explained to her classmates, "Last night for my parents' anniversary we went to a fancy restaurant. You won't believe who was sitting next to our table—Arnold Lobel. You know what? My parents started talking to him and we got invited to his house! And guess what? He's got frogs and toads everywhere—in the bathroom, in the kitchen, even a big bowl full in the living room. He even showed us his next book—*Frog and Toad on the 4th of July!*" Laura proceeded to tell what she remembered of this new story about the friendship between these two animals. She was the envy of her classmates. She had the children sitting on the edge of their chairs. But when Laura's mom came to pick her up at 3 o'clock, Sue found out that there wasn't a word of truth to this six-year-old's story. Yet Laura certainly knows that her classmates are in awe of wonderful writers and she understands the essence of Arnold Lobel's Frog and Toad stories.

Could students do as well with other well-known writers? Could they tell convincing stories about James Howe's next Bunnicula book? Cynthia Rylant's next Henry & Mudge book? A part two to Patricia MacLachlan's *Sarah, Plain and Tall?*

I've also invited students to crawl inside a text, to try to replicate an author's style by adding an extra page. I begin by attempting it myself. In Antoinette's room I read aloud Anne Rockwell's *When the Drum Sang: an African Folktale*. At one point in the story the parents of a lost girl are asking the animals they meet if they have seen their little girl. I tell the children that I have added an extra passage somewhere in the text. Can they guess which part was not written by Anne Rockwell?

Lightly, in pencil, I had added the following monkey scene so the children wouldn't see me pulling out my "phony" text.

A giraffe was munching at the treetops and they called to him, "O Giraffe . . . you with your long neck that looks over the wide plain . . . have you seen our little girl?"

But the giraffe shook his head and went on eating.

They called to a lion in the grass, "Where is our little girl—Tselane who sings so sweetly? Have you eaten her?"

But the lion shook his mane and ran away.

A monkey was jumping from tree to tree and they asked him, "Oh . . . Monkey . . . with your long swinging tail . . . have you bumped into our precious little girl?

But the monkey shook his head back and forth and quickly went on jumping.

On and on the mother and father wandered until they met an elephant. "O Elephant . . . with your great ears . . . have you heard news of our little lost girl?"

But the elephant shook his head sadly and slowly ambled away.

Then they met a hyena, an ugly, unpleasant fellow.

"Hyena, please do you know where our little girl—Tselane who sings so sweetly—where might she be?"

But the hyena only laughed a nasty, sneering laugh and slunk away.

After all the guessing I showed the students my hand-written insert. I then invited them to try it. Very quickly, without even taking pencil to paper, the children began inventing.

"Oh rabbit with your big long ears, have you heard any news about our daughter?"
But the rabbit shook his nose and ran away.

"Oh raccoon, with your great sight in the night. Have you seen our daughter?"
But the raccoon shook his tail and scurried up a tree.

"Oh little bird with your sweet, sweet song. Have you seen our little girl?" But the bird just tweeted and flew away.

The students were not asked to identify Anne Rockwell's techniques, but their words and the look on their faces indicated that they knew what she was doing.

That feeling of "I get it—I know what she's doing" is a breakthrough for many students. Without learning any technical terms or receiving complicated directions—and just for fun—the students participated in Rockwell's text. Without even realizing it, they had begun to listen like writers. Perhaps it was a step on the way to reading like writers.

The four similar passages, one appearing right after the other, enabled the children to imitate Rockwell's technique easily. Whenever I choose texts for this kind of oral play, I look for writers who make it easy. The work of student writers can also be used. In a second-grade class I shared Sandra's book about her sister.

> I have a baby sister. Her name is Melissa. She is two years old.
> She likes to laugh a lot.
> When I wiggle my fingers in her eyes she starts to laugh.
> She likes to drink a lot.
> When she drinks she takes her finger and twirls it around her hair.
> She likes to take bubble baths a lot.
> When all the water is gone she starts to slide . . .

The text continued for several pages. Very quickly students composed additional sentences following Sandra's pattern. Of course, Sandra shook her head each time, "Nope, Melissa doesn't really like that!"

Many writers have written a series of books with recurring settings, themes, or characters. Take *Curious George* by H. A. Rey, for example. If you ask students to invent another book in the series, they might suggest, "You have to have a man with a yellow hat, the monkey has to get into trouble, and there's usually a chase scene and a happy ending." Or if they read Tomi Ungerer's *Crictor,* then his *Emile,* then his *Adelaide,* they might say, "I get it," but their "getting it" would be in a broad sense: "You need an animal who does special things because of his specially shaped body." Then students could do what Laura did with Arnold Lobel's Frog and Toad books, invent a new humorous friendship story using the same characters.

This kind of "getting it" usually occurs in class author studies. Now I want to suggest zooming in to study stylistic devices and literary techniques so that young writers can have the thrill of composing in ways they've never done before.

Another oral mentoring exercise will illustrate my point.

One morning I read aloud several selections from *My Grandmother's Stories* by Adèle Geras. "Bavsi's Feast" begins:

> First of all, let me tell you about my grandmother's kitchen. It was a small, square room with a large sink next to one wall, and a wooden table pushed up to another. Because my grandmother lived on the third floor of an apartment house, the window in one wall was really a door and opened out onto a small balcony. In summer there would be tall, glass jars lined up on a table on the balcony; and in the jars tiny, green cucumbers floated in a pale, cloudy liquid, turning into pickles in the sunlight. If only you could taste the dishes that my grandmother cooked: cinnamon cakes, braided loaves of bread, meats stewed in velvety sauces, fish fried to the color of gold, soup with matzo dumplings, fragrant with nutmeg; and for the Sabbath, the Kugel: a pudding made of noodles and eggs, with just a hint of burnt sugar to give it its caramel color and smoky taste. One of the tasks I enjoyed was helping to mince things. I liked using a carrot to poke whatever we were mincing deep into the silver mouth of the machine clamped to the side of the table. My grandmother liked chopping and talking.
>
> One day, we were making a strudel, cutting up apples to mix with nuts and raisins. "Have you ever thought," she said to me, "what it must be like to be hungry?"
>
> "I'm often hungry," I answered, "I'm hungry now. May I eat the rest of this apple?"
>
> My grandmother laughed. "That's not hunger. That's greed. Let me tell you a story about someone who learned what real hunger meant . . ."

This story begins this way, but so do all the stories in this collection. The children quickly got the feeling of "I get it! I know what she's doing." "She always starts by describing a room in the house, then the grandmother and child start talking and their talk always reminds the grandmother of an old story. Then she tells *that story.*"

"If you want to borrow some of Adèle's techniques," I continued, "how might a story about your grandmother go?" At first the children told rather weak replicas. José began, "My grandmother's house has a stoop with lots of steps. We play ball there, but my grandmother doesn't want us to, so she asked, "Have I ever told you about the time when I was little and I broke my mother's favorite dish? Let me tell you now."

The children at first only noticed the framing structure of Adèle Geras's stories. "What about her writing style?" I asked, "the words she chooses and the way she puts them together?" I reread a few stories and we probed deeper. The children spotted the long sentences filled with sensory details.

José tried again. "My grandmother's brick house has a stoop with seven wide steps. They're made of concrete and she puts big jars of geraniums on the sides. In the summers all the neighbors bring their folding chairs and the kids sit on the stoop. It's always hot out so we buy frosty shakes, chocolate ice cream cones, or popsicles from the Good Humor man."

We also talked about how the author switches from everyday information to "One day." They noticed that the child asks a question that reminds the grandmother of an old story, which she then tells. José continued revising his story out loud, and it took on more of Adèle Geras's style.

We hoped that all this oral mentoring work would prepare students to borrow more freely when they wrote from the authors they admired. In fact, we created a listening center activity that would nudge children toward playful experimentation in their writer's notebooks. In the listening center, there was a shelf of fine picture books and accompanying tapes. They included Holly Hunter reading the *Three Little Pigs,* Meg Ryan reading *Goldilocks,* and Jonathan Winters reading *The Legend of Sleepy Hollow.* We invited the children to select a tape and listen to it several times while they read along in the picture book. Then, with a listening friend, we asked them to answer the question, "What is it about this text that makes it wonderful to read aloud?" Next, we wondered if they could attempt to mimic the reading on a blank tape. Finally, we challenged the students to let this experience inform their notebook writing.

Michelle had gone through this sequence of activities as she pored through the text and tape of Rudyard Kipling's *How the Leopard Got His Spots,* read aloud by Danny Glover. The first page reads,

> In the days when everybody started fair, O Best Beloved, the Leopard lived in a place called the High Veldt. 'Member it wasn't the Low Veldt, or the Bush Veldt, or the Sour Veldt, but the 'sclusively bare, hot, shiny High Veldt, where there was sand and sandy-coloured rock and 'sclusively tufts of sandy-yellowish grass. The Giraffe and the Zebra and the Eland the Koodoo and Hartebeest lived there; and they were 'sclusively sandy-yellow-brownish all over:

After she had listened to the tape several times, Michelle and her partner tried to explain why Glover was able to read so well.

FIGURE 53

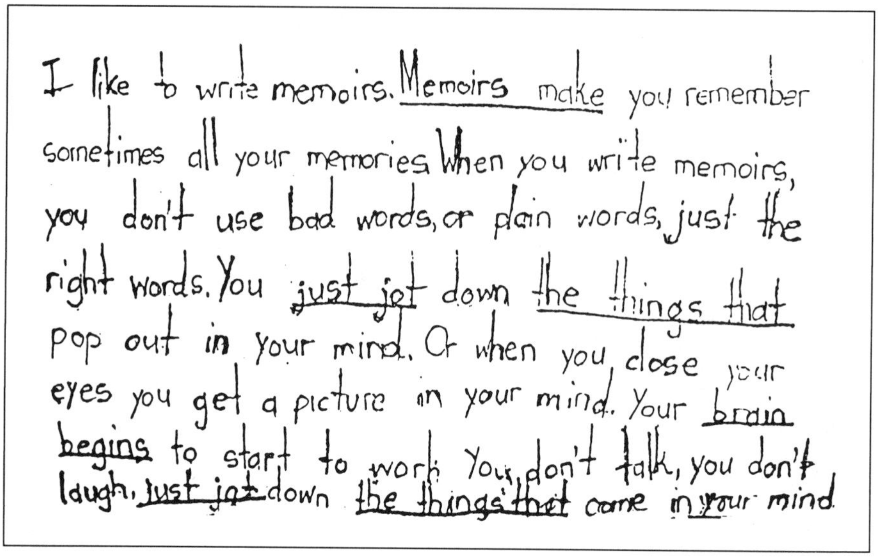

I like to write memoirs. <u>Memoirs</u> <u>make</u> you remember sometimes all your memories. When you write memoirs, you don't use bad words, or plain words, just the right words. You <u>just jot</u> down <u>the things that</u> pop out in your mind. Or when you close your eyes you get a picture in your mind. Your <u>brain</u> <u>begins</u> to start to work. You don't talk, you don't laugh, <u>just jot</u> down <u>the things that</u> come in your mind.

"The author makes your mouth want to do something. It's like a good plate of food and your mouth starts to water."

"The words are half easy and half hard. Some parts are like a tongue twister. You want to try to get it right."

"The author uses repetition—so it's fun—you can remember parts."

"The book is like a party you're invited to. You just can't say No. You want to keep on saying those words."

Then Michelle deliberately attempted to borrow some of Kipling's techniques as she wrote her next notebook entry (Figure 53).

The structure of Kipling's "it wasn't the Low Veldt, or the Bush Veldt, or the Sour Veldt" is obvious in Michelle's "you don't use bad words, or plain words, just the right words" and "You don't talk, you don't laugh, just jot down."

She also attempted to replicate Kipling's alliterative phrases, "Best Beloved," "Leopard lived," "sclusively sandy," underlining the alliterative phrases in her own passage.

In *Illumination,* Walter Benjamin writes, "traces of the storyteller cling to the story the way the handprints of the potter cling to the clay vessel." Michelle and the other fifth graders proved to us that traces of an author can cling to a reader as well.

Sharing Your Own Need to Exercise

Peter Newmeyer begins an article in *The Horn Book Magazine* with the following words, "James Thurber once said of the author of *Charlotte's Web,* 'No one can write a sentence like White, or successfully imitate it. . . . That's a challenge.' " He goes on to list several elements of E. B. White's writing just as teachers do during an author study. According to Newmeyer, White's passages are often marked by surprising images, casual talk, short punch line endings, simple words, long list sentences and what he describes as backtracking—beginning a new sentence with a phrase from the proceeding one.

I decided to challenge myself to imitate E. B. White's style of writing, since I was in a rut in my own writing and bored with sounding like me. For five minutes only I tried to write a passage based on Newmeyer's list of E. B. White's literary techniques.

> President Bush doesn't like broccoli. Not liking broccoli has become big news. It's not as if he said he doesn't like baseball or Boston or reading books. What's the big deal? He probably doesn't like brussel sprouts either.

I wondered if my fifth graders would appreciate my efforts and my reason for trying. Perhaps one way to teach students to "have a go" at learning from the masters is for teachers to demonstrate their own attempts.

I began by reading several E. B. White passages with the students, carefully selecting those that illustrated the elements I had hoped to imitate. Then I shared Newmeyer's thinking. Next I read my own quick attempt and why I decided to try. I told the students that I wasn't doing busywork, that I had assigned myself this task in order to get myself out of a rut, to hear something new in my writing.

The students were quick to point out the elements they thought were well done as well as those they thought over done. They appreciated the backtracking "doesn't like broccoli. Not liking broccoli." They appreciated the casual talk— "What's the big deal?" and the long list sentence, but they thought I had overdone the alliteration. And they didn't think the "surprise ending" was much of a surprise.

Yet, I had been able to demonstrate that writers do set personal goals for themselves and that they can assign themselves quick exercises in the service of meeting those goals. John Gardner, in describing the value of individual exercises for the development of technique says, "Most apprentice writers underestimate the difficulty of becoming artists; they do not understand or believe that great writers are usually those who, like concert pianists, know many ways of doing everything they do."

Trying to imitate an E. B. White passage gave me new ways of composing individual sentences and threading those sentences together. I mimicked a few of E. B. White's techniques, not trying to explore any new meaning for myself. In the best of worlds, one day I'll be confident enough to call some of these techniques into service, consciously or unconsciously, in order to move toward shaping an important piece in a literary way. I will no longer be imitating White's techniques but improvising and inventing my own.

In a recent food column in *The New York Times Magazine* the poet William Matthews describes how he moves from imitation to invention. He begins by suggesting that cooks should "play in the kitchen at imitating dishes first tasted in a restaurant." When he was first learning to cook, he admits, he wanted to prepare what he most liked to eat. In a similar way, the first poems he wanted to write would have been, had he the requisite skill, exactly like the poems he most admired. "But," he concludes, "it would be a slow process indeed, by which I struggled from clumsy imitation to invention, to a point where I wrote poems that, for better or for worse, only I could have written."

The Warnings and the Rewards

My worry in including a section on exercises in this book is that these exercises will become regular whole-class, teacher-assigned activities. But if they remain an occasional tool used to invite students to explore new approaches to their writing they can result in several rewards. A major one is that students will learn how to assign individual exercises to themselves in order to meet personal goals.

Here Angelica, a sixth grader, explains the "practice-writing" she had learned to assign herself.

> When I decided to write journalism for the homeless project, I didn't know how to do it. I had thought nonfiction was encyclopedia writing, that that's what it meant, and I realized that it wasn't, but how to write journalism? I didn't know. So I watched newscasters, and the way newscasters talked, I imagined that on paper. There was one part where they were talking about the Bensonhurst thing, and how there were rallies. I pretended I was writing that, and I put down what happened at the rally. So I made up these stories just to practice being a journalist. "There was a rally in Bensonhurst," and I kept writing what people said and what was happening. After a while it was easy to write like that. When I watched the newscasters I'd see how they often put a little description in with the facts, and I tried to figure out how they got from facts to the description. So in my writing I decided to put it very, very mixed. The newspapers helped more than the newscasters, because in the newspapers I could see it in writing and I could study it better.

These short writing tasks reap other rewards. They let students know what it feels like to be deliberate in writing. It exercises their executive function. They get the feel of the artistic pause. They make deliberate moves to do something in a specified way, a new experience for many beginning writers.

John Gardner points out another advantage of having students work on limited, clearly defined problems. They feel successful. "Students discover how good they are," he says. And good work is empowering. It often leads to more good work.

Yet another advantage of doing exercises is that they provide time for practicing a sought-after literary technique. When the technique is needed as a revision strategy to improve the quality of a work in progress, the writer will feel at home using it. The writer has already explored the technical aspects and can give more attention to determining the appropriateness of this technique for conveying the meaning at hand.

Enriching Author Studies

I feel a bit like a bad host who has offered sandwich bread with no filling. I've suggested only two possible aspects of an author study: We can begin by reading aloud a lot of work by one author and asking the students to talk about what they notice and abstract the author's literary techniques or tendencies. And we can end by inviting students to try to imitate that writer's style, whether orally or in writing. But when a class studies a particular author, there are many more activities that can make that study richer and more productive. In fact, I would probably postpone discussing an author's stylistic techniques until students have been deeply immersed in the texts. Once students have crawled inside these treasured texts in a variety of ways, the process of naming and imitating what they've seen or heard will be a good deal easier.

Last fall, Karla Kuskin was invited to speak at a conference at Teachers College. In preparation for her visit, I found myself exploring lots of ways to help students and teachers study her texts in depth. Many involved returning to activities I've described in the first half of this book, placing Karla's words at the core. For example,

- We used her poems as part of the regular choral performances in the class.
- We wrote from several of her poems, looking for generative seeds for our own writing.
- We used her prose passages to practice reading aloud well.
- We used several of her poems to invite dramatic play.

Her poem "Rules," for example, easily led to a lively improvisation. Children had to think on their feet when, after they had read the poem aloud several times, they were unexpectedly asked to respond to its rules. "Why shouldn't we jump on ancient uncles?" "Why shouldn't we dance on velvet chairs?" and so on.

Rules

Do not jump on ancient uncles.

Do not yell at average mice.

Do not wear a broom to breakfast.

Do not ask a snake's advice.

Do not bathe in chocolate pudding.

Do not talk to bearded bears.

Do not smoke cigars on sofas.

Do not dance on velvet chairs.

Do not take a whale to visit
Russell's mother's cousin's yacht.

And whatever else you do do
It is better you
Do not.

Karla Kuskin

We read her work across the curriculum—her bug poems during science, her multiplication lament during math, her writing on Jerusalem during social studies. Even her picture book *Just like Everyone Else,* written in 1959, launched a lively social studies discussion. The students read critically. The main issue for them was "Is it fair to say that everyone lives with a mother and a father?"

We also found ways to weave Karla Kuskin's life and work into some of the more traditional structures of the reading-writing workshop. We put biographical information gathered from publisher's materials, articles in professional journals, and passages on book jackets to good use during mini-lessons, the short whole-class gatherings that begin most writing workshops. For example, one day we talked about her love for childhood poems. She responded to the sound of language.

There's a line in The Night before Christmas that will stay in my head forever because when I first learned it, I didn't understand all the words.

As dry leaves before the wild hurricane
  fly,
When they meet with an obstacle, mount
  to the sky
So up to the housetop the courses
  they flew,
With a sleigh full of toys,
  and St. Nicholas, too.

I didn't know hurricane. I didn't know obstacle. I didn't know courses, but I just loved the way they sounded. (*Language Arts* [Nov. - Dec. 1979])

In this passage she reveals how topics for her poems are rooted in her past.

There is a verse, one of many, that my Father used to recite to me:

> There was a black beetle
> who lived down the drain.
> quite friendly he was,
> though his manners were plain
> and whenever I'd bathe
> he would come up the pipe
> and together we'd wash
> and together we'd wipe.

Perhaps that "friendly" beetle inspired me, many, many years later to write my own "bug poems." (*The Bulletin: The Children's Literature Assembly* 12, no. 1 [Winter 1986])

When writers add process notes like these, they provide us with insights we can draw from in our mini-lessons (see p. 276). In fact, their words are often so well-crafted they can be read verbatim as the script of a mini-lesson.

Imagine sharing Karla Kuskin's preface to "Thistles" from *Dogs and Dragons, Trees and Dreams:* "As you read a poem aloud listen to the sounds of the words. They have infinite variety. There are short, brittle sounds, soft rolling sounds, stuttering sounds and the sibilance of many s's, long liquid sounds flowing with o's. In some poems there is not so much sense as sound. Tongue twisters use words in this way. This poem begins like a tongue twister."

Her explanation of "Spring Again" from this same anthology would also make a fine mini-lesson: "In order to describe something you have to look at it closely, see it with a clear eye and remember it. Writing and remembering are like Siamese twins; they are so close to each other and so hard to separate. They need each other. Parts of the past are always showing up in the words you write." (To teachers who worry that their mini-lessons take too long, I've recommended that they apprentice themselves to writers who write succinctly about their craft. Kuskin's "How satisfying to say something heartfelt and true in the most stream-lined way possible" applies not only to writing but also to teaching.)

Reading from an author's work before beginning to write can also become a ritual during an intense author study. Jim Bishop, the author of *The Day Lincoln Was Shot,* has said that before writing each day he begins by reading Hemingway, hoping "his style would rub off." Before students take out their writer's notebooks or writing folders, they too can read from the author under study. If their reading has any impact on their writing, students can be invited to bring their discoveries to the share meeting.

During the three weeks of our author study, Kuskin's texts also became im-portant during the reading hour. Her books were available for independent reading and in multiple copies for small group response. Additional copies were gathered from other class libraries, the school library, and the public library. Duplicated copies of book covers were sent home to encourage parents to scout local book shops and libraries. Some of her poems and picture books were tucked into text sets made available during reading: her poem "Catherine" for example, was added to a text set about pretend play and her picture book *The Philharmonic Gets Dressed* became the fulcrum for a text set about musicians.

I even invited the fifth graders to read Kuskin's "I Woke Up This Morning" alongside Jack Prelutsky's "I Should Have Stayed in Bed Today". The children were surprised that two poets shared the same feelings.

I Woke Up This Morning

I woke up this morning
At quarter past seven
I kicked up the covers
And stuck out my toe
And ever since then
(That's a quarter past seven)
They haven't said anything
Other than "no."
They haven't said anything
Other than "Please, dear
Don't do what you're doing,"
Or "Lower your voice."
Whatever I've done
And however I've chosen,
I've done the wrong thing
And I've made the wrong choice.
I didn't wash well
And I didn't say thank you
I didn't shake hands
And I didn't say please
I didn't say sorry
When passing the candy,
I banged the box into
Miss Witelson's knees
I didn't say sorry.
I didn't stand straighter.
I didn't speak louder
When I asked what I'd said.
Well, I said
That tomorrow
At quarter past seven
They can
Come in and get me.
I'm staying in Bed.

Karla Kuskin

I Should Have Stayed in Bed Today

I should have stayed in bed today,
in bed's where I belong,
as soon as I got up today,
things started going wrong,
I got a splinter in my foot,
my puppy made me fall,
I squirted toothpaste in my ear,
I crashed into the wall.

I knocked my homework off the desk,
it landed on my toes,
I spilled a glass of chocolate milk,
it's soaking through my clothes,
I accidentally bit my tongue,
that really made me moan,
and it was far from funny
when I banged my funny bone.

I scraped my knees, I bumped my nose,
I sat upon a pin,
I leapt up with alacrity,
and sharply barked my shin,
I stuck my finger in my eye,
the pain is quite severe,
I'd better get right back to bed
and stay there for a year.

Jack Prelutsky

A final reading activity to enrich an author study invites students to get to know their mentors' mentors, to find out who their favorite writers read, admire, and take lessons from.

When members of our project staff read in an old issue of *Saturday Review* that Eudora Welty admired the last line in Anne Tyler's *Dinner at the Homesick Restaurant,* calling it a tour de force and commenting, "If I had written that sentence, I'd be happy all my life," we all raced for our copies of the Tyler text. We wanted to know what the last line was and why Welty admired it so.

In a similar way, students can research James Agee to understand why Cynthia Rylant says he is most responsible for what and how she writes. They can read Frances Hodgson Burnett's *Secret Garden* and try to figure out why Charlotte Zolotow says this book has so strongly influenced her own writing. They can also research which writers Karla Kuskin reads and try to figure out what she learns from them. The question, of course, is how to get this information. Some students write letters to authors or search through published interviews with them. Many authors also include this kind of information in publicity blurbs or in published memoirs.

When authors visit our schools or speak at conferences, again we can ask, "Which writers do you read, admire, and take lessons from?" This question has become my standard one whenever I meet writers I admire. At a reading conference last year, when the audience was invited to ask questions of a panel of children's writers, I made my usual inquiry. I learned that Bruce Coville reads Natalie Babbitt, Jane Yolen, and Lloyd Alexander. Joanna Cole's favorite book is Maxim Gorky's *My Childhood,* and Bruce Degen has studied Arnold Lobel's illustrations. Ellen Christie admires William Steig and James Marshall but has also learned from the Monty Python comedy troupe that "zany plots are okay." When students and teachers do learn about their mentors' mentors, they can bring their discoveries and hunches to mini-lessons and share meetings.

Once children are filled with the life, work, and writing strategies of their favorite authors, several further activities can bring closure to the author study. Children can have a go at imitating the author, but they can also begin to assess what they've learned during their "apprenticeship" by

- Doing a reflective piece about this writer, trying to put into words what they admire and how they can use what they've learned.
- Taking an old piece and recasting it with techniques learned from this writer.
- Trying to find the same qualities in other writers and presenting their findings to their classmates.
- Sharing a work by the author alongside their own when they sit in the author's chair and explaining the connection between what they have read and what they have written.

In this chapter I have included a rather extensive array of ways to enrich the study of any author. Of course, not all of them need to be done for each author. Time wouldn't allow it, nor are all activities necessary or appropriate for all authors. But over the course of a year, even one or two in-depth studies can make a lasting impression on young writers.

Teachers as Mentors

Edith Wharton has said, "There are two ways of spreading light—to be the candle, or to be the mirror that reflects it." In many ways we are the candles in our classrooms and students the mirrors. They often reflect what we do.

A visit to most share meetings illustrates this point. A child sits in the author's chair waiting for everyone's attention. The teacher is about to see a perfect imitation of his or her own way of settling students down. Perhaps it's the tapping of a foot and the repeated, "I'm waiting . . . I'm waiting." Or the student might give a patient yet serious stare and softly call out the names of inattentive students. Even the amount of time the student is willing to wait and his or her expectations for the level of quiet probably matches the teacher's.

Then the student begins to read the book, and again the teacher sees his or her own technique of holding the book so the pictures are visible and rotating the text so everyone gets a good look. Some children have even mastered the technique of reading the print as the book is held off to the side, facing the children.

Even closing rituals can be precise imitations. My friend Abba Carlquist, a Swedish teacher, was surprised to see the last page of a student's published book. He had written: "Om ni tyckte boken var bra sa rack upp handen" ("If you like this book, raise your hand") Abba realized that she gives this direction each time she finishes a read aloud with her class.

We are powerful models for our students. In Chapter 2, I spoke of bonding with a literate adult and sharing literary ways of being. There I stressed the importance of letting our students know the place of reading in our lives. Now it's time to speak of writing.

In a *New York Times* article, Frank Smith is quoted as saying that "teachers don't provide enough worthwhile demonstrations for their students because they're so busy with drills and tests that they don't have enough time to demonstrate literate activities like browsing through a newspaper, enjoying a good novel, writing a letter to a friend."

We need to make that time. Children need to know that we write letters to friends and letters to the editor, letters of recommendation and letters of request, letters of complaint and letters of sympathy. They need to know we ourselves write in all the genres we invite them to write in—poetry, memoirs, nonfiction.

FIGURE 54

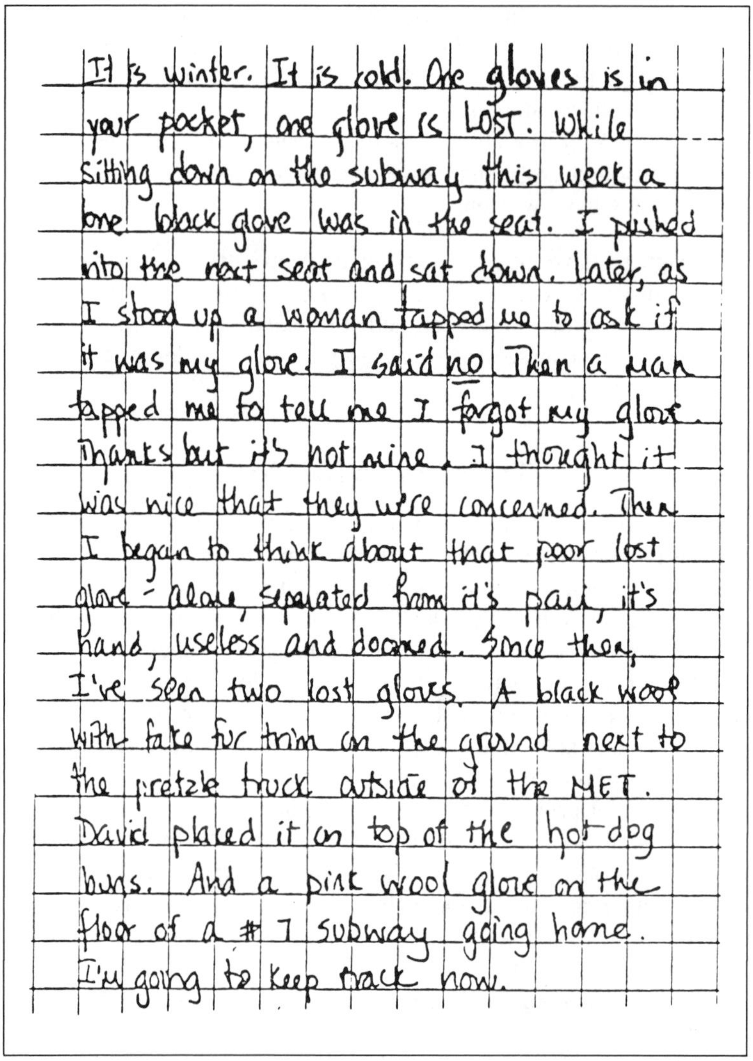

> It is winter. It is cold. One gloves is in
> your pocket, one glove is LOST. While
> sitting down on the subway this week a
> one black glove was in the seat. I pushed
> into the next seat and sat down. Later, as
> I stood up a woman tapped me to ask if
> it was my glove. I said no Then a man
> tapped me to tell me I forgot my glove.
> Thanks but it's not mine. I thought it
> was nice that they were concerned. Then
> I began to think about that poor lost
> glove - alone, separated from it's pair, it's
> hand, useless and doomed. Since then,
> I've seen two lost gloves. A black wool
> with fake fur trim on the ground next to
> the pretzel truck outside of the MET.
> David placed it on top of the hot dog
> buns. And a pink wool glove on the
> floor of a # 7 subway going home.
> I'm going to keep track now.

When we share our attempts with students, they begin to borrow from us as willingly as they do from Byrd Baylor or Langston Hughes, perhaps even more willingly. Sometimes they borrow genres, sometimes techniques. Sometimes they make topic choice connections.

Jacqui Getz, a third-grade teacher, shared an entry from her writer's notebook with her students (Figure 54). Several days later her student Anna read an entry from her writer's notebook (Figure 55). Anna borrowed a seed idea and a reflective stance from a teacher-writer she admired.

In her poem "Of Kings and Things," Lillian Morrison speaks of a neighborhood child who loves to play baseball: "He was better than Babe Ruth, because we could actually see him hit every Saturday morning." Teachers who write and share their writing have discovered the same thing—that they are particularly effective

FIGURE 55

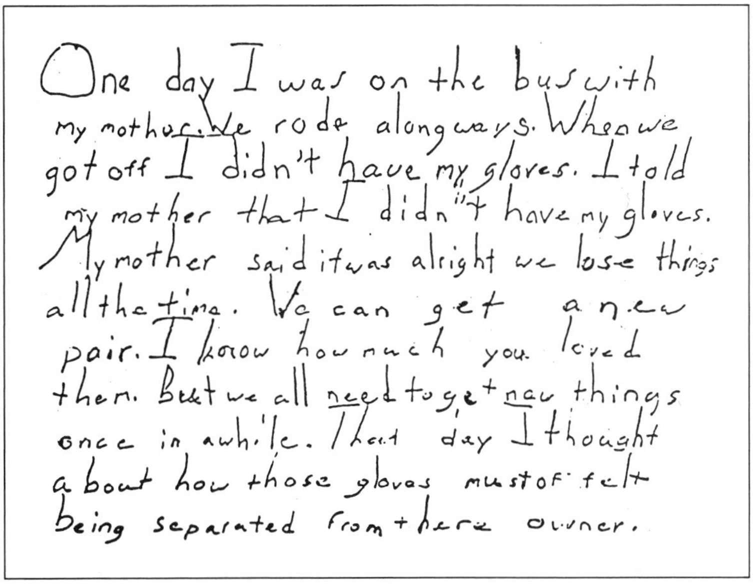

> One day I was on the bus with my mother. We rode along ways. When we got off I didn't have my gloves. I told my mother that I didn't have my gloves. My mother said it was alright we lose things all the time. We can get a new pair. I know how much you loved them. But we all need to get new things once in awhile. That day I thought about how those gloves must of felt being separated from there owner.

mentors because they're always there, ready to share not just their writing but their writing processes. The teacher becomes an important author study. When we share the rough drafts of our work frequently and proudly, we are following Garth Boomer's sound advice: "Teachers must cut off the top of their heads and let kids look inside. Some things," he goes on, "cannot be learned through language, they need to be learned through demonstration."

Students as Mentors for One Another

The teacher is not the only one who is "better than Babe Ruth." Children who write in collegial and supportive environments become mentors for one another. These apprenticeships develop in many ways and for many reasons.

In Andrea Kelly's primary classroom, Raul wrote an alphabet book. At the time he knew few sound-symbol correspondences, so each page of his book had a letter and a random mismatched object to illustrate the sound of the letter. Later on, when he began to understand that the A page should contain objects beginning with the letter *a* and the B page objects beginning with the letter *b*, Joanne Hindley suggested that he return to his alphabet book and review his early attempts. Raul eagerly crossed out and revised. Chris, a rather sophisticated reader and writer, so admired his good friend Raul that he decided to make an alphabet book too. He began by purposely mismatching objects so he too could cross out and have a book like his buddy.

In the lower grades, students greatly influence one another. Ask any primary teacher about the contagious power of one child's use of cartoon bubbles, or one pair of collaborators, or one student's attempt to make a pop-up book. In the upper grades, children continue to want to do what other students have done. Sometimes it's in a "Hey, I could do that" spirit. Joanne Hindley has found that one of the most effective ways to help students understand the value of keeping a writer's

FIGURE 56

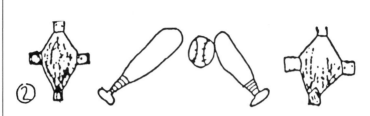

② My grandfather used to to take me to baseball games with 20 thousand other enthusiastic people. Then my grandfather would sit me on his lap. He would put his arms around me and rest his chin on my head. I would just cuddle up closer. Then I could smell the fine aroma of the P.R. soap which smelled like spring roses blooming. Then he would tell who was next to bat. When he would tell me Reggie Jocson was up to bat my eye's would sparkle and I would clap. Every time one of the teams would hit a homerun, I would fly of his lap and clap with my chubby hands. He would just chuckle. Every body in the row that we were sitting in wanted to strangle me, kill me with one glance but my grandfather would just smile with his firm face and hug me.

notebook is to show other students' notebooks alongside her own. "Hey, I could do that" is often the feeling in the room.

In Judy Davis's sixth-grade class, Lucy Calkins found that when a core group of students began writing emotionally and passionately about the plight of the homeless, their words raised the quality of other students' writing.

The range of students' apprentice relationships is diverse and complex. For some the relationships are deliberate, for others seemingly unintentional. On some occasions the mentor is fully informed, at other times he or she remains unaware that someone is borrowing techniques from afar. And students borrow everything from titles, topics, and techniques, to genres, styles of illustrating, and publishing formats.

Serving as mentors for one another can become a major force in a writing workshop. Teachers, in fact, often describe students who are more willing to learn

FIGURE 57

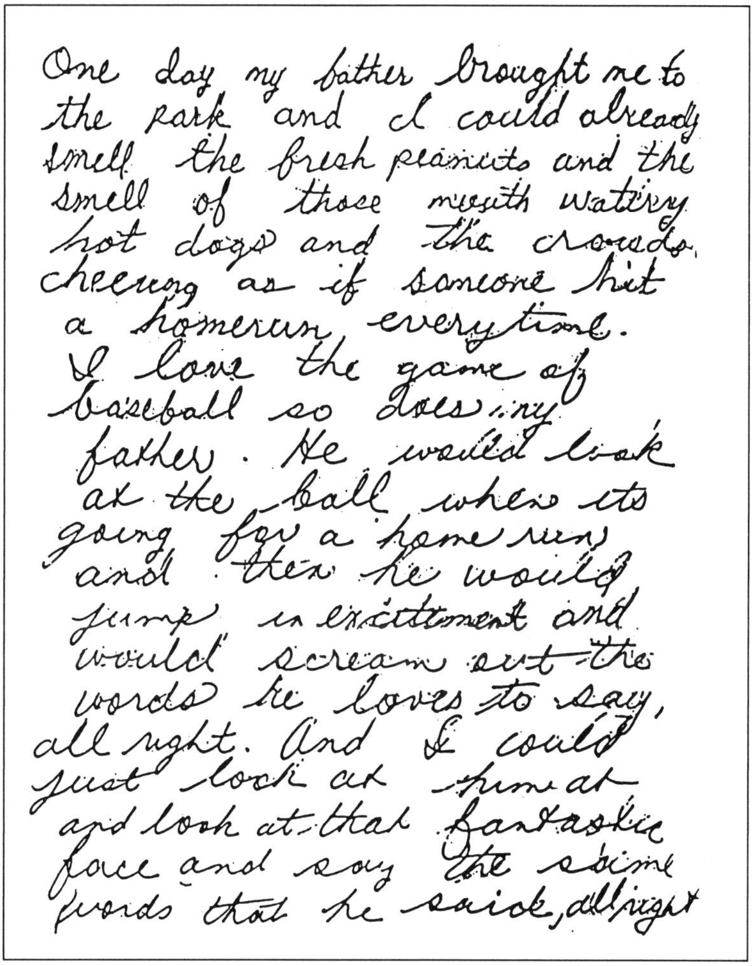

One day my father brought me to the park and I could already smell the fresh peanuts and the smell of those mouth watery hot dogs and the crowds cheering as if someone hit a homerun, everytime. I love the game of baseball so does my father. He would look at the ball where its going for a home run, and then he would jump in excitement and would scream out the words he loves to say, all right. And I could just look at him at and look at that fantastic face and say the same words that he said, all right

from their peers than from the pros. Perhaps student writing seems more within their reach, closer to what young people think is within the world of possibility. And as Nancie Atwell concludes in her book *In the Middle*, "if they're to become borrowers, it's crucial that the good writing be about topics important to them." Some of the most important issues in the lives of ten-year-olds are often issues other ten-year-olds have written about. It's no wonder then that children look to one another for inspiration as well as technique.

When Lucy Calkins came alongside Emil, a fifth grader determined to write about how he and his father share a love of baseball, she discovered several pages of repetitive generalizations: "We love baseball. Baseball is our favorite game. We both love to watch baseball games. We also love to play basketball." Lucy suggested that Emil might be interested in hearing a student's work from *Living Between the Lines*. She read him Tomas's piece (Figure 56).

Emil took lessons from Tomas. He wrote another piece (Figure 57).

Encouraging Students to Become Mentors for Each Other

In many classrooms students seem naturally to view one another as potential mentors. No advice, no suggestions are needed. The students find ways to learn from one another's work. No one assumes celebrity status. In low profile ways, students find what they need among their classmates much the way they find what they need on the library shelves.

I have visited other classrooms, however, in which teachers have intentionally taken steps to ensure that more of their students begin to take writing lessons from one another. First, they've provided more occasions for student work to be read aloud and realized the benefits when an adult reader presents student work. Teachers can often turn a student's words into a powerful text by adding just the right lilt, pauses, and tone of voice. Teachers offer student work during their read-aloud hour, during mini-lessons, and as prepared texts for the listening center. Teachers have also suggested choral class performances of student work.

Second, so that student work is read and reread more frequently, pieces are added to the class library and to appropriate text sets. Multiple copies are also made available for reading response groups.

Student Author-of-the-Week rituals have also been revised to include more in depth study of the student's work. Appreciating a student's efforts involves much more than gazing at a bulletin board display.

One day I suggested to Antoinette's students, "If you were blindfolded and I lifted a piece of student writing from the finished box, one you hadn't read before, do you think you could guess who the writer was? This year we're going to get to know each other so well we probably will be able to guess correctly."

Each Author-of-the-Week study includes some of the following activities:

- The student brings in his or her writing "archive," pieces from past years, so classmates can appreciate changes, growth, variety, and so on.
- The student sends favorite pieces to his or her former teachers asking for a written response. Responses are shared with class.
- Five of the student's pieces are copied and each classmate receives a packet for study and comment.
- Classmates each select a text by a professional writer that for them somehow connects to the student's work. Findings are presented at a share meeting.
- The student's work is included in daily read-aloud sessions, in the week's mini-lessons, or as text for reading workshop.
- Students pursue any or all of the suggestions for enriching author studies of favorite writers. These include choral performances, writing from the student's writing, dramatic play, or studying the student's mentors.

Finally, teachers have encouraged more student mentoring by honoring those apprenticeships that do occur. They make note of students connections to other writers in the room during mini-lessons, conferences, and share meetings. They encourage students to credit their mentors when they compose "About the Author Pages" or introductions for their own formal readings.

Learning to Be Your Own Mentor

In *The Writing Life,* Annie Dillard tells the story of the Washington writer Charlie Butts, who "so prizes momentum, and so fears self-consciousness, that he writes fiction in a rush of his own devising. He leaves his house on distracting errands, hurries in the door, and without taking off his coat, sits at a typewriter and retypes in a blur of speed all of the story he has written to date. Impetus propels him to add another sentence or two before he notices he is writing and seizes up. Then he leaves the house and repeats the process; he runs in the door and retypes the entire story, hoping to squeeze out another sentence the way some car engines turn over after the ignition is off."

Most of us don't retype all we have written, but we do reread. When we sit at our desks, we often find ourselves rereading the best stuff we've already written in order to get our momentum up. We need to hear the voice in our head, to get back on a roll, to go backward in order to go forward. It's almost like being asked to sing the alphabet song starting with *m*. We can't do it. We need to go back to the beginning, to "a-b-c-d-e-f-g," to hear the tune.

Many of us not only reread once to get up steam, we reread our words again and again. Some of us even need to read them aloud. What we're doing, I suppose, is discovering ways to become our own mentors, taking lessons from what we've written before.

Children also need to become mentors for themselves. When I asked students why they were recopying a draft in the past, I was worried that they were obsessing over handwriting or spelling or that they felt pressured to label a sheet "draft two," or that they didn't know any other way to improve their texts. I wonder now if students were using recopying as a way of slowing down their rereading so they could hear the voice in their head. I wonder if they were discovering another way to build momentum.

Of course I'm not advocating recopying, but I do think we need to share with students the benefits of a purposeful rereading of our own work. Students not only need to reread their work in progress, to get back to the place where their writing was going well, they also need to know the advantage of returning to old favorites. Students need to be encouraged to reread their portfolios regularly, taking lessons from their own best work. As I noted in Chapter 8, students need to write with their image of a successful writer in mind.

10

Book Talk That Makes a Difference

*The pleasure of all reading is doubled when one
lives with another who shares the same books.*

Katherine Mansfield

Nineteen eighty-eight was a year filled with long Thursday evenings. Each week I sat at the side of the library conference room at Teachers College, furiously taking notes and reversing the sixty-minute cassettes in my tape recorder, as the members of a reading circle, seven teachers and their leader, talked about the book they had read during the week. From September to June, I listened as they responded to James Agee, Mary Gordon, Toni Morrison, William Kennedy, Elie Wiesel, Nadine Gordimer, Raymond Carver, and many other breath-taking writers. After an hour and a half of book talk, their group leader, Dorothy Barnhouse, would say, "I think it's time to shift to our writing," and for the next hour and a half, Joanne, Mimi, Isoke, Ellen, Sara, Dawn, and Laurie would work on their own writing in progress. Dorothy became their writing teacher, stopping to confer with each of them as she made her way around the conference table. The teachers were attempting to connect their reading to their writing.

In June, these seven women, together with dozens of other reading circle members from around the city, met at the Wave Hill Mansion on the Hudson River for a final celebration. What had the experience meant to them? One after another they stood at the podium and talked of new friendships, new favorite authors, new ways of living their lives in order to make time for their own reading and writing.

And of course they spoke about new ways of teaching. Being a member of a reading circle had meant a lot to them, both personally and professionally, and they planned to incorporate the methodology of their reading groups into their classrooms. They were determined to surround their students with good literature, as the reading group had done for them. They had a renewed respect for multicultural writing. None could imagine having lived the year without Gabriel García Márquez, Jamaica Kincaid, Isabel Allende, Toni Morrison, Louise Erdrich, Amy Tan. They valued the handouts that group members prepared and passed around the table. How much richer their conversation became when they read book reviews and author interviews. They now knew firsthand the importance of responding to their reading in their writer's notebooks alongside their drafts and observations, memories and clippings, free writing and lecture notes.

They learned a number of big lessons as well that would challenge the ways they hosted student reading response groups. These lessons would also challenge the way they used reading response groups to help students make reading-writing connections.

Many of the teachers were writing workshop leaders who later came to literature-based reading workshops. They placed great value on using literature to inform their students' writing, but in their eagerness they often began to explore aspects of the author's craft before allowing students to respond simply as readers. My colleague Roseanne Palamero warns that a similar thing sometimes happens when students read historical fiction. "In our eagerness to get at the facts of the time period, we can forget that the text is a piece of literature first."

Several months ago my daughter recommended a book to me, *Chinese Handcuffs* by Chris Crutcher. As she handed it to me, she said, "But don't exploit it, it's too good." I can still feel the blood rushing to my face. Over the years, my daughter has seen me turn many passages into mini-lessons. She didn't want me to dissect this powerful book. My daughter's advice echoes the wise words of Charlotte Huck, who in discussing Natalie Babbitt's *Tuck Everlasting* says that "children should first have a chance to talk through the issues involved in drinking the magic water and staying young forever . . . Only after they have had a chance to state their positions and give their reasons, should their teachers then raise the question of how the author had made the story so believable as to create that kind of controversy."

In writing workshops, we've learned to pay attention to students' content before we consider their form. In reading workshops we've learned to talk about death and friendship and racism in a book like Lois Lowry's *Autumn Street* before we ask, "How did she create such a text?"

That's not to say that content and form are separate entities. How Lois Lowry writes her novels is related to her meaning, and a discussion of her literary techniques will add richness to our reading and deepen our interpretation. In reading circle discussions, however, we often focus on our personal response before we look at craft in order not to neglect personal response entirely.

The reading circle teachers also came to believe in rereading in order to study an author's craft. They would agree with Sven Birkerts that "literature doesn't kiss on the first date." They would agree with Faye Moskowitz that "not wanting to reread a good book is like saying, 'Paris, I've already been there.' "

This doesn't negate the wonderful experience of reading something for the first time and pausing to admire a surprising verb or a striking metaphor. But as the teachers discovered, in order to really learn from a text they had to live in it, to read it and reread it. They had to know why they liked certain parts more than others and understand how those parts affected them as readers. They had to figure out which literary techniques the writer used to achieve those effects. Those techniques would then become part of the "communal toolbox," as Dorothy Barnhouse called it, and the teachers would learn how to use these tools wisely and well. They suspected that the way they learned from a text probably wasn't all that different from how their students learned.

As the months went on, the group members also found it easier and easier to talk about good writing. At first they seemed awed by Dorothy's fresh ways of naming what she saw in a piece. There were no clichés in her conversation. Instead, she opened the meetings with statements such as, "*Beloved* is like a piece of fabric tightly woven. How did it feel to run your fingers over it this week?" She probed their talk with questions such as, "The author makes a contract with the reader. Do you think the author honored her contract?" She ended one meeting by suggesting, "For next time, why not find a short story you're jealous of?"

As time passed, the same fresh quality began to characterize the teachers' talk. They substituted comments from the heart for canned labels. When group members were struggling with *Beloved*, Isoke Nia counseled, "You have to open your mouth real wide for some books. You can't suck Toni Morrison in with a straw." When the group decided to reread Louise Erdrich's *Tracks*, Laurie Pessah commented, "I take a quick shower every night, but once in a while, I treat myself to a bubble bath. Rereading a great book is like treating yourself to a bubble bath."

Then too, the teachers realized that while on some evenings they spent a great deal of time talking about the author's craft, on other evenings they spent very little time at all. It all seemed to depend on the writer, the text, and where they were in their own writing. They imagined that the same would hold true for the young readers and writers in their classrooms.

The members of this reading circle met recently to talk about reading-writing connections in the classrooms in which they were now working. They couldn't help reflecting once again on their own experiences. "Could the literature we read have had more of an impact on the pieces we were writing?" "If we had it to do over again, what changes would we make?" They all agreed that they would like fewer books and more time for rereading. And more texts closer to what they were writing. In fact, Mimi said, "I was intimidated by Toni Morrison. I was working on a piece about my father's death at the time and I remember thinking that I had a great line that I repeated throughout the piece. It was, "As I sat waiting." I was so proud of those words, and then I read Morrison and it seemed so insignificant."

The others agreed. "Alongside incredible novels like *Beloved*, we probably need to balance our reading with texts that are closer to what we are hoping to write. Perhaps we need more autobiographical sketches, short memoirs, or even those personal essays you see in the newspapers, like Anna Quindlen's 'Life in the Thirties' column or Don Murray's 'Over Sixty.' "

That's not to say that teachers were not making reading-writing connections. Dawn was inspired to write about her own foster motherhood after reading Katherine Paterson's *The Great Gilly Hopkins*. The mother's braid in Eudora

Welty's *One Writer's Beginnings* reminded Joanne of her childhood braids, the ones she draped over her bedroom mirror and was reluctant to part with.

Occasionally, a member of the group did borrow a specific literary technique. Ellen, who was writing about the death of her father, tried writing as an adult looking back, because she admired the first line in Lois Lowry's *Autumn Street:* "It was a long time ago." But most felt that as beginning writers they needed to study the texts longer and more closely. They agreed that their communal toolbox was filled to the brim, but they regretted that they didn't have the courage to dip into it often enough. They wondered how you bring these techniques to yourself as a writer.

Today, when Laurie, Mimi, Joanne, and the other members of this reading circle gather young students to talk about books and the conversation tilts toward craft, their leadership is informed by their participation in their reading circle as well as by their ideas about the special needs of beginning writers.

Working with Children

Teachers never have all the books they dream of. They buy. They borrow. They beg for funds at school board meetings. They write publishers for donations and raid their own children's bedrooms for forgotten treasures. They add student writing and their own work to classroom shelves and school libraries. They cart in old magazines from their neighbors' sidewalk recycling stacks and brake at every flea market and garage sale in town. They even host bake sales and collect bottles and cans to raise funds.

The variety of sources for texts parallels the variety of ways in which they are used. Students read individually and independently. They read multiple copies in small groups. They read whole-class sets as the teacher reads aloud. They participate in shared and guided reading experiences. They read textsets arranged around a common theme or by a favorite writer or within a specific genre. This variety adds richness and texture to the school year.

In our classrooms there have always been varied resources and reading arrangements, but most of our teachers believe that the main way to get children to study an author's craft is to ask the right question. Teachers often came to our staff development workshops seeking suggestions for this perfect question. One evening, the teachers read Bill Martin and John Archambault's *The Ghost-Eye Tree* and were given the following scenario: "You've just read this book aloud to your students, and you've given them ample time for personal response to the text. You're now about to send them off to their reading circle to talk about the author's craft. You've passed out multiple copies to the children. What would you say to get their talk going?"

One teacher offered, "In which part of the story was the author really good at making you feel the children's fear?" and another, "Is there a place in the story where the author said something in a fresh, surprising way?" After bouncing these questions around a little bit, we realized that they were great beginnings but didn't go far enough. In Lucy Calkins's words, they had a "tip-of-the-iceberg" feel to them. We began thinking of these questions as if they were first drafts and then tried to develop more powerful ways of getting at these same issues with our students.

That evening, the teacher who asked about feelings presented a longer, more thoughtful series of instructions that went something like this: "Most stories are about feelings, but the author doesn't say it. Can you go through the story and find places that have strong feelings and share them with your group? Then decide how the feelings are shown. What does the author do to get across the feelings of fear, love, relief and so on?" She imagined that her students would answer, "Through actions, through images, or perhaps through the way language is used." Then she added, "Now look at your own writing. Think about how you get strong feelings across. Find places where you've been successful and share those with your group. Find places that need revising and share those with your group."

The question about language was also revised. Instead of asking, "Is there a place in the story where the author said something in a fresh, surprising way?" one teacher suggested, "When I read something that's beautiful, I mark the parts that are well written. So first in your reading circle I'm going to ask you to do just that. Will you go through the text and mark those parts? Choose just two or three. Then in your group, share those parts and talk about what the author did to make it so beautiful." The teacher imagined that the students would come up with a list that included "comparing things, using surprising language, painting pictures with words." She then ended by saying, "You know, you can do the same thing with your own writing. Find the parts you think are beautifully written and tell what you did. Find the parts that need revising and share them with your group."

The teachers were encouraging a new kind of reading. Patricia Hampl recently wrote about Isak Dinesen in *The New York Times Book Review*. When asked about her writing Dinesen replied, "Read it, read it, and you'll see how it's written!" Hampl continues, "But a particular kind of reading is called for, more investigative than the reading that is enchantment, less mechanistic and reductive than the mentality that speaks of 'the techniques of fiction.' "

The teachers were grappling to discover how to encourage that particular kind of reading. They were struggling to develop a line of questioning that would help students begin to discover how writers work. That evening they realized that there is no perfect question. Instead, they left with a few guiding principles for developing their own. First, questions should invite children to linger in the text, to stick with it. Therefore it is helpful to ask a series of related questions, not just one, and they should be the kind that ask children to search the text. Second, the questions should probably be generic, the kind that can be asked of any text, not just *The Ghost-Eye Tree*. After all, we want students to make reading-writing connections, whenever they read. Third, the teachers realized that just getting children talking about the author's craft was not enough. In order to bring the point home, the students need to consider the implications of a writers style for their own writing, perhaps even taking pen in hand and having a go at trying out what they're discovering. Finally, the teachers realized that the questions would be powerful if they were selected wisely, if they arose from the students' concerns as writers. Students are more likely to learn from their reading if they are invited to talk about the same issues they are dealing with in their writing.

When a teacher finishes reading *The Ghost-Eye Tree* aloud, she may send students to join various reading response groups based on what they're struggling with in their own writing: structure, dialogue, pace, mood. And each group will have its own series of questions. There might also be occasions for students to study a text in very personal, individual ways. "As readers, we all admire different things in a well-written piece of literature. Why not reread the text, jotting down what you admire? Then think through what tools the author used to create this experience for you as a reader. Then meet in your group to share your discoveries."

Teachers left the staff development workshop that evening realizing that not only is there no one perfect question, but asking any question is only the beginning. If the students' talk about books is to make a lasting impression, students needed to interact with the information they are receiving and bring it to their own writing.

The Teacher-Led Response Group

The line of questioning the teachers developed does not require that an adult leader be present during the student response group. Students can work independently or collaboratively and meet to share their discoveries. Yet there are times when teachers might sit in to lead students into deeper ways of responding, searching, probing, and connecting.

One day I hosted a student response group with a cluster of third graders. While the rest of the class read individual books of their own choosing, I read a piece of student writing to the group of five youngsters gathered in the back of the room. I had chosen a piece written by Vera, a second grader from another school in another borough called *The Fifteen Cats* (see Figure 58).

I decided to begin by reading the piece aloud to ensure that these young readers would really appreciate this young writer's work. When I finished I said, "I think this is a very important story. What did you make of it?" Jeffrey, a handsome Malaysian child began, "It kind of teaches you a lesson." "And what's the lesson you learned?" I asked. "Never to steal," said Jeffrey. Jason, an Indian boy sitting across from Jeffrey, agreed but added, "I learned something else. When someone does something good for you, you should do something good for them."

The talk continued around the table as children volunteered their reactions and personal stories. Irene thought the story was mostly about being good and reaping the rewards. The man stops being a thief, so the cats help him. The cats help the man, so they get food when they're hungry. "Like in my house. If I do extra work, I get a reward. If I get a good grade in school, I get to stay up an extra hour."

Eurythia said the book reminds her of the Aesop's fable "The Lion and the Mouse." "You never know when someone's going to help you," she said. Palak thought the group should talk about the poor people who are homeless. "Do you think they're tired of being poor and they might decide to rob jewels like the old man?"

Vera is seven years old, and she has written a piece of literature. I honored her work by treating it as I would the work of Patricia MacLachlan or Judith Viorst. After the children had responded to the content, I moved the conversation to Vera's writing. "You know," I began, "I almost thought about tricking you today. I was going to tuck Vera's story inside a big hardcovered book from the library and let you think a grown-up had written it. I think I could have fooled you. Do you think so? Does Vera's writing have the sound of a library book?"

Instead of predetermining which issues to focus on, as the teachers working with *The Ghost-Eye Tree* had, I first provided time for the students to say what

FIGURE 58

The fiften Cats
By vera

Once upon a time there were fiften cats. They lived in the woods. one day they were hungry so they set out looking for food they looked and looked and looked until they were so tired they had to stop. Then one cat saw a stream and they all started runing to

After they drank they were still hungry so they started to look again but then they saw a dark dark cave. and they went inside. It was spoocky but they still went on. Just then they heard a sound. It was loud and spooky and the cats started to shiver.

FIGURE 58, continued

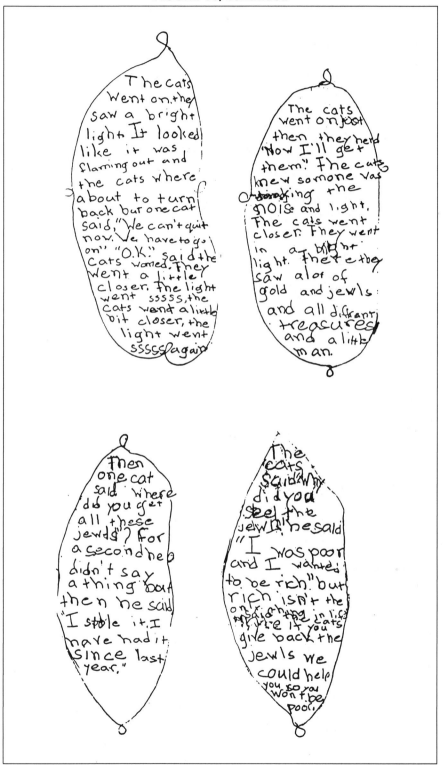

FIGURE 58, continued

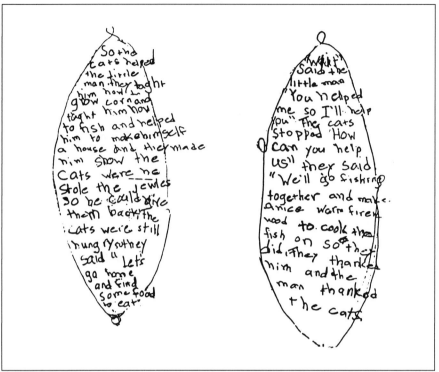

they saw. The children did agree that Vera is a fine writer. I passed out copies of her book so they could spend time rereading. "Why not read with pen in hand? Mark the places she does things you admire." My teaching strategies are marked by a belief in student activity. I asked the students to reread, to mark up, and then to share their discoveries.

Student Discoveries

The students comments included, "It's like a library book because the cats talk. Lots of animals talk in library books."

"She says, 'Once upon a time . . . ' and the cats 'set off.' You hear that a lot in library books."

"She says it's a 'dark, dark cave' and 'looked and looked and looked.' If you're just talking you probably only say it once, but when you write a good story, sometimes you do that—say something two or three times."

"She says the same thing lots of times, but in different places. All over the place she says, 'The cats went on, the cats went on. They went a little bit closer, the lights went SSSSS. The cats went a little bit closer, the lights went SSSSS again.' That's like a book with suspense."

"It sounds like a fairy tale. They tell you a little bit and then they say, 'One day . . . ' and you know something is going to happen."

"I like her words—like flaming out, the light was flaming out. That's beautiful language."

These comments did not just bounce around the table. Instead, I tried to encourage the students to dwell on one issue. "Let's all think about this for a while. How do you feel about repetition of words? Are there other ways Vera created suspense in this piece? What do you mean by 'beautiful language'?"

Georgia Heard teaches children to reread their poems searching for clichés. She suggests they put the clichéd words at the top of a fresh sheet of paper and try to think of other, truer ways to say what they mean. When I ask students what they mean by beautiful language, it is like giving them that fresh sheet of paper.

Eurythia responds, "Well, *flaming* is such a special word." I try to probe her response honestly and gently. "What do you mean, 'special'?"

"It's like she really wanted us to see the color and shape of the lights and so she picked this perfect, special word."

Eurythia was beginning to explain her labels. "Can you say more?" I continued. Finally, perhaps in her urgency to make me understand, Eurythia explained, "Well, it's like my mother when company is coming. She takes out those really special dishes. Every day we use plain ones, but for company she uses the really beautiful ones. I think that's what Vera did, because she wanted her cat book to be special."

Later that day, I talked to Eurythia's teacher about the impression her comment had made on the other children. We admitted that we could never have thought of such a powerful, kidlike metaphor. We knew that her comment was worth a month of mini-lessons. Later that week, I challenged this small group of children to go even further with their study of Vera's craft. First I asked them to search the library stacks. "Can you find professional writers who use the same techniques as Vera and jot their words in the margins of Vera's story?" The children raided the fairy tale section. Jeffrey wrote several quotes from *Snow White* on Vera's first page. He spotted similarities in the conventional opening, "Once upon a time." He also jotted down, "Mirror, mirror on the wall," and "faster and faster she ran," next to Vera's repetition of "looked and looked and looked."

I suggested that the students also search their own writing folders and notebooks for places where they might have used these techniques. Jeffrey discovered that his narrative about a drowning emergency was filled with repeated words. "He went deep, very deep. My father went deep, real deep to save my brother."

I also challenged the students to find places where any of these techniques would strengthen old pieces. Eurythia decided that some "everyday" information should introduce her story that began, "One day I went with my mother to Disneyland." Her story now began, "My mother and I are very happy. We live in Queens with my father. One day we received big news. We were going to Disneyland."

I ended this period of study by reminding children that they could always use their notebook as a place to experiment with any of the techniques they admired.

I had tried to sequence classroom activities to add layers of meaning. The students went from naming what they saw to searching for other examples to trying the techniques out in their own writing. In the past I only talked about the texts. Now I realize that isn't enough. Now I find it helpful to keep asking myself, "Is there more to this? Can I push it further?" I've learned to look for natural pathways of thinking and then follow them.

My teaching also tries to make implicit information explicit. Recently, Di Snowball, the Australian whole-language educator, visited our project. In referring to

Brian Cambourne's stages of learning, she noted that learning is implicit during the immersion stage. "Many struggling readers," she explained, "do not pick things up implicitly. During the demonstration stage we need to make things explicit." Just as Mauricio needed to get inside Kuskin's technique in his author study, so too students need more than immersion during the reading workshop. Most of us are struggling writers. We don't pick up implicitly all that we need to know.

Because of a few star writers, I think we're sometimes fooled into thinking that all our students are connecting to the literature. Some children seem to acquire techniques simply through immersion, as if by osmosis. But what about the others, the ones who don't seem to be able to take lessons from their reading naturally?

Some might not be reading like writers, as Frank Smith suggests, because they are "totally concerned with the act of reading, with getting every word right, or with trying to memorize all the facts." Others might not be reading like writers, because, as Smith continues, they "have no interest in writing what they read or . . . there's no expectation of writing the kinds of texts they read."

There are a great many students, however, who are quite comfortable with the act of reading and who would love to write the kind of material they love to read. Yet we rarely see them attempt to borrow elements of another writer's writing, and when they do, the results are often disheartening.

It is for the students who do not seem to be able to connect their reading to their writing that I find myself offering deliberate challenges when I host reading response groups. I want to help more students build bridges—safe bridges—between what they read and what they write. Often these challenges require students to interact with the information I presented. I ask them to do something with the information in order to claim it as their own. These challenges are as helpful for teachers as they are for students.

One day at Teachers College, twenty staff developers had gathered at our regular Thursday afternoon staff meeting. We began by reading William Stafford's essay "The Door Called Poetry" in *You Must Revise Your Life*. When we had finished we broke into four groups to try to "do something" with what we had learned. One group met with a stack of children's pieces by their side. They explored how the article changed their way of looking at student writing. A second group role-played conferring with students on their drafts, trying to allow Stafford's insights to inform their responses. A third group reread the chapter to explore the qualities of good writing Stafford's essay so clearly illustrates. A fourth group met to probe their personal responses to the chapter.

The staff developers were very excited by this activity. "So much information comes at us," one explained, "that it often washes over us." "This activity made the information stick. It was brought home to each of us."

Another Text, Another Response Group

One Friday afternoon I led a small reading response group from Antoinette's fifth-grade class. Each student had read Donald Hall's *The Man Who Lived Alone,* the story of an eccentric man who lives in a cabin in the New England woods. This time I didn't begin, as I had with the third graders, by asking the students what they got from the story. Instead, I launched the discussion by asking the students to bring any important questions they had to the table. Irvin wanted to know why come some old people can take care of themselves and others seem helpless. Orlando wanted to know if animals count as friends, because maybe he really didn't live alone. Yuri asked, "Is it better to be like the old man and just depend on yourself than to rely on your family for everything?"

The students spent almost forty minutes answering their questions, moving back and forth between the text and their own life experiences in order to make their meanings clear. Afterwards, I channeled their talk toward a discussion of Hall's style. "What do you admire in Donald Hall's writing?" I began. "How was he able to write such a powerful piece?" The children began flipping through the pages of their books, rereading passages and pointing out what they liked. They noticed that it's possible to write a good story without dialogue. They thought each page was a poem. They liked the way the last page repeated images from throughout the book.

On the following Monday, I returned to the same group. "As I was rereading this book over the weekend," I began, "I couldn't help but notice that Donald Hall uses a few similar techniques throughout. I thought it might be helpful for us to study these techniques closely to see if we might some day feel the need to borrow them."

I then passed out a sheet of excerpts from the text. One page was filled with passages containing what the students later named "strings of sentences":

He learned how to do just about everything.
He could shoe a horse, or a mule.
He could make a pitchfork, handle and tines.
He could build a whole shotgun from scratch.
He could make a house, or a road, or a wall.

Sometimes in the winter he would eat tomatoes out
    of his Ball jars three times a day.
Sometimes peas.
Sometimes applesauce.
Sometimes he would buy a case of cornflakes or one
    of graham crackers and eat nothing else until
    he finished the case.

I had prepared this handout thinking it might be easier for children to appreciate a new technique when they see several examples of it, one right next to the other, rather than spread throughout a text.

Not only was it easy for the students to notice Hall's use of strings of similar sentences, but they also saw other unexpected things as well. They spotted an internal structure to the passages. "He goes from small to big," Orlando said. "Yeah," Yuri agreed, "shoeing a horse to making a pitchfork, to building a shotgun, to building a whole house. Small things to big things." The students pointed out a similar build-up from peas to applesauce to whole cases of food.

The students were quite comfortable in talking about what they saw in the excerpts. They had more difficulty, however, when I probed further. "What effect does this technique have on you as a reader?" I asked. I had learned to ask this question of the students because Dorothy Barnhouse had asked it of teachers at a recent teacher workshop. She helped teachers discover that it's not enough to notice a technique. If a technique is to become important and useful to writers, they need to appreciate when and why and how to use it and what effect it has on readers.

First-grade teacher Julie Liebersohn spends a lot of time helping her students understand the why behind class directions, rules, and writing suggestions. "When I was a little girl my mom always used to tell me to leave the light on in the garage when I came home from school. I never remembered to do it," she explains, "until my mother finally told me why. 'If the garage is dark,' she said, 'I trip over the boxes when I come in late.'" Julie never forgot to leave the light on again. Julie, like her students today, remembers to do things that make human sense.

Quality talk about quality writing results when students not only say what they see but wonder why the author chose to use these techniques. Students need to explore the effect the writer has created and to speculate on the tools used to achieve this effect.

And so when students examined Hall's "strings of sentences," I persisted. Again I asked, "What happens to you as a reader when you see something written in such a manner?"

The students responded to my questions with rather predictable comments that didn't really answer the question. "I like this way of writing because I like repetition," or "It's good writing because it has lots of details."

I was determined to move the students beyond familiar labels, so I kept on probing. They struggled to find the right words to make me understand. Eventually our talk became more honest. Yuri described the buildup from small to big as an orchestra working toward a crescendo. Orlando saw it more like mountain climbing: "You start at the bottom and you work hard to get to the important top. When you read these pages," he went on, "it's like Donald Hall is letting you know, 'I mean business. I have important things to say.'"

The students followed the same procedure when I handed them a second sheet containing what they later named "list sentences." Again I highlighted the technique by grouping several passages on one handout. They talked about the effect of a poetic sentence like

> But mostly he stayed at his camp
> and dreamed about Old Beauty the intelligent mule
> and Grover Cleveland the owl
> and seven kinds of apples on one tree
> and a hundred thousand nails
> and two dozen pelts
> and eight wasps' nests
> and thirty clocks
> and one-hundred-and-forty-seven old newspapers . . .
> He kept his beard winter and summer now, because
>   it was easier,
> and as he got older and older and older, it grew so
>   long that it covered the darns on his shirt.

Samantha suggested, "Donald Hall probably wants us to read it quickly like a shopping list, so we'll remember how much stuff he had so we won't think he was so alone." Yuri added, "I think he wants us to be amazed by this old man so he leaves a lot of empty space to give us time to think."

The students had moved beyond mere labels. My colleague Lydia Bellino was awed by the insights in the students comments. "Their talk reminds me of a meeting I had with my own adult reading circle. We had read John Steinbeck's

Cannery Row and he too uses very long sentences. I remember members of my group describing the technique as a 'clicking of the camera' or an 'assembly line of images' that brought out a trudging feeling in the reader."

I brought the student response group to a close by asking them if they could ever imagine using these two techniques or any others they had discovered in Hall's writing. I didn't ask the students to write but merely to talk about their potential use, since I agree with John Gardner that "thinking about the exercises can sometimes be as valuable as sitting down to do them." Orlando was the first to respond. "I might string some sentences together in my report on crime in New York City. I might say,

> You'll hear ambulances screeching,
> You'll hear sirens roaring,
> You'll hear people calling out for help!

or I could make a long listing sentence like, 'What New York needs to stop crime is Batman, Robo Cop, Superman, Teenage Mutant Ninja Turtles, Robin, Ghostbusters, He-Man, Firewoman, Iceman, Spiderwoman, and, last but not least, Spiderman.' That would show the reader I mean business."

Imagining an appropriate use for Hall's techniques gave Orlando and his classmates a chance to interact in concrete ways with the information presented. I could also have invited students to

- Write about Donald Hall's literary style noting what you admire and hope to borrow.
- Go over your own writer's notebook looking for places that connect with Hall's techniques.
- Name the techniques you admire in Hall's writing and carry them into your next notebook entry.
- Find other writers you think write like Donald Hall. Jot down similarities.
- Try to quickly mimic Hall's techniques in your own writing.

Adding Layers to Response Groups

Teachers have discovered that they can add richness to a discussion of one author's craft by tucking in a piece of related reading. Imagine talking about Hall's technique after reading a book review of *The Man Who Lived Alone*. Students can reread the text with the reviewer's ideas in mind. Do they agree or disagree? Do they see things they haven't seen before?

Imagine talking about Hall's techniques after reading a page or two from a text on good writing. If students read a page of suggestions from Don Murray they could talk through examples of "the particular detail, the release of feelings, or the use of senses as a bridge to the reader."

Imagine talking about Hall's techniques after we ask a friend to jot "reading as a writer" notes in the margins of the text, much the way Don Murray has done in *Read to Write*. In this fine text Murray includes his thoughts as he reads through several literary selections, sharing how he studies the masters. We can ask any colleague who takes her writing seriously to jot down in the margins what she sees in Hall's text. The point of all this, as Murray reminds us, is not that students should copy our colleague's way of reading, but that they learn to read with a writer's eye.

Imagine talking about the literary techniques Hall used in *The Man Who Lived Alone* after reading another picture book by the same author, *Ox-Cart Man,* noting similarities and differences in tone, technique, and topic.

Teachers can also generate valuable talk by asking students to read background information on an author along with a text. Biographical sketches, acceptance speeches, author interviews, and journal articles often contain insights into an author's writing processes, intentions, preparations, and frustrations.

Looking Back

This chapter began with a discussion of adult reading circles and perhaps it's fitting that it ends with them. For many of our teachers, their own weekly reading groups continue to serve as an inspiration and example of what they eventually hope will take place in their classrooms.

At one such meeting, a group of teachers had just read "Natural History," an award-winning short story by Vicki Vinton, a fiction writer and member of the Writing Project. After much talk about family relationships, Marianne, a teacher from Connecticut, shifted the conversation toward Vicki's craft. She began not by pointing out any particular stylistic technique but by sharing the overall effect this text had on her as a reader. "It's such a silent story," she began. Other members of the group agreed. Vicki's story evoked a sense of mystery and eerie silence. The group then studied the text closely, trying to figure out what Vicki had done to create such an effect. One teacher thought the fact that the characters lacked first names created the silence. Another described a kind of unraveling of information as the sentences leaked out onto the page. Still others noticed the sparse use of dialogue. "When people speak," Hindy List commented, "it's like glass breaking." The group also proposed that the characters' lack of much internal thought added to the sense of silence.

Talk about Vicki's craft folded back into individual interpretations of her story, adding new layers to their responses. In their book *Grand Conversations* Ralph Peterson and Mary Ann Eeds note, "It is possible to read MacLachlan's *Sarah, Plain and Tall* without attending to how the story is moved along by the simplicity of the prairie setting, without being aware of the part music plays in symbolizing the loss felt by Caleb and Anna, or without being aware of the importance of color in building our anticipation as well as in bringing unity to the text. But," they conclude, "much of the richness of the book will be lost if these levels are not explored." Analyzing literary technique is not only for aspiring writers, it is also for those aspiring to read texts more deeply.

Adult response groups often move into rather sophisticated ground. Discussion of Vicki's techniques fed into the group's ideas about the meaning of the text, but it also led group members to wonder about Vicki's writing process—and their own. Did Vicki deliberately set out to create silence? Was she conscious of the techniques that members of the group had pointed out? Could they use some of these techniques if they were interested in creating a similar atmosphere?

Most suspected that stylistic devices, such as the sparse use of dialogue, are organic to a particular piece of writing. Perhaps Vicki notices, consciously or unconsciously, that something works and then refines its use. As Meltzer reminds us, "Literary technique cannot be applied like a coat of paint." The group doubted that it would be possible to apply a technique as if it were a step in a cookbook recipe. They decided that if you admire an effect, it might make sense to try it in your own writing. But you have to become a critical reader of your own writing. You have to be willing to say, "No, that doesn't work in this piece." As Dorothy reminded us, "You have to learn to listen to your writing and you have to teach children to listen to theirs."

If children are too quick to slap any stylistic device they admire onto a piece, the results may be disheartening. How often have we wished that we hadn't taught sharp leads when every paper in the class begins with a sound effect or a bizarre, catchy question? That we hadn't stressed adding details when class pieces turn into ten pages of bed-to-bed minutiae? That we had never talked about strong verbs when we see children removing every "said" and replacing it with distracting alternatives.

In a recent newspaper column, Ellen Goodman wrote about the popular television show, "America's Funniest Home Videos." She noted that the videos were once rather zany and eccentric, but now something has changed. Many viewers, it seems, bent on winning the weekly $10,000 prize, are no longer capturing real-life moments but staging them. It doesn't work. The videos appear canned and inauthentic. "They come packaged, produced," she writes. Texts by young writers can also appear canned and inauthentic, packaged and produced, if we don't encourage these writers to begin to evaluate the appropriateness of the techniques and tools they borrow.

Teachers who have participated in adult reading groups want their students' talk about books to be as layered as their own. They want students to move from content to craft and back again, to crawl inside a text to get at literary technique, to reread their own writing carefully and borrow techniques wisely.

Teachers who push for authentic discussion of reading and writing feel that they're breaking ground. Their students often begin the year without knowing there's such a thing as literary technique. They have had little experience in recognizing these techniques or realizing their power. Our teachers often begin the year by giving students lots of support. As the year goes on, students begin to internalize the process of reading like a writer and teachers can step out of the way.

One Child's Efforts

It would be a good idea if children would write books for older people, now that everyone is writing for children.

G. C. Lichtenberg

There were several feisty fifth graders in Antoinette's class, children who would rather be playing in the park than sitting in school. Amaury, a curly-haired boy from the Dominican Republic, was one of them. As a writer, he had no superstar status. Early in the year he kept a writer's notebook because everyone in the class kept one, not, unfortunately, because he found writing satisfying.

The following notebook entries were selected from the many Amaury wrote during the first few weeks of school. They create a realistic portrait of this young writer.

This first entry (Figure 59) indicates that Amaury expects his notebook to be read by others. Why else would he introduce himself? Besides letting us know he loves sports, Amaury also reveals that he's an honest and straightforward writer. Not every child would admit that he eats junk food and hates school.

The second entry (Figure 60) gives me a hint of Amaury's understanding—or misunderstanding—of notebook keeping. At first he used his notebook like a diary, recording one event from each day. This entry does suggest that Amaury sees

FIGURE 59

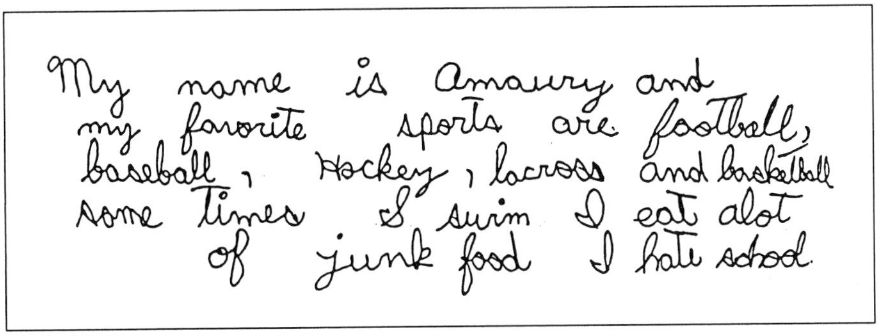

> My name is Amaury and my favorite sports are football, baseball, Hockey, lacross and basketball some times I swim I eat alot of junk food I hate school.

FIGURE 60

> Today I went To Najibs House Najib is a good Friend and Nelson But Befor that I was at Nelson's House and He was playing with His dog, So he picked up coco and The dog did Number 1 on him. IT was so funny !!!) I Thought He was lying at First but Then His Hand was all wet.

humor in everyday things, but I begin to wonder if he's trying to shock the adult reader: junk food, hating school, and now a bit of bathroom humor.

In the next entry (Figure 61) Amaury is still recording one event from each day. So far his notebook keeping is limited to very short narratives, but his entries are letting me know that not all the students in the class respect people's differences, nor do they have appropriate ways of resolving conflicts. Amaury's writing also reveals a rather sexist attitude, which suggests that if this class is to grow into a successful writing community, Antoinette and I need to address the issues of camaraderie and respect that I described in Chapter 2.

FIGURE 61

Today we ~~Helped~~ Helped
a teacher with boxes it
was Fun ve got in trouble
we made to much noise
Najib snuffed peland then
I ~~H~~ kicked him.
He screamed like a little girl
the teacher told Him to
go back o up stairs Peland
is So slow after we
finish he was still walking
up the stairs.

FIGURE 62

I woke up this morning
at 8 a 8:10 Threw the blanket
off and Herked out of bed
got dressed comb d my hair
brushed my hair,
~~ever~~ Ever Since
That all I said was
by mom, After that I
came back and said
High mom, then she
cooks while I play
nintendo. Then I eat play
again then go to sleep.
The next morning I get
up at 8:13.

FIGURE 63

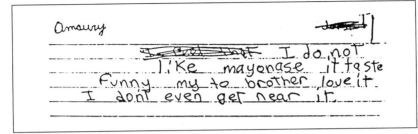

Amaury

I do not
like mayonase it taste
Funny my to brother love it
I don't even get near it

FIGURE 64

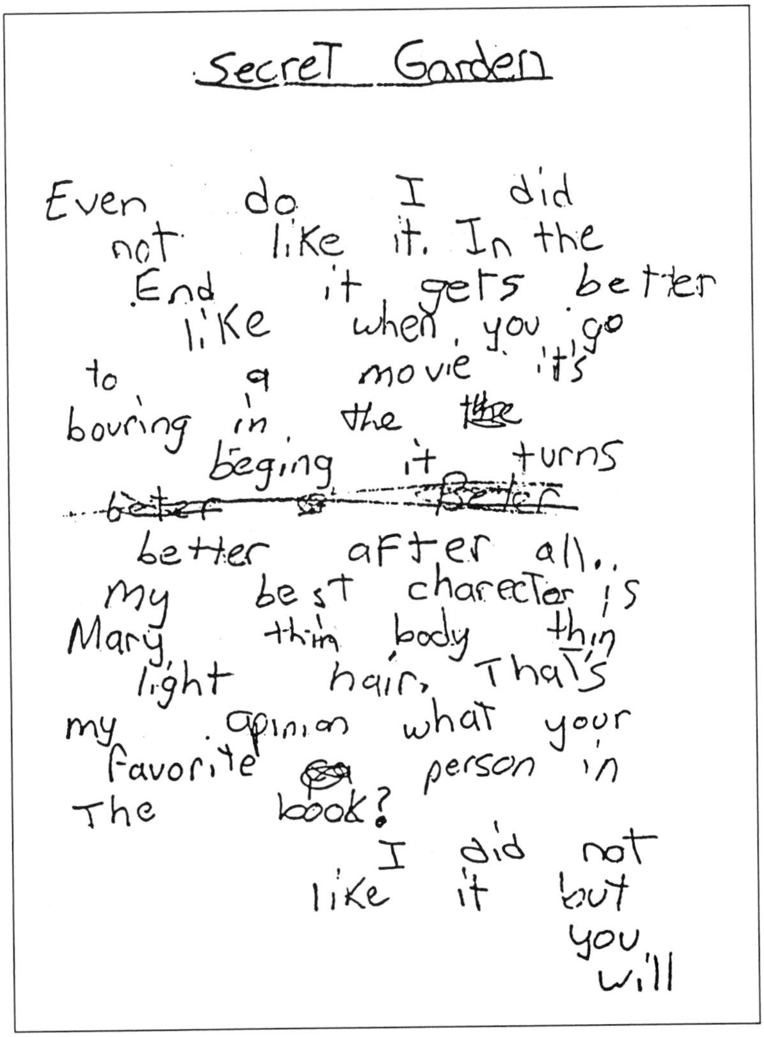

Secret Garden

Even do I did
not like it. In the
End it gets better
like when you go
to a movie it's
bouring in the the
beging it turns
better after all..
My best charecter is
Mary, thin body thin
light hair. That's
my opinion what your
favorite person in
The book?
I did not
like it but
you
will

FIGURE 65

Raccons are cute animals that have problems like They go into the garbage eat twinkies oreos and Bigmacs these animals have cavites, broken teeth gum Disease.

FIGURE 66

D.R.

The D.R. is a country That is in the carribean islands it is very nice There but the muscitoes a ~~teste~~ terrible down there , te they bite you during the night.

IF I wa a muscitoe D.R. is Hawen all the Food you want. mostly people From toronto, canada go there. muscites are mostly drinking canadian blood.

FIGURE 67

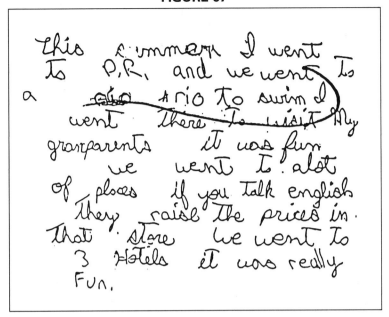

The fourth selection (Figure 62) reminds me that I could focus on weaknesses, but I must also discover Amaury's strengths as a writer. I could read this entry and worry about the confusion between homophones, the misplaced capital letters, or Amaury's use of his notebook as a place to log in bed-to-bed happenings (he is not even highlighting one event now but reporting quickly on an entire day). Instead, I need to try to appreciate his use of the surprising verb ("hurled") and his attention to precise details ("8:13").

When I read the entry in Figure 63 I can look and see nothing or everything. I can think, "So what? Why bother to write this?" Or I can marvel at Amaury's breakthrough. He finally appreciates the fact that a notebook is a perfect place to capture fleeting thoughts. Not every entry in a writer's notebook needs to be a narrative. Amaury has also begun to record observations about his family life.

Antoinette had read Frances Hodgson Burnett's *The Secret Garden* aloud to the class. Amaury, who had learned to respond to his reading in his writer's notebook, made the entry in Figure 64. As his comments reflect, he follows the traditional book report format, but he also demonstrates a lovely use of metaphor: getting into a book is something like getting into a movie. ("Even do" reflects a true New York pronunciation of "even though").

Amaury wrote the entry in Figure 65 in response to a newspaper article about tooth decay in raccoons. As I described in Chapter 3, we encouraged students to respond in their writer's notebook to all the reading they did. Although we had encouraged students to follow appealing newspaper stories over several days or weeks, Amaury, like most ten-year-olds, selected stories that were unlikely ever to appear again, self-contained specialty articles that required little background information. Amaury's entry is mostly a summary of the facts contained in the article. Just as he has learned to write book reports, Amaury has also learned the traditional format for a current events summary. Although he lets us know that he finds raccoons to be cute animals, he adds no additional thoughts, opinions, or suggestions. Whenever I show Amaury's notebook pages at workshops, teachers smile in recognition. Every classroom, it seems, has a few students like Amaury.

One day Amaury began writing about life in the Dominican Republic. His notebook jotting took on new energy. He had discovered an issue that really mattered. Keeping a notebook became almost as good as playing baseball in the park. It was as if he were the child in Byrd Baylor's *I'm in Charge of Celebrations,* the one who was "breathing some new kind of air." One entry led to many entries.

In the entry in Figure 66 Amaury is no longer recording facts alone. He comments on the situation and once again reveals his sense of humor.

In the middle of Amaury's fairly traditional recording of his summer vacation in Figure 67 is the surprising one-liner: "If you talk English they raise the prices in that store." This line and his comment in the previous entry about tourists from Canada suggest that Amaury is a fine observer who pays close attention to the world around him.

The selection in Figure 68 shows that Amaury's entries have begun to increase in length. He has a lot to say about the Dominican Republic. The underlined and circled sections are those Amaury thought worth using when he decided to draw upon this material to work towards a finished piece. He marked them as he reread his notebook in search of gems.

By the entries in Figures 69 and 70, Amaury has committed his notebook almost exclusively to gathering more thoughts on life in the Dominican Republic. He has learned to dwell in his topic while letting his thoughts wander from the plane ride, to the gardens, to the river, to the guard protecting the houses. He writes freely, not stopping to worry about handwriting, spelling, grammar, or punctuation. These are things he'll tend to when he works on a finished piece.

At one point, Amaury thought he had exhausted all his resources. He had nothing left to say about life in the Dominican Republic. I suggested that he talk to Nelson, another child who had spent time in his country. He included exact quotes from his interview with Nelson in his entry in Figure 71.

Amaury wrote the entry in Figure 72 after he read Frané Lessac's *My Little Island.* He did a lot of reading along with his notebook writing. It became common practice in this class. Once students had made a commitment to a topic, they searched for related literature.

Amaury's classmates, his teacher, and the school librarian all searched for helpful material. By week's end, he had a small stack of texts related to life on a tropical island in general, not just the Dominican Republic. He read Eloise Greenfield's poems set in the Bahamas in *Under the Sunday Tree.* Amos Ferguson's paintings in this book were as generative for Amaury as the poems. He read Caribbean poems in Lynn Joseph's collection *Coconut Kind of Day* and in Grace Nichols's *Come on into My Tropical Garden.* He also pored over Frané Lessac's *Caribbean Canvas,* rich with paintings, proverbs, and poems. We also tucked in a few nonfiction articles about the Dominican Republic.

His reading helped Amaury in several ways. The related literature generated further thoughts. Not only did Amaury read these materials in class, but we encouraged him to share them with his family and friends. Family conversation would no doubt provide more grist for his literary mill. In addition, these texts also gave

FIGURE 68

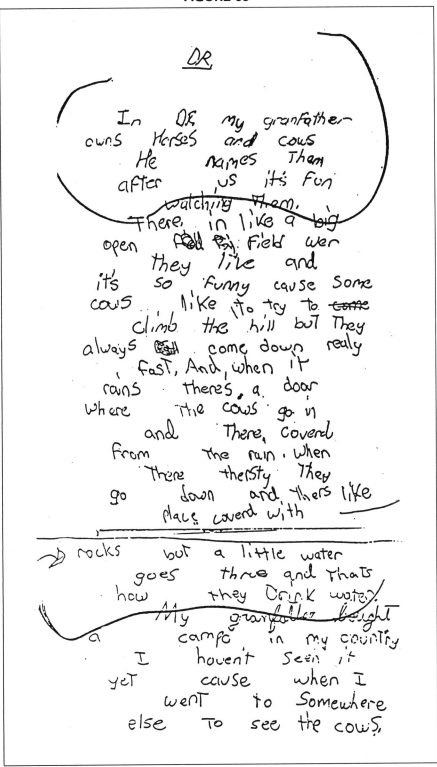

DR.

In DR my granfather owns Horses and cows He names Tham after us it's Fun watching them. There, in like a big open Field wer they live and it's so funny cause some cows like to try to climb the hill but They always come down realy fast, And, when it rains theres, a door where The cows go in and There, coverd from the rain. When There thersty They go down and thers like places coverd with rocks but a little water goes thrue and Thats how they Drink water. My granfather bought a campo in my country I havent seen it yet cause when I went to somewhere else To see the cows.

FIGURE 69

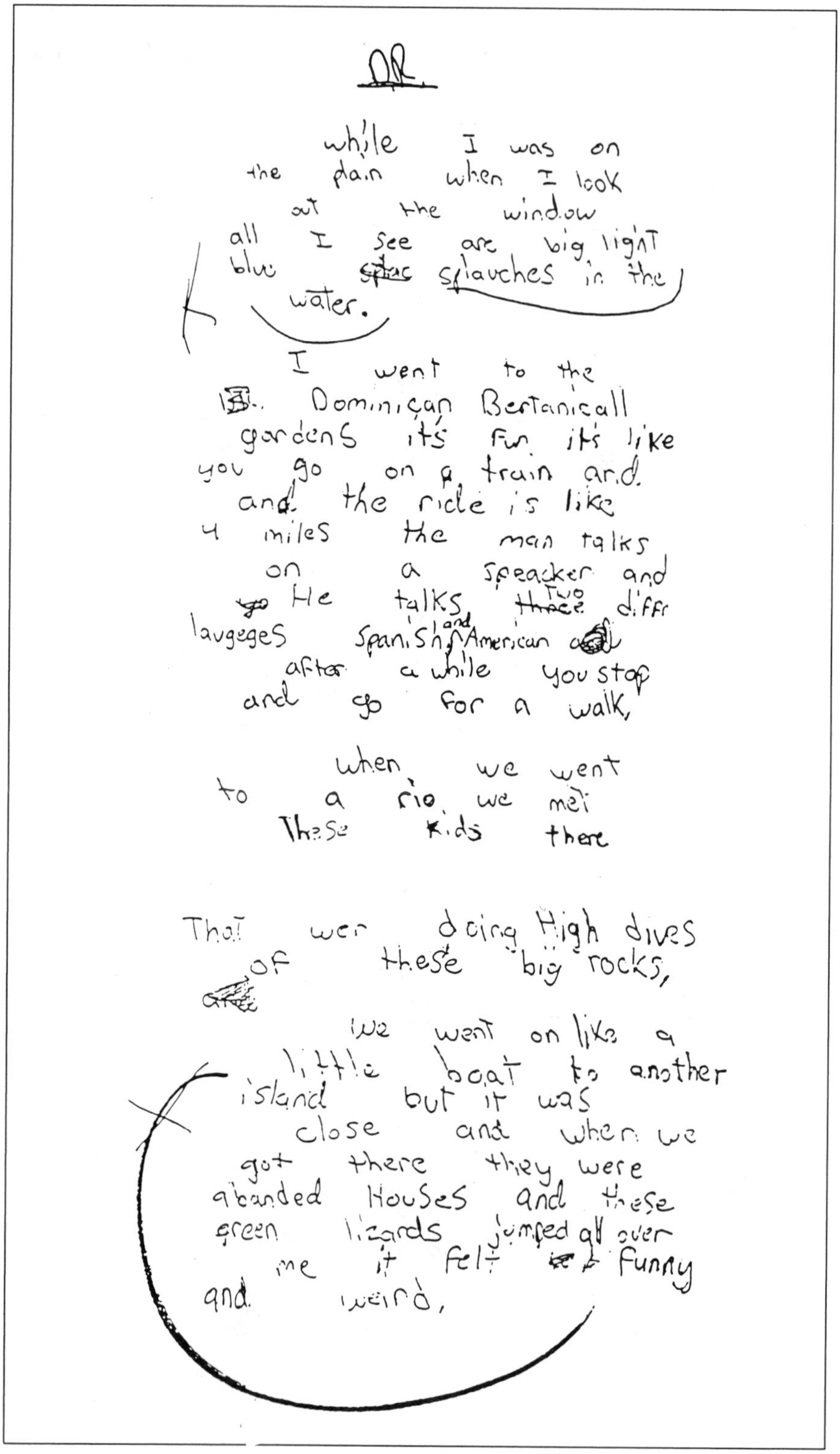

_DR._

while   I   was   on
the   plain   when   I   look
out   the   window
all   I   see   are   big light
blue   ~~spac~~ splauches   in   the
water.

I   went   to   the
Dominican   Bertanicall
gardens   it's   fun   it's like
you   go   on   a   train   and.
and   the   ride   is   like
4   miles   the   man   talks
on   a   speacker   and
~~go~~ He   talks,   ~~three~~ Two   diffr
laugeges   Spanish and American and
after   a   while   you   stop
and   go   for   a   walk.

when,   we   went
to   a   rio   we   met
These   kids   there

That   wer   doing   High   dives
of   these   big   rocks,

we   went   on   like   a
little   boat   to   another
island   but   it   was
close   and   when   we
got   there   they   were
a'banded   Houses   and   these
green   lizards   jumped all   over
me   it   felt   so   Funny
and   weird,

FIGURE 70

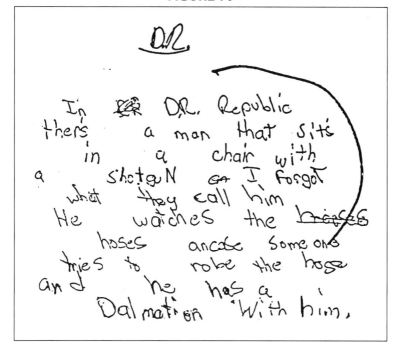

FIGURE 71

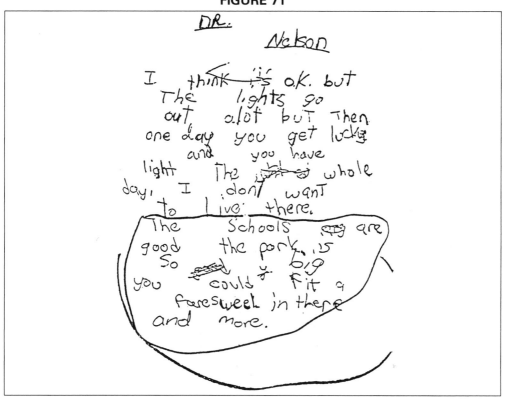

him a sense of the range of potential genres. When Amaury is ready to turn his material into a finished piece, or several finished pieces, he can consider trying his hand at poetry, picture books, nonfiction articles, letters, and the like. Just as important, the related texts seemed to raise the quality of his own notebook writing. Somehow when you read good stuff about your own topic, you're nudged to write good stuff. You realize it's possible to do well; you want to do well yourself. Amaury's writing appeared richer, in part, because he borrowed precise names of things and a few well-turned phrases. But he also learned to slow down, to capture scenes.

The study texts even seemed to influence Amaury's handwriting. His work became more legible, its smaller, neater words spaced evenly and consistently. Not only did he want his writing to sound like these published works on island life, he also seemed to want his writing to look like the published works.

FIGURE 72

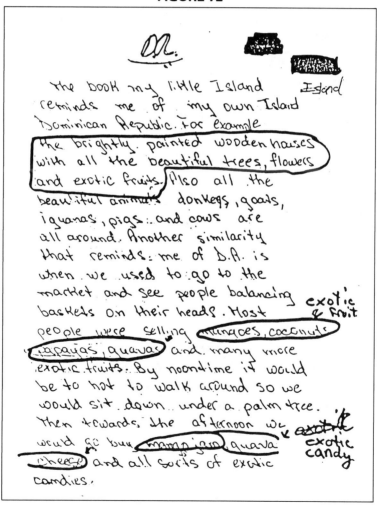

Frané Lessac's *My Little Island* seemed to have the most resonance for Amaury. For his finished piece, he not only found inspiration in the picture book genre, he also imitated the shape of the book. His narrative moves quickly from scene to scene, from one part of the day to the next. He also borrowed several of Lessac's precise details: "brightly painted wooden houses," "mango jam," "guava cheese." Amaury also seemed to be inspired by the island poems he read. In a final notebook entry he wrote the poem in Figure 73.

Several days later, Amaury thought he was ready to shape his material into a finished work. He wove a few entries together into a draft showing a day in the life of a Dominican child (Figure 74).

But he wasn't satisfied with his first attempt at writing a picture book. He realized that he hadn't put the material in his writer's notebook to its most powerful use. He had simply written whatever popped into his mind, occasionally using a passage from his writer's notebook. Amaury wasn't as yet attempting to create a work of art.

Two weeks later, Amaury completed a six-page picture book (the text appears in Figure 75).

I read Amaury's finished work several times, wondering how he was able to do what he did. How was he able to move from reluctant writing to a weak first draft

FIGURE 73

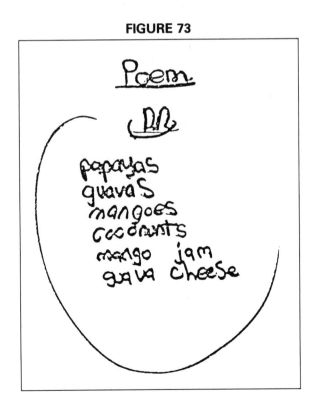

FIGURE 74

I wake up listening to
The cherping of a rooster,
And my 7 Friends come to
play. I had an temper cause
There was no tekvision
So we decided To do
Something Fun So my Mommy
Said take your batheng suts.

AFtewords I was made
cause I thought we wer going
to the pool, But it was Fun
we went to the D. britanikul
gardens there was this
man. I dont now, how he does
it he talks like 3 laugeys
at onee I was So
confuesed I turned my head
and ignored him. But Then
The real fun came, we went
on a bridge with water
under us it had big blue
splauches in the water.
We wont down and had a
barbucue every body jumped
in the water. It was cold
but that did not stop me
I got use to it I never
wanted To come out, again but
I had to we wer leaving,

When we got back
to my granmother's house
She sent us to The market
to buy things like mangoes,
coconuts, guavas and papayas
those are exotic Fruits
with the change wich
I hade no pormission To take,
But enyway, I bought
mango jani and guavau cheese

FIGURE 74, continued

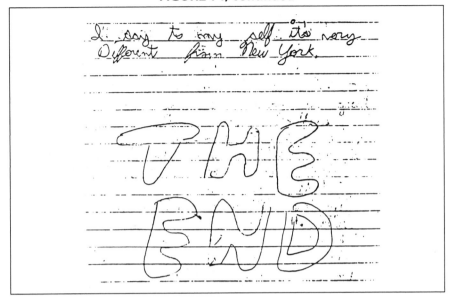

to a picture book to be proud of? He was successful, I reasoned, in part because he had a lot of things going for him.

He was invested in his topic. The notebook writing, reading, and rereading allowed him to discover what was really important in his life.

He was given lots of time to linger on his topic, writing pages and pages of entries.

He attended a school where wonderful literature on similar topics is available and can be taken home, and he was encouraged to let this reading inspire his writing.

He was able to select the genre that worked best with his subject and he chose one he was familiar with, having studied picture books in fourth grade.

He was in a class that honors talk. He didn't need permission to get up and talk to Nelson about the Dominican Republic or to share his notebook entries with his classmates.

He was in classroom where children write for real audiences. His finished work will be celebrated, added to the class library, translated into Spanish, and mailed to his grandparents as a gift.

But there was more than this. We made a deliberate effort to encourage Amaury to live with the consciousness of a craftsperson. We spent lots of time giving him and his classmates the kinds of experiences that inspire them to stop and ask "How can I write about this?" "How shall I say this well?" These experiences were provided through the familiar workshop structures of conferences and mini-lessons.

A true confession

It's true, I did wonder how Amaury was able to do what he did. It's also true that I wondered about a few of Amaury's classmates who were not able to do what

FIGURE 75

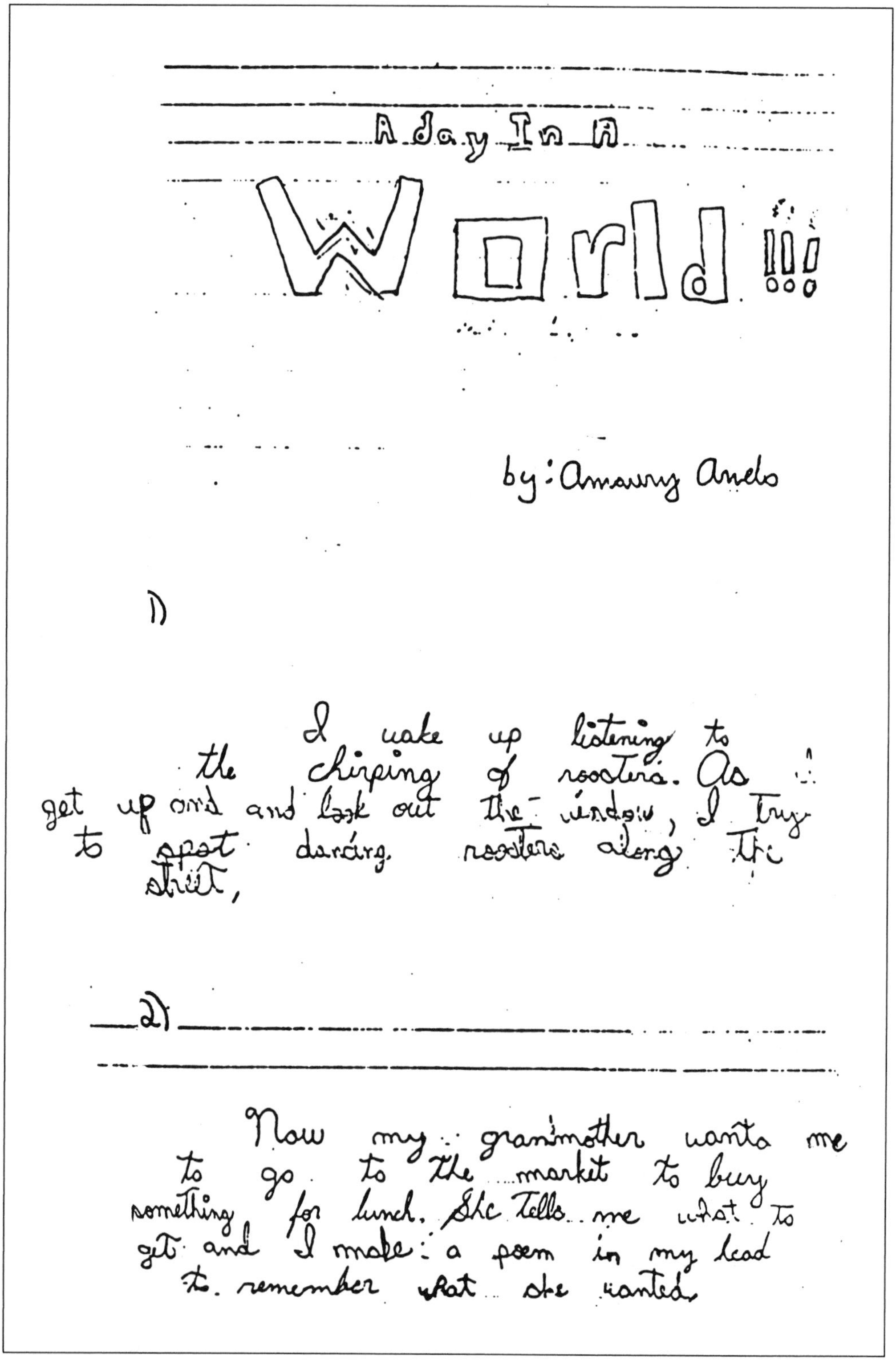

A day In A

World !!!

by: Amaury Ando

1)

I wake up listening to the chirping of roosters. As I get up ond and look out the window, I try to spot dancing roosters along the street,

2)

Now my granmother wants me to go to the market to buy something for lunch. She Tells me what to get and I make a poem in my head to remember what she wanted

FIGURE 75, continued

papayas
guavas
mangos
coconuts
mango jam
gauva cheese.

As I walk along I notice the brightly painted wooden houses with all the beautiful trees and flowers in The gardens. On the way I say to my self its! very different from New York.

3)

On the way back we meet our grandfather and he gives us a ride. We pass by a school. The school yard is so big you could fit a ferris wheel and more in there.

A whole entire army of lizards is climbing on the school.

4)

My grandfather decides to take us to where he has his cows and horses and other things. He named a cow after me. I wanted to be a horse.

FIGURE 75, continued

After, we decide to climb the hill that besides the rio. Its easy but my mother had Trouble because you have to grab a rope and go down a thin edge that was very slipery. But my mother makes it after all. We see big blue splashes in the water.

5)

Finally the darkness hovers over the sun and the time is 11:46 PM. We are playing a game, called Piña Colada. At 12:22 PM my grandmother is screaming "Get in side." The night watch man is saying "Go in", too. Its too late anyway it is too late. So we go in.

6)

At night we get snuggled up in bed but those mosquitoes are having more fun then us. They get all different varieties of blood from the tourists like Canadian Spaniard's even some Texan blood.

Finally I fall asleep and the day is over.

he did. Some weak first drafts turned into weak second drafts. Despite all of the same advantages that surrounded Amaury—topic investment, real reasons to write, an abundance of related literature, ample time to talk, and so on—a few students never did produce finished work of such literary merit. I continued to worry about these students, checking in more often with them as I made my conference rounds.

At the same time, however, I began to realize that not all students would change this dramatically as writers during any one school year. I was comforted to know that this small group of writers took pride in keeping a writer's notebook, saw their lives as worth writing about, and had favorite writers and texts. That's a lot for any one school year. Next year, perhaps, this year's group of struggling students will find their stride as writers. With continued support, next year might be the time these students begin to build bridges between what they read and what they write.

12

Record Keeping and Routines of Conferring

*I suggest that the only books that influence us are
those for which we are ready, and which have gone
a little farther down our particular path than we
have yet gone ourselves.*

E. M. Forster

I wondered about including a chapter on conferring in this book. After all, this is a book about using literature to inform students' writing. Although there are countless occasions to refer to literature during a writing conference, not every conference involves literature. And yet, a chapter on conferring seems most appropriate. After all, Amaury and his classmates were attempting to write their own literary pieces, and conferences are a prime way for teachers to support those efforts.

Starting with What We Do Well

It is a Wednesday afternoon meeting of staff developers. We are waiting for the others to arrive. As we sit around the library table finishing our sandwiches and cups of coffee, I can't help but overhear Arion and Llewelyn talking.

Arion is complaining that she never gets around to writing all the thank-you notes she plans to write. "How come?" Llewelyn asks. Arion talks of being too busy, of having too many other things on her mind. "I know what you mean," Llewelyn adds. "Life is like that, but there must be a way to make time. Arion nods in agreement and finally adds, "Maybe I'll keep some stationery on my night table and begin writing just one or two notes every night."

The others arrive. We begin our meeting on how to teach teachers to confer.

I start by relating Arion and Llewelyn's conversation.

"I think we've complicated the idea of conferring. Teachers need to see that they've been conferring their whole lives. They need to recall moments when they've been good listeners and moments when they've helped someone see options, make decisions, and take risks. Llewelyn was a good listener. She acknowledged her colleague's problem, and that recognition brought Arion's own solution to the forefront. Of course, conferring about writing is usually not that simple. But we have to begin with the belief that we can do it, that indeed, we've been doing it well for many years."

In her Crosswicks Journal *A Circle of Quiet,* Madeleine L'Engle remarks,

> I remember learning to skip rope. It's not too difficult when you hold the rope yourself. But then there's learning to jump into a rope swung by two other children, learning to jump in without breaking the rhythm and tripping over the rope. It can't be done unless you have that special kind of creative courage which is unselfconscious; the moment you wonder whether or not you can do it, you can't.

I've often thought that L'Engle's comment on jumping rope applies as well to learning to confer: "the moment you wonder whether or not you can do it, you can't."

Some of my best writing conferences have occurred, in fact, when I wasn't thinking about having a writing conference at all.

A few years ago, while home on spring break, my son Michael began complaining about a research report he had to do on an American author. He had chosen Ring Lardner because of their shared interest in baseball but was struggling to find something new to say. "So much has been written about him already."

As we chatted at the kitchen table, Michael was browsing through the newspaper. At the time, the headlines were filled with news of the presidential primaries.

"You know," Michael said, "Ring Lardner got one vote for president in the Democratic National Convention in 1928."

"You're kidding."

"No, it's true—and it's really not that outrageous. I could imagine Lardner in the White House. He had a lot of qualities that could have gotten him elected."

"Like what?" I asked. And Michael was off. He began telling me about Lardner's sense of humor, his popular speech, his all-American interest in Florida vacations and our national pastime, baseball. He also talked about how much easier it would be to get elected when your name is already a household word.

Before Michael returned to school he had written a first draft. He called it, "Ring Lardner: He Could Have Been a Contender." Our "conference" required no sophisticated techniques. I had merely been a respectful listener, trusting that he had important things to say.

To confer well about writing, teachers need information about the writing process, about literature, about the qualities of good writing. But it begins with trusting your instincts. It begins with believing you're a respectful human being who knows how to listen and respond wisely and gently. The other more technical information can be tucked in along the way.

In Randall Jarrell's *The Bat-Poet,* the bat recites his poem about an owl that almost caught him to the mockingbird, who gives him a technical response: the rhyme scheme is effective; he appreciates the iambic trimeter in the last line. The bat-poet feels terrible. "What do I care how many feet it has? The owl nearly kills me, and he says he likes the rhyme-scheme!"

We don't need lists of rules on how to respond, nor do we need to wait until we're saturated with writing tips.

Earlier, I suggested that if our students don't care about reading and writing, it won't make any difference how brilliant our mini-lessons are. In the same way, it doesn't matter how brilliant and sophisticated our technical information is if we don't respond to children in gentle and nurturing ways. That comes first and it comes naturally to good teachers.

Our staff development meeting continued. I suggested that one way to begin an in-service course on conferring might be to have teachers recall those moments in their own lives when they conferred well.

In fact, we began to recall those moments. We spoke of late-night talks with teenage children with broken hearts, and long distance calls to old friends who had lost parents or spouses. We also spoke of people we know that are easy to talk to. Perhaps surprisingly, we ended up talking about our favorite hairstylists, landscapers, and caterers, who begin by asking, "What did you have in mind?" and then listen to our ideas.

When I arranged a party for my son's college graduation, the caterer didn't begin by asking if I wanted to serve stuffed mushrooms or quiche as an hors d'oeuvre. Instead he asked, "What kind of party did you have in mind? Formal, informal? Sit down or buffet? After I had described the image I had in mind, he went on to help me see my options, to guide me in my choices. Isn't that what teachers of writing need to do?

The staff developers agreed that it was very important for teachers to leave in-service courses believing that they could confer, that conferring is not all that complicated. "The moment you wonder whether or not you can do it, you can't." What seems to get in the way are feelings of being rushed, anxious, or overwhelmed.

Keeping Tabs on Conferences

Notebooks were new to all of us. I recall one evening sitting at my desk trying to plan my next day's visit to Antoinette Ciano's fifth-grade class. Thirty-five students, all keeping notebooks. I was to help them move from gathering notebook entries to writing a finished piece. I no longer had a neat stack of thirty-five drafts to skim at home. Instead, students wrote pages and pages on diverse topics and in diverse styles. I sat at my desk trying to sketch my conference plans. It was hard to remember all I needed to know. Who is having a hard time keeping a notebook? Who is struggling to find important things to say? Who is bursting to work on a finished piece?

I closed my eyes and tried to visualize the class. I jotted down students' names according to their seating arrangement. I listed clusters of students table by table and tried to recall what they were up to. Where were they on the continuum that moved from gathering entries to shaping material into a chosen form? The results of my jottings appear in Table 2. (The children's names run vertically down the left side.) I prepared a sheet like this for each of the five tables in the room.

Running horizontally across the top of the page is the continuum of questions I found myself asking about each student. They are not steps, and they do not require separate conferences. They can happen all at once or not at all. I did not intend to display them to the class. Instead, I tucked them on my clipboard as I made my way around the fifth-grade classroom. They helped me feel in control and keep tabs on conferences.

Using the Chart

At a recent workshop in Denver, Colorado, a teacher surprised my by asking, "Does the chart work for you on your own writing? Did you ask these questions of yourself as you wrote *Lasting Impressions?*" After a bit of thought I was relieved to find that, although I hadn't actually needed to ask myself these questions, had I done so I would have answered "Yes" to all of them. In order to write the text, I did indeed value my notebook jottings, reread my notes regularly, discover important issues, figure out why they mattered, linger in them, and read other materials alongside them. When I realized that all this might add up to a text, I did take a deliberate stance, sift through for the best stuff, imagine the publishing possibilities, and closely study other published texts. Then of course, I did a lot of drafting, revising, and editing.

The chart works for my own writing but it's not necessary for my own writing. After all, the chart is not intended to be a set of procedures. It is a record-keeping device to help me keep tabs on the process and progress of a group of thirty-five young writers.

As I moved from table to table around the room, I often jotted down short comments or reminders or made quick check marks to indicate that the questions had been answered. An occasional question mark also reminded me of work to be done. My notes were particularly helpful in the evenings as I planned the next day's workshop, but I also found myself glancing at them during class as I approached each young writer.

Table 3 illustrates the kinds of quick notes I took on Amaury during the three-week period in which he discovered his writing topic and completed his picture book.

Slowing the Questions Down

Certainly, I didn't ask these exact questions of each student. Instead, each served to remind me of the kinds of nudging that might help each young writer. Each question stood for a larger area of interest. They were not a prescribed script. In fact, I deliberately tried to ask questions in a variety of ways to avoid the rote response.

Whenever I share this record-keeping chart at workshops or in-service courses, I ask teachers to jot down their own ways of finding out where students are as notebook keepers. Many of their ways of speaking and the words they use have become part of the discussion that follows.

TABLE 2

KEEPING TABS ON CONFERRING~ HELPING STUDENTS CRAFT LITERATURE

TABLE 1	Does the student value helping notebook?	Does the student reread regularly?	Has the student discovered special entries?	Has the student wondered why this issue matters?	Is the student lingering with the issue?	Will literature help this writer?	Does the student understand literary stance?	Does the student appreciate the gems?	Can the student imagine possibilities?	Does the student need closer genre study?	Has the student attempt a draft?	Is the student making decisions?	Is the student actually ready to edit? publish
AMAURY													
ZANVI													
NAJIB													
JENNIFER													
DANIELLE													
EMIL													
JEANINE													

TABLE 3

KEEPING TABS ON CONFERRING ~ HELPING STUDENTS CRAFT LITERATURE

TABLE 1	Does the student value help? notebook?	Does the student reread regularly?	Has the student discovered special entries?	Has the student wondered why this issue matters?	Is the student Lingering in the issue?	Will literature help this writer?	Does the student understand literary stance?	Does the students appreciate the gems?	Can the student imagine possibilities?	Does the student need closer genre study?	Has the student attempted a draft?	Is the student making deliberate decisions?	Is the student ready to edit? publish
AMAURY	9/24 skimpy entries used lits a diary	has begun to reread	9/26 Dominick misses his great parents seem important	interviewed Nelson gathering literature brainstorm — letting yourself be reminded	bring in my little I imagine grandma baking to take the sting	?	circled powerful ideas love his choices	chose powerful picture but genre?	remembers last year's wrote strong. needs genre(?)	10/3 wrote without using best stuff	10/10 - 2nd draft very different go over with him with kindness

The chart quite naturally falls into two parts. The first six questions focus on helping students discover important issues in their writer's notebook. The remaining questions focus on shaping those entries into a literary work. Once the class and I were used to moving from notebook entries to finished writing, this scaffolding would no longer be necessary. If all went well, much of this work would be internalized.

Does the student value his/her notebook?	Does the student reread regularly?	Has the student discovered special entries?	Has the student wondered why this issue matters?	Is the student lingering in the issue?	Will literature help this writer?

The first time I ever conferred with Amaury about his writing, I wanted to know if he honored his notebook. That is, did he value it as an important writing tool or was he keeping it because his teacher asked him to or because his classmates were? Did he use it as a container for his thoughts and ideas or did he tear out pages for math homework or notes to friends? Did he use it as a diary or as a new kind of writing folder, filling it exclusively with short personal narratives? Had he found a way to make notebook keeping a regular part of his life in school and out, or did he usually forget to take his notebook home? Was it brimming with writing or did the writing slow to a trickle?

I wanted to know if he honored his notebook, but at the same time I wanted to honor his beginning attempts. I didn't want to find myself saying, "No, you're not supposed to use your notebook for that." Instead, I wanted to celebrate his efforts, both what he wrote about and how he wrote. I wanted to acknowledge the breakthroughs he's made and the risks he has taken. I wanted to marvel at the unique ways he had discovered to use his writer's notebook.

If Amaury had not been honoring his notebook, I would know the direction our conference needed to go: "How can you make this tool work for you?"

Does the student value his/her notebook?	Does the student reread regularly?	Has the student discovered special entries?	Has the student wondered why this issue matters?	Is the student lingering in the issue?	Will literature help this writer?

Children rarely reread their diaries. If they do, it's often several months or even years later, and they reread to catch a glimpse of what they were doing or thinking back then. Notebooks are meant to be reread all the time. When I flip through the pages of a student's notebook, I can spot the rereaders. They often have jotted notes running up and down the margins. They have drawn arrows connecting one page to another or added secret codes attaching one thought to another one several pages ahead. They have scrawled questions and comments across pages, "I can't believe I wrote this" or "What was I thinking?" Some have even written reflective passages based on their rereading of entries.

The rereaders know that the notebook is a tool for writers and they know that tools are only helpful if they're used. The rereaders have learned to say more, to write in response to their own writing, just as they write in response to the literature they read. They reread to find new connections and notice continuous threads in their thinking. They reread to be inspired by their favorite parts and to gain momentum for the writing to come.

Even when Amaury discovered his interest in the Dominican Republic and made a commitment to dwell on that topic, he kept on rereading his notebook. He knew he might gain new insights on life in the Dominican Republic when he reread his thoughts on visiting a good friend's home. He knew that even a glimpse of a New York school scene might remind him of memories.

If Amaury had not been rereading his notebook, I would probably have asked him to begin, and I'd have lingered a few minutes to demonstrate the value of rereading.

Does the student value his/her notebook?	Does the student reread regularly?	Has the student discovered special entries?	Has the student wondered why this issue matters?	Is the student lingering in the issue?	Will literature help this writer?

Students in our writing workshops reread their notebooks searching for "hot" topics, ones worth lingering over. They are on the lookout for a sense of urgency, a compelling need to write more in order to understand more.

Some students, particularly those who have some experience of writing workshops, have an urgent need to return to familiar ground. They long to label that yellow sheet of paper "draft one" and begin experimenting with leads. They long to have a finished piece of work, all edited and copied over in their best handwriting. But teachers have learned not to rush children into focusing on a topic prematurely.

Some students pick an issue merely by taking inventory. "I have seven baseball stories. Okay, I'll work on a baseball piece." Those students need to know that the importance of an issue is not measured by volume. A line, or even a word, may tell the writer that something significant is rooted here.

Other students decide on a project because it's the popular thing to do. Everyone at their table has settled into a "writing project," and they want to join the fun. So they select the first topic that comes to mind. Unfortunately, it is hard to make that kind of project a labor of love and the drudgery usually shows up in their writing.

Most students also overlook the potential of form for suggesting a "hot" writing idea. It's rare for a child to notice that he's good at capturing authentic dialogue and could try his hand at writing a play or that she gets great pleasure from close observation and could develop a writing project from this strength as a writer.

When I moved alongside Amaury and celebrated the entry in which he "hurled" out of bed at exactly 8:10, I was not surprised to read, "darkness hovers over the sun and the time is 11:46 p.m." When we point out for students what we see as their writing strengths, it's more likely that they'll call upon these techniques in their writing.

Does the student value his/her notebook?	Does the student reread regularly?	Has the student discovered special entries?	Has the student wondered why this issue matters?	Is the student lingering in the issue?	Will literature help this writer?

When Amaury announced that he was planning to do a project on the Dominican Republic and Najib chose crime in the neighborhood and Jennifer claimed her best friend as her "hot topic" it became our responsibility to help them understand why they were so personally invested in these issues.

When I asked Amaury, "What's pulling you to spend so much time thinking about the Dominican Republic?" I was helping him to understand why this country mattered to him. He began to realize that his topic was not the Dominican Republic at all, it was his love for his grandparents who have created such a special life for the grandson that visits from America.

Teachers can tell in a minute when something really matters to students. They can see it in the their eyes, in the way they sit, sometimes in the way their voices choke up.

Several years ago, a young student wrote about going to the supermarket with her mom to buy lamb chops, returning home, and eating the lamb chops while her mom stood by watching. She told me that her mom has been out of work and they had been living on pasta and canned soups. "Mom is so happy that she has a job now. She couldn't wait to serve me lamb chops, my favorite." Behind every story is a story. As Emerson said, "Under every deep, a lower deep opens."

Of course, young writers don't always know about that "lower deep." In our conferences we need to get that conversation going.

Does the student value his/her notebook?	Does the student reread regularly?	Has the student discovered special entries?	Has the student wondered why this issue matters?	Is the student lingering in the issue?	Will literature help this writer?

In telling the story of Amaury, I suggested that he was given lots of time to linger on his topic and write pages and pages of entries. As I walk about the classroom, I also need to make sure students know how to dwell deeply in the topic they've selected. I need to ask myself, "Will this writer be able to write from a rich abundance of ideas? Does the writer have strategies to keep on going on?

In one-on-one conferences as well as in small group gatherings and whole-class mini-lessons, I remind students who've made a commitment to a topic they care about that they now need to linger with that topic and gather new insights and ideas. Of course, students need to be taught how to linger, how to live their lives so that their experience reminds them of their topics.

One day during workshop time, I invited Amaury and two other young writers to join me at the round table in the back of the room. Each of these students had announced they had found a really important issue in the pages of their writer's notebook. I now needed to make sure the students had ways of living on their issues.

I began my small group conference by pulling out a small prop, a toy bench with three dolls sitting on it. The dolls were clearly multi-ethnic. One appeared Asian, another African, the third Caucasian. "You're walking in the park today, and you're leading a writerly life. This scene catches your eye. You pause to think about it. What would you probably think?" Najib, who was obsessed with crime in his neighborhood, began, "I'd think that three little girls shouldn't be sitting in the park alone and I'd probably tell the one with the gold earrings to take them off."

Jennifer, who was writing about Kareen, an African-American friend, suggested, "I'd probably think how wonderful it is for girls from different backgrounds to be friends, how much they can learn from one another."

Amaury spoke about skin colors. "That scene reminds me that in the Dominican Republic, people with different skin colors can be part of the same family."

I was trying to teach students that everything you see can remind you of your topic, if you let it. I was trying to teach them what Vicki Vinton had taught the members of the Writing Project: "When you're writing, all roads lead to Rome."

On the following day, I met once again with this small cluster of students. If three students in the class really knew how to get inside their topics, they in turn could share what they were learning whenever they conferred with their classmates.

That morning I began by telling the students that I put contact lenses in my eyes each morning to help me look at the world in clearer, sharper ways. "So too," I continued, "When you're committed to a topic it's as if each one of you puts a kind of contact lens in your eyes each morning. Amaury's is coated with his grandparents in the Dominican Republic, Najib the crime in his neighborhood, Jennifer her best friend." When you look at your world, for the time being you'll be seeing it and thinking about it in new ways.

I then asked Amaury to share his morning rituals. "What would you probably think about? I asked him. "Remember, you're seeing your grandparents' life in the Dominican Republic. You're going to let everything remind you of that." Amaury looked at me, confused. "Okay, what's the first thing you do in the morning?" I asked. "I listen to the weather report," offered Amaury. "When you hear this cold, rainy forecast, what are you thinking?" Amaury understood. "I'd be thinking how warm and sunny it probably is in the Dominican Republic." Amaury went on to tell us how eating cold cereal would make him daydream about his grandma's fried donuts and putting on his sweatshirt and jeans would remind him of the shorts and sandals he wears every day in the Dominican Republic.

Young writers need a host of strategies for gathering information. They need to know how valuable it is to talk about their topics to anyone that will listen and to interview people with related experiences. And they need to know how valuable it is to read related literature.

Does the student value his/her notebook?	Does the student reread regularly?	Has the student discovered special entries?	Has the student wondered why this issue matters?	Is the student lingering in the issue?	Will literature help this writer?

In telling the story of Amaury, I suggested the important role literature played in helping him look at his topic. The books, stories, and articles he read not only helped him think, they provided examples of potential genres and served to raise the quality of his own writing about island life. After reading his short stack of books, Amaury clearly began writing more fluently and with richer sensory details.

The same would probably happen with adults. If I were writing about growing up in New York City, Kate Simon's *Bronx Primitive,* Alan Lelchuk's *On Home Ground* and Alfred Kazin's *A Walker in the City* would remind me of moments and impressions I've long forgotten. Content-related texts jog an adult's mind just as they do a child's. It's also true that as I read these books I might pick up some ideas about genre or some literary techniques along the way that would improve the quality of my writing. What happened for Amaury can also happen for adults.

At the same time, there is a clear difference in the way children and adults learn from their reading. I would learn a great deal from reading other writers' stories about growing up in New York, but I could also learn a great deal from all of my reading. Adults are able to identify literary techniques whatever the content. Children, however, seem much more comfortable learning from a text that is directly related to their content. This is particularly true when they are studying texts on their own, without adult guidance.

I remember working with Tina, a third grader, who was imagining what it would be like to have a brother. When she ran out of thoughts, I wondered if Crescent Dragonwagon's *Diana Maybe* would help her generate some additional ideas. "No," Tina said, "that book is about imagining what it would be like to have a sister. I'm writing about a brother." Luckily, not all children insist on as close a match as Tina did. But when we send children off to the library to search for ideal texts, most usually pick those that are closely related to their topic. Many children prefer these content-related texts well beyond their need to generate more ideas, even when they're studying a particular genre or a specific literary technique.

If we place a young student who has decided to write a picture book about kittens in a roomful of picture books, it should not surprise us if the student studies picture books about kittens. Students do not always realize they can learn from any fine picture book. Even if Maurice Sendak were their favorite writer, some students would not choose just any Sendak title. (If Sendak had written about kittens, that would be a different story!)

It seems easier for students to identify the mood, the style, the form, or the literary techniques in a text if it is on the same topic as the one they're writing about. Doing so with a text on a different topic is much harder.

Amaury was one of those students who believed you can only learn from books closely related to what you are writing about. Even though Mem Fox was his favorite picture book writer and *Wilfred Gordon McDonald Partridge* his favorite picture book, Amaury chose to take lessons from Frané Lessac's *My Little Island* alone.

Borrowing a literary technique from an unrelated text requires not one leap, but two. If Amaury had noticed a stylistic device in Mem Fox's book and decided to try it in his writing about the Dominican Republic, he would have to identify it and then adapt it to his content. I rarely see young writers make this apparently complicated move on their own.

Mauricio's ability to see the techniques at work in his nontopic-related Kuskin texts and then apply them to his own writing (Chapter 9) was probably aided by his deep familiarity with Kuskin's work and the distinctiveness of her style, but most of all by the support of his teachers. He was not alone. In that same chapter, the children who took part in oral-mentoring exercises appeared to be able to borrow literary techniques and apply them to new content. Carlos, for example, took elements of Joanne Ryder's style and applied them to Humpty Dumpty. Again, these children had many support systems. The teacher was leading the exercise. The children were listening to several models. The whole class was pitching in. Their efforts had a safety net. Oral-mentoring experiences like these, in a large group, can help prepare students to one day abstract techniques on their own.

In Chapter 9, I described how Lucy Calkins was able to help Emil improve the way he wrote about watching a baseball game with his father by showing him another child's efforts. But this text was not the only one that helped Emil.

When children chose to write about a particular topic, we made a public call for help. We posted a graffitilike board outside the classroom asking for suggestions as well as contributions. In part it read:

> We're looking for literature on many different topics. We promise to treat your books, magazines, articles, excerpts, poems, etc. with tender loving care.
>
> *Name*   *Topic/Issue*
>
> Emil   Sharing your love of baseball with your father.
> Amaury   Life in the Dominican Republic or any other tropical island.
> Jennifer   Having a best friend.
> Zanvi   Cats as best friends.

Emil's study stack included pieces that were not simply about baseball but about relationships explored through a shared interest in baseball. A book about how to play baseball or biographies of baseball heroes would probably not be as evocative for Emil as texts dealing with people's responses to baseball. Emil read Gary Soto's short story "Baseball in April" from his collection with the same title, several poems from *Sprints and Distances,* an anthology of sports poems, Karen Lynn Williams' short chapter book, *Baseball and Butterflies,* and excerpts from Rick Wimmer's *Baseball Fathers, Baseball Sons.* Perhaps the piece that was the most evocative for Emil was a *New York Times* essay by Ralph Schoenstein entitled, "The Day My Daughter Discovered Baseball," about a parent and child sharing their love for the sport. It was a first person account, rich with ballpark scenes and conversations.

It became apparent to me as I worked my way around Antoinette's classroom just how essential it is for teachers to know the field of children's literature or at least know how to reach out to other school or community experts. Kaity was doing extensive nature observations of her fish, Najib was writing an anticrime letter to the editor, Jeanine was writing fiction about a mother-daughter relationship, Benny was writing a letter to his baby brother. If one way to help children write is to offer them content-related literature, the titles of helpful texts need to be on the tip of our tongues and at our fingertips. And as I suggested in Chapter 5, we also need to invite students in on the search.

In fact, when children are involved in creating their own study stacks—with a little bit of help from friends, teachers, librarians or parents,—we don't worry that other peoples' "ideal texts" are unduly influencing their tastes as readers and writers. When the texts are wide-ranging, children can select the ones that are closest to their own ideal. (Study stacks can later be added to classroom libraries. They make natural text sets to be used by response groups during reading workshops.)

From Subject to Ideal Text

When children make a commitment to a topic, they often fill many pages of their notebooks with writing about their subject. They've learned to linger. At some point as we confer, we need to know if they feel ready to work toward a finished piece and if they intend to do something wonderful with their material. The time has come to think less about the subject and more about the ideal text they're working toward. At this time, I shift my conference questions to the second part of the record-keeping chart.

The students now need help moving from writing notebook entries to working on a literary text. This help is offered one-on-one in conferences as well as in small-group sessions and whole class meetings. Although on the conference chart the questions are listed separately, when I confer these categories overlap. I've separated them in the following discussion in order to better attend to each. (These categories are easier to separate during mini-lessons. See Chapter 13).

Does the student understand literary stance?	Does the student appreciate the gems?	Can the student imagine possibilities?	Does the student need closer genre study?	Has the student attempted a draft?	Is the student making deliberate decisions?	Is the student ready to edit? publish?

It would be neat and simple to say that taking a literary stance—making the deliberate decision to work on a piece and carrying out that decision—occurs after students have gathered all their material. They sit back and ask, "Now, what should I do with all this? How can I say it well? How can I write something that will move my readers?" It would be neat and simple, but it's probably not completely accurate. My guess is that as soon as students discover that what they're writing is important and has potential, their attitude toward their work changes. They position themselves to write well.

The quality of Amaury's notebook writing began to improve as soon as he was aware that eventually he'd want to do a good job. It's as if he knew he'd eventually need rich sensory details, strong images, and fresh insights.

As I confer with a child who is about to begin selecting, shaping, and drafting, I wonder if he has literary ambitions. Here is where the overlapping of categories begins to take place. I ask Amaury if he can imagine turning his material about his grandparents' life in the Dominican Republic into the kind of text that could be added to the class library? Does he have a feel for his best stuff? Can he imagine what genre would serve as the best container for these gems? It quickly becomes apparent that children who have rich literary backgrounds find this easier to do. It's hard to position yourself to work your best material into a chosen form, if you're not aware of the traditions and conventions of various genres. Children who've never attempted to write in a literary way might need to begin with some of the whole-class experiences in taking a literary stance (See Chapter 13).

Does the student understand literary stance?	Does the student appreciate the gems?	Can the student imagine possibilities?	Does the student need closer genre study?	Has the student attempted a draft?	Is the student making deliberate decisions?	Is the student ready to edit? publish?

Sylvia Cassedy, in *In Your Own Words* tells a story about Michelangelo. She explains that the sculptor " . . . used to imagine that every block of stone he set out to carve contained a fully formed statue waiting to be released. All he had to do was chip away everything that wasn't statue, and there it would be—a horse, an angel, a beautiful woman, or a tiny cherub."

Young writers too need to learn to chip away. They need to go through their notebook pages looking for those entries that will best help them express their meaning. Sometimes an entry, or a combination of entries, leads a student to select a certain genre. Sometimes students decide on a genre and then sift through their entries searching for those which will help create the ideal text they have in mind.

When I stop to confer with students who are about to begin working toward a finished piece, I often ask them to flag the pages that have the most potential. Ideally, these notebook pages should be duplicated and spread across a long work table so the writer is able to see all the material at once. This helps children who have not as yet chosen a genre as well as those who are thinking of ways to shape their material into the genre they've chosen.

Some children have had little experience in reading their own writing critically and they find it difficult to choose their own best stuff. If many students fall into this category I'd probably offer mini-lessons to provide this experience (see Chapter 13). I would also use conference time to help them sift through their material. Perhaps I'd suggest, "Why not read the pages aloud listening for powerful bits?" or "Why not meet with a friend and go over the pages together?" or "Why not choose a few favorites and imagine them as leads to pieces of writing. Do any seem to take off?"

Does the student understand literary stance?	Does the student appreciate the gems?	Can the student imagine possibil- ities?	Does the student need closer genre study?	Has the student attempted a draft?	Is the student making deliberate decisions?	Is the student ready to edit? publish?

Like Amaury, some children are very quick to select a genre. Either they have favorite ones or they are filled with a previous year's study or they really have heard an inner voice call out, "This deserves to be a poem," or "This would make a great picture book." When I confer I find myself congratulating students for having made firm decisions. Then I ask them to improvise their as yet unwritten draft. "How might it go? Using your storyteller voice or a public speaking stance, can you invent just a little bit of it right now?" This request not only reminds students to keep that literary stance, it also helps them evaluate the appropriateness of their choice and realize the need for closer study of the chosen genre. I also probe students' appreciation of an array of possible genres: "Can you imagine using your material in additional pieces in different modes?"

I frequently confer with students who are struggling to choose a form for their material. Sometimes the material itself is unusually challenging. At other times the difficulty stems from the writer, who is sometimes reluctant or inexperienced. My job is to help them think through their options.

If difficulty in choosing a genre is widespread, I attend to it during whole-class mini-lessons (see Chapter 13) or pull together a small group of students in need of the same help. At other times I address the problem in a one-on-one conference. The challenge here is to open up the problem. I might find myself making sugges- tions, "Perhaps you need to browse through the library shelves or some of the published class anthologies. Maybe someone else's form will make sense for your project." Or "Perhaps you can make a list of all the genres you're familiar with. Then reread that list and star the ones that have possibilities for this project. Call me over to help you think them through." Or "Perhaps you need to try to write what Peter Elbow calls an 'instant version' of your material. Without stopping to read through them just yet, can you sketch your ideas out in several different modes? See where that leads."

When writers are unusually inexperienced or reluctant, I am more direct. These students seem to need more nudging to help them think about the possible purposes, audiences, and genres for their writing. I might say, "I think I hear some poems in here. Do you?" or "Your entries are filled with vivid dialogue. Have you thought of shaping them into a skit to be performed by the children in the class?" or "I wonder if you'd like to shape some of your entries into a letter to your friend who has moved away?" When I do suggest genres, I offer the ones that seem most appropriate or most accessible.

Students are usually successful when they attempt simple poetic forms, short skits, or letters. Letters are a particularly effective way for students first learning to shape notebook material into finished pieces. Letters allow for a clear point of view and a clear sense of audience. Students become personally involved in their writing and receive authentic and personal responses. Letter writing also allows students to stretch, highlight, and rearrange their notebook entries without too many restrictions or conventions.

Does the student understand literary stance?	Does the student appreciate the gems?	Can the student imagine possibilities?	Does the student need closer genre study?	Has the student attempted a draft?	Is the student making deliberate decisions?	Is the student ready to edit? publish?

When students were first learning to turn their notebook entries into literature, we had done no whole-class genre studies to support their efforts. Amaury had decided to write a picture book. Jennifer, seated next to him, was writing poems. Across the table, Najib was determined to write a letter to the editor calling for an end to neighborhood crime. Later in the year the entire class would pull together to study poetry, picture books, and forms of non-fiction writing in a more formal way. They would use their notebooks to work toward these specific modes. But for now, there were several different genres being pursued simultaneously.

When no whole-class genre study is taking place, it's easy for teachers to become anxious as they move about the classroom, stopping to confer with their young writers. They don't have time to teach individual students all they know about poems and plays and picture books. It would have been easy for Antoinette and me to panic. How can so much be going on in one room? How can we help all the students do a good job?

We didn't panic. Instead, we made some promises to ourselves.

First, we agreed not to worry that students were working in genres without the benefit of whole-class study. When I confer with Jennifer, who is writing poems about her best friend, I can't worry that she doesn't know about line breaks and white space. I can teach her a bit as I confer, but she can't possibly learn as much as she would if she were surrounded by poets and poetry. That will come later, in December, and then again in March (see Calendar, p.305). We kept reminding ourselves that students could always pull out previously written pieces and revise them by applying information they learned later.

Second, we promised to give children access to literature in all the genres they were attempting. We needed to trust that Jennifer would learn about poetry on her own if she were reading fine poems. For now, our responsibility lay in stocking classroom shelves with all kinds of texts.

Third, we agreed to make arrangements for students to meet with others who were having a go at the same genre whenever possible and to support the efforts of these small clusters of students.

Since I can't possibly teach Jennifer all she needs to know about poetry in brief conference visits, it becomes essential that as I confer, I suggest places in the classroom, and in the school, where she can learn in the company of other poets. I might suggest, "Why not get together with Eileen and Yoorak? They're also writing poems. Take some time during the workshop to form a study team. You can gather at a round table in the back of the room or on the floor in the hallway. Be sure to bring along the poems you admire."

When students do gather together to talk about work they admire they're also laying the groundwork for productive peer conferring. Rather than talking about fixing up errors, students are helping each other work closely with the texts they admire. Amaury can form a study team with other picture book writers, as can those writing letters or memoirs. I might also suggest that members of each study team work together during their reading workshop and read in the same genre they're writing in.

During workshop time, I can confer with small clusters of children. When I talk with each group I can suggest additional ways for them to do closer study. Perhaps I'd suggest that the young poets spend a few days in Ms. Gonzalvez's room. She's doing a formal poetry course. Perhaps I'd lend the group a copy of Georgia Heard's *For the Good of the Earth and Sun*. Certainly these serious poets would appreciate Georgia's thoughtful advice. So too, the picture book writers could read excerpts from Jane Yolen's *Writing Books for Children*. The letter writers could study Sylvia Cassedy's chapter on letter writing in *In Your Own Words*. (See To Gather Advice from Professional Writers, p. 270)

Perhaps too, I'd invite confident poets from around the building, including children and teachers, to talk with members of the study team about how they learn from their reading or to respond to student drafts.

Antoinette and I also promised to support students' efforts to study genres on their own by devoting some mini-lesson time to teaching children how to go about studying a genre, any genre (see Chapter 13).

Does the student understand literary stance?	Does the student appreciate the gems?	Can the student imagine possibilities?	Does the student need closer genre study?	Has the student attempted a draft?	Is the student making deliberate decisions?	Is the student ready to edit? publish?

The last three questions that helped me to keep tabs on my conferring are those with which I am most familiar. Have students attempted a draft? Are they making deliberate decisions? Are they ready to edit, then publish? In the past, in fact, these questions often served as the starting point when I conferred. They match the "draft, revise, edit, publish" cycle associated with the writing process.

When I approached young writers I wanted to know if they had written a draft. I wanted to know if they were making deliberate decisions about that draft. In other words, I wanted to know if they were critically rereading and revising their work in order to get closer to the ideal text they had in mind. (If many students were not aware that writers make conscious and deliberate decisions about their drafts I would teach the kind of mini-lessons that remind students of the need to

FIGURE 76

Best friends
Best Friends are
made of
of caring and responsability,
caring and responsability,
Best Friends are made of
caring and responsability,
and I am not telling a lie

FIGURE 77

When she grows up, I hope that
she will be sucessful in what ever
she does. With all the racigom
in this country I think that just
because Karen's is a different
color then me doesn't me that
we can't be best friends. Everyday
she looks fantastic. We are
like two chains that are unseperable
and I mean unseperatable. She is
great. I would thought I would I never
say this but I have some kind of
fear about losing her I don't know
why but I think it is because
I have never had a friend like
this before and maybe that is the feeling
that I am worring about not seeing her
next year. I have a lot of thoughts
going through my mind about her
I I made her a poom yesterday
about her and I gave her

be deliberate; see mini-lessons beginning on p. 283). And finally, I wanted to know if students were ready to edit their work in order to publish it.

The writer's notebook slowed the students' writing process down. They were no longer turning every idea they had into a draft. When they thought they were ready, they began to take some of their material and shape it into a first draft. Some chose to write their first draft in their writer's notebook. Many chose to return to the familiar yellow-lined paper and writing folder.

At this point, we can anticipate a few predictable problems. Some students, like Amaury, forget the literary stance and merely combine bits and pieces of notebook entries to fulfill their early image of a first draft, usually a story with a beginning, middle, and end. They had gotten used to personal narratives of a certain length. They had learned about good leads and "endings that sound like endings." In mini-lessons as well as in conferences, these students need to be reminded to use their best material and to make deliberate decisions about that material in order to write well.

Some students disregard the notebook as a tool for writing when they begin to draft. Drafting is familiar ground. It's what they did last year and they return to last year's image of it. Jennifer, for example, completely ignored her rich notebook entries when she decided she was ready to draft her first poem about having a best friend. When I pulled up alongside her I was surprised to see her poem (Figure 76).

FIGURE 77, continued

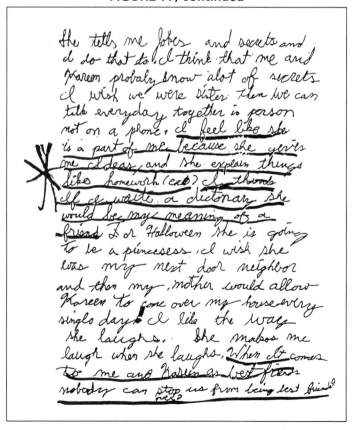

There was a major "aha" when I asked her why she wasn't using some of the lyrical lines and passages in her notebook to write poems about her friend. The look on her face said, "Now I get it, now I know why you asked us to keep a notebook."

Jennifer then went through her notebook pages carefully, underlining and placing asterisks next to the parts that had potential (Figure 77). She decided to use each of her favorite lines as the key thought in four simple poems. Her drafts appear in Figure 78.

As Jennifer's drafts indicate, she has been a critical reader of her own writing. She has become a decision-maker about her own emerging texts. She crossed out her first attempt at writing about the meaning of friend. It wasn't good enough. (In fact, Jennifer told me that as she composed she occasionally closed her eyes and wondered how Langston Hughes would write about Kareen. His poems about friendship had been her favorites in her study stack.)

When Jennifer was satisfied with the meaning of her poems, she needed to take editing very seriously. It was then that she needed to correct the spelling of "unseperatable" and "batterey." She needed to check her punctuation and use her best handwriting to copy her poems onto appropriate paper. After all, these poems were to be gifts for her best friend, Kareen. Jennifer learned to draft by selecting her best material and shaping and reshaping it.

FIGURE 77, continued

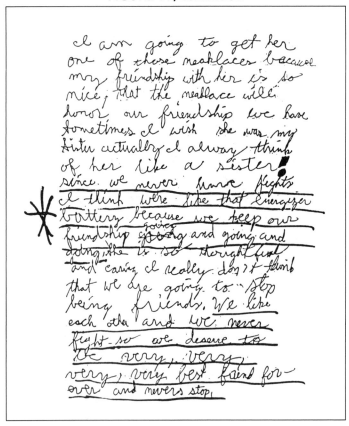

When she was satisfied, she gave the same careful attention to editing and publishing (Figure 79).

When Literature Is at the Heart of Our Conferences

In the early pages of this book I compared literature in the classroom to the Vega-Matic on the kitchen shelf. Both are handy, both get many jobs done. Nowhere is the versatility of literature more apparent than when we confer with students.

In the last section, I described the specific kind of conferring that helps students move from writing notebook entries to writing finished pieces. Literature appeared at several points on my record-keeping chart. Students read literature to generate more ideas, to study genre possibilities, and to closely study a particular genre.

Whether or not students keep a writer's notebook, literature plays a key role when we confer with students. The following lists suggests more than a dozen reasons why we might refer to literature in conferences.

- To spark ideas for their own writing.
- To generate more thoughts on a particular topic.
- To gather specific bits of information.
- To study traditions of a genre.

FIGURE 77, continued

FIGURE 78

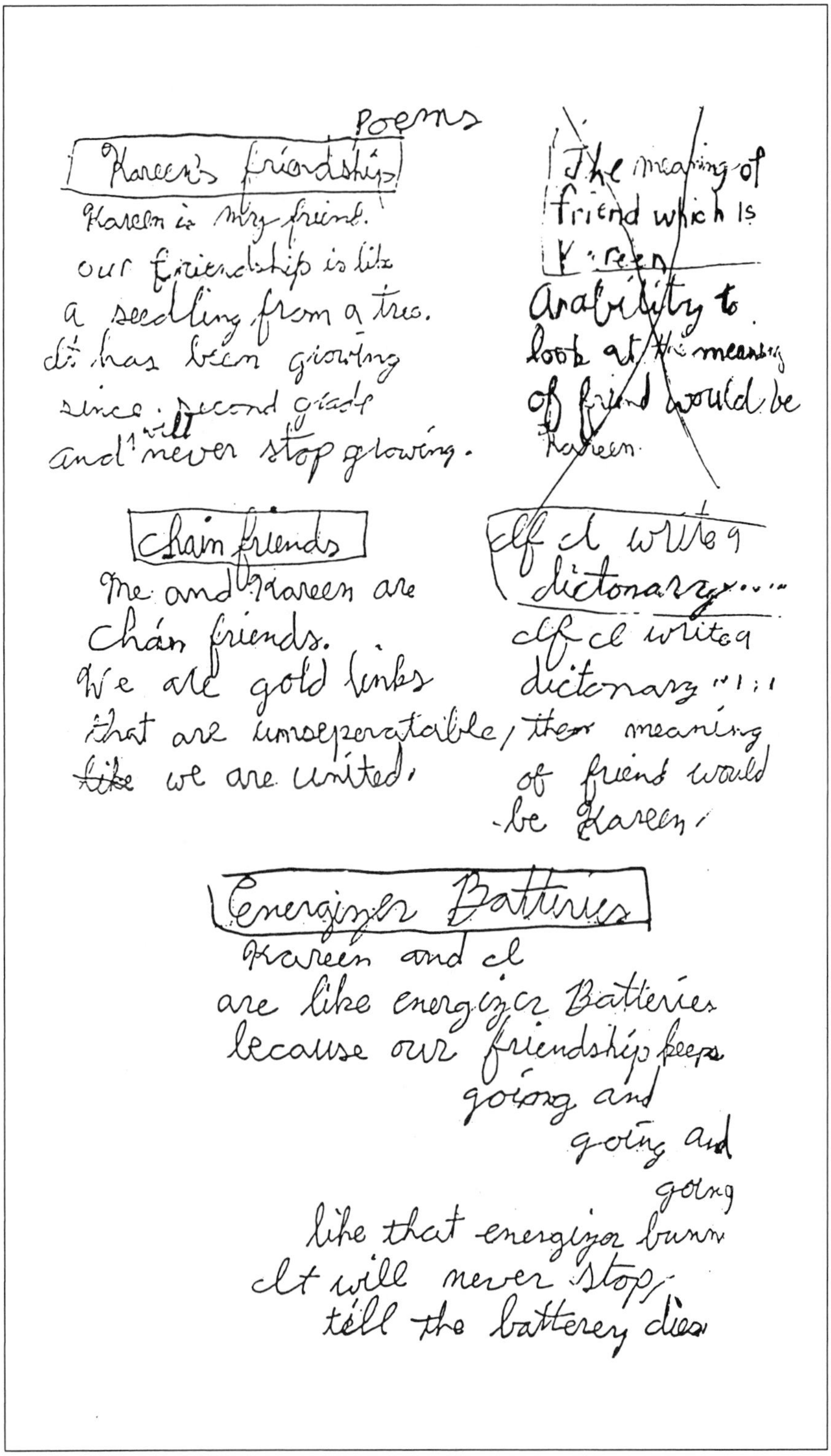

poems

[Kareen's friendship]

Kareen is my friend.
our friendship is like
a seedling from a tree.
it has been growing
since second grade
and will never stop growing.

| The meaning of
friend which is
Kareen
Arability to
look at the meaning
of friend would be
Kareen.

[Chain friends]

Me and Kareen are
chain friends.
We are gold links
that are unseperatable,
like we are united.

If I write a
dictionary.....
If I write a
dictonary ''!'!
their meaning
of friend would
be Kareen.

[Energizer Batteries]

Kareen and I
are like energizer Batteries
because our friendship keeps
going and
going and
going
like that energizer bunn
It will never stop,
till the battery dies

FIGURE 79

Kareen's Friendship

Kareen is my friend.
Our friendship is like
a seedling from a tree.
It has been growing
since second grade
and will never stop growing

Chain Friends

Kareen and I are
chain friends.
We are gold links
that are inseparable.
We are united.

Energizer Batteries

Kareen and I
are like energizer batteries
because our friendship keeps
                    going and
                      going and
                        going.
Like that energizer bunny
it will never stop
till the battery dies.

If I Write a Dictionary

If I write a dictionary
the meaning of friend
would be Kareen.

Poems by Jennifer
                    grade 5

- To study specific literary techniques.
- To learn from a particular writer.
- To imitate in order to get out of a rut.
- To study shape or design options.
- To gather advice from professional writers.
- To learn editing skills.
- To appreciate publishing options.
- To be challenged.
- To be inspired.

To Spark Ideas

In Chapter 4, I explored the notion of students using literature to explore their own thinking. Reading helps students realize they have their own stories to tell. As I walked around Antoinette's classroom, I often suggested to students who were facing a writer's block that they use the literature they love to spark new ideas. Joanne Hindley, my colleague from the Teachers College Writing Project, does so with Lorenzo, a second grader.

Joanne: So, Lorenzo, what's going on?

Lorenzo: [Shrugs shoulders. Blank paper on desk.]

Joanne: I see you have a blank piece of paper here again. What are you thinking you might write about today?

Lorenzo: [Shrugs again. Giggles when notices that a peer is listening. I waited about twenty seconds before continuing. Lorenzo continues to stare down at paper and pulls top of marker on and off.]

Joanne: Well Lorenzo, do you think you need help coming up with a topic today?

Lorenzo: [Shakes head "no."]

Joanne: So, what will you do then when I walk away? [Pause.] What's going to help get that pencil moving?

Lorenzo: [Shrugs shoulders again.]

Joanne: Well Lorenzo, since you're not sure what you're going to do next, I'm going to help you get started. You haven't been getting much writing done lately and I'm a little worried about that. Do you know why it is that you haven't been writing at writing time?

Lorenzo: Can't think of nothing to write about.

Joanne: Well, that's a common problem with writers, Lorenzo. It happens to me sometimes too, so I think I can help you out with this. I usually try to think of things that matter to me a lot in my life. People or events. I know you've done a little bit of writing like that this year, haven't you?

Lorenzo: Yeah, but I don't have any more ideas. I used them all up.

Joanne: Maybe it's time to find other ways of coming up with an idea. You can use your own memory, but sometimes you can use things to get your memory going. I want you to go to our class library and find three books that you really like, and then find a friend that you think likes them also, and bring them all back over here in five minutes. I'm going to talk to Allison now, but I'll be ready for you. Okay?

Lorenzo: [Nods "yes."]

Joanne: So Lorenzo, let's see what you have here.

Lorenzo: *I Can Swim, Cats Are Like That,* and *Grandpa.*

Joanne: I remember that a lot of other people like those books too, when we read them at story time. And Peter, you came along too. Did Lorenzo tell you why I asked him to bring a friend over?

Peter: Nope.

Joanne: Well, I asked him to find three books he really likes, and bring a friend over who he thinks also likes them.

Peter: Yeah, I like them.

Joanne: Well maybe you and Lorenzo can sit and talk about them for a minute.

Peter: I like the swimming book best.

Lorenzo: Yeah, cause it's funny. Remember the time we went to that swimming pool? And Jessica, she fell in and didn't know how to swim? We were all laughing at her, but then the man pulled her up and she was coughing and it sounded like she was going to throw up!

Peter: Yeah, but then it wasn't so funny.

Lorenzo: Not really. She could have died or something. I can swim really good. That wouldn't happen to me.

Peter: [Picks up *Grandpa.*] I think this book is weird. I think he dies at the end 'cause of that empty chair. My grandpa died a long time ago. But I wasn't sad because I really didn't know him.

Lorenzo: My grandfather lives in Puerto Rico. He might come visit this summer.

Peter: How come you like this cat book? I don't know it.

Lorenzo: Me either, but I like cats.

Joanne: Well Lorenzo, it seems to me, from listening to you talk to Peter, that you have a lot to write about. You mentioned that you like cats, and I'd love to know more about that. You also talked about your grandfather living in Puerto Rico, and about Jessica falling into the pool. I do what you did just now. Sometimes when I'm stuck for an idea to write about, I look at some books to see if they make me think of something in my own life. So you actually have a lot of ideas today for writing. Which one will you work on now?

Lorenzo: [Shrugs shoulders.]

Joanne: Well Lorenzo, not writing at writing time is not an option, so you have to pick one of them.

Lorenzo: Jessica swimming.

Joanne: Okay great, get me the paper you'd like to use from the writing center and bring it to me.

[Lorenzo returns with paper.]

Joanne: Okay, this is the deal. You brought me a three-page book. By the end of writing time, I want you to have filled at least the first page. You'll need to work really hard to get all that done, but I know you can do it. So, what are you going to do now when I leave you?

Lorenzo: Write about Jessica.

Joanne: Great. Get going!

Joanne demonstrated how literature gets your mind going. Lorenzo now knows he has many stories to tell.

To Generate More Thoughts on a Topic

Although study stacks helped children realize that there are several genre options and inspired them to write well about their topics, the main reason we created them was to help students linger over a topic they had already discovered. We wanted to help them generate more thoughts, deepen those thoughts, and discover new ideas and angles, new problems and points of view.

Any time I come alongside a youngster with a full-blown obsession, I know I can ask, "Do you think it might be helpful to read other people's writing on this issue?" Sometimes the answer is "No." Most times it's "Sure."

As I have suggested, we tried to get materials as close to their topic as possible. Emil wasn't writing about baseball, he was writing about sharing his love for the sport with his dad. Zanvi wasn't writing about cats, she was writing about cats as best friends. The entry in Figure 80 demonstrates how literature helped her think new thoughts.

To Gather Specific Bits of Information

Years ago I clipped a *Newsweek* column by Robert Klose, a biology instructor. He wrote in part,

> For me, scientists are among the most interesting people on earth. They are incorrigibly curious and energetic, so much so that their energies spill over into nonscientific pursuits. They not only peekaboo into the contents of the living cell, but play the cello or struggle with translations of German poetry as well. These associated activities aren't tangential; rather, they are an expression of the scientist's greedy need to know, which is everything.

I've often thought I could substitute the word *writers* for the word *scientists.* Writers too have a greedy need to know, which is everything.

In Pat Conroy's novel *Prince of Tides,* a young man describes his poet sister's reading habits.

> There was a fruitful exchange between her reading and writing. She had developed the appealing habit of collecting books on subjects she knew nothing about. I found one book, heavily underlined, on the life cycle of ferns, and one called *The Sign Language of the Plains Indians.* There were six books on various aspects of meteo-

FIGURE 80

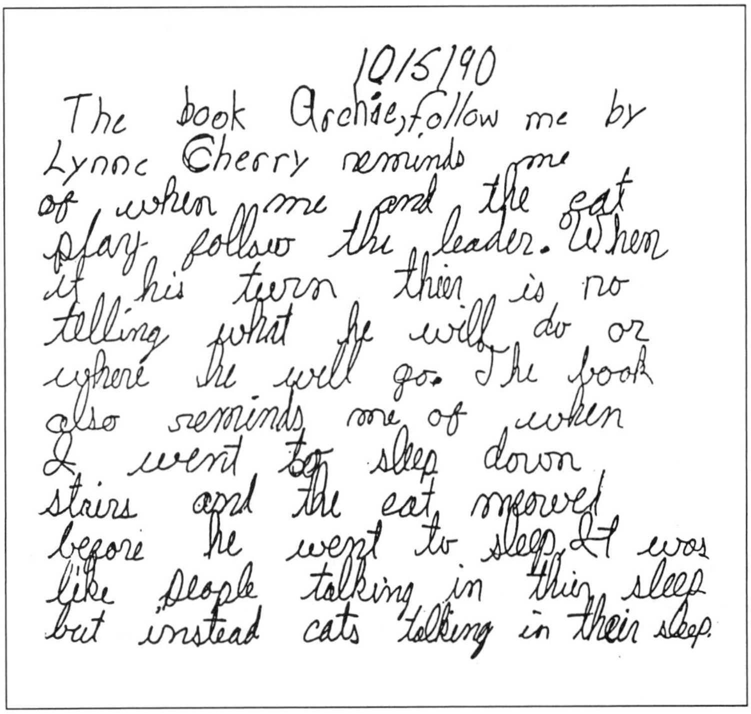
10/5/90
The book Archie, follow me by Lynne Cherry reminds me of when me and the cat play follow the leader. When it his turn thier is no telling what he will do or where he will go. The book also reminds me of when I went to sleep down stairs and the cat meowed before he went to sleep. It was like people talking in thier sleep but instead cats talking in their sleep.

rology, three books on sexual deviation in the nineteenth century, a book on the care and feeding of piranhas, a *Mariner's Dictionary,* and a long treatise on the butterflies of Georgia. She had once written a poem about the butterflies that came to my mother's garden on Melrose Island and through the notes in the book's margins I discovered how my sister picked up a working knowledge of swallowtails, hairstreaks, and coppers. She used her books well and no fact was too obscure to escape her passionate scrutiny. If she needed a ladybug in her poetry, she would buy ten books on entomology to find the absolutely correct ladybug.

Savannah, Conroy's character, illustrates Samuel Johnson's thought, "The greatest part of a writer's time is spent reading in order to write; a person will turn over half a library to make one book."

In the same way, when we confer with students, it's not unusual to suggest that they read reference materials and other nonfiction texts in order to weave precise names and authentic details into their drafts. When Julian brings us a draft of a fiction piece in which a boy saves his friend from drowning, we might encourage him to read a chapter in a first aid book. Julian needs to know what a drowning person looks like and how to help. When Stacey wants to write a science fiction short story about landing on a mysterious planet, we might suggest she read newspaper articles about real-life astronauts and texts that authentically describe space travel. When Francisco shares a draft of a personal narrative about his family trip to Disneyworld, we might suggest that he would write with more authority if he included the precise names of rides and attractions he's read about in a travel brochure.

All this of course has implications for our class libraries and our conferring. We need to reserve a shelf for the kinds of reference materials young writers need. We also need to feel at home with conferences that send a student off to search those shelves to gather specific information.

To Study the Traditions of a Genre

Earlier, I suggested the need to encourage young writers to study the genre they're interested in. In one conference, I help Nelson, Amaury's friend, sort out his genre options. Nelson is the kind of student who would like to read wrestling magazines all day. He reads them during math and social studies, any chance he gets. It came as no surprise to see his most recent notebook entry: "Last night I watched wrestling. My sister was screaming. I couldn't hear, so I started screaming. Then the whole family was angry. I think the Hulk won. She better not scream tonight."

Shelley: Nelson, I see you're writing about wrestling again. It really is a big part of your life.
Nelson: Yup.
Shelley: I wonder if all your writing about wrestling is the same kind of writing.
Nelson: I dunno.
Shelley: Can we look through your notebook?
Nelson: Okay.
Shelley: Are all the wrestling entries in one section or are they spread throughout the notebook?
Nelson: They're everywhere. No special place.

Shelley: Nelson, how about preparing for our talk? Here are some stick on notes. Can you mark each page that's about wrestling and jot down what kind of writing you're doing? Then I'll come back and we'll talk.
Nelson: What do you mean?
Shelley: I'm sorry I'm not being clear. Should we do some together?
Nelson: Okay.
[At this point Nelson turns to a few wrestling entries.]
Shelley: This one sounds like a sports reporter to me, giving a blow by blow description. And this one sounds a bit like a how-to book, how to be a great wrestler. Can you continue rereading each entry and decide what kind of writing you were doing? Then we can talk about the kind of writing you really care about, the kind you want to study this year.
Nelson: I'll try.

When I returned, Nelson had found several more "sports reporter" entries and an additional list of "how-to instructions." He also labeled a few pages about favorite wrestlers as "biographies." Some entries, like the one about his sister screaming, were labeled "diary-pages."

Shelley: What kind of writing do you care most about? What kind would you like to study this year?
Nelson: The biographies. I like writing about famous wrestlers.
Shelley: Have you ever seen that kind of writing done professionally?
Nelson: Sure, [hugging his wrestling magazine]. They're all in here.

Over the next few days, Nelson was given time to study the traditions of his favorite genre. He looked over two feature columns in his favorite wrestling magazine, "The Personality Profile" and "A Talk With . . ." interview. We then talked about the techniques he admired and how he would apply them to tell the story of"Macho Man Randy Savage."

In this conference with Nelson, I first had to help him realize that wrestling could be written about in many ways. Once he had picked what interested him most, I needed to suggest that he take lessons from the reading he admired.

To Study Specific Literary Techniques

In working with a student who's struggling with a specific literary technique, how lucky we feel if we know our library well. When a child attempts a flashback but that attempt is weak, it is wonderful to know a few books in which the writer uses the technique successfully. The conference really becomes a matter of connecting the student with a place where he might get help. Earlier in this book, I quote Lucy Calkins, "The job of a writing teacher is to put herself out of a job." Nowhere is it more apparent than when we're helping a student study a specific literary technique. If we have five hundred quality books in our classroom library, we have five hundred colleagues to help our students grow in their skills as writers.

I pull up alongside Katherine. She has attempted to weave her notebook entries into a personal narrative about her move to New York City but senses that the draft moves too quickly. She doesn't know how to slow the narrative down. In my tote bag, I happen to have a list of first-person narratives. I send her off to the school library to take out any of the following books:

- *Just Us Women* by Jeannette Caines
- *Me and Nessie* by Eloise Greenfield
- *My Island Grandma* by Kathryn Lasky
- *Three Days on a River in a Red Canoe* by Vera B. Williams
- *Katie in the Morning* by Crescent Dragonwagon
- *Tight Times* by Barbara Shook Hazen
- *Watch the Stars Come Out* by Riki Levenson
- *The Terrible Thing That Happened at Our House* by Marge B. Blaine
- *Fireflies* by Julie Brinckloe
- *Little Nino's Pizzeria* by Karen Barbour
- *Frannie's Fruits* by Leslie Kimmelman
- *When I'm Sleepy* by Jane R. Howard

Katherine returns with seven of the twelve. I need not confer with her for several days.

The same scenario could occur when children are attempting to circle the ending back to the beginning, use flashback, or weave dialogue into their family scenes. How wonderful it would be to send them off to the school library with a list. Better yet, how wonderful it would be to have a basket of books at hand for their close attention.

To Learn From a Particular Writer

Sometimes a student is struggling with a particular technique, and rather than suggest an array of texts for him to study, we are reminded of one particular writer.

In *On the Teaching of Creative Writing,* Wallace Stegner suggests: "It is common practice to send a student out to learn a particular technique by studying a particular writer who was good at it: Joyce, say, for stream of consciousness or Conrad for the tricks of multiple narrators."

With our youngest writers, it is often easier to make the kind of suggestion Stegner speaks of if we were conferring about illustration. The student is struggling with a cartooning technique and we suggest that they study William Steig or James Stevenson. Or the student is attempting to fill whole pages with strong, bold colors, and Byron Barton, Heidi Goennel, or Marisabina Russo come to mind.

How wonderful it would be if we could do likewise with writing techniques. Perhaps if we spent more time talking with confidence about writers and their writing we'd be able to suggest appropriate writers for students to study. Perhaps we'd suggest Robert Cormier to the student who's struggling with building suspense, Charlotte Zolotow to the student who wants to have gentle yet powerful endings, and Lois Lowry to the student who wants to know how to write in a regional dialect. And how wonderful, if this kind of information becomes part of the students' world as well.

Dorothy Barnhouse, the wonderful writer and teacher of writing who has taught members of the Writing Project so much over the last few years, revealed to her reading circle that she goes to Alice Munro to study story structure and to Louise Erdrich to study language. How lucky Dorothy is to know where to look when she needs help. When students spend more time talking with confidence about writers and their writing, perhaps they too, will know which writers to turn to and which to recommend to their friends.

When I confer with young writers I sometimes suggest they study a particular writer because their writing reminds me of that writer. To be told your writing is similar to that of a professional writer is of course, quite a compliment. Children not only sit up a few inches taller, they eagerly rush off to read that writer's work. With our very youngest writers, I've been able to play a "your writing reminds me" sort of game at share time. After the students share their writing, I respond, "Your writing reminds me of . . ." and then I have to think very quickly on my feet. Occasionally, I have to resort to similarities in topic or publishing format rather than literary technique. "Your writing reminds me of Ezra Jack Keats because you both write about snowy days" or "you both illustrate with collage."

I try as often as possible to point out more abstract connections. "Your writing reminds me of Judith Viorst's because you both use long meandering sentences." I then invite them take home a few books by the chosen writer. On the following day, I make it a point to confer about what they discovered as they read this writer. Eventually, other children join in on the game. They become quite good at suggesting, "Your writing reminds me of. . . ."

When I confer, I also find myself suggesting to students that their writing reminds me of a particular text.

When I first saw Jerry's entry about his hair (Figure 81), I was reminded of a page in Sandra Cisnero's *The House on Mango Street.*

Hairs

Everybody in our family has different hair. My Papa's hair is like a broom, all up in the air. And me, my hair is lazy. It never obeys barrettes or bands. Carlos' hair is thick and straight. He doesn't need to comb it. Nenny's hair is slippery—slides out of your hand. And Kiki, who is the youngest, has hair like fur.

But my mother's hair, my mother's hair, like little rosettes, like little candy circles all curly and pretty because she pinned it in little pincurls all day, sweet to put your nose into when she is holding you, holding you and you feel safe, is the warm smell of bread before you bake it, is the smell when she makes a little room for you on her side of the bed still warm with her skin, and you sleep near her, the rain outside falling and Papa snoring. The snoring, the rain, and Mama's hair that smells like bread.

Sandra Cisneros

FIGURE 81

My haircut is nice everyone says that it is nicely shaven. I only like the shave but the front and top look awful I like the back of my head it feels so spiky. It reminds me of when I was little when my father hugged me I felt the itchiness of his mustache that's how my hair feels like.

FIGURE 82

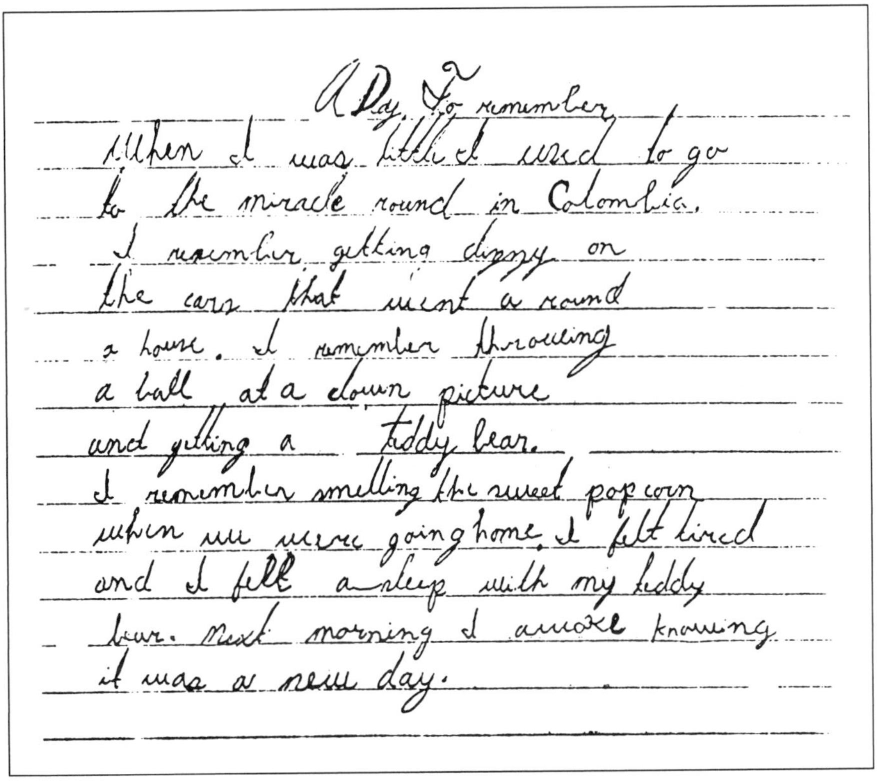

> A Day To remember
>
> 1. When I was little I used to go
> to the miracle round in Colombia.
> I remember getting dizzy on
> the cars that went a round
> a house. I remember throwing
> a ball at a clown picture
> and getting a teddy bear.
> I remember smelling the sweet popcorn
> when we were going home I felt tired
> and I fell a-sleep with my teddy
> bear. Next morning I awoke knowing
> it was a new day.

At first it was merely a topic similarity that brought the text to mind. Upon closer study however, I was able to say to Jerry, "You're both so good at paying incredibly close attention to hair and you're both so good at using hair to talk about tender feelings."

Jerry felt good about himself as a writer and he was interested in taking a closer look at *The House on Mango Street*. Now, he too, would write a collection of short family vignettes.

Alejandro didn't know what a fine writer he was. He was selecting his best childhood memories from his notebook for a memoir.

"They're not very good," he said as he handed me several looseleaf papers. He had been painstakingly copying out a collection of short first draft memories. Alejandro naturally writes well. His tight, shaky handwriting contrasts with the ease with which lovely words flow from his pen. But he doesn't think of himself as a gifted writer. Instead he complained, "I just keep saying the same thing over and over. Like in this one," pointing to 'A Day to Remember' (Figure 82), "I keep saying, I remember this, I remember that. That sounds like a little kid."

I read Alejandro's piece to myself. I found myself pausing at the first line. I closed my eyes, trying to savor his "miracle round," not merry-go-round. When I finished the piece I read it aloud to Alejandro. He still wasn't convinced that it was powerful, poignant writing.

I read several more pages.

FIGURE 82, continued

> Hoptal Playground
>
> When I was four years old I used to go to a hospital in my country named Club noel. I remember that that hospital had a park and I used to go there. I remember the fresh air hitting my face and my little shoes getting muddy. I remember the slide getting muddy when I was running up and down the slide and the swings getting tied together after I spun around. I remember my hat getting dusty playing frisby with it. What a child hood I had.

"Alejandro, would you consider reading your memoirs aloud to the class? I think it's as good as any book in our library."

"Mine?" Alejandro asked, "I don't think so."

Later that day, I kept recalling Alejandro's words. These lines kept replaying in my mind:

> I remember getting dizzy on the cars that went around a house. I remember throwing a ball at a clown picture and getting a teddy bear. I remember smelling the sweet popcorn when we were going home. I remember the fresh air hitting my face and my little shoes getting muddy. I remember the slide getting muddy when I was running up and down the slide and the swings getting tied together after I spun around. I remember my hat getting dusty playing frisbee with it.

And finally it hit me. His writing reminds me of Paul Auster's *The Invention of Solitude.* The next day I told Alejandro that I had his voice in my head all night and that his writing brought to mind the work of a wonderful writer. Then I read to him a few pages of Auster's work.

> He remembers learning how to tie his shoes. He remembers that his father's clothes were kept in the closet in his room and that it was the noise of hangers clicking together in the morning that would wake him up. He remembers the sight of his father knotting his tie and saying to him, Rise and shine little boy. He remembers wanting to be a squirrel, because he wanted to be light like a squirrel and have a bushy tail and be able to jump from tree to tree as though he were flying. He remembers looking through the venetian blinds and seeing his new-born sister coming home from the hospital in his mother's arms. He remembers the nurse in a white dress who sat beside his baby sister and gave him little squares of Swiss chocolate.

FIGURE 82, continued

> Apple Madness
> When I was little I used
> to climb apple trees and get apple's.
> I used to put them in big
> baskets and separate each rotten
> one so the other ones would not
> get rotten. When I took
> the first bit I felt the sweet warm bite I
> took. When my mother went to work,
> she did not leave anything to eat.
> I used to make apple sauce.
> It was good. Years past. Soon, soon
> winter was coming again.
> The apples soon were gone. The
> leaves disappeared.
> You could see the dried ugly branches.
> Inside I felt hot. Outside I felt cold
> seeing the beautiful tree gone.
> The neighbors had cut it down because
> catepillars used to crawl in their houses.
> Soon winter was opening and spring
> was closing. Lucky for me a new
> tree was growing.

Alejandro beamed. I explained what I saw in his writing.

"Your work reminds me of Auster's not just because you both repeat the lines, 'I remember' or 'He remembers.' No, it's more than that. I think you both have a way of selecting just the right precious memory. You both know how to move your readers."

Alejandro needs to know his strength. He needs to know what other people see in him as a writer.

To Imitate in Order to Get Out of a Rut

One afternoon Antoinette sent a small group of students who were in need of some extra help with their writing to the library. I frequently arrange for struggling writers to work in the school library. There's nothing like having just the right book at hand. Some of the students were having trouble generating notebook entries. They didn't know what to write about. Others felt that nothing in their notebooks deserved to be worked into a finished piece. Still others felt that important issues were emerging in their entries, but they didn't know what to do next. Perhaps the most difficult and overriding problem of all was that the members of this group, for varied reasons, did not feel good about themselves as writers.

Luis was a member of this group. When I sat down next to him to talk about his work, I found it difficult to make eye contact with him. He kept his head bent down toward his sweatshirt, masking his brown eyes and olive skin. When he finally did look up he seemed expressionless, with no energy for his writing.

His early notebook pages were filled with many short entries including a few rhyming poems. The excerpts in Figure 83 give a sense of his writing as well as his joyless attitude toward school.

Mixed in with these early entries were several longer ones that were rooted in responses to literature. In the entry in Figure 84, for example, Luis responds to Christina Rosetti's poem "Hurt No Living Thing."

Luis's notebook reminds us that for some students, responding to their reading often results in their longest and most powerful entries. Literature serves as a seedbed now and forever, not just when the teacher introduces the notion early in the year (See Chapter 4).

Aside from his entries in response to literature, Luis seemed to pick up speed when he made a commitment to write a lot about his dad. Many of the students in his class had already found important issues in their writer's notebook and had begun to use the notebook as a place where they could focus on one important issue. Luis too had settled in comfortably, writing almost exclusively about his dad for several pages (Figure 85). Like most reluctant young writers he seemed to feel more comfortable using a notebook in thinking about this particular issue in his life, rather than relying on whatever happened to float into his mind.

In anticipation of an eventual finished piece about his dad, Luis had even prepared a special book cover. With his father's help he sawed a clipboard in half. Then, using thick electrical tape, he attached both halves to create a hardcover binder for his work to come.

Luis felt that it was time to turn his material into that finished piece, but he wasn't satisfied with what he had written. None of it seemed good enough to deserve that fine and formal cover. None of it seemed to hint at a genre. As Luis put it, "It's just boring—me and my dad this, me and my dad that." He had no favorite lines or favorite paragraphs. And yet when he talked about his dad his face lit up. He made his first eye contact with me.

Two thoughts went through my mind and I shared them with Luis. "How wonderful to have found a topic you really care about and how wonderful to want your writing to be the best it can be." My response, I think, has something to do with seeing the glass half empty or half full. Luis lacks confidence as a writer, he finds his writing boring, he doesn't know what to do next. But looking through the optimist's lens, I see a young writer who has become a critical reader, who stops to evaluate the quality of his text. I see a young writer who has learned to pause, to wonder what he might do next, rather than writing "any old thing."

FIGURE 83

I love Fridays because
you dont have to do
your homework that day.
And I can play.

Manhatten

Manahattin is full of
skyscraper. With people in
it.

My neighbor has a dog, and the dog
was chasing a little mouse, then
the mouse hid under these pile of woods
then the mouse thought he was safe

then the mouse got out
and the

When I was baby I use to
be fat becuase I ate
alot of food. But now
am not fat and I eat
alot. Why did I get to skinny
from fat.

FIGURE 83, continued

Right now the teacher
told to write and
I don't know
what to write
so I am writing
this

Today we had a lot
of fun becuase we made
a CANDY House. it was
great. When I was doing it
my hands were all with
sugar. Mine wasnt so great
but it was okay.

I like winter but I like
summer better. becuase in summer
you get to play and go on trips
and the days are sunny and
you can go to beaches. But
in winter you go to school
and stay stuck in school

FIGURE 83, continued

If I like football. alot because its fun and you get run, catch, and thorow. I like it very much. I like being reciever and quarterback. I like the Giants, Raiders, San-Fransico 49ers. I play it sometimes in school or at home.

Poems

① Big large .sometimes small
   that would eat you whole

② A bear is ~~cuddly~~ ~~cute~~ soft and
   ~~cute~~ cuddly too. So when you're
              scared it's there for
   you.

③ When the night begins to   fall
   The city starts to glow
   But the night   is
   not   alone   at
   all.

FIGURE 84

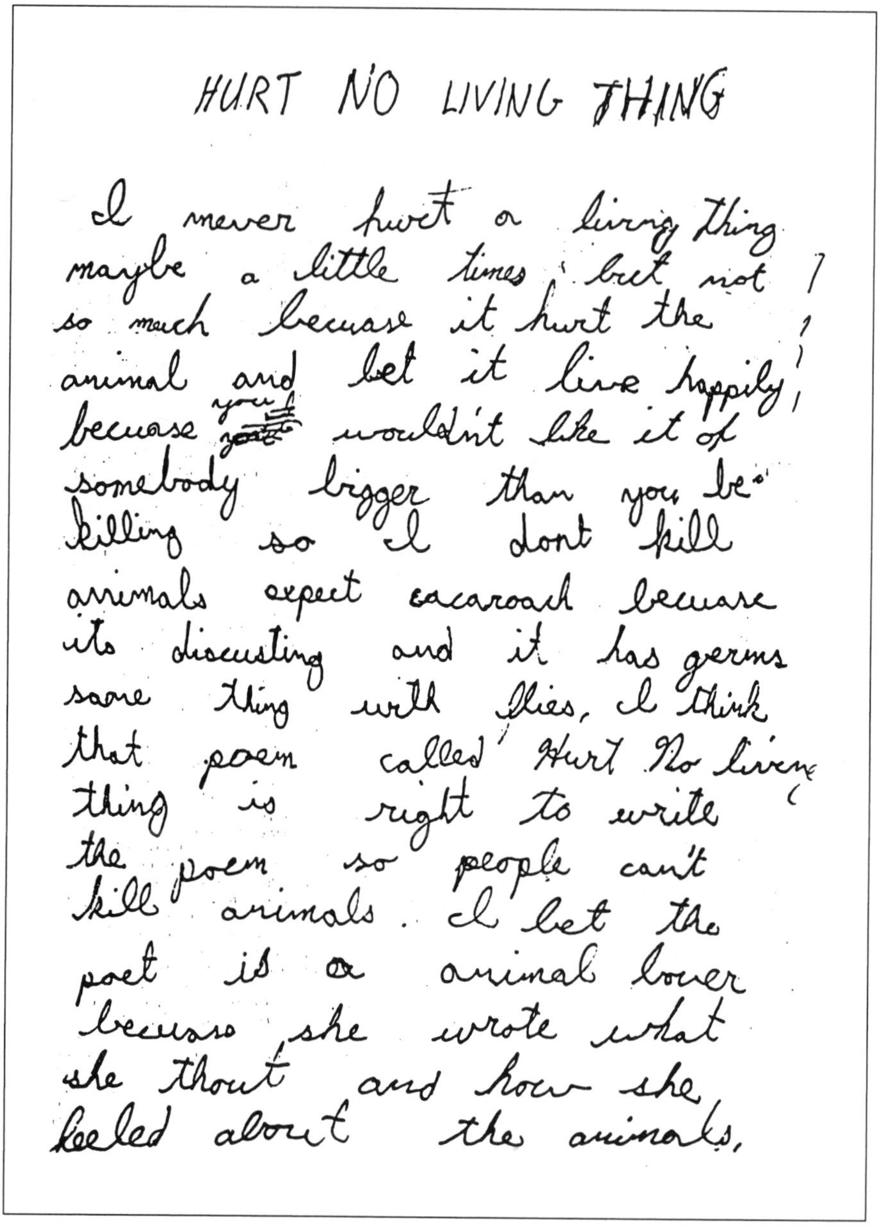

HURT NO LIVING THING

I never hurt a living thing maybe a little times but not so much because it hurt the animal and let it live happily, because you wouldn't like it if somebody bigger than you be killing so I dont kill animals expect cacaroach because its discusting and it has germs same thing with flies, I think that poem called Hurt No living thing is right to write the poem so people can't kill animals. I bet the poet is a animal lover because she wrote what she thout and how she feeled about the animals.

I thought the best way I could help Luis was to convince him that he could write about his father in ways that he would not consider boring. First I got him talking and I gave him back his words. "Tell me about some of the important moments with your dad, Luis. Don't worry about the writing just yet." Luis told a story about playing in the park with his dad. "Dad's all sweaty, right? He gets real tired, right? So he stops to drink an ice cold soda and then when he gets a goal he starts screaming and jumping. He gets all happy." (Luis, as do many children his age,

FIGURE 85

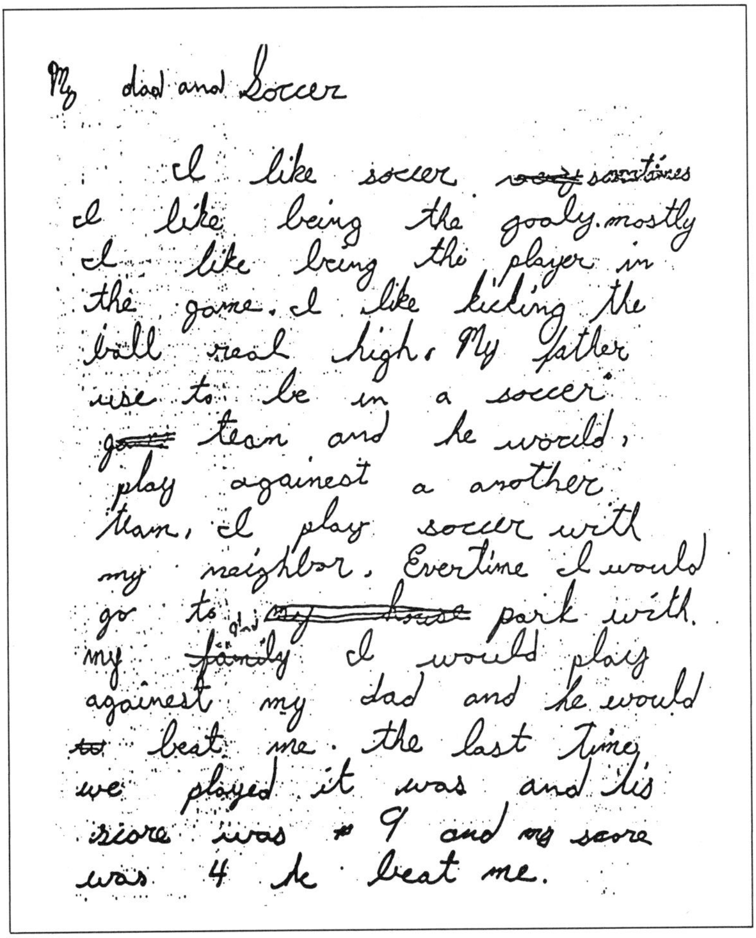

> My dad and Soccer
>
> I like soccer. ~~every~~ ~~sometimes~~
> I like being the goaly. mostly
> I like being the player in
> the game. I like kicking the
> ball real high. My father
> use to be in a soccer
> ~~game~~ team and he would
> play againest a another
> team. I play soccer with
> my naighbor. Evertime I would
> go to ~~did~~ ~~my~~ ~~house~~ park with
> my ~~family~~ I would play
> againest my dad and he would
> ~~to~~ beat me. the last Time
> we played it was and his
> score was # 9 and my score
> was 4 he beat me.

used an occasional, "Right?" to ensure that I was really listening as well as to propel his story forward.) He went on for several minutes. Then I read his words back to him. I even handed him my quick notes. He knew that he could tape these notes into his writer's notebook. He could even draw on them to write. Luis needs to realize that a notebook is the perfect container for the stories he tells so well. He needs to understand that his stories can meander off in lots of directions and that he need not worry about sentence structure and spelling and grammar just yet.

Next I deferred to all the professional writers whose works line the library shelves. I asked Luis if there was a writer he admired, one he wished he could write like. He shrugged his shoulders and murmured the familiar "I dunno." (There's a joke about why children have short necks—from all the years of shrugging their shoulders to say "I dunno.") "Why not walk around the room?" I suggested, "Maybe you'll be reminded of a book you've read." He came back empty-handed.

FIGURE 85, continued

My Dad

My dad is real nice. He's fun.
Everytime we go to the
park he would play with
even he was tired then
he would play with me
any sport. I love my
dad for that. Evertime
he comes back from work
he would bring me something.
Or sometimes he would take
me to his work. I would have
fun there and I would help,
most people know me there
because sometimes I would go there
on Saturdays I like going to
his work because I help
him. Or when he notices
I'm bored he gives me a
pile of diffrent sizes of wood so,
I can make something (nails hammer)

Then I walked around with him, stopping to pull a book or two off the shelf. I was looking for some sign of familiarity or enthusiasm. I was also looking for texts that were in some way topic-related in order to make it easier for Luis to learn from the pros' literary techniques.

Two books were all we needed. Luis had heard his teacher read Judith Hendershot's *In Coal Country*. *Guess Who My Favorite Person Is* by Byrd Baylor was new to him, although he knew other books by this writer.

What I suggested next was clearly an exercise, although very different from the Karla Kuskin challenge I had offered Mauricio. Luis was not ready to do what Mauricio had done. He was not about to fall in love with an author, read a lot of her work, abstract her techniques, then write in the author's image. No, this was quite

FIGURE 85, continued

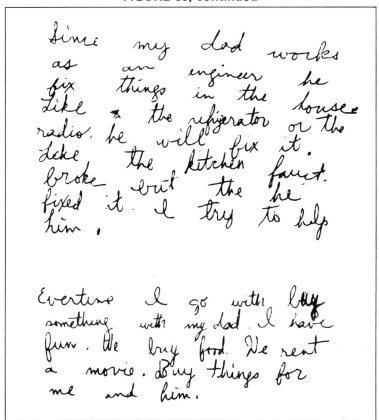

different. I selected the texts. In fact, I selected specific passages. "One way you might feel better about your writing is if you try on a lot of different writing styles. Let's see if we can find some that work for you. Later you can create your own. I wonder if you can write about your father the way Judith has written about the father in this book?"

I opened to this page in the Hendershot text.

> Papa dug coal from deep in the earth to earn a living. He dressed for work when everyone else went to bed. He wore faded denims and steel-toed shoes and he walked a mile to his job at the mine every night. He carted a silver lunch bucket and had a light on his miner's hat. It was important work. He was proud to do it.

Luis, a quiet, mellow child, seemed more eager than usual. Having an accessible pattern to follow gave this less than confident writer the leg up he needed.

Fifteen minutes later Luis had written the entry in Figure 86. He certainly borrowed freely from Hendershot, not just the idea of writing about one's father preparing to go to work, but even many exact phrases.

Luis sensed he had done a good job. He knew this notebook page sounded different than the others, although he couldn't articulate why. He seemed gleefully surprised when I offered an explanation. "This is one of the few times you've

FIGURE 85, continued

> Sometimes I feel sorry
> for my dad because he
> has to work very hard.
> This is how it gos: From Monday
> to Friday he has to wake
> up at 4:30 a.m. and come
> back home around 4:30. He
> works in Manhatten. And he
> also works on Saturdays and
> work almost for 11 hours and
> once in a blue moon he
> works on Sundays. So many
> times I go with him I
> almost know whole Manhatten.
> I know how to return
> to Queens from Manhatten
> by car and by train.

written about your dad in the past tense, and yet, there is an everyday quality to it. Just like in Hendershot's passage, the reader feels that this goes on day after day. I think it's also one of the first times you've written about your dad and you're not on the page. That gives us a very different feel."

The Byrd Baylor text was more of a challenge for Luis, since it was not so closely related to his topic although it was about a relationship between an adult and a child. I said, "Perhaps Byrd Baylor can teach you lessons about how to recreate special moments between people. Why not try to do some of the things she has done?" I opened to the following passage:

> I happened
> to be
> in an alfalfa field,
> barefoot,
> sort of
> lying down
> watching
> ladybugs
> climb

FIGURE 85, continued

My Father likes the same sports I like. Like Football, Baseball. On Sundays me and him would set on the couch and see television. Mostly we see Football. When Lunch is ready we eat. And if we dont have a thing to do or not busy we continue. When I'm seeing and he has to do something and he can't see more later I tell him who won. Like yesterday he had to go to his work and I stayed home. And when he came back I told him about the parts he missed.

Indianapolis Colts 40 · N.Y. Jets

yellow flowers
when
I saw
this little farm kid
who was also
barefoot,
sort of
lying down
watching
ladybugs
climb
yellow flowers,
helping them up again
when they fell off.

"Want to see
my favorite
one?"

FIGURE 86

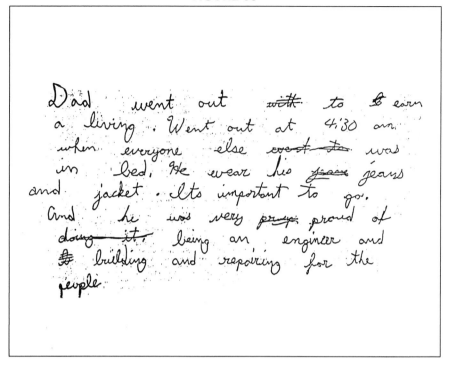

At the end of our library visit, Luis had written the entry in Figure 87.

Not only did Luis borrow Baylor's poetic shape, he also uses quite a bit of her gentle repetition. He also ended his passage with conversation, just as Baylor did.

What did this exercise do for Luis? He learned to borrow someone else's tools to create his own meaning. That's no small accomplishment. He also began to feel better about himself as a writer and that too, is no small accomplishment. Now it will be important to watch Luis to see if he continues to be comfortable trying on other people's styles for fun, for the sake of experimenting. It will also be important to see if he returns to any of the techniques he has played with and if any make their way into his finished piece about his dad. For now, he's slipped only one page between those clipboard covers, the dedication page (Figure 88). His tentative plans are to write a picture book composed of a series of vignettes about his dad.

Luis was challenged to imitate other writers as an exercise in order to shift him out of his writing rut. As I noted in Chapter 9, the main reason to assign an exercise is so that students learn how to assign individual exercises to themselves in order to meet their personal goals. It would be ideal if one day, on his own, Luis found writers he admired and found ways to learn from them. Right now, Luis still needs a bit of nudging and support from others.

There are writers in Luis's class, however, who were able to seek out writers and texts on their own. When I stopped to confer with Francisco he was attempting to borrow a bit of Christina Rossetti's form in "What Are Heavy?"

FIGURE 87

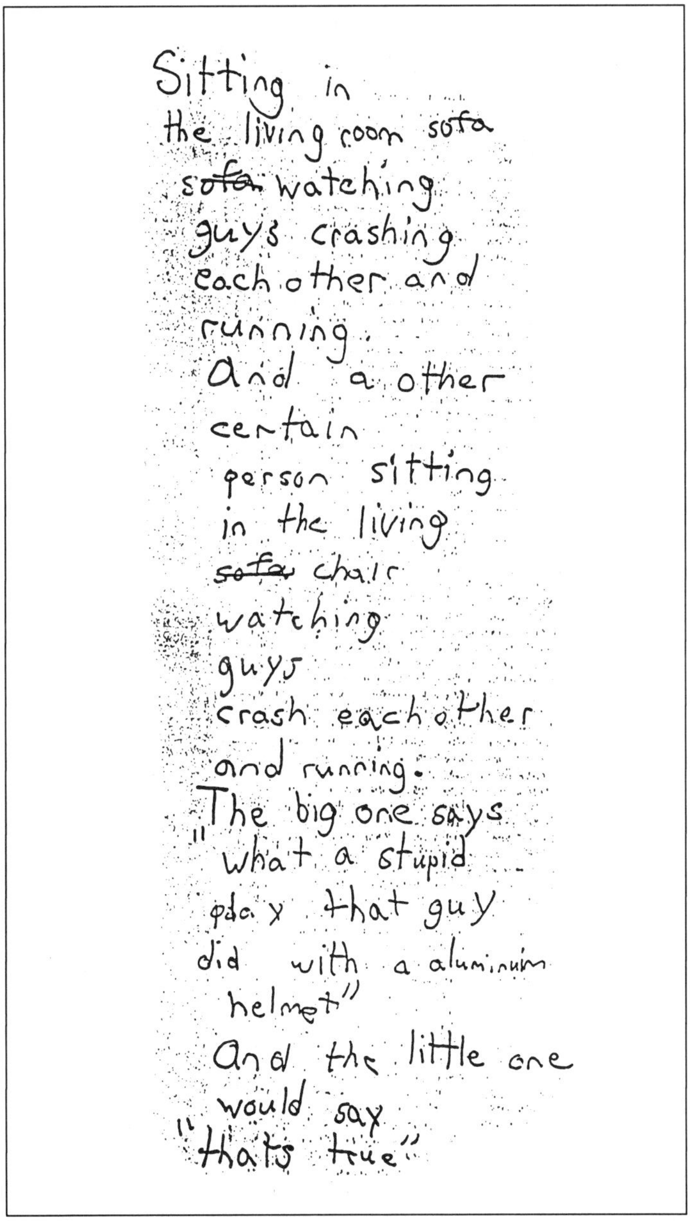

Sitting in
the living room sofa
sofa watching
guys crashing
each other and
running.
And a other
certain
person sitting
in the living
sofa chair
watching
guys
crash each other
and running.
The big one says
"what a stupid
play that guy
did with a aluminum
helmet"
And the little one
would say
"thats true"

What Are Heavy?
What are heavy? Sea-sand and sorrow;
What are brief? Today and tomorrow;
What are frail? Spring blossoms and youth;
What are deep? The ocean and truth.

In his notebook Francisco was writing about his upcoming move to Florida. He wasn't quite sure what form his writing project would take. Just for fun, he wrote another entry (Figure 89) in his notebook.

FIGURE 88

Dedication:
To Dad,
With Love.

FIGURE 89

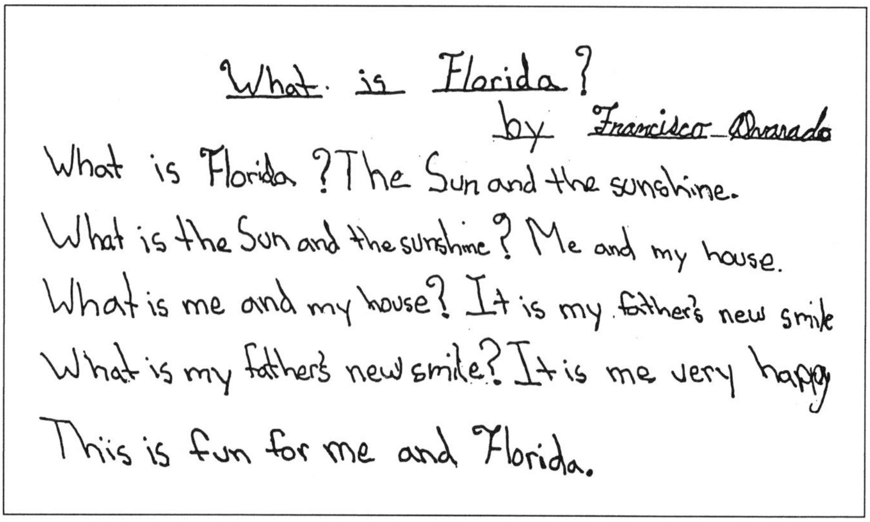

What is Florida?
by Francisco Alvarado

What is Florida? The Sun and the sunshine.

What is the Sun and the sunshine? Me and my house.

What is me and my house? It is my father's new smile

What is my father's new smile? It is me very happy

This is fun for me and Florida.

Francisco's poem never made it into his final writing project. He wrote it in a playful manner, just for the fun of experimenting—as it should be.

To Study Shape or Design Options

One of the difficulties in leading a whole-class mini-lesson on shape or design options in picture books is that many children deliberately set out to write with a specific shape in mind. When children intend to write a cumulative tale or a text in which the ending circles back to the beginning, no matter what the story is about, the writing is often strained.

How much more powerful it is, as we confer one on one with students, to see the hint of a shape appearing naturally in a student's writing. Then we can point out what we see and even suggest several texts the student might want to study in order to tighten or accentuate that shape.

A student is writing about his grandfather, who is moving into his home. In our conference, he begins to speculate on what his grandfather is thinking about the same event. We might suggest that he read Judy Blume's *The Pain and the Great One* to see how Blume presents different points of view.

Or a student begins writing about her new baby brother, suggesting that there are good things and bad things about having a new member of the family. We might recommend other books that have a good news/bad news design. The student could, for example, read *My Mom Travels a Lot* by Caroline Feller Bauer, and *Here I Am an Only Child* by Marlene Fanta Shyer. These texts demonstrate two very different options for organizing "good news/bad news" thoughts.

Often it's not enough just to send children off to read these texts. I find it helpful to add, "After you've read those books, let's talk." In this way I can help students think through how they might bring these polished techniques to the rough draft they've already begun. Children are usually quite comfortable and eloquent when they talk about the techniques they've studied, even though the books are not usually content-related. They have been reading with their antennae out, deliberately studying a design option that their teacher has highlighted.

Sometimes a student has no plans for designing a finished work, and we don't see a hint of a shape as we confer. No genres come to mind, no patterns emerge. Reading fine literature at this point, especially topic-related literature, is often appealing and instructive to young writers.

When Jerry wrote his entry about hair, we suggested he read Sandra Cisneros's "Hairs" in *The House on Mango Street*. He didn't just enjoy the story, he was also able to recognize its design. He realized that he too could write a series of very short, seemingly unrelated vignettes about his childhood. When he made this design decision we also suggested he study *Memories of My Life in a Polish Village* by Toby Knobel Fluek, Eloise Greenfield and Lessie Jones Little's *Childtimes,* and Brenda Seabrooke's collection of poetic narratives, *Judy Scuppernong.*

When Kaity decided that the notebook entries she cares most about are the pages of close observation about the fish in her uncle's tank, I suggested she take a look at Barbara Brenner's *A Snake Lover's Diary* and Bernard Heinrich's *An Owl in the House: A Naturalist's Diary.* These texts not only illustrated finely detailed writing, they also suggested a way for Kaity to shape her material into a manageable form.

FIGURE 90

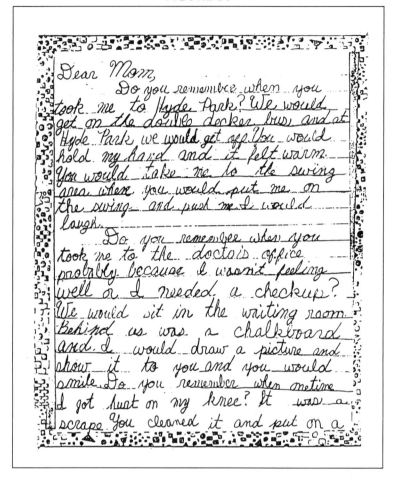

When children are struggling with the architecture of their pieces it is also helpful to have available the kinds of texts that allow them to get inside the shape of a professional writer's work.

In Antoinette's classroom we kept a cardboard box filled with unbound picture books. We separated the pages of the books so that students could spread them out on a back table or on the hallway floor and see the entire text all at once. (Two copies of each book allowed us to show both sides of the page at the same time.) We slipped each page into a see-through plastic sleeve for protection and permanency.

These pages came in handy when we conferred with a student who was considering the amount of attention he had given to different parts of his own text. A student can more easily take a critical look at the shape of his own writing after he has studied the work of other writers. A student can look at how Susi Gregg Fowler weighted each of the seasons in *When Summer Ends* when he spreads out the pages of her book. He can do likewise with Ben Schecter's *Grandma Remembers*. Does Schecter give equal attention to all the stops on his tour of a beloved

FIGURE 90, continued

old house? It's easy to see the design of a book when you can group sections together and slip pages in and out.

Antoinette and I also kept a file folder filled with the typed texts of several favorite picture books. After students had read and reread the books, we typed the entire texts onto one sheet. Students seem to find it easier to note the shape of the whole, as well as patterns or repeated literary devices, when they can look at all the pages at once.

When I stopped to confer with Sophia, she was struggling with a repeated refrain. The question "Do you remember?" was studded throughout a letter she was writing to her mother. She wanted to know how frequently the question could be asked, if she could alter the words slightly at times, and if the amount of text following each repeated question needed to be of equal length.

I suggested that she read the typed texts of books that had a line repeated throughout: Charlotte Zolotow's *I Like to Be Little,* Heidi Goennel's *Sometimes I Like to Be Alone,* and Cynthia Rylant's *When I Was Young in the Mountains.* After she had studied these works we met to talk. Her letter to her mom appears in Figure 90.

FIGURE 90, continued

> Then it would be time to cut the cake. Everybody would be singing "Happy Birthday to you" and "How old are you now?" I would be nervous and shy to say "I am **** years-old" so Mom you would sing it with me. It would make me feel better. So then I would blow out the candles. You would hold my hand to cut the cake so I wont get hurt. Your hand felt warm and soft.
>
>   Remember when we traveled on the airplane? Bilal you and I. Bilal sat on your lap and I would sit in the seat next to you. When I fell sleepy I would rest my head on your shoulder. It would feel warm and soft. It would be very comfortable. When it was time to eat —

To Gather Advice from Professional Writers

Lucy Calkins has likened the teacher's role as conference partner to that of the switchboard operator who helps callers make appropriate connections. Throughout this chapter I have tried to demonstrate that our job is to connect students with people and places from which they can learn. Not all information needs to come directly from us. We can send children off to the library, to other writers, to other experts in the school building. We can also send children off to read professional literature that was intended for adult audiences.

Some of my most dog-eared issues of *Language Arts* are those in which a writer has shared suggestions for learning a particular genre. They're dog-eared because they've been added to my class library and children are invited to read them. As I confer, I can refer mystery writers to Jack Wilde and Tom Newkirk's "Writing Detective Stories" (March 1981), nonfiction writers to Margaret Queenan's "Finding the Grain in the Marble" (November 1986), science fiction writers to Dorothy Mark's "When Children Write Science Fiction" (April 1985), fiction writers to Sharon Taberski's "From Fake to Fiction" (October 1987), and so on. Over the years I've highlighted passages in these articles and I refer

FIGURE 90, continued

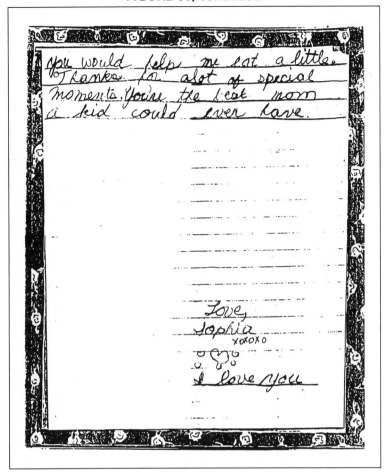

students to these highlighted sections. Sometimes I suggest they read the article in its entirety.

Students can also profit from texts written for adult audiences. I have book-marks in Don Murray's "Some Notes for Student Writers" in *A Writer Teaches Writing* and others in Murray's "Twenty-Six Ways to Start Writing" in *Write to Learn*. I've sent students off to read William Zinsser's chapters "The Lead" and "Writing About a Place" in *On Writing Well*. I've suggested that students read Jane Yolen's chapter "Picture the Picture Book" in *Writing Books for Children* and Georgia Heard's chapter on poetic forms in *For the Good of the Earth and Sun*. I often highlight the accessible passages for young readers. After they read, I suggest that we meet to talk about what they're learning or that they share their reading with other students attempting to write in same genre.

Of course, guides to writing aimed at young writers in particular are also an important resource in our writing workshops. I've sent students who are writing letters to read Sylvia Cassedy's chapter on letter writing in *In Your Own Words*, and I've often referred students to Jacqueline Jackson's *Turn Not Pale, Beloved Snail*.

To Learn Editing Skills

Literature is an important resource when we want to teach editing skills to students. A dictionary and a thesaurus are not the only books we can refer students to during editing. How much easier it is for students to appreciate punctuation and paragraphing when they see how these are used by their favorite writers. How much easier it is to suggest that students fine-tune their choice of verbs and nouns when they have been impressed by the precision of language in the works of well-known writers. Who better to illustrate a grammatical point or a punctuation technique than an accomplished writer whose work has been carefully edited?

But students need to approach all editing in a joyful manner. Some seem to think of it as tedious drudgery. This image of editing needs to change. It is particularly with these bored students that I stress my own thrill at finally being ready to tighten my work. Editing is celebratory. I'm always grateful to have reached these final moments. I not only demonstrate my own editing procedures, but I often share thoughts on editing offered by professional writers the students admire.

Lilian Moore says,

I believe that editing is a kind of sculpture. If there's a line with a bump in it and you have a sense of form, you smooth it and give it shape.

Jacqueline Jackson suggests,

When you're fishing, you don't stop to clean a fish as soon as you catch it. You keep throwing in your line as fast as you can while the fish are biting. If you come to a hard spot you can't figure out, but the idea's still there ahead of you, solid ground beyond the pig wallow, leap and go on. When all the creative energy's used up you can go back and rewrite and polish to your heart's content, fill in the gaps, clean the fish.

Then too, much of editing requires the "auditory inwardness" I described in Chapter 6. Sven Birkerts reminds us that to write well one needs to hear "the rightness of a phrase" and be able to "reject a dissonance." Some of this occurs as students compose. Much of it occurs as students edit. Editing needs to include attention to the sounds of language. Children who've listened to literature read aloud seem better equipped to make changes in their final drafts simply because "it just doesn't sound right."

To Appreciate Publishing Options

I remember as a child being awed by the human body section of the encyclopedia. I loved the series of plastic overlays. As I lifted each one, I could see under the skin, into each organ, along each muscle and nerve, and finally down to the skeleton.

I'm still awed today when books surprise me, not just by their content but by their format.

When I first started teaching, I filled a back shelf with "Books with Surprising Shapes." I had board books, unusually long and narrow books, accordian-paged books, and books in the shape of a ladybug, or a firefighters hat, or a beach ball. My favorites were the fairy tales that opened like the spokes of a wheel with a ribbon attached to tie the text into a complete circle. Today I'd add the pop-up books, the scratch and sniff books, and probably Eric Carle's latest, *Cricket,* complete with a sound effect.

I don't share unusual books with students so that they will do unusual things with their own texts. Rather I want to remind them that they have options. Publishing requires decision making. There is more than one way to publish a text. Browsing through books in the class library reminds students of these options.

I look at my own bookcase and see Don Graves's wonderful books in the series, The Reading/Writing Teacher's Companion. I spot the useful blue pages in the back of Regie Routman's books. I recall the "hand-written" revision notes appearing on the pages of several of Don Murray's texts. I see the photograph of Nancie Atwell and her students on the cover of *In the Middle* and the children's drawings on the covers of Georgia Heard's *For the Good of the Earth and Sun* and Tom Newkirk's *More Than Stories*.

When I confer with students who are about to publish their work, I want them to think seriously about the possibilities of paper, layout, print, and illustration. I want them to think about the frills of publishing: the dedication, table of contents, prologue, epilogue, about the author page, and of course, title. Once again, the class library becomes an important resource in helping students make their decisions. When we take publishing seriously, we begin to treat the literature of children as children's literature.

To Be Challenged

Young students can become complacent about their writing. They can become used to lots of carefree writing that doesn't invite them to take new risks or grow as writers. When we approach children who churn out piece after piece of plateaued writing, we need to offer bigger challenges.

I've heard Dorothy Barnhouse ask writers to find stories they're jealous of, and I've heard JoAnn Curtis refer to "challenge books," those that would launch writers on ambitious writing projects. I've opened many conferences by talking to children about the book they're currently reading. "Do you ever wonder if you could write like that?"

When Lucy Calkins approached Zanvi, the fifth grader had settled comfortably into a writing project about her love of cats. She discovered in her notebook writing and rereading that she thought of her kittens as good friends. As Lucy read through the pages of Zanvi's notebook she celebrated the way the young writer had expanded the images in her entries. Zanvi had learned to say more and more about small moments.

Zanvi had begun with a short entry (Figure 91).

FIGURE 91

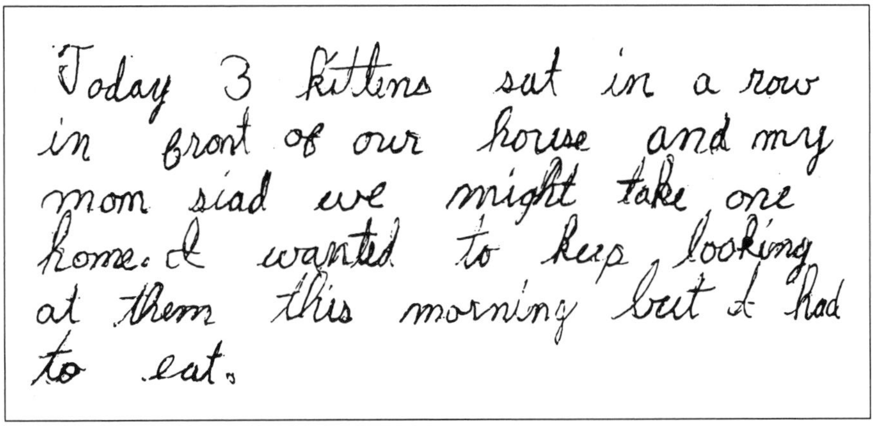

Today 3 kittens sat in a row in front of our house and my mom siad we might take one home. I wanted to keep looking at them this morning but I had to eat.

FIGURE 92

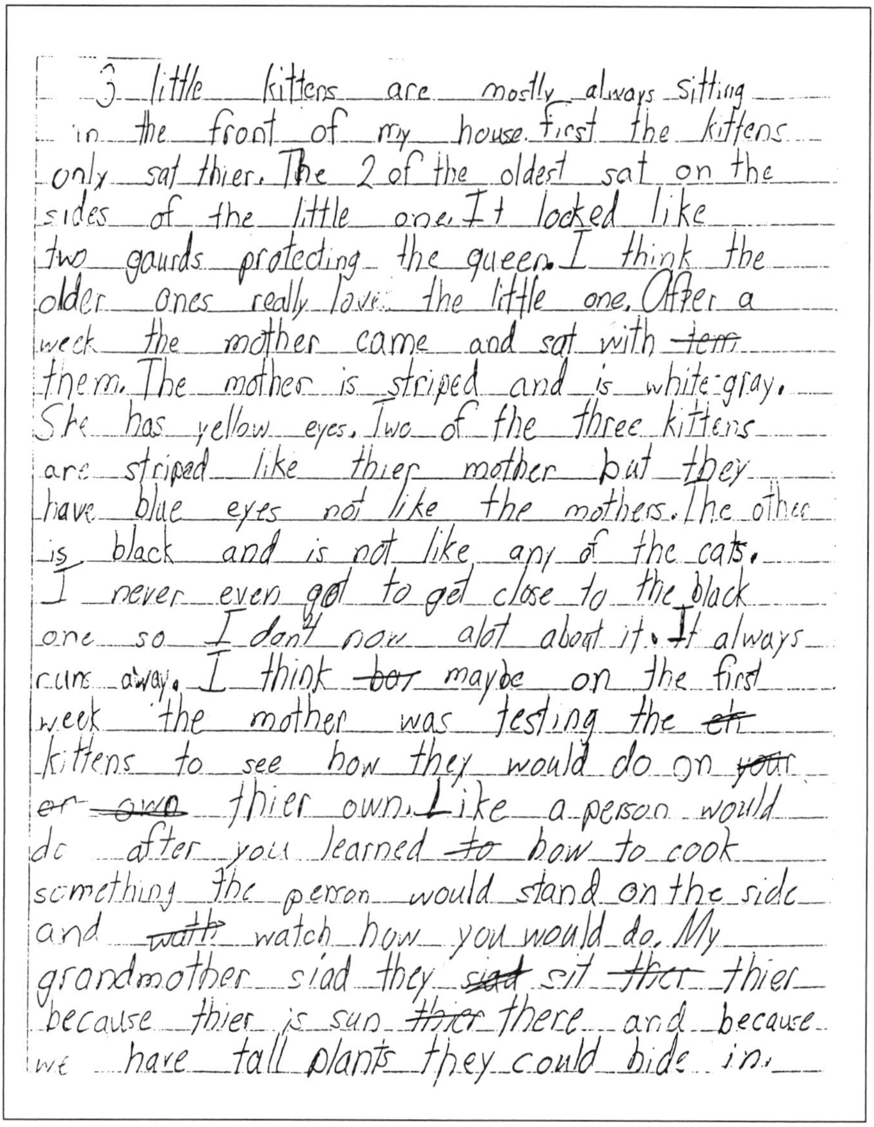

> 3 little kittens are mostly always sitting in the front of my house. First the kittens only sat thier. The 2 of the oldest sat on the sides of the little one. It looked like two gaurds protecting the queen. I think the older ones really love the little one. After a week the mother came and sat with ~~tem~~ them. The mother is striped and is white-gray. She has yellow eyes. Two of the three kittens are striped like thier mother but they have blue eyes not like the mothers. The other is black and is not like any of the cats. I never even got to get close to the black one so I don't now alot about it. It always runs away. I think ~~bot~~ maybe on the first week the mother was testing the ~~et~~ kittens to see how they would do on ~~your er own~~ thier own. Like a person would do after you learned ~~to~~ how to cook something the person would stand on the side and ~~with~~ watch how you would do. My grandmother siad they ~~siad~~ sit ~~thier~~ thier because thier is sun ~~thier~~ there and because we have tall plants they could hide in.

She then freshed the scene out (Figure 92).

Zanvi admitted that these fleshed-out scenes were her favorite passages. Lucy asked her to think about the genre that would best allow her to use this kind of writing. Zanvi quickly chose the picture book, which she had spent a great deal of time with the year before. But Lucy wondered if it was time for a bigger challenge. "Yes, that's one good option," she said to Zanvi, "but what about also writing something longer, like a short story? In a short story you could do the kind of rich layering, the adding on and saying more, that worked so well for you in your notebook."

Lucy then challenged Zanvi to read Cynthia Rylant's *Every Living Thing,* a collection of short stories each about a relationship between a person and an animal. They planned to meet to talk about Rylant's writing. Lucy would lay Zanvi's writing alongside Rylant's. Together they would think through ways for Cynthia Rylant to become this ambitious fifth grader's writing teacher.

To Be Inspired

In the introduction to *Inventing the Truth,* William Zinsser speaks of the writers "who nudged him down the path" to his life's work. He is speaking of baseball writers, those sports journalists who wrote for *The New York Herald Tribune, The New York Times, The New York Sun,* and *Baseball* magazine. Robert Cormier speaks of the "writers who put you in the mood to write." Patricia MacLachlan talks of being inspired by Natalie Babbitt, Cynthia Rylant, and James Agee.

Children also need moments of inspiration. When we approach students who are not in the mood to write, one effective way to shift their mood is to fill them with good writing. This is an opportunity once again to "bathe, immerse, and soak" them in fine literature.

We can send some children off to the listening center to hear the words of their favorite writers read aloud. Others can profit from rereading their own best work. Some may be more inspired by their peers. They can take time to read class magazines or anthologies. Occasionally, I've even sent students from room to room, spending an entire morning listening to different teachers read aloud. I can't imagine a student not being inspired to write after such a luxurious listening spree.

Early in this chapter I admitted that I was once asked if the questions on my conferring chart work for me as I move from notebook entries to a finished piece. Now I can also be asked if all the reasons I've mentioned for sending students off to read could also apply to my own writing. Again the answer is yes. During the year and a half I've been working on this book, of course, I had to stop my writing to take care of my reading. I had, as Frank Smith describes it, lots of "unwitting collaborators."

As we travel up and down the aisles of our classrooms, we often suggest that young writers read for particular purposes. If the job of a writing teacher is to put herself out of a job, we can hope that students will begin to assign reading to themselves in order to meet their own personal goals as writers.

13

Expanding the Notion of Mini-Lesson

Simply put, I try to write the kind of books that I like to read. I go to books for training the way a ball player goes to the ball park for practice. I don't try to imitate other writers, but I am always trying to learn from others.

Robert Cormier

Five years ago if someone had asked me to name the single most important way I help students connect their reading to their writing, without hesitation I would have answered, "Through my mini-lessons."

Back then, if asked to demonstrate how to build bridges between what students read and what they write, I would have relied on an old favorite, "a sure-fire mini-lesson." I'd gather the students near and begin.

"You know, when I was a little girl my mother would make all my clothes for me. And I'd get a very special, proud feeling when I walked into school because no one would have the very same clothes. And today, I get that very same proud feeling when I write and I think I've said something in a way that no one else has ever said it. And even when I read someone else's writing and I think they've said something in such a unique, original way, I get that very same proud feeling.

"Just this morning," I'd continue, pulling a book out of my tote bag, "I was reading *Little Bunny's Loose Tooth* by Lucy Bate. When I got to the part where the bunny loses her tooth and the author writes, "I have a window in my mouth," I wanted to shake that writer's hand. "Good for you, Lucy Bate," I wanted to say,

"I'm so proud of you. What a way to describe a missing tooth." Then I'd end the brief lesson by saying something like, "I just know that today when I come around to talk to you about your writing, you'll be using fresh, surprising language" and I'll be able to shake your hand and say, 'good for you.' And some of you will want to try to say things in fresh, surprising ways and we'll be able to talk about that. Go get started on your writing!" Lesson over.

Thinking back on those carefully framed words, I'm embarrassed to admit that at the time I thought the lesson effective. I used a natural tone of voice. The students paid attention and smiled at the right moments. And the mini-lesson, which lasted only a few minutes, concluded with an appropriate tag-line to connect the information to the students' work. I thought I had added literature to the writing workshop and taught children the power of language. The only problem? The lesson made very little difference in the students' writing.

I was clearly engaging in what Janet Emig has so rightly described as "magical thinking." I talked about fresh and surprising language expecting the children to "get it." People who take their writing seriously, however, don't think about language for only four or five minutes before they sit down to write. Instead, they live their lives in ways that value language—all day, every day, at their desks and away from them.

Over the last several years Lucy Calkins has been reminding us that the qualities of good writing are no different from the qualities of good living. We want to control time in our writing; we want to control time in our lives. I often share with teachers and students E. M. Amedingen's poem, "Gifts from my Grandmother":

> Grandmother, you gave me the wealth of detail.
> You taught me to love grass and moss, ants, and
> butterflies . . . You gave me my first trees and my first
> sunset, mushroom hunts and the bliss of long walks.

How can we teach students about details in short lessons and yet hope to give them this wealth?

I often explore with teachers and students why Laura Ingalls Wilder was able to write with such precision and clarity about her childhood years. Alice Pace Nilson suggests that constantly interpreting the world to a blind sister fostered and fine-tuned Wilder's ability to describe people, places, and happenings along Plum Creek.

Norman Rockwell's father read passages from Dickens aloud as his young son sketched, and some experts speculate that Rockwell's ability to paint with such precise and authentic detail has its roots in Dickens's intricately detailed descriptions.

When Lucy Calkins asked, "How can we give our students the lived chunks of life that will enrich their vision of good writing?" teachers were pushed to rethink their classroom routines. They no longer relied solely on the mini-lesson to help students explore quality writing and make reading-writing connections. Instead, they began adding complementary rituals, activities, and structures to their school day.

Some changed the way they taught reading, exploring ways of inviting students to talk about an author's literary techniques during their reading workshops (see Chapter 10). Others carved out additional time for engaging students in the joyful performance of literature (see Chapter 6). Still others invited children to engage in long-term investigations of good writing (see Chapter 5).

Some teachers felt the need to build in occasional two- or three-day seminars on writing issues, allowing big blocks of time for students to linger over some quality of good writing or live with a beloved book. Some teachers eliminated mini-lessons altogether, replacing them with study times so that small clusters of students could get together to talk about good writing and then make deliberate attempts to apply their learning to the work at hand. But most did not eliminate the mini-lesson altogether. They had come to value and treasure the opening ritual that brings a community of readers and writers together physically and spiritually. They had too many fond memories of huddling together with students in the meeting area sharing tears and laughter. They saw this gathering as the prime time for adding a sense of direction, rigor, and especially information to the writing to come. Instead of eliminating mini-lessons, teachers rethought, redesigned, and refocused them.

Redesigning Mini-lessons

The mini-lesson based on *Little Bunny's Loose Tooth* closely resembles the short whole-class gatherings I taught for many years. Each day I would read aloud a snippet from literature and mention that the writer had used this or that quality of good writing. One day it was telling details, the next a good lead, fresh language, or lots of showing, not telling. My mini-lessons have changed a great deal since those early days.

First, I now know that really understanding good writing requires more than a mini-lesson. Ideas need to be studied deeply. We can't teach an idea by teaching one mini-lesson and then adding that idea to a student checklist or classroom poster. There can't be a bumper sticker that says "Do it with Details."

We need to add breadth and depth. Students need to realize that the qualities that make good writing involve complex issues. Writers struggle over which details to include or omit, which are significant, which insignificant, which are useful, which useless. Students can engage in an entire course of study on how authors handle details. During mini-lesson time, they can look at lots of different books or several books by the same author to study this one quality. They can compare one author's use of details to that of another, including the work of classmates. They can pore over their own portfolios studying their own use of details.

A second change in my mini-lessons is that when I do introduce some aspect of good writing, I've learned to do it with care, avoiding quick clichéd labels at all costs. In a comedy routine on the old "Saturday Night Live," Father Guido Sarducci dreamed of the first five-minute university where you would learn the key phrases that most people remember: in economics, "supply and demand," in American history, "the North wore blue, South wore gray," in Spanish, "¿Cómo esta Usted?" The routine was more tragic than funny. I used to worry that writing workshop graduates would also be filled with key phrases. In fact, several years ago, in *The Writing Workshop: A World of Difference,* I wrote,

> New York City teachers have always tried to teach their students the qualities of good writing. They used to do this by simplifying these qualities into catchy phrases and presenting them as "tricks" authors use to make their pieces better. Five years ago, it would not have been surprising to find a laminated checklist hanging in a prominent spot in the writing center, filled with reminders such as "Sharpen your Lead," "Prune the Clutter," "Show, Don't Tell." Unfortunately, these labels led to

caricatures of good writing. Pieces written by children around the city began to look similar to one another. They tended to begin with catchy leads, with "Wow," "Whoosh," or "Kerplash," and to contain a detailed chronology of one small event in the child's life. Now, New York City teachers avoid simplifying qualities of good writing into items that can appear on a checklist.

Instead of using clichéd labels, we try to talk about good literature in ways that are honest and authentic. I no longer offer the definitive "This author added details/used fresh language/painted pictures." Instead I try to talk from the heart in ways that are more tentative and speculative. I try to talk to students in writing workshops the way I talk to neighborhood children on my front porch, in honest ways without any jargon.

When teachers ask me what qualities of good writing they should teach, I suggest that they read Don Murray's *Learning by Teaching,* and William Zinsser's *On Writing Well,* but most of all, I suggest they find pieces of literature they love and dig deep. "Speak from the heart. Let children know why you're moved by this writer or this text. And then of course, invite them to join you."

One additional suggestion I make to teachers who are struggling to strike formulaic labels from their literary talk is to pair student writing with professional writing. Somehow it seems easier to avoid jargon when we're talking about a piece of writing by a child we know well. It's hard merely to say Jacob uses "colorful language" when we know how hard it was for him to write about the loss of his cat and how hard he worked at finding just the right words.

Once I spoke to children about Patricia MacLachlan's *Sarah, Plain and Tall.* I said: "What I love most about this book is that the author helps me get to know the people so well. And I think she does it by choosing the tiniest things that say so much about her characters. I love knowing that, 'the sheep made Sarah smile' and that, 'she sank her fingers into their thick, coarse wool. She talked to them, running with the lambs, letting them suck on her fingers. She named them after her favorite aunts, Harriet and Mattie and Lou.' Not just anyone would let sheep suck on their fingers, or name sheep after their favorite aunts. I feel that I know Sarah so well."

Along with MacLachlan's work I also talked about Eric's. I let the students know that I love Eric's writing because he too helps me get to know people well. He too chooses small things that say a lot about his characters. I then read a bit of Eric's writing.

> Paul is a tough, neighborly, punky, and "Chip off the ol' block" kind of kid. He has blond hair, wears the same kind of shoes every day and goes around making muscles.

"Not just anyone wears the same kind of shoes every day and goes around making muscles," I added. "I also feel that I know Paul well." As my mini-lesson continued, the conversation turned toward the issue of how writers sift through what they know or think about a character in order to include the most telling thoughts.

The third change in the way I now teach mini-lessons involves their shape and tone. They are no longer exclusively brief lecture-style presentations. Instead, two or three times a week my "mini"-lessons last twenty minutes or more; they are different from traditional mini-lessons not only in length, but also in feel. They are much more interactive. Lots of voices take the floor, not just mine. I am trying to end what my colleague Joan Backer so aptly describes as "frontal teaching on the rug." Gathering children in a meeting area does not ensure authentic language experiences.

I remember a sign hanging in my high school Spanish class: "En la boca cerrada, no entran moscas" meaning "Flies don't enter a closed mouth." I've learned that not much else enters a closed mouth either. Children need to interact with the information presented in mini-lessons. They need to talk through ideas and strategies before putting pen to paper.

Earlier in telling about my mini-lesson on Patricia MacLachlan's and Eric's work I suggested that "the conversation turned." Conversation is the crucial word. Lots of voices need to take the floor. In Chapter 9, I describe oral mentoring exercises as having a parlor-game feel. Increasingly, many mini-lessons took on a similar tone.

Perhaps my mini-lessons have changed most dramatically, because I've discovered many more reasons to teach short whole-class lessons and many more resources to rely on in designing them.

Listed here are more than two dozen reasons for teaching mini-lessons in room 409. All were in the service of helping these fifth graders learn from literature as they worked on their own writing.

Mini-Lessons . . . Many Reasons

To build community.
To demonstrate your
   own literacy.
To take students' breath
   away.
To develop students' oral
   memory bank.   } Particularly at the beginning of
To get at students' literary   the year—usually involves
   histories.   reading alound and telling stories.
To demonstrate a love of
   language.
To build students' own
   image of good writing.

To launch the writer's
   notebook.
To provide real reasons
   to write.   } Particularly when notebook
To generate more writing.   writing is introduced.
To honor students' efforts.
To encourage rereading.

To teach students how
  • to search for special
    entries.   } Particulary when students are
  • to find the significance   choosing writing projects.
    of those entries.
  • to linger on an issue.

To teach students how
  • to take a deliberate stance
    toward writing literature.

- to appreciate the gems in their writing.
- to imagine genre possibilities.
- to make deliberate decisions about their writing.
- to study a genre on their own.

} Particularly when students move from notebooks to finished pieces.

To do formal genre studies.
To study the qualities of good writing.
To study an author.
To teach students about drafting, revising, publishing, editing.
To promote self-evaluation.
To demonstrate reading-writing connections.
To learn to peer confer.

} Ongoing through the year.

Studying the qualities of good writing was only one of many reasons to pull young writers together. We can design lessons in which literature is used to build community, reveal students' literary backgrounds, demonstrate our own passion for reading and writing, help develop students' "oral memory banks," invite students to play with language, encourage mentor relationships, inspire notebook writing, or simply take their breath away.

We can also design mini-lessons that help students move from gathering notebook entries to shaping their own literary work. These reasons for teaching mini-lessons correspond to the conference goals described in Chapter 12. When we weave our way around the classroom conferring with young writers, we often note issues worth working on with the entire class.

We don't have two separate lists of instructional objectives, one for mini-lessons, one for conferring. We need to simplify our thinking about these workshop structures. Sometimes we teach at whole-class meetings, sometimes we teach one on one, and sometimes we gather a small group of students together during workshop time. If information is worth sharing, it's worth sharing at any time.

Below, I've also listed the resources I rely on when I put together mini-lessons. I've included this list to highlight the wide-ranging possibilities available to writing teachers. For example, if I want to encourage rereading I might refer to my own experiences as a reader, a conference held with a student on his or her reading, or a story about rereading from a journal article. Likewise, if I want to help students explore publishing options I might look to other experts at school, students' finished work, or the literature students are reading.

Mini-Lessons . . . Many Resources
- Teachers' own experiences as a reader.
- Teachers' own experiences as a writer.

- School, community, and university experts.
- Students' notebooks, drafts, and finished work.
- Students' responses in booktalk sessions, conferences, and share meetings.
- A wide range of reference materials.
- A wide range of children's literature.

Mini-lessons that helped Amaury

I recently saw a performance of John Guare's play *Six Degrees of Separation*. There's a memorable moment when one of the characters asks a fabulous art teacher what her secret is. She explains that she has no secret; she simply knows when to take their paper away.

Sometimes we feel the same way. The children discover something important in their lives. They pack more and more around their seed idea, writing entry after entry. Then they begin to work toward a finished piece of writing. Sometimes when we see their finished work, we wish we had taken their papers away sooner or reminded them to include some of the lines we found so powerful.

But of course the challenge is for the young writer to know when to stop, how to shape and arrange the text with powerful lines.

When students in room 409 began discovering important topics on the pages of their writer's notebook, I knew it was time to shift my mini-lessons away from the activities at the top of the list and toward those listed in the middle (see page 280). It was time to help them cast their important ideas in literary ways. For a period of about two or three weeks, all mini-lessons were geared toward providing students with the strategies they would eventually need in order to take the material in their notebooks and turn it into works of art.

But the class was not studying any one topic. Amaury had invested his energy in the Dominican Republic. Najib was interested in stopping crime in his neighborhood. Jennifer was gathering thoughts about her best friend. Emil was exploring the love of baseball he shares with his dad. Some children hadn't yet found really important issues in their notebooks. Each day they continued to write on a wide variety of topics using a wide variety of writing styles.

Neither were these young writers studying any one genre at this point. Many of the students, in fact, had not as yet made any decision about which genre would best support their individual ideas and writing styles.

It is not surprising that the students needed new kinds of mini-lessons or that these echoed the questions on my conferring chart (Chapter 12). Sometimes we handled problems individually. Sometimes we explored an issue with the entire class. Frequently, an issue raised in an individual writing conference would spark ideas for whole-class lessons or an issue raised in a whole-class lesson would be fine tuned and reinforced as we conferred individually with students.

The new mini-lesson categories

Learning to take a deliberate stance toward writing.
Learning to appreciate the gems in your writer's notebook.
Learning to imagine genre possibilities.
Learning to make deliberate decisions about your writing.
Learning to study a genre on your own.

Taking a Deliberate Stance

One of the first things these fifth graders needed to know was that there is such a thing as deliberately trying to write well. People intentionally try to cast their words in literary ways. This kind of writing has a different feel than writing an entry in a notebook or recopying notes in better handwriting.

Several years ago we discovered that one of the reasons students were not making deliberate attempts to cast important pieces in literary ways is that we never let them know this is what we were hoping would happen. It hadn't occurred to us that we needed to announce it. Just as New York shopkeepers used to post little placards in their windows, "Aqui se habla espanol," (Spanish is spoken here), writing workshop teachers realized that perhaps students needed the message "Aqui se escribe la literatura" (Literature is written here).

Not all of our children come to us understanding that every once in a while, something matters to you so much you want to write about it in a way that it will move your readers. You want to write about it so well that your teacher can share it during read-aloud time and add it to the library shelf.

When children have a sense that they want to write well, there is a big payoff. They begin to live with the consciousness of a craftsperson, paying greater attention to share meetings, mentors, and mini-lessons.

A first-grade teacher I know launches her students in writing by taking them on a walking tour of the classroom. At each stop, she talks about the kind of writing the children might do. "On the bulletin boards you'll probably post announcements or messages, in the cooking center recipes and shopping lists, near the piano lyrics for songs, and you'll no doubt write letters to place in the class mailboxes." Then she dramatically enters the class library. "And here, you'll be doing a very, very special kind of writing." Her students understand early on that you do something different when it's a book for the library, when it's a book the teacher may read aloud to the class or a friend may borrow to take home.

Fifth graders need to have that same understanding. In *On the Teaching of Creative Writing,* Wallace Stegner speaks of the things a writing teacher can teach. He includes "literary tools and techniques and strategies and stances." Students need to know about that literary stance.

When students were about to begin their drafts, I decided to teach mini-lessons in which I laid bare the notion of literary stance. One morning I gathered students and I told them that I had recently bought a long black velvet cape—a Laura Ashley design—and that it was very expensive. "But," I explained, "I was able to get it at half-price because it was damaged. There was a large tear on the right shoulder." Then I said, "I was in such a hurry to wear my new cape I thought I would just buy some trimming to sew on both shoulders to hide the tear. That would be good enough. But then my mother came to visit. She thought long and hard. She turned the cape inside out. She examined the seams. She had me try the cape on. She measured the width of every panel. She toyed with different ideas. Then she gathered together the right tools—the perfect needle and the exact color of thread—and began. She made the cape just a little bit smaller, taking in seams on both shoulders with careful stitches, absolutely eliminating the tear. No one would know it had ever been there."

"My mother," I explained to the students, "takes her sewing very seriously. To her it's not worth doing if you don't try to do it well. She wants her finished work to be perfect, to be beautiful. Time and again I've heard her say, "It's as good as store-bought, even better."

I then asked the students if they know people or have had experiences themselves about which they have decided, "This time I'm going to do it splendidly instead of just any old way."

Mauricio talked of building a snowman. Every winter since his move from Ecuador to New York he has built a snowman. "But last year," he explained, "I wanted to build the biggest and the best on the block." It took all day and he had to search for just the right scarf, carrot, buttons, and stones. He even gave that snowman his own Yankee baseball cap. That's how special it was.

We heard about an aunt who polishes her finger nails but who for special occasions paints intricate designs and adds diamond studs. We heard about a father who prepares breakfast every day but who on Sunday morning makes fancy omelets filled with cheese, mushrooms, and tomatoes.

Then the children speculated on how people work when they want to do something special and not just any old way. How do people work when they want the Sunday morning breakfast feel and not the everyday breakfast feel? You don't mend an elegant garment with a hasty patch. Nor do you write well by hastily fixing up a quick draft, adding a lead here, a few details there. Instead, you write well by positioning yourself to write well. It begins with intention: "Today I want to write a fine picture book, one that will move my readers."

The next day we shifted to creating great stories. We talked about how it feels to sit at your desk, knowing you want to do your best work ever. The room filled with voices. We swapped stories, recalling our best work from years past. Stacey's was a poem from second grade. Jorge's was a sports column for the school newspaper. Miranda's was a picture book about her grandfather's garden.

I told the students a story about my colleague Joan Backer, who excitedly told me how she had changed as a writer. "I had this surprising urge over the weekend. I was about to write a quick bon voyage note to a friend and it hit me, I could try to write a really fine note. While my friend was vacationing, I was having dental surgery and so I began fiddling with this line: 'While you're sailing on the Chesapeake Bay, I'll be sitting here with chipmunk cheeks and ice packs.' It took me much longer to write that note, but it felt great to drop it into the mailbox."

I also read the students a letter I had recently written. "At first," I explained, "I was planning to write a quick memo to remind colleagues of an upcoming meeting. Instead, I decided to write a letter that matched the literary occasion it was announcing."

Dear Reading Circle Leader,
Summer was made for those who love to read. Aboard a train to Stockholm I delighted in Oscar Hijuelos's *The Mambo Kings Play Songs of Love* and on a flight from Fort Worth I discovered Lee Smith's *Oral History*. On my back porch I got lost in Wallace Stegner's *Crossing to Safety* and Lois Lowry's Newbery winner, *Number the Stars*. Everywhere I traveled, I asked people what they were reading. I've got titles, and authors and stories to share. And of course, you do too.

We're hoping that you'll mark your calendar and plan to be with us at Teachers College all day Thursday October 18th beginning at 9:00 in the morning. Karla Kuskin, the joyful poet and writer of picture books, will be with us as we explore her content and craft and look closely at the world of reading-writing connections.

Our group of booktalk leaders will remain at 2:30 when the larger crowd leaves. We'll then have time to swap our titles and authors and stories, to snack on strawberries and champagne punch, and finally to have a more intimate gathering with Karla.

We're hoping you'll attend. After all, autumn too was made for those who love to read.

Please call the office to R.S.V.P. and let us know if you'd like to bring along another member of your reading circle.

See you then.

Sincerely,

Shelley

I told the children how pleased I was when friends told me that they liked my letter. I was glad I had worked a little bit harder.

We then talked about the kinds of things we remembered doing when we were determined to do a great job. We talked of rereading, of listening to that little voice in our heads, of choosing words carefully, selecting those that had just the right sound and meaning. We talked of taking extra time and not being satisfied with any old thing. We talked of bringing the Sunday morning breakfast feel to our writing.

Appreciating the Gems

Last year my friend Ruth Daniels described for me the scene as she was leaving school with her students for a class trip. The children had noticed that the schoolyard was a mess, strewn with broken bottles and burned newspapers. One girl called out to Ruth, "Hey Ms. Daniels, we should start a campaign to stop this literacy!"

Ruth knew the line was a gem. When I heard it, I agreed. I quickly imagined it as a tag line under a cartoon in a magazine for teachers. For me it didn't have the potential to be a poem or a picture book, it was clearly a cartoon caption.

Appreciating gems and then imagining what you might do with them are precisely what our students need to do if they're to turn notebook entries into fine writing.

One Thursday morning Martha Serpas, a poet and member of our staff, reminded us that poets are particularly tuned in to recognizing gems. The staff was interested in learning some conversational Spanish so they could speak with more of our city kids. I brought in a very old booklet that had been given to me when I first began teaching in New York City twenty-four years ago. It was an alphabetical list of so-called "useful" English teaching expressions with their Spanish equivalents: Don't forget—No te olvides, Don't run—No corras.

We sat browsing through the pages, commenting on the rather didactic and harsh tone and practicing some of the more useful expressions.

Martha interrupted, "Listen to this poem I found." She read the following alphabetical list of "Don'ts," then paused and read, "Erase it." Martha had found a poem.

- Don't forget.   No te olvides.
- Don't go now.   No vayas ahora.
- Don't hit him.   No le des.
- Don't jump.   No brinques.
- Don't push.   No empujes.

- Don't run.   No corras.
- Don't shout.   No grites.
- Don't speak Spanish.   No hables español.
- Don't touch.   No toques.

- Erase it.   Bórralo.

Writers' ears and eyes seem to be constantly tuned to recognizing unexpected and powerful language and thought. Children who write need that same sensitivity.

Of course, if you've ever listened to young children swap jokes, you realize that what touches children is not always the same as what touches adults. And what resonates for us doesn't always resonate for them. One day a group of teachers joined me as I invited youngsters to talk about the settings of their pieces. We talked about how just the right detail can help the reader really get a feel of the place. Irvin, a child from the Dominican Republic, offered this detail: "Bumpy roads and abandoned babies." The visiting teachers all sighed at the same time.

For them this was an incredibly powerful line. Many of us would have given a day's pay to have written it. Irvin, on the other hand, didn't even realize he had said something special. I paused to explain to Irvin and his classmates why this line touched the adults so deeply. We responded deeply and personally to the poverty in his country and at the same time we admired the shock of putting babies next to bumpy roads, the strong image, and the sound of all those *b*'s next to one another.

Although I think it was appropriate to let the children know why the adults admired that line, I think it is more important for them to have the opportunity to select their own gems and explain their choices.

One day I began an extended mini-lesson period by inviting a student to read aloud several notebook pages. Just for fun, the other children would point out lines, images, or anecdotes that stood out for them. Kerstin volunteered. Kerstin had gone to the orthodontist a week before Christmas to have her bands tightened. "What color rubber bands do you want?" the doctor asked. "I don't care," said Kerstin, "Rubber bands are rubber bands." When Kerstin arrived home and greeted her mom, the look on her mom's face told her something was wrong. She ran to the mirror. In honor of the holiday, the doctor had filled her smile with alternating bands of red and green. Many children agreed that her orthodontist entry had "precious gem" status.

It was a gem of an entry. The children loved the topic. They loved her surprise ending. They loved the dialogue between Kerstin and her doctor. Perhaps most of all they loved peering into Kerstin's mouth.

On another day, knowing that the students had recently spent a week with a substitute teacher and that children pay unbelievably close attention to substitute teachers, I asked the children as they sat gathered in the meeting area to jot down in their notebooks as full a description as they could. (It had become customary to bring notebooks and pencils to all mini-lessons. If these short gatherings are to be more interactive, if children are to respond to the information presented and attempt to bring the information to their own composing, their notebooks need to be close at hand.) Then the children reread their jottings and were invited to put lines that stood out on the chalkboard. Among the gems they listed were "straight, wild hair," "shoes that go clunk," "hollers like crazy," "winter brown eyes," and "always joking 'Don't call me a hairy monster.'"

Amaury and his classmates had lots of practice in appreciating the gems in classmates' writing and in professional texts, so they felt more at home doing the same with their own writing.

Early on after Amaury had decided to write a picture book, he sifted through his notebook pages, underlining, circling, and starring the lines and passages that stood out, the ones he thought had potential, and the ones too good to pass up. He learned to cup his hands around the powerful lines in his notebook, the ones most appropriate for the picture book he had in mind. He was able to sense that there was something special about a "grandfather who names cows after kids," that "green jumping lizards" was vivid, and that "a park with room enough for a ferris wheel" was evocative. He was able to decide that "mangoes, coconuts, and papayas" should somehow be included. Many children did not choose a genre so early or so readily. Some began by selecting their best material and then wondered which genre would be most appropriate. But all students needed to be able to imagine the world of possibilities.

Imagining the Possibilities

Children not only need experience in recognizing and appreciating the gold in their notebooks, they also need to know that those nuggets have rich potential. Just as gold can be turned into earrings and pendants and necklaces, notebook entries and combinations of entries could be turned into poems and letters and picturebooks.

I live in an old sea captain's house on a beach at the southernmost tip of New York City. When I bought the house it wasn't even grounded for electricity. The walls were covered with century-old peeling, cracking wallpaper, and the rooms were filled with dark, heavy furniture. And yet I thought it had potential. I could imagine the possibilities for every room. I was only able to do this because I had an image of wonderful old houses in my mind. For years I had been taking house tours, reading magazines and attending slide shows.

If children are to be able to imagine what a writer might do with an anecdote about a little girl with a mouth full of green and red rubber bands or with pages of entries about life in the Dominican Republic, they need an internalized sense of options. If I needed an ideal home in my mind's eye, writers need what Dorothy Barnhouse calls an ideal text.

Of course children who read fine literature over and over and who are read aloud to again and again are constantly building in a sense of options and gathering ideal texts. At the same time, young writers need to be convinced that the bits and pieces in their notebooks can indeed be turned into literature. They need to believe that their loose thoughts and unfinished passages can be turned into splendid works of art.

In *The Way to Write for Children* Joan Aiken comments, "Very soon, you will have found that selecting the germinal idea is no problem. But then what? One idea on its own is not enough." We spent a lot of time, orally and often collaboratively, pitching in to take a student or teacher gem and work it through in a parlor-game spirit, just for the fun of it.

Kerstin donated her orthodontist story to the class pot. She had no intention of writing about this issue so she offered it to the class, and we played with it. I began one mini-lesson by asking the students, "What if you made Kerstin's braces anecdote into a work for the library shelf? Do you see it as a poem, a play, a picture book, a nonfiction text, a newspaper article?" The students thought a picture book seemed most appropriate. This first time, I started them off. "Once upon a time, there was a village with no Christmas spirit. No one decorated their windows, no one baked cookies, no one exchanged gifts. One day a new little girl came to town. She looked like an ordinary little girl. Well almost . . ."

The students quickly took over. "I know," Emil, called out, "That's gonna be the girl with the red and green things on her teeth." "Yeah," said Stacey, "and she's gonna give the holiday spirit to people whenever she smiles." "Yeah, some magic power," added Javier.

It's amazing how writer's block disappears when you're fiddling with someone else's ideas. Students who were reluctant to take risks took risks. Students who rarely spoke pitched in. Nothing was written or evaluated. Students were learning to do in a friendly community what they needed to learn to do on their own. They were learning to do orally what they would later do in writing. To turn material into story without simultaneously worrying about spelling and handwriting was a real comfort, particularly to struggling children. Children propelled one another and the story forward. Their voices kept those silent and scary composing moments, those "I give up, this is too hard for me," moments from paralyzing these young writers.

They began to see telling a good story as within their reach. They began to see writing well as within their reach. The storyteller's voice helped them maintain their literary stance.

Other mini-lessons also helped children imagine how they might develop seed ideas.

We played a quick searching game, "Who's got an entry you could imagine as a letter to someone? A poem to be read at a wedding? A newspaper article?" Children read their entry and talked through its development.

We used issues of *Cricket* magazine to help explore possibilities. Children came to the meeting area carrying their notebooks and an issue of the magazine. Each issue is usually devoted to a particular topic, thereby demonstrating the many ways writers have chosen to write about cats or spring or flight or dragons. During the mini-lesson children were asked to speculate on which of the genres in their magazine might also be appropriate for the topics they were discovering in their notebooks. (For this mini-lesson to be effective, students must come prepared.)

Sophia listed the genres she found in an issue of *Cricket* devoted to insects. She then starred those she thought would be appropriate for conveying her thoughts about her mother (Figure 93).

We showed several texts in which the writer had taken traditional tales and tried them in new forms, like *Belling the Cat and Other Aesop's Fables,* retold in verse by Tom Paxton, Gwen Straus's *Trail of Stones,* in which fairy tales appear in verse, *Jack and the Beanstalk* retold in verse by Beatrice Schenk de Regniers. We then talked through the possibilities of turning poems or newspaper articles into picture books and picture books or novels into plays.

We asked children to select one entry and attempt to recast it quickly in several forms. (Again, students prepared for this mini-lesson in advance, as a homework assignment.)

FIGURE 93

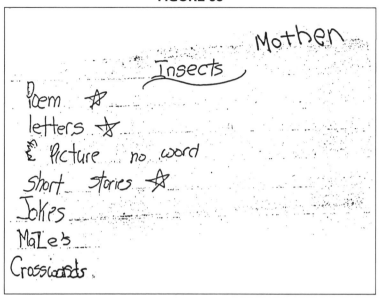

Danielle began with an entry about mistakenly pruning her mother's in-
door plants (Figure 94). She turned this entry into an apology note, a poem, and
a short skit.

After we heard her three pieces we asked Danielle to evaluate her efforts.
Which genres seemed more appropriate? Which best conveyed her meaning?
Which altered her meaning? Which genre would she like to study further?

We spent a great deal of mini-lesson time playfully experimenting together. We
imagined possibilities for the entries young writers tossed into the class grab-bag
as giveaways. But we also helped writers think through possibilities for the pieces
they were determined to write.

Mini-lessons began to resemble share meetings. One student sat in the
author's chair seeking help from other writers. Sometimes their problems were
small and uncomplicated. Kaity sat in the author's chair one morning and read an
entry from her notebook. She didn't know what to do with it. "It's so funny," she
began, "I think I should do something with it, but it's little, it's not a real project."
Kaity's entry captured some family conversation. She was sitting in the backseat
of the family car with her young brother begging her parents to buy her an Apple,
meaning a computer. Her brother interrupted, "No, buy a watermelon." One
student suggested that Kaity begin a special collection of funny things her brother
says as a surprise present for when he grows up. Another suggested that she try
to write a funny poem à la Jack Prelutsky or Shel Silverstein. Kaity finally decided
to turn her entry into a caption for a drawing contest (Figure 95).

Some students required more help. When a student said, "This is really important to me. I have all these entries and I don't know what to do with them," we
devoted mini-lesson time to helping them think through their possible options.
Occasionally a struggling reader and writer would take the author's chair and then
we also lingered just a bit to help get them started.

FIGURE 94

I remember when I was small. I was only 5 years old. I was watching my mother cut the bushes outside. I took the sciccors from the junk draw and started cutting the leaves off my mothers plants. When my mother came in and saw all these leaves on the floor she got mad. She put every single leaf in a cup and she had all these cups around the house. She took the sciccors away from me and went downstairs in the basement and went into the backyard. She saw her neighbor with his weed cutter cutting down the weeds. My mother asked Bill if she could cut the weeds for him. He said sure. My mother started cutting the weeds. When my father came home he told him that I cut my mothers plants and that she was doing this to get the angen out of her!

FIGURE 94, continued

Cut!
Cut!
Cut!
Look there are 3 leaves on the floor

Cut!
Cut!
Cut!
Look there are more leaves on the floor.

Cut!
Cut!
Cut!
Better clean it up before mom gets mad

Cut!
Cut!
Cut!
Oh, no! clean it up quick

Cut!
Cut!
Cut!
You're grounded for the rest of your life

FIGURE 94, continued

Setting: I am living
room with my
mother, and I me.
I had just cut
my mothers plants.
I am as asking
my mom if I
did anything
bad and She keeps
on nodding.

me and mother

_____

skit
Me: Did I do anything bad?
Mom: Yes you did. Look
at these _____.
Me: Who cut all those bars?
Mom: You did!
Me: I am sorry. Can I glue
them back together again.
Mom: No you can't, but
you can go into your
room and stay there
till you are 9.
Me: Mom you don't mean
that!
Mom: Of course
I don't. Just stay
there till you
are 21.
Me: MOM!

FIGURE 95

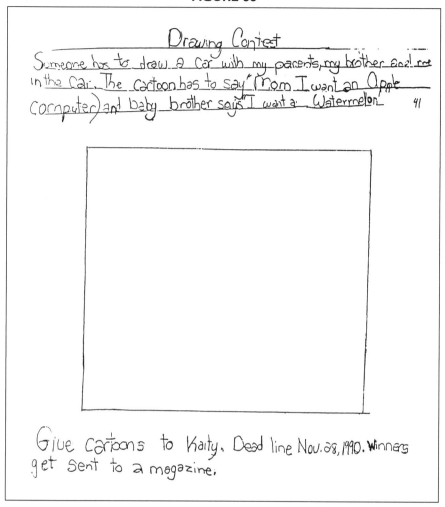

Drawing Contest

Someone has to draw a car with my parents, my brother and me in the car. The cartoon has to say "Mom I want an Apple computer) and baby brother says "I want a Watermelon." 4l

Give cartoons to Kaity. Dead line Nov. 28, 1990. Winners get sent to a magazine.

James was one such student. He had written a great deal about feeling like a loser in baseball. He told us that he's always on the losing team and that his team often loses in the last inning. James began by sharing a few entries. He had added little stick on flags to the pages in his notebook he wanted to read so he didn't have to spent a great deal of time flipping back and forth trying to find his material.

When James was finished, Barry asked, "What kinds of writing do you like?" His answer was "rap songs and picture books." "Could you write about losing baseball games in those ways?" Barry asked. James wasn't sure. "Perhaps we can help you get started," I suggested.

As students snapped their fingers, James began to composed a rap song: "When your team / does always lose / You go home with / the baseball blues." Students' comments and contributions kept James from giving up. Their enthusiasm added energy to his efforts.

James needed safety nets around his composing. Finger-snapping was all he needed for his rap song, but the picture book required a little more help. He quickly reread his selected notebook pages. Then I suggested that he put away his notes and handed him a library book as a prop. "Can you begin to tell us your story? Pretend it's a book in the library. Turn the pages as you go."

James began, "Long ago, last summer / there was a boy named James / who had fuzzy hair / and a big Afro." James turned the page of his prop book. A dog appeared in the illustration and in order to keep his story going he wove a dog into his own baseball-defeat story. "He had a dog named David that played catch with him. He always went to the park and played with his dog. One day he joined the San Francisco sluggers. They had the worst record in Little League history. Then his dog David gets hit by a car and he dies."

James stopped. His classmates' questions helped him continue. "What does the dog have to do with it?" "What about the last-inning stuff?" James hedged a little and Tyrone helped him out. "What if he hears the bad news right before he gets up to hit in the ninth inning?" "Yeah," James went on. "Then I could hit a home run in honor of his memory."

With this workable story in mind, James and his classmates were willing to pause and wonder which parts needed to be slowed down and which quickened. "If the dog's death is going to make such a drastic change in James," I wondered aloud, "will the reader have to be more convinced that his love for his dog was so strong? Is that part developed enough?"

"You could add more old memories of the boy and the dog together." Barry suggested. "Yeah," James replied, "I could put in more of the good things they did together."

James left the meeting area determined to write his picture book text. He'll not only need to weave his baseball entries into this new story he's created, he'll need to add some "boy loves dog" images. It was a big challenge and yet James seemed eager to meet it. His friends were in on the plans, and he didn't want to disappoint them.

Will James feel complete ownership or authorship of his finished picture book? At this point in his writing life, the belief that his seed ideas are worthy and the experience of joyfully reworking these ideas within a supportive community seemed more important than total individual ownership. Having a successful finished piece, even one that required a little help from his friends, seems better than having no finished piece at all.

This lesson was valuable not only for James, but also for the thirty other children who participated. What they were doing collaboratively they would eventually need to learn to do on their own. They would need to spread out their entries and reread them asking "What might I do with all of this? Would a poem be appropriate? A picture book? A letter? All three?"

Making Deliberate Decisions

Children need to imagine possible genres for their writing projects, but they also need to know how to move their thoughts toward the ideal text they have in mind.

Once writers make the deliberate decision to cast something in a literary way, they continue to make conscious and deliberate decisions about language and form and style because those choices will enhance what they're trying to say. Writers reread their work critically looking for moments of possibility. Revision is filled with deliberate decisions.

Musical arrangers deliberately choose brass when they want to add power to a piece, flute for speed, or strings for romance, so too young writers need to know what is available to them.

Choosing between the present tense and past tense is a deliberate choice. So is choosing short clipped sentences over long meandering ones, or a first-person narrator over an omniscient one.

Young writers also need to know that they're allowed to stretch and highlight and eliminate and exaggerate and substitute and tighten and manipulate their language and their material to create the effect they're after. Amaury needs to know that it's okay to take his strong line about the big blue splashes of water and use it about the river even though it was about the view from the airplane, that it's okay to use a poem as your grandma's shopping list. He needs to feel free to take unrelated events and make them seem as if they had all happened on the same day. All these decisions enhanced his meaning and conveyed the precise feeling he was after.

The children in Antoinette's classroom needed to know about poetic license and the artistic pause. They needed to know that the material in their notebook is malleable and that writers are decision makers.

The children knew I was writing about them. Every once in a while I read aloud a draft I was working on. One day during mini-lesson time I shared an excerpt from Chapter 2 on reading aloud.

> Each time I read aloud I lit a candle. It was a mushroom-shaped candle covered with an intricate African pattern in deep reds and blues. The shopkeeper in Johannesburg told me that as it melts and the light shines through, it will be as beautiful as a Tiffany lamp. I explained to the fifth graders "the candle will help create the magical and mystical aura that reading aloud deserves."

> I can recall only one day when the student's attention wandered as I read aloud. It wasn't quite ten-thirty in the morning, but the still summery weather quickly withered us as we sat cross-legged, clammy shoulder to clammy shoulder, in the back of the room. I felt my shirt sticking to my back and I began wishing I hadn't worn stockings. The children, dressed in their new school clothes—bright sweatshirts and stiff new jeans—started to use their notebooks as fans. I knew it was time to blow out the candle and take a break.
> I brought out a small, ragged, black book. "Is it your Bible?" the children asked. "No, but it is a special book. It's where I keep the poems I love."

The children smiled and nodded with recognition. They were flattered. The room filled with lots of "Yeah, I remember that." But I think there was something else going on. Because the children had lived through the scene I had described there seemed to be an extra dimension to the experience in hearing me tell about it.

Perhaps it's like attending a World Series game or opening night of a Broadway play and then reading about it in the next day's newspaper. It was as if my draft were a second draft for them. They had lived through draft one. It was a concrete way of helping them to see that writers take their material and intentionally try to shape it in literary ways. When Amaury appreciates how sitting at the back of the classroom can be captured on paper, he's beginning to understand what's available to him as he tries to capture a day with his grandparents in the Dominican Republic.

The students knew I didn't settle for any old thing that popped into my head. They understood that I worked at the sounds, the details, the tone. They came to appreciate inside their bones that writers omit and fudge, twist and highlight, slow down and speed up. In fact, at one point, a student asked, "Who said, 'Is it your Bible?'" The truth was—a child in the class next door. "You're allowed to do that? You're allowed to make it seem like it happened here?" The students learned that writers call upon a host of tools to convey their meaning, to create the effect they're looking for.

During another mini-lesson, I told students that I make a deliberate choice when I dress for a speech or a workshop. I'd never wear jeans when I deliver a carefully written keynote, nor would I wear high heels at a hands-on workshop. For me, the presentation wouldn't be the same. It wouldn't feel right. When a writer writes in a particular style it's a deliberate choice. It adds to the meaning. A different style would make a different piece.

I then shared with the fifth graders the labyrinthine Linda Rief published in the September 1990 issue of *Language Arts*. I displayed it on the overhead so they could see the form.

> My husband asks me why I have to go into school sometimes on Sundays to prepare for the week to come because he doesn't understand that I believe the curriculum comes from the kids and not off some ditto sheets to be handed out year after year which is probably why he brings me home a gift which is a book entitled The One-Minute Teacher which he thinks will cut down considerably on the time I spend in the classroom so I'll have more time to iron the shirts I sprinkled and put in the refrigerator three years ago because that's what my grandmother taught me to do with 100% cotton shirts that have to be ironed but they've been in the refrigerator so long no one is sure anymore what the green fuzzy lump is in the plastic bag and all of us are too afraid to open it because the last time I stuck my hand in a plastic bag to find out what it was it was a dead chicken my son had refrigerated so he could take it over to the pathology lab at UNH to find our why the chicken died and to see if it would infect the rest of his flock which in some cases probably wouldn't be such a bad idea because the neighbors are getting a little irate at the rooster that has stationed himself in our pine tree and cock-a-doodle-doos day and night which I'm sure is why one neighbor called at 3 a.m. and said "If you don't shut that rooster up, I'll do it for you" to which I said "Please do" because it isn't ours as the man who delivers wood left the rooster with the logs even though we told him we didn't want any more roosters and we can't catch him and shut him up either and the rooster is keeping us from sleeping too which is making me too tired to iron the shirts which are still in the refrigerator. . . .

Linda wrote in a long meandering rush ideally suited to her state of mind. In this one long sentence one surprising idea spills into the next surprising idea. "Would it be as effective if she wrote it in a more conventional way? Would it be the same piece?" I asked the students.

Working with fourth-grade teacher Isoke Nia, Vicki Vinton helped children understand the deliberate decisions writers make by sharing two of John Steptoe's popular picture books, *Mufaro's Beautiful Daughters* and *Stevie*. The children could see that the writing in the two books was markedly different. Their teachers helped them realize that neither book could have been written any other way and still achieve the same effect. Steptoe intentionally chose the form and style that supported his content.

The children in Antoinette's classroom had an open invitation to share several works by one writer that showed a diversity of styles. This is very different from the way they used author studies (Chapter 9). There, similarities in style across an author's works enabled children to pay more attention to literary techniques.

One day, Javier brought in two poems by Jack Prelutsky. He suggested that the poet deliberately matched the form to the content of the poems.

Twaddletalk Tuck

I'm Twaddletalk Tuck and I talk and I talk
and I talk when I run and I talk when I walk
and I talk when I hop and I talk when I creep
and I talk when I wake and I talk when I sleep
and I talk when it's wet and I talk when it's dry
and I talk when I laugh and I talk when I cry
and I talk when I jump and I talk when I land
and I talk when I sit and I talk when I stand
and I talk and I talk into anyone's ear
and I talk and I talk when there's nobody near
and I talk when I'm hoarse and my voice is a squawk
for I'm Twaddletalk Tuck and I talk and I talk.

Slow Sloth's Slow Song

I . . . . am . . . . a . . . . . . sloth . . . .
a . . . . sloth . . . . am . . . . I . . . .
I . . . . live . . . . in . . . . trees . . . .
But . . . . I . . . . can't . . . . fly . . . .
I . . . . do . . . . not . . . . run . . . .
I . . . . am . . . . so . . . . slow . . . .
But . . . . I . . . . am . . . . where . . . .
I . . . . want . . . . to . . . . go.

The other students agreed. A poem about a slow sloth should have short, spread out words. A poem about talking too much should have long, repetitive, squashed together lines. If the poet had written them differently they wouldn't have the same effect. They'd be different poems.

Our files of background materials on authors also provided ideas for teaching mini-lessons on making deliberate decisions when you write. Author interviews, profiles, book reviews, publicity blurbs, and journal articles often include a writer's explanation of the choices he or she has made.

After several of the students had read Randall Jarrell's *Animal Family,* illustrated by Maurice Sendak, I shared an excerpt from an article by Sally Holmes Holtze in *The Horn Book Magazine:* "Sendak and Jarrell decided to place the text in small, contained blocks at the center of the page; the words would look like a tight little island . . . surrounded by extremely wide, white margins, representing the world outside. The squarish, fat shape of the book itself became the family's little house." This served as a fine example of the deliberate decisions writers make to enhance their meaning.

The children also needed to recognize the different ways writers manipulate language in order to create certain effects. They were fascinated to learn about the power of the present tense. I shared with them Sarah Ellis's findings about the use of the present tense in another article from *The Horn Book Magazine*. She writes that the present tense creates an immediacy, a rhetorical quality, a dreamlike, mystical effect and quotes Ben Yagoda: "To describe an event in the past tense means taking a kind of responsibility for it." The present tense creates "the illusion of pure objectivity." Ten-year-olds were not too young to understand Ellis's conclusion: "The past tense seems to say, 'This particular thing happened and I will tell you about it.' The present tense seems to say, 'Things happen.'"

Yet another way I showed students that the choices writers make really do make a difference involved a bit of "What if?" exploration. The students had read and reread Cynthia Rylant's *The Relatives Came*. We talked about her careful choice of words. Grapes, for example, seemed the perfect fruit to recur throughout the text since they come in bunches, like big families. We talked about her long, long sentences, which make readers feel as if they're taking a long, long journey. We talked about how Rylant uses the same words and phrases at the beginning and at the end and how that seems to comfort the reader and provide a satisfying shape to the book. It feels as if you're returning home, going over familiar ground. Then we thought about some "What if?" scenarios. What if Rylant had used apples instead of grapes? What if she had used short choppy sentences? What if she hadn't repeated any images?

A final way I demonstrated the power of an author's decisions involved biographies. I challenged students to read several biographies about the same famous person over a long holiday break and jot down the distinct choices that the individual authors made. The students' notes provided a week's worth of mini-lessons on the use of time, anecdotes, quotations, tense, point of view, and description.

The Place of Genre Study

Over the last several years I have seen an incredible number of student take-offs on Cynthia Rylant's Caldecott honor book, *When I Was Young in the Mountains*. The titles vary only slightly, "When I Was Young in Puerto Rico," "When I Was Young in Coney Island," "When I Was Young Down South." These young writers haven't necessarily studied the picture book genre. Rather they've studied this one particular picture book. It calls out to be imitated. Just as certain writers are accessible because their writing has very distinctive features (see Chapter 9), certain individual texts are also accessible because they have very distinctive features. The students quickly grasp the shape of the whole text and the repeated refrain, "When I was young in the mountains." They understand the series of vignettes, snapshots almost, which follow one after the other. The students in turn, take memories from their own childhoods and thread them together with a repeated refrain. Somehow their writing is more successful than usual.

Children frequently choose to borrow language patterns from individual picture books, such as Bill Martin, Jr.'s *Brown Bear, Brown Bear* or Judith Viorst's *Alexander and the Terrible, Horrible, No Good, Very Bad Day*. This kind of borrowing is sometimes successful, although it can also result in rather strained efforts, particularly if the entire class feels obliged to use the same form no matter what they are writing about. As Frank Smith points out, "children learn what is demonstrated." The demonstrations provided by the authors of these books are particularly loud and clear. The children can't help but notice their distinctive features and think, "I can do that."

The "I can do that" feeling is very important in our reading-writing workshops. Children need to believe that they're growing as writers, that they're learning new things. They need to feel proud of their work. The "I can do that" feeling can stem from several sources in a writing workshop. A student looks at an individual title and senses, "I can write a book like that." A student looks at an entire body of work by an author and thinks, "I can write like her." Or a student comes across a new mode of writing and senses, "That one is for me. I'm going to try that."

One of the reasons we've long been advocates of genre studies at the Writing Project is a strong belief that in any one writing workshop children need lots of ways to be excellent. The child who struggles with personal narrative can shine as a poet.

But not all genres are easily accessible to young writers. The formal study of memoirs, picture books, and various nonfiction genres often require several weeks or months of intense work. Many forms of poetry also require this deep study.

And yet, when the children in room 409 began moving out of their notebooks during the first few months of school and into self-chosen writing projects, we knew a multitude of genres would be sprouting everywhere. We guessed that the children would be attempting personal narratives, letters, and picture books as well as poetry.

As I've already mentioned, Antoinette and I made some promises. We would invite students to return to old pieces when we studied genres more formally later in the year. We would surround children with fine literature in every genre and arrange for them to meet with others interested in the same forms. We also promised to devote mini-lesson time to supporting students' efforts.

Paving the Way for New Genres

We had begun the year looking at genres rather playfully. I was determined to convince students that they could succeed at learning new modes. True to the parlor-game spirit, I invited students to fool around with some short, accessible forms.

One day as a mini-lesson we played that old paper and pencil game, Dictionary. I selected the word *mulligatawny*. I read the real definition along with two I had made up: "a curry-flavored soup of East Indian origin; a small squeaky voiced bird found in marshlands; and a man's three-cornered hat worn on festival days in Northern Ireland." After several rounds of guessing and then revealing the true meaning, I invited students to have a turn. We picked difficult words, and students tried to fool their friends by writing dictionary-like definitions. They very quickly got the "dictionary definition genre" down pat.

On another day I entertained them with the attempts of some very young students to write math word problems. Their favorite one was written by Charles (Figure 96). We talked about why these word problems sounded like the ones they recalled from their workbook days and they eagerly composed their own out loud.

We also had fun with "back of the book blurbs." I shared several written by professional authors and some written by former students. We talked about the

FIGURE 96

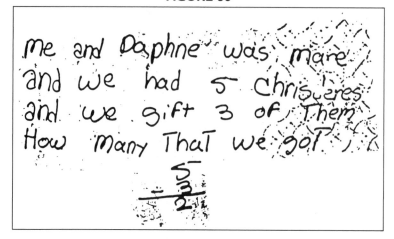

me and Daphne was mare
and we had 5 chrisveres
and we gift 3 of Them
How many ThaT we got

$$\frac{5}{\begin{array}{r}-3\\\hline 2\end{array}}$$

FIGURE 97

This book is about two
girls that were always
best friends until
One of them had to
move. You'll find out
the rest of the story
in this book.

Oh, Kelly would you stop
crying Susie said. Why
is Kelly crying? Find out
when you read the
book!

This book is about
Kara and Janine
doing many things
together. Kara
walks her dog
and Janine asked
if she could walk
the dog too. Are
they going to take
a chance a piece?

form, content, and purpose of this short genre. I then invited students to bring in
finished pieces from years past and to compose a quick blurb. Figure 97 illustrates
several examples.

When children tried their hand at dictionary definitions, math problems, and
back-of-the-book blurbs, they were not being asked to use their notebook material
at all. Yes, they were being challenged to follow new formats, and yes, they felt
good about their attempts. But more was needed if they were to learn how to
shape their notebook material into desired forms. So I challenged students with
several additional short and easily accessible forms of writing that allowed them to
dip into their notebook pages for material.

We started with About the Author pages. We talked about the difference between saying something in a flat, predictable way and saying something in a fresh, unexpected way. We all talked about moments in our lives when we had been struck by the way people spoke: by a unique telephone greeting rather than "hello," by a subway conductor's new way of announcing stops, and by the flight attendant who made us really pay attention to safety procedures.

We then invited students to search the library for unusual, well-written About the Author pages, avoiding those that contained bland paragraphs telling where the author lived and a listing of other books.

The students loved Vera B. Williams and Jennifer Williams's author page in *Stringbean's Trip to the Shining Sea.* They learned why the authors thought they could collaborate well. They also loved the book jacket notes in Lois Ehlert's *Fish Eyes,* which explain the roots of the author's interest in her topic and how she went about learning more about her topic. From the back page of Kay Chorao's *Cathedral Mouse* they realized that author notes can include sources of inspiration. From Leah Komaiko's *I Like the Music* they learned to add surprising personal bits of information. From Riki Levenson's *My Home is the Sea* they learned about the possibility of including direct quotes from the author.

The students made lists of the kinds of information that seemed appropriate for About the Author pages. They brought in old About the Author pages they had written in years past. They looked through their early notebook entries for bits of writing that might be included. They wrote short drafts. They learned to deal with constraints. (Some About the Author pages are text-specific. They were writing generic ones and not including information about how a particular book came to be.) They experimented with writing about themselves in the third person. Their final versions were mounted next to their photograph and placed on file for future publications.

Jennifer's first attempt is illustrated in Figure 98. She revised her blurb as shown in Figure 99.

FIGURE 98

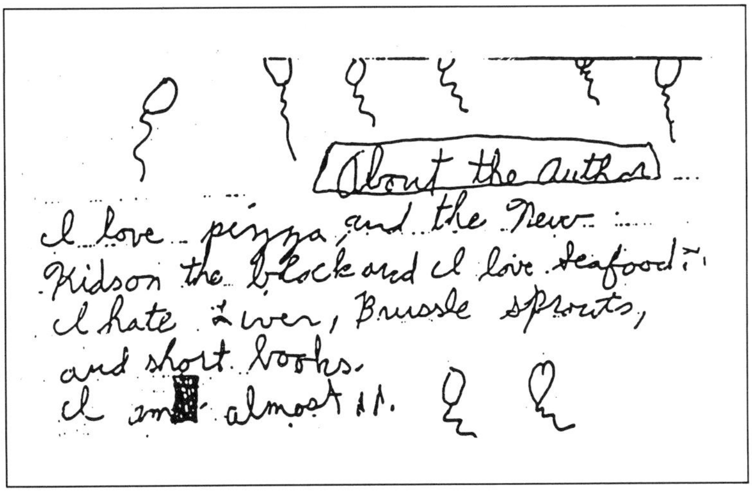

FIGURE 99

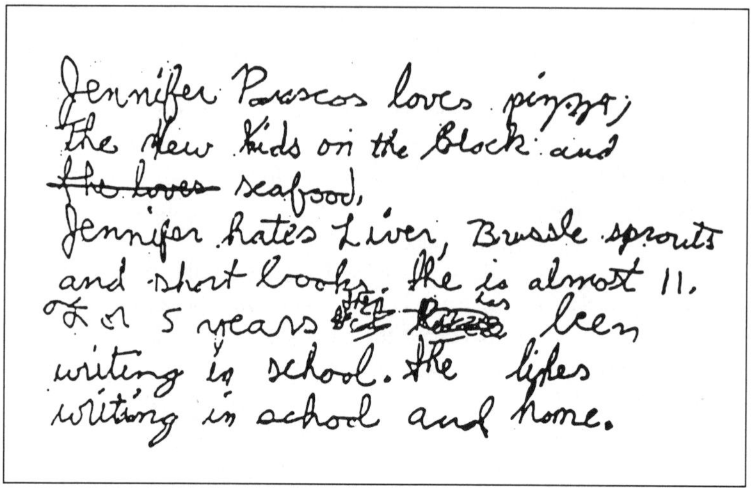

> Jennifer Pascos loves pizza,
> the new kids on the block and
> ~~he loves~~ seafood.
> Jennifer hates Liver, Brussle sprouts
> and short books. She is almost 11.
> For 5 years ~~she has~~ been
> writing in school. She likes
> writing in school and home.

FIGURE 100

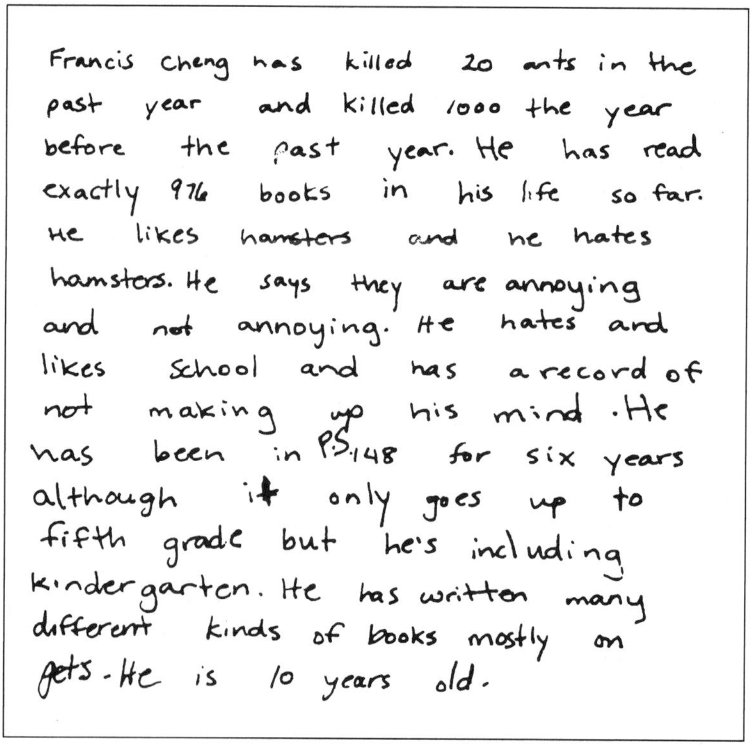

> Francis cheng has killed 20 ants in the
> past year and killed 1000 the year
> before the past year. He has read
> exactly 976 books in his life so far.
> He likes hamsters and he hates
> hamsters. He says they are annoying
> and not annoying. He hates and
> likes school and has a record of
> not making up his mind. He
> has been in P.S. 148 for six years
> although it only goes up to
> fifth grade but he's including
> kindergarten. He has written many
> different kinds of books mostly on
> pets. He is 10 years old.

Francis's About the Author page is shown in Figure 100.

This simple writing project gave students an early taste of making their own reading-writing connections. They studied a simple genre and abstracted the essence of that genre for their own use.

Other short and accessible genres that gave students real reasons to select and shape their notebook entries into finished works included letters to family and friends and classroom vignettes, short descriptive passages to be published in the school newspaper.

Most children feel at home writing letters. They think, you simply start with "Dear," and end with "Sincerely" or "Yours Truly." Practically anything goes in between. We began by sharing a few well-written letters (see p. 308). Then we encouraged students to reread their notebook pages searching for scenes and ideas that would make worthwhile letters. The letters they wrote were mailed to the real people to whom they were addressed.

Classroom vignettes were another form of writing children took to eagerly, although it required more demonstrations than letter writing. We explained that two or three vignettes might appear in each edition of a school newspaper to give the rest of the school a feel for what happens in room 409.

Again, we began by sharing well-written classroom scenes from literature. These included passages from Lois Lowry's *Autumn Street,* Beverly Cleary's *Muggie Maggie,* Eleanor Estes's *The Hundred Dresses,* Pam Conrad's *Staying Nine,* Kathryn Lasky's *Pageant,* and Eloise Greenfield's *Childtimes.* Students then reread their notebook pages searching for snapshots of classroom life.

Jennifer turned some comments about silent reading time into a vignette (Figure 101).

Benny had never written about school life in his writer's notebook, but he accepted the challenge of recording a classroom scene for the school newspaper. His description of an art lesson appears in Figure 102.

All the genres introduced to the children so far had been rather uncomplicated. Students could hold the image of the entire form in their mind's eye. There was a clear sense of "We can do that." They would have much more ambitious writing challenges later, but for now they needed this safety net.

When students begin the year with long, complicated writing projects before they've found their stride as writers, they often lose their energy and interest. They grow bored and unproductive. Dead, drawn-out writing projects can become the norm. What students need above all are successful, joyful experiences.

After these short forms, I shifted mini-lessons toward thinking through with students what to do if they wanted to learn a more formal genre on their own. I reminded the students how we had prepared to write those About the Author pages during the first weeks of school. We recalled searching for published examples we admired and listing the kinds of information that seemed appropriate. We then noted the techniques we admired and students searched for bits of notebook material they might use. Finally we began drafting our own.

We used mini-lesson time to run through how students might design their own course of study for different genres. Their suggestions included the following:

1. Read a lot in the genre.
2. Form a study group with other students interested in the same genre.
3. Meet to talk about your favorite reading selections.
4. Swap selections.
5. Ask the teacher for suggestions.
6. Find out if other people in the building are experts in the genre.
7. Try to figure out what makes the genre special.

8. List techniques you admire.
9. Try to use some of the techniques in your writing.
10. Confer with members of your study group.

A final reminder to children: "Whatever you've learned about good writing so far this year and in years past applies to all writing. Even though there are different traditions and conventions in poetry and letter-writing and newspaper articles, good writing is good writing."

FIGURE 101

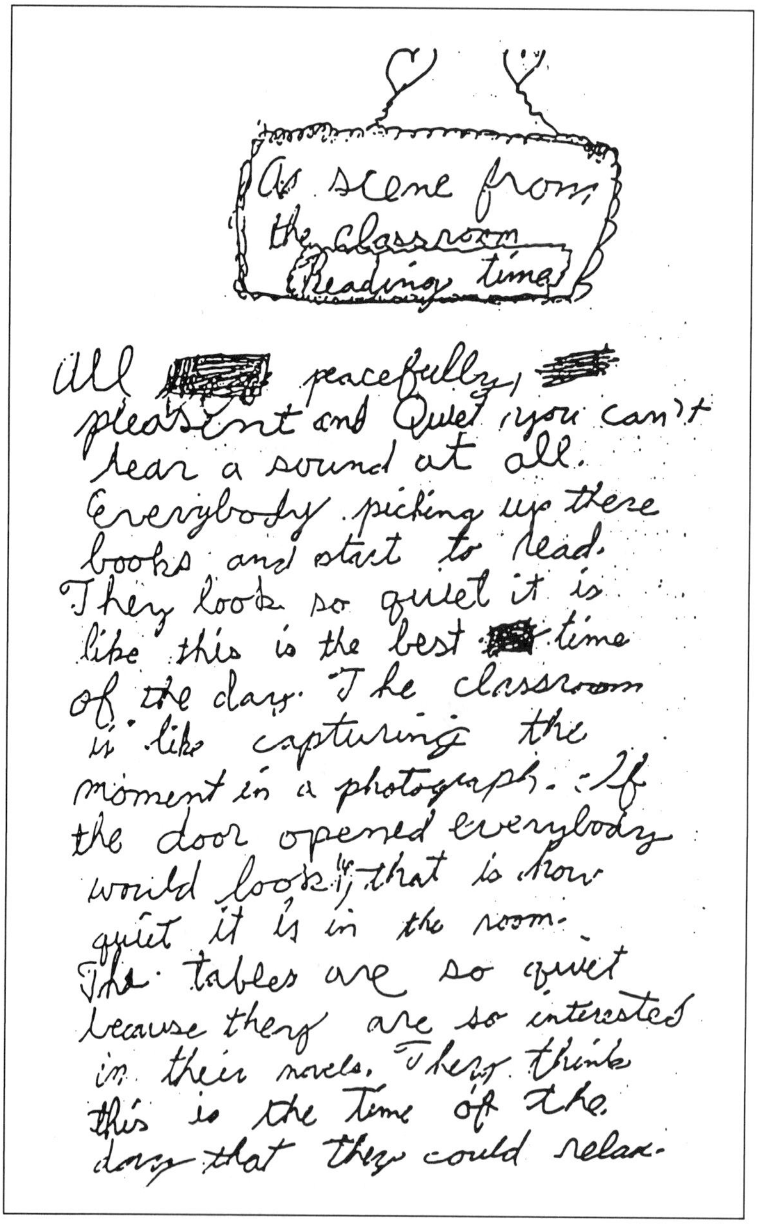

FIGURE 102

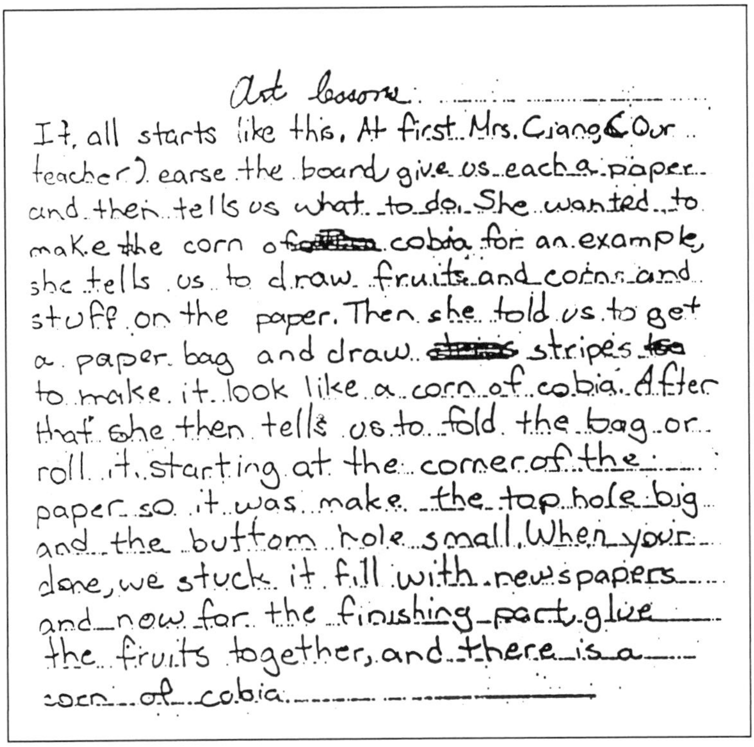

Art lesson:
It all starts like this. At first Mrs. Cjang (Our teacher) earse the board, give us each a paper and then tells us what to do. She wanted to make the corn of cobia for an example, she tells us to draw fruits and corns and stuff on the paper. Then she told us to get a paper bag and draw stripes to make it look like a corn of cobia. After that she then tells us to fold the bag or roll it starting at the corner of the paper so it was make the top hole big and the buttom hole small. When your done, we stuck it fill with newspapers and now for the finishing part glue the fruits together, and there is a corn of cobia.

A Genre Calendar

Over the course of the year, our fifth-graders studied genres according to an emerging schedule.

September October November	Open-ended/Self-chosen genres
December	Poetry
January February	Nonfiction genres
March	Poetry again
April May	Picture books
June	Open-ended/Self-chosen genres

In September, October, and November, no long, formal genre studies took place. Students were just getting to know one another, finding their stride as writers, and becoming invested in their notebooks and their topics. Genre-based mini-lessons were not geared toward any complicated or sophisticated genres but toward playing with shorter, less formal ones, and toward learning how to study a genre. During this time, students wrote short pieces in many different formats. The most popular genres early in the year were letters, simple poems, and short personal vignettes. Amaury wrote his six-page picture book as well as a simple poem and a letter to his grandparents (see Chapter 11).

In December the whole class studied poetry. Many of the children had written poetry in past years, so one month seemed to be enough for an initial return visit. We devoted mini-lesson time exclusively to poetry. Many students used their poems as part of holiday greetings or prepared them as gifts for friends.

January and February were devoted to nonfiction writing. Antoinette's students were immersed in multicultural ethnic studies. They produced family profiles, cookbooks, interviews, and newspaper articles.

In March, we once again returned to the study of poetry. There's much to be said for revisiting a genre during the same school year. My close friends know that I only invite them to one formal dinner party a year because I serve the same meal to guests throughout the year. Each September I design a new menu. Last year it included poached salmon with a dill sauce, stir-fried asparagus, rice pilaf, and a lemon poppy seed bread. I served that same meal five or six times, each time getting just a little bit better. Eventually, I perfect my shopping list, prepare just the right amounts, time everything exactly, choose the right wine, and know exactly which serving bowls to use. It's a very efficient and rewarding way to entertain. By the third or fourth party, I feel quite accomplished.

I've long believed that over a course of a year, genres also need another visit. Young writers feel quite proud and accomplished when they try their hand at writing poems in October, in March, and perhaps again in June. They can note breakthroughs, advances, and changes in style and technique when they look over their poems. They can see clearly how they're growing as poets.

There's also a lot to be said for working within one genre for several months. The pressure to cover the curriculum often keeps young writers from doing more than getting their feet wet. In April and May the students began a course of study on picture books. Many had studied this genre in third grade and again in fourth, so they brought a lot of information with them. We encouraged them to reread any picture books they had previously written, keeping possible new revisions in mind.

In June students used their notebooks to work toward self-chosen genres. Many opted for real-world writing—graduation speeches, invitations to parties, autograph verses, pen pal letters, thank-you notes, and pieces prepared as parting gifts.

Mini-Lessons

Reading-Writing Connections, With or Without Notebooks

Not all teachers invite students to keep a writer's notebook. There is no one way to run a successful writing workshop. But in all the writing workshops I visit, notebooks or not, all students are encouraged to take lessons from their reading. Whether students begin by keeping a writer's notebook or by filling folders with drafts or by engaging in class-wide thematic studies, it seems important that they know how to build bridges between what they read and what they write. Whether or not students keep a writer's notebook, it's important that they all position themselves to appreciate the strong parts of their writing, to imagine genre possibilities for their ideas, to learn to make deliberate decisions about their drafts, and to know how to go about studying a genre on their own.

Teachers throughout the grades devote lots of mini-lesson time to this world of reading-writing connections. These lessons need to be designed in response to our students' reading and writing. There is no guide called "1001 mini-lessons for every occasion." Each classroom is unique, and teachers tailor their lessons to meet their students needs. What we decide to teach in a mini-lesson depends on what we see happening in our classrooms. We read students' writing. We eavesdrop on their peer conferences and reading response groups. We stand in our doorways and observe. Then we know what to teach.

Encouraging Students to Talk About Writing

In Chapter 10 I explored the challenges of encouraging children to feel at home talking about good writing. Children can talk about what they see, value, and admire in the small circle of their reader response groups and in whole-class gatherings at mini-lesson time.

Antoinette and I found it a great challenge, however, to get multilayered discussions going during the short mini-lesson block of time, even when these whole-class gatherings were extended to twenty minutes. Students often seemed ill at ease talking about quality writing. They seemed to prefer talking about the conventions of familiar genres. They easily spotted the "once upon a time" and "happily ever after" in fairy tales. They eagerly pointed out the white spaces and line breaks in poems, and the charts, glossaries, and diagrams in nonfiction texts. They seemed less comfortable talking about the qualities of good writing that cut across genres. As I suggested in Chapter 10, some students were so filled with clichés they couldn't get beyond "colorful language" and "sharp leads." Others had little confidence in their ability to read critically. They didn't know that their opinions were worthy.

We discovered one effective way of getting a rich give-and-take going in a short amount of time: capitalizing (perhaps surprisingly) on weak writing. As Robert Scholes reminded the audience at last year's University of New Hampshire Conference, "you don't build a bridge without studying bridges first, and not just the bridges that have worked but those that have fallen into the river." Writers, he went on to suggest, need the same thing. We can learn a lot by looking at weak writing.

With our very young writers, in fact, we found that weak writing often led to lively and eager talk. Children spoke more confidently and seemed to have an easier time getting their voices on the floor when they could quickly spot weaknesses or gaps in writing. They browsed through old student magazines and anthologies looking for pieces that, according to them, "could use a little work." They talked about how they might help these aspiring writers. (The technique actually served as solid rehearsal for learning to peer confer gently.) They read negative book reviews of children's literature and closely examined the aspects the reviewer found to be weak. (Unfortunately they were sometimes too intimidated by the words of the reviewer to disagree.)

Another successful way of encouraging children to talk as they read and reread was to put contrasting pieces of literature in their hands side by side. I remember being asked to write a position statement when I ran for the Nominating Committee of the National Council of Teachers of English. I scratched out a rather mediocre one full of empty words. I didn't realize how poor my first attempt was until I happened upon Janet Emig's beautifully phrased one. Seeing the two side by side helped me realize what's possible. In our work with children, we also found it helpful to place weak next to strong, dead next to alive, in a point-counterpoint fashion.

We frequently selected two very short excerpts and displayed them side by side on two overhead projectors.

Jean Craighead George:

Near the coyote den dwelled a tarantula, a spider almost as big as a man's fist and covered with furlike hairs. She looked like a long-legged bear, and she was sitting near the top of her burrow, a shaft she had dug straight down into the ground. The hot desert air forced her to let go with all eight of her legs. She dropped to the bottom of her shaft, where the air was cooler. The spider survives the heat by digging underground and by hunting at night. The moist crickets and other insects she eats quench her thirst.

Encyclopedia:

TARANTULA, tuh RANtyoo luh, is the largest of the spiders. It is named for the city of Taranto, in southern Italy, where it was first closely studied. Many tarantulas are still found there. Any of the large, hairy spiders found in large numbers in the southwestern United States and in Central America are called tarantulas. They often reach the United States in shipments of bananas. One species of tarantula that lives in South America has a body 2 inches long, and legs that spread 7 inches. The largest of all these spiders lives in Guiana and has a body 3-1/2 inches long. Such spiders sometimes catch small birds. Tarantulas capture their enemies by grasping them. They live in little wells in the ground, lined and covered with silky webs.

It seemed easier for students to express what they admired about the passage on tarantulas in Jean Craighead George's *A Day in the Desert* when they read it alongside an encyclopedia entry about tarantulas. One student described the encyclopedia as strict. "It's like someone pointing their finger at you and saying, 'You'd better learn this.' Jean's comes out slowly. It's gentler."

Another said, "Jean's is like you're on a safari and at the end you're saying, "Oh great, I found it! While in the encyclopedia it's just there, someone just hands it over, like a computer printout."

It also seemed easier for children to say what they saw when they looked at two strikingly different letters from camp. These two versions appear in Sylvia Cassedy's *In Your Own Words.*

Dear Mom and Dad,
The kids in my bunk are okay. The scenery is nice. Every day we have arts and crafts. The food stinks. Well, I have to go now.

Love,
Tanya

Bunk D
Camp Windsong
East Lake, VT 05899
July 3, 19–

Dear Mom and Dad,
Yesterday I got Silly Putty caught in my hair, but Harriet got it out. It took her a whole hour, and she had to miss swimming, but she said she couldn't stand the

thought of me with a lump of Silly Putty stuck in my hair for the rest of my life. It wasn't just because it was her Silly Putty. She's really a good friend.

Sometimes, if we get up very early, we can see a mist rising from the lake. It reminds me of a whole bunch of ghosts going for a swim.

I have already made four lanyards in arts and crafts. They are all blue and green, because those are the only colors left. The big kids got to all the pink and silver first.

One thing I miss up here is your cooking. For the past three nights we have had powdered mashed potatoes mixed with water. It tastes like detergent. On Sundays they serve ordinary meals, but they give them fancy names. "Beef Jamboree" is really meat loaf.

Love,
Tanya

Once students seemed at ease talking about paired excerpts our work became more ambitious. We distributed a few handouts, grouping several passages together. We no longer needed to include weaker writing as a springboard to conversation. Students became used to hearing one another talk about writing without hesitation or cliché. Then we shifted their attention toward only the very best.

One of the first handouts we talked about at length was one we had read earlier in the year. (I invited the children to reread the collection of classroom scenes listed on page 303.) Asking children to do some preparatory reading in advance of the mini-lesson guaranteed that more students could participate. It was also interesting to see how their approach to the same texts had changed.

When students joined me in the meeting area for our whole-class mini-lesson I asked, "What surprises you about the different ways in which people have captured classroom moments? Which writers do you admire?" Talk came easy. Classroom life is a naturally hot topic for students and there were many points of contrast, since the content and style of the writers were diverse. On subsequent days, I prepared similar handouts on city street scenes, grandparents, and family meals.

Zanvi described Eloise Greenfield's story about a bad experience in a class play as "peaceful, not like rock music." "Yeah," Jeanine agreed. "It's not all spruced up."

A Play

When I was in the fifth grade, I was famous for a whole day, and all because of a play. The teacher had given me a big part, and I didn't want it. I liked to be in plays where I could be a part of a group, like being one of the talking trees, or dancing, or singing in the glee club. But having to talk by myself—uh uh!

I used to slide down in my chair and stare at my desk while the teacher was giving out the parts, so she wouldn't pay any attention to me, but this time it didn't work. She called on me anyway. I told her I didn't want to do it, but she said I had to. I guess she thought it would be good for me.

On the day of the play, I didn't make any mistakes. I remembered all of my lines. Only—nobody in the audience heard me. I couldn't make my voice come out loud.

For the rest of the day, I was famous. Children passing by my classroom door, children on the playground at lunchtime, kept pointing at me saying,"That's that girl! That the one who didn't talk loud enough!"

I felt so bad, I wanted to go home. But one good thing came out of it all. The teacher was so angry, so upset, she told me that as long as I was in that school, I'd never have another chance to ruin one of her plays. And that was such good news, I could stand being famous for a day.

Eloise Greenfield, *Childtimes*

Time and again in mini-lessons, just as in reading response groups, I probed children's responses. I wanted them not only to share their responses to the writing but also to talk about the author's use of technique. I guided the mini-lesson using the following sequence of questions.

- Do you think she deliberately wrote it that way or that's the way it happened to turn out?
- Can you ever imagine wanting to create this same effect in a piece you might write?
- What techniques might you borrow?

Danielle was the first to respond. "I think she deliberately wrote it that way because it was a sad day for her. She was embarrassed. She didn't want people looking at her. So, you leave your writing plain, not all spruced up—You don't paint a picture for the readers. That's a good match."

"Can you ever imagine wanting to create that same plain, peaceful tone?" I asked Danielle.

"Maybe I'd need a sad feeling like that if my cat died or I failed a test in school." To the third question, the issue of technique, Danielle responded, "If I wanted to do the same, I'd use simple words, no fancy describing words—just tell the truth straight out."

Jeanine shifted the group's attention to the passage by Lois Lowry.

"She refuses to drink her milk at snack time," they wrote home to my parents.

"Why won't you drink your milk at school? You always drink it at home, my mother said.

"It tastes different. I don't like it."

She sighed and wrote a note back requesting that I not have to drink school milk. It was true that it tasted different. The paper container, the straw that collapsed and grew soggy, and the wax that peeled in flakes from the carton all conspired to give a strange papery taste to the warmish milk they placed in front of us at the little kindergarten tables. Even listening to the gurgling sounds that the other children made through their straws as they emptied the container brought a feeling of gagging to the back of my throat. It was the milk at the very bottom that tasted the worst. By then it was mixed with spit.

Lois Lowry, *Autumn Street*

Jeanine commented, "It makes you feel sick, like you're drinking that awful milk." Again I asked the group, "Do you think she deliberately wrote it that way or is that the way it just happened to turn out?"

Emil was the first to respond, "No, she worked at it—lots of drafts probably, because she really wanted you to taste that bad milk."

"Can you ever imagine wanting to create that kind of effect in a piece you might write?" I asked.

Emil couldn't, but Jeanine could, "Maybe if I were babysitting and had to change a baby's diaper. I might want the reader to feel the same way I do."

"Would you use any of Lowry's techniques?" I continued.

"Probably lots of details like she does," Jeanine thought. "I'd tell what things looked and smelled like and what I was thinking while I was doing it."

Jeanine and her classmates seemed to get more out of mini-lessons because they were asked to explain the labels they used so easily. Of course, we were delighted that Jeanine noticed Lowry's rich sensory details. What's more useful to

Jeanine as a writer, however, is that she understands why Lowry bothers to do what she does and that those same techniques are available to her as a writer.

We created several other mini-lesson rituals that invited children to talk about fine writing.

- Students were invited to do as Cynthia Rylant suggests, "take their breath away." They could sign up to read aloud any material they thought would get their peers sitting on the edge of their chairs, savoring every word. The reader would then explain what he or she admired in the piece and the listeners would join the conversation.
- Students were challenged to select a powerful piece of literature and then jot down what they thought was good about the text without using any clichéd phrases. Students would then share the literature along with their jotted notes.
- Students volunteered to create mini-anthologies. Groups prepared small collections of pieces that demonstrated particular qualities or literary techniques. Each collection contained excerpts by different writers in various genres. During the mini-lesson, the excerpts were displayed on the overhead projector and then the anthology was added to the reference section of the class library.

Promoting Self-Evaluation

Several years ago Don Murray said that after all these years he has realized he's not a teacher of writing but a teacher of reading. We all sat up, startled. We began to question our own teaching practices. Do we spend enough time teaching students to be critical readers of their own writing? Do we spend enough time teaching students to read other peoples' writing critically?

Since that time, much has been said and written about the need for evaluation in the writing workshop, particularly self-evaluation. Teachers have begun to weave evaluation into everyday activities, drawing a thin line between teacher evaluation and self-evaluation. Students are now being encouraged to evaluate the reading-writing connections they make.

Self-evaluation happens at the end of an author study when teachers turn to the student writers and ask if they have used techniques similar to those of the author. It happens in conferences when students are asked what goals they've set for themselves as writers and what mentor relationships they might enter to help them reach those goals. It happens during reading response groups when students are asked to search through their writing folders for techniques similar to those in their reading. And, of course, if can be part of mini-lessons.

Antoinette's fifth graders know that twice a month they need to bring a clipboard and pen to their Friday morning gatherings. Every two weeks, she asks one question that gets her students thinking about their own growth as writers. Many of her questions probe the lessons they are learning from their reading. Throughout the year, the students have used mini-lesson time to write responses to questions such as:

- What new genre would you like to learn? How would you go about studying it?
- Have you been influenced by other student writers? Where does their influence show up?

- Who is the professional writer you admire most right now? What are you learning?
- Think about the writing you are doing right now. Does it feel like the kind of piece you want to shape in a literary way? Why or why not?
- Have you had moments when you were aware that you were reading like a writer? Explain.

Antoinette often invites one or two children to share their responses and then collects the others. As she reads them over, she selects some students to host mini-lessons and others to sit in the author's chair during share meetings. Many of the students' responses serve as points of departure in individual reading-writing conferences in the weeks ahead.

Whenever Joan Backer uses mini-lesson time to remind students of a literary technique or a particular quality of good writing, she suggests that they spend a few minutes at the beginning of the workshop searching for examples in their own writing. Students then volunteer to read aloud their discoveries at the share meeting that ends the writing hour. Students share pieces in which they used a surprising metaphor, stayed within one point of view, or used authentic dialogue. When Joan reminds students of these issues, she is careful not to present them in oversimplified ways. Instead, she intentionally talks about them in varied, tentative ways, demonstrating the difficulty in coming up with precise definitions.

Sixth grade teacher Judy Davis has created a monthly ritual that invites students to read their own work as well as the work of others with a critical eye. On the first Monday of the month, she posts three short pieces by professionals or students on the side bulletin board labeled, "Looking for Connections." Occasionally she includes excerpts from longer works. The month I visited she had mounted the opening passages from Patricia MacLachlan's *Arthur for the Very First Time*, the typed text of Cynthia Rylant's *When the Relatives Came*, and the poem "Ladybug" by Francois Dodat.

During the month, Judy makes copies of these texts available for individual study. Students know they should be on the lookout for writing of their own that connects in any way with the displayed pieces. Throughout the month students volunteer to explain the connections they have discovered at whole-class gatherings. Jane shared a piece about her own family gathering that was like Rylant's. Pedro said calling his tall uncle, "the skyscraper of the family" was like calling a ladybug a tiny island, and Rosa thought her own dialogue was as funny as MacLachlan's.

As the year goes on, students fill a class scrapbook with their own pieces and put those they connect with next to them. They write a brief note explaining the connections. Judy often refers back to these pages as she confers or leads mini-lessons, response groups, or share meetings.

Demonstrating Reading-Writing Connections

In Chapter 9 I suggested that teachers need to be mentors for their students. We can share our writing and what informs our writing with our students. We can let them in on our own reading-writing connections.

One day I visited my colleague, Joanne Hindley, as she taught a mini-lesson to a group of fourth graders. "You know," she began, "some people think being jealous is a really bad thing, but I think that sometimes you just can't help being a little bit jealous. And it's not such a bad thing. When I was a young child, I was a little bit jealous of the children who could roller-skate better than I could, and I was a little bit jealous of the children who could paint better than I could. I remember thinking, 'I wish I could do that.' And now that I'm a teacher, I still think that being a little bit jealous is not such a bad thing, especially when you read. Some books I look at and I think, 'I wish I could do that,' but some books I look at and I think 'I might be able to do that.' Like the book *Fireflies* by Julie Brinchloe. When I first read that book, I found myself wanting to read it over and over again. I stuck little yellow stick-ons to the pages I wanted to share with my friends. I kept asking myself, 'How did she do it? Why am I so moved by it?' "

"Above all," she continued, "What I learned from Julie Brinchloe's *Fireflies* is that if you care about something, you can write about it in a way that makes other people care. I never realized that you could write about something as small as catching fireflies and make it seem so beautiful and important." Joanne then read a few excerpts from her own writer's notebook in which she had tried to capture something small by writing about it in an important way.

Joanne was demonstrating what it means to read like a writer and what it means to have a beloved book. In addition, she showed the teachers observing her demonstration lesson just how valuable it is to share the connections you make between your own reading and writing with your students. How can we encourage students to connect what they read to what they write if we do not? How much easier it is to develop a mini-lesson when we have our own experience to draw from. How much easier it is for students to feel comfortable connecting their reading with their writing when they're surrounded by adult models doing the same.

Just as I talked about how E. B. White jogged me out of the writing rut I was in, I could also share the many ways other writers have helped me to write. I could gather students near and explain how, after reading Oscar Hijuelos's Pulitzer prize-winning *The Mambo Kings Play Songs of Love,* I got that "me too" feeling and filled many pages with stories my father told me about his move from Cuba to New York City. Or I could let children know how, after reading Kim Chernin's *In My Mother's House*, I began writing about my mother and my daughter and their relationship with one another. I could tell them about how I apprenticed myself to Georgia Heard in order to write about conferring and how she helped provide an ideal for my writing as well as specific literary techniques I could borrow. I could also share the moments when my reading inspired me to make changes in something I'd already written, how after reading several of Anne Tyler's books, for example, I reworked a family story trying to create more of that comfortable, familiar, everyday world I so admire in her work. I might even talk about how writers can help with the editing process. As I read Robert MacNeil's *Wordstruck*, I couldn't help but notice his verbs: foghorns *grump,* children *hurl* acorns, words *puncture* pretension, warships *limp* into harbor, and parents *plant* magic into children's minds. I could then share a draft in which I focused on verbs, looking for more precise and powerful ones.

 Our students can join in the fun. Teachers can take the role of casting directors, making sure to invite young guest-lecturers who can demonstrate the full range of ways that literature influences writing. Jeanine can explain how Ann Martin's *Babysitters Club* helped her understand why she might keep a writer's notebook. Mauricio can talk about his attempts to mimic an author's style. Amaury can share the influence Frané Lessac's *My Little Island* had on his own picture book.

The more time we take to listen to our students and observe their activities, the more reading-writing connections we will discover. Mary Beth is reading a book on teenage pregnancy in order to write a fictional piece with authentic details. Her mini-lesson would remind students that writers read to fill in the gaps.

Inga wrote a parody of Bill Martin, Jr.'s *Brown Bear, Brown Bear*:

> Root, root, what do you see?
> I see a stem, looking at me.
> Stem, stem, what do you see?
> I see a leaf, looking at me.
> Leaf, leaf, what do you see?
> I see a petal looking at me.
> Petal, petal, what do you see?
> I see the whole flower looking at me.

Her mini-lesson can open up the classroom conversation to parodies, sequels, retellings, and versions.

I've often thought about inviting my daughter to class to tell the story of her college application essay. She wanted to write about a recent visit to the black townships of South Africa, but she had trouble getting started. At around the same time, I had brought home an article written by Mary Savage, a colleague in the Writing Project. Mary had written about her literacy work in Nicaragua. Her piece began, "Nicaragua changes you." J.J. asked if it was okay to borrow that line. Her essay began, "Soweto changes you."

When students stand in front of their classrooms, they need not share only their successes. Their intentions can be as informing as their finished work. When Jeremy announces to his classmates that he's trying to make a more suspenseful piece, it's a decision that allows him to make reading-writing connections. He is ready to seek out those writers who can teach him what he's bent on learning.

Looking Closer at Resources

So far, I've attempted to expand the notion of mini-lessons by exploring the wide range of reasons to teach them. I've discovered that another way to break away from orthodox thinking about mini-lessons is to look closely at the resources we rely on as we attempt to meet the needs of our students.

Whenever I take a good hard look at any of the resources listed on p.281, I realize that there are as yet untapped ways to help students improve the quality of their writing.

Throughout this book, I've suggested that we make students more active in our writing workshops. They too can lead mini-lessons and their ideas can inform us as we design our own. Teachers who do research in their own classrooms, who pay attention to what students read and write—and to what they say about what they read and write—not only discover new reasons to teach mini-lessons, they also discover information worth sharing with the entire class.

Reference material, in all its forms, is one of our richest resources. Where else would we turn when our students need more information about the writing process, about genres, or about children's literature to support their efforts? Our resource shelf can include textbooks on writing and literature, journals, magazine articles, book reviews, the notebooks and memoirs of published authors as well as author publicity, promotional material, and videos.

Sometimes the literature we read may not be considered "professional," but we can use it professionally. One day, to help a group of students understand mentor relationships, I launched my mini-lesson with an article from *The Wall Street Journal*. The columnist, Ronald Shafer, maintained that most late-night television comedians owe a debt of gratitude to Steve Allen—that Johnny Carson's "The Great Karnac" has its roots in Allen's "The Question Man", that Arsenio Hall's audience participation is reminiscent of similar Allen bits, and that David Letterman's crazy stunts and on-the-street interviews are also Steve Allen legacies. After explaining who Steve Allen was, I told the young students, "Comedians have mentors as do writers. We admire others, we borrow bits and pieces. We innovate and make their ways our own, in our own voice and style."

It's easy in our rushed and often overextended lives to carve out only enough reading time to keep up with our professional journals. That's a mistake. Newspapers, magazines, works of fiction and nonfiction offer ideas and insights for our teaching lives.

Perhaps our greatest resource is children's literature in all its forms. Earlier, I suggested that my resources for teaching mini-lessons are much more varied than lines or passages from a picture book. Although this is true, it doesn't negate the power of just the right line or passage from just the right picture book or poem or short story at just the right moment. Children's literature is so important, it deserves a bit more attention.

Children's Literature as a Resource

This entire book has been about using literature as a resource to inform students' writing. By literature I mean more than just the books that line our workshop walls. I also include literature read aloud on records and tapes, literature displayed on overhead projectors, picture book pages slipped into see-through plastic sleeves, excerpts prepared as hand-outs, student- and teacher-made anthologies, as well as the texts of favorite picture books typewritten onto single sheets. All of these can serve as resources when we design whole-class lessons. Imagine duplicating the typewritten text of a well-known picture book and handing a copy to each member of the class. In preparation for a mini-lesson, students could be asked to mark up parts they admire, free-write in the margins, or cut the text apart to study its shape. Students can share their discoveries during the mini-lesson.

Our literature resources also include texts that lend themselves to being used differently. Occasionally, I come across a book that somehow calls out to be used for one purpose, and for one purpose alone. For years I've had a bookmark slipped into one page of Doris Orgel's *The Uproar*. The narrator describes the baby-sitter, Mrs. Onion.

> Mrs. Onion's name was really something else. But she usually wore a sweater over her dress, and a coat over the sweater, and a raincoat over the coat in case of rain. And before she sat down she peeled the raincoat off the coat, the coat off the sweater, and the sweater off the dress—

Although the book is full of good writing, I usually reach for it whenever I want to introduce children to the use of metaphor. Children quickly understand why Mrs. Onion is such a perfect name.

Or I turn to Crescent Dragonwagon's *Diana Maybe* whenever students get caught up in the "I did this, then I did that . . ." kind of personal writing. This book tells the story of a little girl's desire to meet her half-sister. It's told from a young child's point of view, but it's noticeably different from the first-person narratives most children write, since it is told without the usual barrage of facts and list of conclusions. Instead, the young child reveals her thinking and how she got to this place in her thinking. She stands back to reflect on her life and to imagine what life is like for her half-sister. The book encourages young writers to step back and share their own thoughts and imaginings as they tell a good story.

I suspect that each of us probably keeps a shelf of special books, ones we turn to for very particular reasons. In addition, we may each have a few books we find ourselves turning to time and again for many, many reasons. I turn now to a final, yet crucial mini-lesson resource, the well-worn book.

The Well-Worn Book

Several years ago, when I first took a copy of Kathryn Lasky's *My Island Grandma* from a dusty shelf in the Teachers College library, I knew I had discovered an old treasure. I easily imagined reading to students the passage in which the grandmother makes a sleeping bag for the young child out of a floral print fabric. The little girl comments, "It's just like sleeping in a flower cave." I knew I'd read aloud the child's description of the ground. It was "green and soft with moss that feels like velvet blankets under my feet." "Perfect!" I remember thinking. "It's beautiful and it's short, just right for a mini-lesson. What a perfect book for teaching the power of fresh, surprising language."

But then I shared the book at one of our weekly staff meetings and my colleagues helped me to see the narrowness of my plan. I began by reading aloud just the first few pages and asking my colleagues what they heard. They wouldn't respond until I had shared the entire text. *Lesson number one:* Don't lift isolated bits and pieces. "Mini" shouldn't mean "trivial." A good piece of literature needs to be appreciated in its entirety (children need to hear all of *The Uproar* before I highlight Mrs. Onion). "Mini" shouldn't mean "short cuts."

We then returned to the first page to talk about what we noticed. We talked for an hour and never got to the second page. *Lesson number two:* You can see a whole lot of things in any book, on any page, in any one passage. Yes, some books seem to lend themselves to teaching particular qualities, but many fine books are unlimited storehouses that contain a rich array of lessons for writers.

The opening passage in *My Island Grandma* reads:

I have a grandmother who swims in dark sea pools. She takes me with her early in the morning. She has strong hands that hold me tight and safe in the cool deep water while I learn to swim. Today she held me with two hands and I kicked my feet. Tomorrow when she holds me with one hand I will almost float.

Dorothy talked about Lasky's use of time. She noted that in one short page Lasky moved from timelessness to today to tomorrow. Lucy appreciated the honesty of the piece. Isn't it true to the spirit of a young child learning to swim? Aren't the hands that hold you just what would be on a youngster's mind? Ralph was intrigued by the placement of the camera's eye. The opening lines are far away and then the camera zooms in on the hands. Jenifer delighted in the sensuality of the page, the dark sea pools, the deep water.

Lesson number three: Talk is important. We needed time to talk at length, to realize what we have noticed, to find our own ways of saying what we saw. When time is short, we resort to clichés. No one at that meeting needed to say "sharp lead" or "colorful language." Talk also helped us appreciate this text as one of those "storehouse" books that are full of lessons for writers. Just as you never use up a good topic in writing, you never use up a good text in teaching about good writing.

Now, whenever I work with teachers and their students, I look for the well-worn books that are well-loved by the classroom community. Those dog-earred texts are often the deepest well.

Making It
All Possible

Keeping Your Dreams

We believe in books. Somehow we want to make childhood better, and we believe that a book given at the right moment can work magic in a child's life.

Ann Schlee

m occasionally asked to serve as a guest speaker at elementary school graduations in New York City. I hesitate to say yes because the ceremonies are always held during the last week in June when temperatures soar and the humidity becomes unbearable. The children, dressed in their elegant new party outfits and shiny patent leather shoes, seem to suffer most. Proud, well-meaning parents and grandparents surround them clicking cameras and steadying video camcorders as the graduates march into the poorly ventilated and crowded auditoriums.

But there are some invitations I can hardly refuse. When Antoinette's students graduated, along with one hundred other fifth graders, I was thrilled to speak at the graduation. For them, it was easy to find the words to say.

I not only carried notes with me as I approached the podium, I carried a large white gift box topped with a red ribbon.

It's customary in my family," I told the audience, "to give gifts to graduates. And so I've brought some for you."

All eyes were on the box as I lifted the lid. I hoped they weren't expecting one hundred and thirty-five gift certificates to Bloomingdales or gold pens from Tiffany's. Instead, I brought gifts that were hand-picked for graduates of P.S. 148.

The first was a stack of light-blue fliers from the New York City Public Library, suggesting the names of"must-read" books for preschoolers. "Children who graduate from P.S. 148," I explained, "have grown to love fine literature. Now that you're leaving us you have the responsibility to share that love with someone else. I hope each of you will find a young friend this summer and help them get started."

Next, I pulled out 135 envelopes held together with a thick rubber band. "Another thing you've learned in this school is just how important people are in your lives. Your teachers are going to miss you," I continued, "and so each one of you will receive an envelope addressed to your teacher. They expect to hear from you."

I then lifted 135 lovely bookmarks donated by several publishing houses. "Graduates of this school need no explanation for these."

The third handout was a list of wonderful city sites, including museums, gardens, libraries, theaters, galleries, monuments, and concert halls. "You've also come to appreciate in this school that learning doesn't only take place inside a classroom. You live in one of the most important cities in the world. I hope you'll hang this list over your desk at home and make a point of visiting these sites as you continue to learn and grow in the middle school."

Finally, I took out a stack of small index cards. Younger students had helped me attach a copy of Aileen Fisher's poem "June" to each one.

> The day is warm
> and a breeze is blowing,
> the sky is blue
> and its eye is glowing,
> and everything's new
> and green and growing . . .
>
> My shoes are off
> and my socks are showing . . .
>
> My socks are off . . .
>
> Do you know how I'm going?
>   BAREFOOT!

And I said to the students, "In this school you've learned to honor fine literature not because it's a subject on your report card but because reading is one of life's pleasures. And when you're grown up I hope you'll continue to find yourselves turning to literature. I hope literature will be a comfort to you on days when you're sad or lonely or days like today when you're especially joyous and carefree. So to start you off on some life-long reading, I've prepared this poem for you to keep in your pocket."

I then displayed the poem on the overhead projector and orchestrated a gala choral read. I assigned lines to parents, grandparents, brothers and sisters, aunts and uncles, with the graduates reading aloud every other line and ending with a rousing cheer of "BAREFOOT!"

When I first planned the closing chapter of this book, it seemed appropriate to end with scenes like this graduation day. It made sense, I thought, to close with some of the end-of-the-year activities that pay tribute to school years filled with literature.

May and June, the closing months of our school year, are the months when bottles of white-out are sold, primer typewriters are borrowed, laminating supplies are ordered, and duplicating machines break down from overuse. May and June are filled with author celebrations, publishing parties, class anthologies, and poetry readings.

I thought at first I would describe a few of these popular end-of-the-year celebrations and even tuck in one or two more surprising closing rituals. I wanted people to know about the teacher who spends the last day of school rereading with children the poems, chants, and picture books they had read together on the very first day of school. I wanted people to know about the students who spend the last day of school swapping short stacks of books for summer reading and about those who end the year by filling the chalkboard with titles of all the books they've read together during the year and then trying to guess one another's top three favorites. I wanted people to know about the students who end the year by ceremoniously donating a copy of their best work to the school library and others who autograph copies of their favorite works and hand deliver them to their former teachers throughout the school. But it seems to me that as teachers we delight in inventing our own ways to bring closure to a school year. We're good at that. Celebrations come easy.

Instead, I've chosen to devote this last chapter to the more difficult task of getting ready for the next school year. Endings also imply beginnings, new beginnings. If we are to immerse children in fine literature in the fall, we need to use some of the precious white space that the summer months provide to rethink our hopes, plans, and needs.

The ending of this book is a particularly significant ending for me. It marks the end of my role as co-director of the Teachers College Writing Project and a new beginning as well. I'm about to take on the role of director of the Manhattan New School, an alternative public elementary school in the heart of New York City. In the last several weeks I've spoken to more parents than I have in my twenty-four years of working in the New York City schools. "What makes your school different?" they rightfully ask. "Literature will be at the heart of this school," I tell them. It will be one of those schools Yetta Goodman would describe as, "dripping with literacy."

That kind of school is a dream. There's a line sung by Bloody Mary in *South Pacific,* "You've got to have a dream, if you don't have a dream, how ya gonna have a dream come true?" I think every teacher who considers it a privilege to be around young people has dreamed of starting a school from scratch. Several of us from the Teachers College Writing Project family have given ourselves the gift of possibility. We're going to start our own school. We're going to see what's possible. We do have a dream.

Right now, I'm dreaming of a school as beautiful as the Tattered Cover bookstore in Denver, Colorado. I'm dreaming of a school so well-equipped that it brings to mind the Charles Hotel in Cambridge, Massachusetts, where you just dial 1-2-3-4 from the phone in your room and a local bookstore will deliver any of 50,000 titles within a half hour's time. I'm dreaming of a school where all through the year teachers keep that summertime high feeling they get when they read and write and talk together as they do at Breadloaf, at Martha's Vineyard, at the university in New Hampshire, and at our own summer institute in New York.

I'm dreaming of the kind of school Frank Smith would call his ideal, the one that he says "would be very simple. It would have no room for anyone who was not a learner, whether student, teacher, administrator, or visitor, in primary school, the intermediate and secondary grades, and right through university as well. School should be learning emporia where people go when they want to engage in the spirit of learning, from which anything that would suppress or inhibit learning would be excluded. I cannot imagine any child not wanting to be part of such a school."

And now as the summer months approach, I have a fantasy of long, breezy afternoons stretched on a chaise lounge on my back porch with a stack of "must-reads" and "rereads" on one side—Rex Brown's *Schools of Thought,* Denny Taylor's *Learning Denied,* Nancie Atwell's *In the Middle,* Jane Hansen's *When Writers Read*— and on the other a stack of yellow legal pads and some sharpened pencils. The summer months feel like the perfect time to sketch plans for our dream school. Now's the time to pull back and ask, "How are we going to make our dreams come true? How do we create a simple school in a complicated city? How do we create a school with literature at the core, a school where children, teachers, and parents read and write alongside one another?

At a recent International Reading Association convention in Las Vegas, Don Graves delivered another breathtaking address. I was no longer listening as a teacher or a teacher of teachers. I was listening as the director of a brand new school. I thanked Don for reminding me about priorities. His eloquent message was strong. We need to rethink our use of time and space in schools. "We need to take the long-term view." He called for bigger vision, schools where children learn in and out of school, today and tomorrow, for themselves and for their world communities.

How are we going to make our dreams come true? How are we going to create a simple school in a complicated city? The questions, of course, are not mine alone for the answering. In the best of worlds, children, parents, teachers, district experts, community members, and university personnel would sit with me on that back porch and together we'd sketch our hopes and plans for our new school year together.

For now, I can only speak for myself. For now, I feel obliged as well to only speak about literature. After all, this is a book about using literature in ways that make lasting impressions on students' writing. Undoubtedly, such crucial issues as decision making, evaluation, inquiry, respect, morale, curriculum design, parental involvement, research, and staff development will all be part of making the dream come true. Undoubtedly too, when we ask "How do we make our dreams come true?" part of our answer will be to practice what we've preached, to weave literature into the fabric of the school day.

In this book I've shared ideas on using literature in the reading-writing work-shop. Teachers, hopefully, will sift through them, borrow a few, or what is more likely, innovate, experiment, and create their own wise ways of placing literature at the heart of their reading-writing communities. The Manhattan New School will be a place for us, all of us, to do the same. Now as I approach the role of director, I've begun to ask myself, "How can I help? How can I support other people's efforts as well as carve out time for my own teaching and learning?"

Over the years, I've met many frustrated teachers, teachers with wonderful ideas but confronted by too many school or district obstacles, which prevent them from making deep, long-lasting change. Now's our chance to challenge those obstacles. Now's our time to "put up or shut up."

Whenever our Writing Project teachers gather to plan a genre course of study, whether in poetry, memoir, or nonfiction writing, they find it helpful to think about the mentors, tools, and rituals that will make that course successful. So too, in creating a new school, one with literature at its core, I have found it helpful to think once again about mentors, tools, and rituals. I've begun scribbling on those yellow legal pads. I've begun asking myself, "How can I make sure that every member of the Manhattan New School has the mentors they desire and the tools they need? How can I help create schoolwide rituals and structures to support their efforts?"

Mentors

Earlier I suggested that students need to enter mentor relationships with professional writers, with their teachers, and with one another. But mentors are not just for students. They're not just for writers. All of us at the Manhattan New School, including the director and all the teachers, will need mentors as we create a schoolhouse with literature at its core.

I'll need mentors. I'll need to recall the building administrators I've admired over the years and I'll need to call on them for information as well as inspiration. I'll need to recall the principal who carves out time to read aloud to students, one on one, every afternoon, all afternoon. And the one who finds time to write original plays for his students to perform and sends out holiday greetings adorned with quotes from children's literature. And the one who has the energy to host adult reading circles at the end of those long, hard days.

And then there are the principals I know especially well. How does my colleague Sal Romano stretch those limited substitute dollars in order to send a dozen teachers to a conference at the college? How does he cover so many teachers on Friday mornings so they can participate in their own reading-writing workshops? How does he get permission for his fifth graders to sleep over in the whale room of the Museum of Natural History with their favorite nonfiction texts in their backpacks?

How does my friend Tanya Kaufman find the funds to have an up-to-date professional library alongside her well-stocked children's collection? How does she maintain her expertise in content as well as in the process of change? How does she host so many visitors so graciously and elegantly?

I'll need mentors and so will the classroom teachers. I suppose that's why I've been so fussy about selecting teachers to work at our new school. I want teachers to have potential mentors everywhere, in every classroom, in every corridor.

At a recent Colorado Reading Council meeting, Tomie dePaola, in stressing the need for high quality in children's literature, told a story about Stanislavsky. When the great Russian acting coach moved the best people he had from the Moscow Art Theatre into the Moscow Children's Art Theatre he was naturally asked, "Why?" He answered, "I did it because only the very best is good enough for children."

At our new dream school, only the very best will be good enough for children. When I was asked to post the criteria for job applicants I was tempted to quote some thoughtful words from Laura Benson, a wonderful teacher of teachers from Denver, Colorado. Laura writes that the best teachers remind her of her most beloved characters in cherished books, "like the boy in Chris Van Alsburg's *Polar Express,* forever able to hear the sleigh bell; like Searchlight in *Stone Fox,* devoted, loyal, and completely giving; the little engine in *The Little Engine That Could;* Atticus Finch in *To Kill a Mockingbird;* and *Wilfred Gordon McDonald Partridge.* They explore truth. They treasure questions. They drink knowledge and breathe insight. Learning is part of them. Naturally."

I was also tempted to hang out a sign that read, "Wanted: teachers like Miss Kaprowski" and then below it hang Richard Abrahamson's poem, "Perfume and Orange Juice."

I sip my orange juice and smile.
I'm still in love with you,
Have been since the second grade.
When we were licorice and crayon smells,
You were mints with a hint of perfume.
You hugged me; I worshipped you.

You had us write poetry. I was smitten,
I wrote:

"Miss Kaprowski you are neat.
I like everything about you,
Even your feet."

Remember when Paul Cloverhouse and I
Secretly followed you home?
You stopped outside the drugstore,
Called your two young Hardy Boys over,
Invited us inside for ice cream sodas.
Wrapped in perfume, you drank orange juice.
In ecstasy I promised you I'd be a poet.

Now I drink my sweet orange juice, smile.
And hope that my words can bring back the perfume.

Of course, the teachers' union wouldn't stand for such literary postings. Instead the selection criteria read in part: "Demonstrated experience using a process approach to reading and writing instruction and a willingness to participate in teacher support networks, adult reading and writing groups, teacher as researcher projects, and summer institutes."

We need to demand the best because our teachers will become mentors for each other and for our students.

There's a Japanese Buddhist belief that in heaven there is "a network of pearls, so arranged that if you look at one you see all the others reflected in it." I would hope that in our new schoolhouse, each of us will begin to reflect what we admire in one another. All of us will have opportunities to become mentors for one another. We won't give in to those who say a genius is someone a hundred miles from home. We won't give in to those who say you can't be a prophet in your own land. We need to create school buildings where teachers not only are willing to learn from one another but expect to learn from one another. We need to create school buildings where teachers are called upon to share their unique areas of expertise. Of course, parents and community members are part of the potential mentor pool as well.

In her autobiography *Blackberry Winter,* Margaret Mead describes her childhood education.

> Mother thought about every place we lived, not only in terms of its school, but also as a more or less promising source of "lessons." In Hammonton I had music lessons and also lessons in carving, because the only artist the town boasted was a skillful wood-carver. In Swarthmore we were taught by an all-round manual training teacher under whose tutelage I even built a small loom. In Bucks County I had painting lessons from a local artist and later from an artist in New Hope. And one year Mother had a local carpenter teach Dick and me woodworking. She was completely eclectic about what we were taught in these lessons, provided the person who was teaching us was highly skilled.

Margaret Mead's mother had the right idea. When students registered for school we asked each parent to list their own interests and abilities, ones they'd be willing to share with the students and staff. We're hoping it will become a Manhattan New School tradition for parents to host special seminars. The musician can teach students and staff to turn text into song. The carpenter can help us build bookcases and Big Book easels. The photographer can demonstrate a new way to illustrate texts. The secretary can strengthen all our word processing skills.

Parents and community members can also become part of our adult reading-writing circles. What better mentor for young children than a parent who comes to school to share their writing and talk about their reading?

Tools

My wishlist for the Manhattan New School began with the finest teachers. It began with an image of a schoolhouse where teachers take care of their own literacy and professional growth, where children are surrounded by passionate readers and writers and do what we do. Now I need to ask, "What will those teachers and students need? What tools and resources will make their dreams come true?"

Craftspeople honor their tools. Our tools say who we are and what we believe in. If you or I wanted our families to eat more healthy foods, the tools in our kitchen would show a commitment to good nutrition. Perhaps we'd fill our counters with carob and bran, vegetable juicers and steamers, recipes for tofu and brown rice, and coupons for the local health food store. The things in our kitchen say so much about the kind of eating we hope to do.

I recently heard a news report about a building being erected for the Audubon Society. Environmentalists are going to great expense to build in special chutes that will sort and recycle office trash. The tools we use say so much about what we value.

So too, the tools in our schoolhouse say so much about the kind of teaching and learning we want to do. We've built a huge loft for the principal's office, one with a book rack all around. We're also scrounging for a large conference table and lots of bookcases. I hope the message will be clear. This is a workroom for reading and writing and special projects. This is not a room for paperwork and record keeping alone.

Of course, there are other tools that embody our belief that literature needs to be at the heart of our reading-writing communities. The most obvious are reading materials. Unfortunately, public schools have very little money these days. Small alternative public schools have even less. And so our campaign has already begun. We're looking for donations, all kinds of donations. I've even bought a beautiful illustrated stamp that reads, "This book was donated by. . . ."

We're looking for picture books, plays, poems, chants, short stories, novels, memoirs, reference materials, magazines. We're looking for texts for children and teachers and parents. I've been asking for donations from publishers, bookstores, and high school students with outgrown bedroom collections. We're looking for bargains at library sales, flea markets, and discount stores. We're crating books from home, getting ready for the big move to Manhattan.

We're expecting to organize community-wide drives for donations. Our neighborhood is filled with huge apartment complexes. Surely, there are residents who toss stacks of National Geographic and the Smithsonian Magazine into their incinerator rooms. Surely, they'd prefer to donate them to the local schoolhouse.

Even when library funds are non-existent, I want teachers to know that "just happen to have" feeling. I want them to be able to put their fingers on just the right materials for their students. I also want students to know that "searching the stacks" feeling, to be able to make their own wonderful discoveries.

And then there are the beautiful touches. Reading posters on the walls. Bookends on the shelves. Rooms filled with rocking chairs, over-stuffed sofas, magazine racks, and reading lamps. We live in a big crowded city. Certainly, there are folks with items to spare. Now's the time to find them.

Of course our students won't be just reading literature, they'll be writing literature as well. And so our wishlist grows.

In my ideal schoolhouse not only every teacher, but also every child would have his or her own filing cabinet, a desk with drawers, fine writing implements, personal computers, and easy access to telephones, stationery, and duplicating machines.

But for now, we'll settle for lots of recycled paper—one-sided fliers, the backs of junk mail, outdated office forms. For now, we'd like those unused markers, pens, pads, and broken crayons that fill everyone's junk drawers at home. For now, shirt boxes will house source materials, shoe boxes will serve as portfolios, and liquor store cartons will be our mailboxes. Now's the time to send "Please Save" letters to prospective parents and to begin that all-inclusive school supply list, the one that goes home the very first week of school. This time, though, we'll remember the clipboards, the masking tape, and the beautiful blank daybooks. Now's the time to set autumn dates for publishing parties, not to celebrate finished pieces, but to create publishing materials. Parents and teachers can spend evenings at the school, sharing potluck dinners and creating bound blank books in lots of shapes and sizes.

We're starting a school on a very limited budget. We're looking for free books and free writing materials. We're also asking "What else is available?" We need to make good use of all our community resources.

We may not have money for consultants, but we do have libraries and museums and parks nearby. Now is the time to browse in our public libraries. We need to know the quality of their collections, their hours, their policy on school visits, even their librarians' names. Now is the time to wonder whether we can tap into the expertise of local museum educators in ways that support the literacy work in our schools. Now is the time to imagine our students reading poetry amid the wild-flowers and exotic trees of Central Park or conducting research at the Central Park zoo, dairy, reservoir, or conservatory.

Rituals and Schoolwide Structures

George Mansfield is well known in Denver as a master principal. Each summer when I visit, teachers eagerly share another story or two about his wisdom and his leadership. Perhaps my favorite involves the five yearly professional half-days. "I'm going to use the time to study the violin. What are you going to do?" he asked his staff. George Mansfield supports his teachers efforts to be life-long learners. I hope to do the same for teachers and students.

Mentors and tools are of little use I suppose, if teachers and children don't have the opportunity to make the most of them. Each teacher together with his or her own students will create individual classroom rituals and ways of working. There is a place, however, for schoolwide rituals and structures, ways of living our lives together that will help turn this reading, writing, learning community into a reality.

As a staff development project, we came to value the notion of rituals. In our work in New York City schools, we worked hard to create predictable routines that children and teachers could count on.

When I was about to turn forty, I began complaining to my husband that I was getting out of shape. And so for my birthday, he bought me an exercise machine. I overheard him say to our son, "In a week it will be up in the attic." I knew he was probably right, but I was determined to prove him wrong. I placed the large, cumbersome, chrome and black machine in the middle of the guest room, facing the television set. "Jeopardy" airs every evening at 7:00 P.M. It's one of the few quiz shows I enjoy. I decided to exercise each evening from 7:00 to 7:30. In fact, I did rowing to the first round, leg-lifts to Double Jeopardy, and awful, painful sit-ups to the few Final Jeopardy moments. Evening exercises became a ritual. Jeopardy kept me honest.

Once my guest room ritual became known to my family and friends, the phone calls stopped between 7:00 and 7:30, no one interrupted, no one visited.

It's so easy to promise ourselves to do the things we know are important, to keep in touch with old friends, to take long walks after dinner, to start playing the piano again. Unless these become rituals in our lives, it's easy for other things to get in our way. We lead crowded, jam-packed lives. Rituals support our good intentions.

We can support teachers intentions to put literature at the heart of the curriculum when we create appropriate schoolwide rituals and structures. We can become a school that "drips with literacy" in lots of small ways. We can institute once-a-month read-aloud breakfasts with parents. We can insist that fundraisers mean bookfairs. We can define homework as at-home reading time. We can invite students to memorize a poem a month. We can place magazine racks in all the waiting areas.

Yes, we can do lots of small things, but we can also look to bigger areas of support. We can rethink the role of the administrator. We can rethink the use of the school library. And perhaps most important of all, we can design ways to give teachers' own learning and literacy top priority in our school building.

The Director's Role

Everything seems possible now, as I sit on my back porch in July. I close my eyes and try to imagine myself in the role of director. I quickly try to dismiss the first image that comes to mind. I see myself in a grey business suit sitting behind a huge desk filling out endless evaluations, surveys, reports, and applications.

Instead, I close my eyes and try to imagine those moments that directly support teachers' efforts to put literature into the hands and hearts of their students.

I imagine myself seated at a conference table with school board members, parents, and district representatives. Many policy decisions either support or hinder teacher's efforts. So I'll voice my "no" to basals, "no" to workbooks, "no" to pressures to show off with elaborate bulletin board displays and auditorium extravaganzas, "no" to class sets of text books, "no" to endless test sophistication materials and "no" to signing up for every special program that comes our way.

Of course, there will be lots of things to say "yes" to. "Yes" to attending professional conferences, "yes" to real books for teachers and children, "yes" to staying with your class for more than a year, "yes" to big blocks of time for following your interests, and "yes" to seeing teachers as an essential part of all these policy decisions.

But the scenes that are the easiest and most pleasurable for me to imagine are the teaching scenes. One of the real advantages to having a small school is that the director, the principal, can more easily live up to the title of "instructional leader." And the only way to be an instructional leader is, I think, to stay close to teaching. Instructional leaders need to instruct. They need to teach.

I can imagine working alongside teachers in their classrooms creating structures that allow us to collaboratively teach, research, and write together. There are many reading-writing issues to explore, and it's important for teachers to have professional company in their classrooms. Teachers need a chance to bounce ideas off one another, to see their students through another pair of eyes. (The real challenge is not just for me to spend time in classrooms but for all the teachers to have a chance to visit in one anothers' rooms.)

I can imagine as well, carving out teaching moments for myself outside the classrooms. I'm hoping to work with small clusters of children throughout the afternoon. That's why the principal's office has been turned into a workroom. Perhaps a handful of children across the grades will show an interest in publishing a school newspaper, preparing a visitors guide, or rehearsing a readers' theatre performance. Then too, as I move in and out of the classrooms, perhaps I'll discover children who share common interests. I could use this teaching time to bring together students across the grades who want to tackle a new genre, study a favorite author, or follow a common obsession.

Perhaps one afternoon a week I'll work with parents instead of children. I'm dreaming of a writing workshop for parents, inviting them to create original reading materials for those young children anxious to learn to read. I can picture kindergarten students showing off the Big Books and jumprope rhymes written by their parents.

I also have a fantasy about creating a schoolwide community time for the first twenty minutes of each school day. The one hundred and fifty members of our entering class will meet me each morning in an empty oversized kindergarten classroom. We'll gather on the floor to sing songs, to tell jokes, to try tongue twisters, and to talk about items in the local newspaper.

This opening ritual will allow children to share a literary heritage. Children belong not only to a class, but to a school, and not only to a school, but to a community. This opening ritual will also give teachers some white space in their hectic lives. Most arrive very early in the morning and stay very late into the night, but there's never enough time. Now they'll have an opportunity to observe a child they're concerned about, to talk to a parent, to arrange that museum visit, to fill out that bus request form, to talk to a colleague, to have that extra cup of coffee, to find a better parking spot, to call home to check on the sick child they're worried about, or to start their own day singing or reciting or listening to a good story.

Of course, for administrators to have teaching roles, these rituals need to be public knowledge. "Don't call Shelley from 8:40 to 9:00. She's working with the children in the Community Room. Don't interrupt her from 1:00 to 3:00. She's hosting small study groups in the workroom."

Rethinking the School Library
When my daughter turned eleven, she got her ears pierced and then was forever losing her earrings. Each morning I'd remind her to make sure the posts were in tight. Each evening I'd suggest she put the matching sets away carefully. Nothing seemed to help. And then as a gift she received a beautiful jewelry box, the kind with lots of velvet-lined drawers divided into small square sections. Miraculously, or so it seemed, she rarely lost another pair of earrings. She took pride in organizing and reorganizing her now perfect collection—pearl earrings in one section, gold in another; pinks and reds in another drawer. None of my reminders, none of my words, were as effective as having the right container.

The lesson I learned from watching my daughter parallels one I learned from speaking at faculty conferences. The arrangements made for these meetings were always as important as the words I prepared. It's a lot easier to listen in a well-ventilated room with mugs of fresh-brewed coffee and platters of home-made pastries.

In the same way, the literature collections that fill library shelves are only as good as the structures we create to make those texts easily available and functional. I worry about things that are filled but never used: portfolios, notebooks, and libraries that are filled but never, or rarely, used.

Now we're starting a library from scratch and it seems like the perfect time to create a custom-built one designed to meet the needs of the teachers, children, and parents who will use it. Since our school opens as a kindergarten through third grade, we know we'll have lots and lots of picturebooks, but we also know that these need not be arranged alphabetically by author's name.

Instead, we can house our books in categories that work for the people who will use that building. We can put a set of bookends around all the alphabet books, the counting books, the how-to-books, and the picture dictionaries. We can also arrange books to support our work with author studies, language play, or the shape of texts. We can also categorize texts around topics young children tend to write about. There would probably be baskets of books about new babies in the family, moving to new neighborhoods, grandparent relationships, and caring about pets. These texts will cut across genres and contain poetry, fiction, and nonfiction, pieces by professionals as well as young writers.

And then, of course, we'll need sections reserved for parents and teachers. I imagine an ideal parent section filled with books and articles that suggest ways for parents to support teachers efforts and newspapers and wonderful writing in all the first languages of the student population.

The teachers' section would be rich in multiple copies of professional literature, as well as poetry, novels, and nonfiction. Teachers can pool and file reference material on children's literature. They can house author packets of bibliographies, book reviews, and promotional materials. There might also be class sets of carefully selected and laminated poems, newspaper articles, and short stories so teachers need not continually prepare their own for close study.

We'll also be rethinking the design of our library. Several years ago an article appeared in *The New York Times* entitled, "In Hasidic Homes: Ritual is the Shaper of Design." The writer described how Orthodox Jewish homemakers design their living quarters to facilitate religious rituals: double kitchens for Passover observances and large open spaces for huge Sabbath gatherings.

The design of our libraries should also reflect the rituals we intend to create. If we believe, for example, that classes should hold their writing workshop once a week in the school library, then tables should be arranged for peer conferring, and the library should be equipped with an author's chair and the necessary writers' tools. If we believe that performance is important in the students' reading and writing lives, then libraries might have platforms as stages and microphones for delivery and movable furniture to create a theater arrangement.

And if we agree with Di Snowball's important research on reading aloud, then our school library will be designed for parent volunteers to read aloud one-on-one with children in the early grades. Di, the wonderful Australian educator, researched the interaction between parents and children during read-aloud moments at home. She then followed those same children to school to study the read-aloud hour there. Di can't stress enough the value of the one-to-one read aloud experience. Even with the finest teachers, children do not get the same emotional support and language extension in a large group that they do when they are the only one being read to. If that's the case, then library hours can be set aside for these intimate read-alouds, complete with cozy rockers and baskets of carefully selected texts.

Taking Teachers' Learning Seriously

My work began with choosing fine teachers. It will continue with building in many sources of support. As I drive to work each morning, I see the special blue zone reserved for taxis and buses during rush hour. I've often wished there could be a special blue zone for teachers—a clear pathway that enables them to whiz to work free of the stress, delays, and parking nightmares that are part of New York City commutes. City Hall never gives teachers what they deserve. That's up to us.

At graduation ceremonies at Brown University, parents who are educators are invited to march in the processional. It's their way of honoring teachers, and it's very rare. The public and the press never pay enough tribute to the teaching profession. That's up to us.

Parents ask me how this school will be different. They also ask, "Will there be specialists to enrich the curriculum? Will there be trips? Will there be adequate libraries?" It occurred to me that the questions parents ask in the interest of their students are probably the very same questions I need to be asking about the teachers if they are to demonstrate themselves as readers, writers, critical and reflective thinkers. Teachers also need specialists to enrich their curriculum, bulging adult libraries and frequent trips to conventions, workshops, and other school rooms they admire. Our school is five blocks away from the Metropolitan Museum of Art. If we do things right, that building will enrich the lives of teachers and those of our young students.

My son Michael spent one elementary school year with a teacher who was obsessed with playing chess. He didn't learn very much else that year, but in some very real way he learned everything that year. He learned what it means to learn, what it means to be passionate about learning. He learned what it means to linger, to think deeply, and to have priorities.

We are not planning to be taken up by teachers' obsessions, but we are hoping to create a building where teachers feel alive, where they are public learners. We are hoping to create a setting where teachers can demonstrate their excitement about learning along with their students.

I recently ordered a gift for the teachers at our new school. It's a business card. On it is the teacher's name and the name of our school. But I've also included a quote from Maimonides: "I've learned much from my teachers, more from my colleagues, but most from my students."

The challenge is to design schoolwide structures that enable teachers to keep on learning from their teachers, their colleagues, and their students, that enable teachers to read and write and research together.

For the last decade, the Teachers College Writing Project has been doing staff development work in New York City schools. Perhaps the greatest obstacle to helping teachers take care of their own learning has been time. The school day is crowded with curriculum and commitments, the school calendar divided into other people's priorities and pressures. Teachers rarely have enough time to get together, to talk about, reflect upon, or do research for their own teaching. My first challenge in making time is to eliminate the busywork, not just from childrens' lives but also from teachers' lives.

Several years ago, I came across an entry in a third-grader's notebook capturing a family scene, a conversation with her father (Figure 103). Jennie didn't have time to sing with her dad because she had to alphabetize her vocabulary words. Unless we eliminate those elaborate auditorium extravaganzas, show-off bulletin boards, intricate lesson plans, and endless new curriculum agendas that fill our mailboxes, teachers will not have any time to sing—to take care of their own learning. How can teachers teach students how to connect their reading to their writing if they have no time to read, no time to write?

Most New York City teachers are given free periods several times a week—prep periods, short for preparation. The traditional image of a prep period used to bring to mind teachers hunched over manuals, copying instructional objectives

FIGURE 103

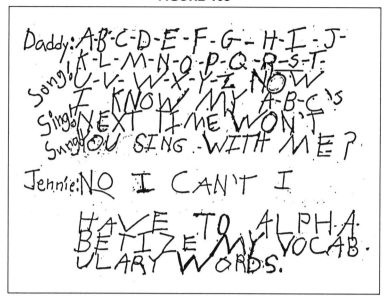

Daddy: A-B-C-D-E-F-G-H-I-J-
Song! K-L-M-N-O-P-Q-R-S-T-
Sing! U-V-W-X-Y-Z NOW
Sing! I KNOW MY A-B-C's
Sung! NEXT TIME WON'T
Sung! YOU SING WITH ME?

Jennie: NO I CAN'T I
HAVE TO ALPHA-
BETIZE MY VOCAB-
ULARY WORDS.

into their plan books, running off materials at the duplicating machine, or cutting, pasting, and lettering teacher-made materials. I think we need a new image.

Teachers who read professional texts and write professional articles are preparing for their teaching. Teachers who meet to talk about their students, their teaching techniques, their own reading, their own writing, are preparing for their teaching. Teachers who visit one another and receive feedback from one another are preparing for their teaching.

We don't just need a new image, we also need new ways to arrange time for teachers' learning. Perhaps at the new school I'll schedule as many prep periods back to back with lunch hours as possible. It's hard to feel productive in forty-five-minute blocks of time. An hour and a half makes quite a difference. Perhaps I'll hire the kinds of specialty teachers who can host large numbers of students at one time, so that several teachers can be freed up at the same time. Musicians, storytellers, and physical education instructors can teach large groups while classroom teachers meet to talk about their reading and share their writing. Perhaps our faculty conference time will be focused into weekend retreats, so that teachers can study shared interests in long stretches of time. Then too, I need to rethink ways for teachers to spend full days away from their buildings, guilt-free, to visit other sites, attend workshops, and speak at national conferences.

We're hoping to assemble a core group of substitute teachers. Some will be those the children know well, the frequent "subs" who are familiar with school routines and can keep classrooms running well. Others can be specialists who offer enriched courses of study. When teachers know the dates they will be away from their classrooms well in advance, we can hire people who can offer specialized courses, running five or six days perhaps, spread out over the course of a year. There won't just be a "sub" covering a class, there will be a magician, or an environmentalist, or an astronomer, or a dramatist leading children through these all-day seminars. And we need to take care of all these part-time teachers. We need to support their daily work, honor them, send them cards on their birthdays.

We can also help teachers take care of their own learning when we provide fine professional libraries, encourage teacher as researcher projects, host visitors in ways that help teachers see the power of their teaching, and join city, state, and national networks of teachers with similar educational dreams.

Perhaps, most of all, we'll help teachers take their own learning seriously and continue their summertime highs when we maintain university connections throughout the year. When my children were born I made sure to give birth at New York University Hospital. My neighbors in the outerborough asked why I didn't just go to the local hospital. "It's a teaching hospital," I explained. "that's where people have cutting-edge information."

We're hoping that the Manhattan New School will become a teaching school-house, a place where student teachers, graduate students, and professors join in to help us make our dreams come true.

A Few Last Words

I often end workshops by sharing one of my favorite reading-writing files; samples of very young students' attempts to end their books. Many show variations on spelling "The End."

DN

The ine

THAAND

tHe ANNe

Some show delightful ways to illustrate "The End."

Some borrow endings from favorite books, as a *Madeline* reader did:

and thats all
there is, there
isn't any more

Some reflect clever, often outrageous endings.

- Did you like our
store?
yes or no
Sine here___

If you liked
my Book
you get a
prize, and
if you do not,
like my book
you get mud.

The ending that seems most appropriate for this book, however, is shown below.

To B CNTN
VD

We take courses. We attend workshops. We read books. We get lots of information. But the really important information comes later on. It comes when we take that seed information back to our classrooms, when we experiment and innovate and invent, when we make it our own. The story really is "to be continued."

There is no one way to run a writing workshop. There is no one way to weave literature into the writing workshop. There are only two essentials: quality literature and reflective teachers.

Quality texts are nonnegotiable. There's a joke told about two Israelis. The first one says to the second one, "I was walking in the desert and a lion began to chase me. I was so scared, I ran up a tree." The second one responds, "Wait a minute, there are no trees in the desert!" To which the first one replies, "What else could I do?" We may not have enough money to fill our library shelves with wonderful books. We may not have enough time to use the ones we have. But "what else can we do?" It's nearly impossible to help students become life-long readers and writers if they don't have access to wonderful literature. It's nearly impossible to help teachers feel alive and professional if they don't have access to wonderful literature. It's also nearly impossible to help students raise the quality of their writing if they don't have access to wonderful literature.

Reflective teachers are also nonnegotiable. They are always asking "Why?" They are always stepping back to ask, "What's working that I can build on? What's not working that I can eliminate?"

Thomas Edison once said, "The most prominent event of my life-long labor is that I now know 50,000 things that don't work." Those of us who have been studying the writing process approach could probably say say the same. Proudly.

If literature is to make a lasting impression on young students' writing—and on their lives—we need to keep surrounding them with the finest, and we need to keep teaching on the frontiers of our thinking. Our work will always bear the label, "To Be Continued".

BIBLIOGRAPHY

Professional Literature

Agee, James. 1989. *Let us now praise famous men*. Boston: Houghton Mifflin.

Aiken, Joan. 1982. *The way to write for children*. New York: St. Martin's.

Anderson, Carl A. 1990. *Young writers in adolescent literature: Models for student writers*. ALAN Review, Spring, 12–14.

Atwell, Nancie. 1987. *In the middle*. Portsmouth, NH: Heinemann.

Auster, Paul. 1982. *The invention of solitude*. New York: Avon.

Baker, Russell. 1982. *Growing up*. New York: Signet.

Beattie, Ann. 1990. *Picturing Will*. New York: Random House.

Benjamin, Walter. 1969. *Illuminations*. New York: Schocken.

Birkerts, Sven. 1989. What, me read? *Harvard Magazine,* Sept/Oct, 35.

———. 1987. *An artificial wilderness: Essays on twentieth-century literature*. New York: William Morrow.

Boomer, Garth. 1985. *Fair Dinkum teaching and learning*. Portsmouth, NH: Boynton/ Cook.

Booth, David, and Bob Barton. 1990. *Stories in the classroom*. Markham, Ontario: Pembroke.

Burrows, Alvina Treut. 1979. Profile—Karla Kuskin. *Language Arts* 56:934–940.

Calkins, Lucy McCormick with Shelly Harwayne. 1990. *Living between the lines*. Portsmouth, NH: Heinemann.

Chernin, Kim. 1983. *In my mother's house, a daughter's story*. New York: Harper & Row.

Cisneros, Sandra. 1991. *The house on Mango street*. New York: Random House.

Cleary, Beverly. 1985. *Why are children writing to me instead of reading?* The New York Times Book Review, 10 Nov., 42.

Conroy, Pat. 1986. *Prince of tides*. Boston: Houghton Mifflin.

Courtney, Ann. 1985. Profile: Patricia McLachlan. *Language Arts* 62:783–787.

Cox, Susan Taylor. 1989. A word or two with Eve Merriam. *The New Advocate* 2 (3): 139–149.

Cullinan, Bernice E. 1989. *Literature and the child. 2d ed*. New York: Harcourt Brace Jovanovich.

Danielson, Kathy Everts. 1990. Author illustrator profile: Marc Brown. *The Dragon Lode* 8:14–15.

Didion, Joan. 1979. "On keeping a notebook." In *Slouching towards Bethlehem*. New York: Simon & Schuster.

Dillard, Annie. 1989. *The writing life*. New York: Harper & Row.

———. 1987. *An American childhood*. New York: Harper & Row.

———. 1987. "To fashion a text." In *Inventing the truth: The art & craft of memoir,* ed. William Zinsser.

Ellis, Sarah. 1989. News from the north. *The Horn Book Magazine* 65: 659–661.

Erdrich, Louise. 1988. *Tracks.* New York: Henry Holt.

Five Owls Staff. 1991. Writing from experience: A bibliography. *The Five Owls,* Jan/Feb.

Fleischman, Paul. 1986. Sound and sense. *The Horn Book Magazine* 62:551–555.

Fox, Mem. 1992. *Dear Mem Fox.* Orlando, Fl.: Harcourt Brace Jovanovich.

Gardner, John. 1983. *The art of fiction.* New York: Alfred A. Knopf.

Giovanni, Joseph. 1986. *In Hasidic homes. ritual shapes design.* New York Times, 19 June.

Goldberg, Natalie. 1990. *Wild mind—living the writer's life.* New York: Bantom.

Gorky, Maxim. 1954. *Childhood.* Moscow: Progress.

Hagen, Uta. 1976. *Love for cooking.* New York: Collier.

Hall, Donald. 1988. *String too short to be saved: Recollections of summers on a New England farm.* Boston: David R. Godine.

Halpern, Daniel, ed. 1988. *Our private lives.* New York: Ecco.

Hampl, Patricia. 1981. *A romantic education.* Boston: Houghton Mifflin.

Heard, Georgia. 1989. *For the good of the earth the sun.* Portsmouth, NH: Heinemann.

Heron, Kim. 1989. Van Allsburg's express. *New York Times Magazine* 24 Dec., 12–29.

Hijuelos, Oscar. 1989. *The Mambo kings play songs of love.* New York: Farrar, Straus, & Giroux.

Hoffman, Eva. 1989. *Lost in translation.* New York: E. P. Dutton.

Holtze, Sarah Holmes. 1985. A second look: The animal family. *The Horn Book Magazine* 61:714–716.

Huck, Charlotte. 1981. Literature as the content of reading. *Theory into Practice* 16 (Summer): 363–371.

Jackson, Jacqueline. 1974. *Turn not pale, beloved snail. A book about writing among other things.* Boston: Little, Brown.

Judson, Sylvia Shaw. 1988. *The quiet eye.* Washington, D. C.: Regnery Gateway.

Kazin, Alfred. 1969. *A walker in the city.* Orlando, FL: Harcourt Brace Jovanovich.

Kingston, Maxine Hong. 1975. *The woman warrior.* New York: Random House.

Klose, Robert. 1987. The joys of science. *Newsweek,* 26 Oct.

Krieger, Elliot. 1988. Gone with the wind . . . As sequel might have been. *Rocky Mountain News Sunday Magazine,* 12 June.

Kuskin, Karla. 1986. Poetry and literary heritage. *The Bulletin* 12: 7–9.

Lamme, Linda. 1989. Illustratorship: A key factor of whole language. *Instruction Childhood Education,* Winter, 83–86.

Lelchuk, Alan. 1985. *On home ground.* Orlando, FL: Harcourt Brace Jovanovich.

L'Engle, Madeline. 1972. *Crosswicks Journal Book 1—A circle of quiet.* New York: Harper-Collins.

Lloyd, Pamela. 1987. *How writers write.* Portsmouth, NH: Heinemann.

London, Jack. 1970. Call of the wild. New York: MacMillan.

MacLachlan, Patricia. 1986. Facts and fictions. The Horn Book Magazine 62:19–26.

MacNeil, Robert. 1989. *Wordstruck.* New York: Viking Penguin.

Marks, Dorothy. 1985. "When children write science fiction." *Language Arts.* April, 355–361.

Matthews, William. 1991. Poetic license. *The New York Times Magazine,* 17 March, 73–74.

Mead, Margaret. 1972. *Blackberry winter: My early years.* New York: William Morrow.

Meltzer, Milton. 1976. Where do all the prizes go? The case for non-fiction. *The Horn Book Magazine* 52:17–23.

Mitgang, Herbert. 1989. "Theory and practice in writing of diaries." *The New York Times,* 21 January.

Moffett, James. 1987. *Active voices II.* Portsmouth, NH: Boynton/Cook.

Moran, Charles. 1990. "Reading like a writer." In *Vital signs I—bringing together reading and writing,* ed. James L. Collins. Portsmouth, NH: Boynton/Cook.

Morrison, Toni. 1987. *Beloved.* New York: Alfred A. Knopf.

Moyers, Bill. 1989. *Vartan Gregorian educator. A world of ideas.* New York: Doubleday.

Murray, Don. 1990. *Shoptalk: Learning to write with other writers.* Portsmouth, NH: Heinemann.

———. 1986. *Read to write, a writing process reader.* New York: Holt, Rinehart and Winston.

———. 1984. *Write to learn.* New York: Holt, Rinehart and Winston.

———. 1982. *Learning by teaching.* Portsmouth, NH: Boynton/Cook.

———. 1968. *A writer teaches writing: A practical method of teaching composition.* Boston: Houghton Mifflin.

Newkirk, Thomas. 1989. *More than stories; the range of children's writing.* Portsmouth, NH: Heinemann.

Newkirk, Thomas and Jack Wilde. 1981. Writing Detective Stories. *Language Arts* 58:286–292.

Newmeyer, Peter. 1987. E. B. White: Aspects of style. *The Horn Book Magazine* 13:586–591.

Painter, Charlotte. 1985. *Gifts of age.* San Francisco: Chronicle.

Paterson, Katherine. 1989. *The spying heart.* New York: E. P. Dutton.

———. 1981. *Gates of excellence: On reading writing books.* New York: Dutton Children's Books.

Paton, Alan. 1987. *Cry, the beloved country.* New York: MacMillan.

Peterson, Ralph and Maryann, eds. 1990 *Grand conversations, literature in action.* New York: Scholastic.

The Primary Language Record, Handbook for teachers. 1989. Ilea/Centre for Language in Primary Education. Portsmouth, NH: Heinemann.

Queenen, Margaret. 1986. Finding the grain in the marble. *Language Arts* 63:666–643.

Rief, Linda. 1990. Cutting Loose: Getting it write. *Language Arts 67:* 473.

Roberts, Royston M. 1989. *Serendipity, accidental discoveries in science.* New York: John Wiley.

Romano, Tom. 1982. *Clearing the way.* Portsmouth, NH: Heinemann.

Rylant, Cynthia. 1990. "The room in which Van Gogh lived." In *Workshop 2: Beyond the basal: By and for teachers,* ed. Nancie Atwell. Portsmouth, NH: Heinemann.

Schoenstein, Ralph. 1988. "The day my daughter discovered baseball." *The New York Times.*

Schon, Donald. 1984. *The Reflective practitioner: How professionals think in action.* New York: Basic.

Silvey, Anita. 1987. An interview with Cynthia Rylant. *The Horn Book Magazine* 63: 695–702.

Simon, Kate. 1983. *Bronx Primate: Portraits in a childhood.* New York: HarperCollins.

Smith, Frank. 1983. Reading like a writer. *Language Arts* 60: 558–567.

Smith, Lee. 1983. *Oral history.* New York: Random House.

Smith, Louisa. 1980. Child writers in children's literature. *Language Art* 57: 519–523.

Stafford, William. 1986. *You must revise your life.* Ann Arbor, MI: University of Michigan Press.

Stegner, Wallace. 1988. *On the teaching of creative writing.* Hanover, NH: University Press of New England.

———. 1987. *Crossing to safety.* New York: Random House.

Steinbeck, John. 1986. *Acts of King Arthur and his noble Knights.* New York: Ballantine.

Taberski, Sharon. 1987. From fake to fiction. *Language Arts* 64: 586–596.

Taylor, Denny. 1990. *Learning denied.* Portsmouth, NH: Heinemann.

Terry, C. Ann. 1989. "Literature: A foundation and source for learning to write." In *Children's literature in the classroom: Weaving Charlott's web,* ed. Janet Hickman & Bernice Cullinan. Norwood, MA: Christopher Gordon.

Tway, Eileen. 1981. Come write with me. *Language Arts* 58: 805–809.

Updike, John. 1990. A bookish boy. *Life magazine.* Oct.

Van Der Post, Laurens. 1978. *A Story like the wind.* Orlando, FL: Harcourt Brace Jovanovich.

Vinton, Vicki. 1989. Natural History. *Prairie Schooner* 63 (4): 3–14.

Wason, Ellen Linda. 1988. Using literary patterns: Who's in control of authorship. *Language Arts* 65: 291–301.

Weathers, Winston. 1980. *An alternate style: Options in composition.* Portsmouth, NH: Heinemann.

Weisel, Elie. 1960. *Night.* New York: Hill & Wang.

Welty, Eudora. 1986. *One writer's beginnings.* New York: Warner Books.

Wendelin, Karla Hawkins & Kathy Everts Danielson. 1990. Fictional writers as models of writing. *The Dragon Lode* 8:1–13.

Wimmer, Dick. 1988. *Baseball fathers, baseball sons*. New York: William Morrow.

Wolfe, Tom. 1987. *Bonfire of the vanities*. New York: Farrar, Straus, & Giroux.

Wood, Don and Audrey Wood. 1986. The artist at work: Where ideas come from. *The Horn Book Magazine* 62: 556–565.

Woolf, Virginia. 1958. *Granite and rainbow essays*. Orlando, FL: Harcourt Brace and Jovanovich.

Yolen, Jane. 1973. *Writing books for children*. Boston: The Writer.

Zinsser, William. 1987. *Inventing the truth*. Boston: Houghton Mifflin.

———. 1976. *On writing well*. New York: Harper & Row.

Children's Literature

Abercrombie, Barbara. 1990. *Charlie Anderson*. New York: Margaret R. McElderry.

Ahlberg, Janet and Allan Ahlberg. 1978. *Each peach pear plum*. New York: Viking Penguin.

Author's Eye series. 1988. New York: Random House Media.

Babbitt, Natalie. 1975. *Tuck everlasting*. New York: Farrar, Straus, & Giroux.

Barbour, Karen. 1987. *Little Nino's pizzeria*. Orlando, FL: Harcourt Brace Jovanovich.

Barracca, Debra and Sal. 1990. *The adventures of Taxi Dog*. New York: Dial.

Bash, Barbara. 1990. *Urban roosts: Where birds nest in the city*. Boston: Little, Brown.

Bate, Lucy. 1975. *Little Bunny's loose tooth*. New York: Scholastic.

Bauer, Caroline Feller. 1985. *My mom travels a lot*. New York: Puffin.

Baylor, Byrd. 1986. *I'm in charge of celebrations*. New York: Charles Scribner's Sons.

———. 1985. *Guess who my favorite person is?* New York: Aladdin.

Bemelmans, Ludwid. 1977. *Madeline*. New York: Penguin.

Blaine, Marge. 1975. *The terrible thing that happened at our house*. New York: Parents Magazine.

Blos, Joan. 1987. *Old Henry*. New York: Mulberry Books.

———. 1979. *A gathering of days, a New England girls journal, 1830–32*. New York: Charles Scribner's Sons.

Blume, Judy. 1985. *The pain and the great one*. New York: Bradbury.

Brenner, Barbara. 1970. *A snake lover's diary*. New York: Harper & Row.

Brighton, Catherine. 1987. *Five secrets in a box*. New York: E. P. Dutton.

Brown, Ruth. 1991. *Alphabet times four, an international ABC*. New York: Dutton Children's Books.

Browne, Anthony. 1985. *Gorilla*. New York: Alfred A. Knopf.

Bulla, Clyde. 1985. A grain of wheat. Boston: David R. Godine.

Bunting, Eve. 1990. *The Wall*. New York: Clarion.

———. 1989. *The Wednesday surprise*. New York: Clarion.

————. 1984. *Jane Martin, dog detective.* Orlando, FL: Harcourt Brace Jovanovich.

Burnett, Frances Hodgson. 1962. *The secret garden.* New York: Harper & Row.

Caines, Jeannette. 1982. *Just us women.* New York: HarperTrophy.

Calvert, Patricia. 1989. *The snowbird.* New York: Penguin.

Carle, Eric. 1990. *Very quiet cricket: A multi-sensory book.* New York: Philomel.

Carlstrom, Nancy White. 1990. *Light stories of a small kindness.* Boston: Little, Brown.

Cassedy, Sylvia. 1990. *In your own words, a beginner's guide to writing.* New York: Thomas Y. Crowell.

Charlie, Remy. 1969. *Arm in arm.* New York: Parents Magazine.

Cherry, Lynne. 1990. *Archie follow me.* New York: Dutton's Children's Books.

Chorao, Kay. 1988. *Cathedral mouse.* New York: E. P. Dutton.

Cleary, Beverly. 1990. *Muggie Maggie.* New York: William Morrow.

————. 1988. *A girl from Yamhill.* New York: William Morrow.

Cole, Brock. 1987. *The goats.* New York: Farrar, Straus, & Giroux.

Collins, Judy. 1989. *My father.* Boston: Little, Brown.

Conrad, Pam. 1988. *Staying nine.* New York: HarperTrophy.

Cooney, Barbara. 1982. *Miss Rumphius.* New York: Penguin.

Cowley, Joy. 1980. *Mrs. Wishy Washy.* Auckland, New Zealand: Rugby Education.

Crutcher, Chris. 1989. *Chinese handcuffs.* New York: Greenwillow.

Dahl, Roald. 1984. *Boy, tales of childhood.* London: Puffin.

de Paola Tomie. 1983. *The legend of the blue bonnet: An old tale of Texas.* New York: Putnam.

————. 1973. *Nana upstairs and Nana downstairs.* New York: Putnam.

DiSalvo, Diane. 1991. *Uncle Willie and the soup kitchen.* New York: Morrow Junior Books.

Dragonwagon, Crescent. 1990. *Home place.* New York: Macmillan.

————. 1987. *Diana, maybe.* New York: Macmillan.

————. 1983. *Katie in the Morning.* New York: Harper & Row.

Dunham, Meredith. 1987. *"Picnic—how do you say it?"* New York: Lothrop, Lee & Shepard.

Eastman, P. D. 1966. *Are you my mother?* New York: Beginner Books.

Ehlert, Lois. 1990. *Fish eyes.* Orlando, FL: Harcourt Brace Jovanovich.

Els, Betty Vander. 1981. Knives on the right, forks on the left. *Cricket Magazine* 9 (3): 10–13.

Engel, Diana. 1988. *Josephina the great collector.* New York: Morrow Junior Books.

Estes, Eleanor. 1944. *The hundred dresses.* Orlando, FL: Harcourt Brace Jovanovich.

Fitzhugh, Louise. 1964. *Harriet the spy.* New York: HarperTrophy.

Fleischman, Paul. 1988. *Rondo in C.* New York: Harper & Row.

————. 1986. *Rear-view mirrors.* New York: Harper & Row.

———. 1980. *The Half-A-Moon Inn*. New York: Harper & Row.

Florian, Douglas. 1990. *City street*. New York: Greenwillow.

Fluek, Toby Knobel. 1990. *Memories of my life in a Polish village*. New York: Alfred A. Knopf.

Forman, Michael. 1991. *One world*. New York: Arcade.

Fowler, Susi Gregg. 1989. *When summer ends.* New York: Greenwillow.

Fox, Mem. 1985. *Wilfred Gordon McDonald Partridge*. New York: Kane/Miller.

Frank, Anne. 1985. *Anne Frank: The diary of a young girl*. New York: Doubleday.

Fraser, Betty. 1990. *First things first*. New York: Harper & Row.

Fritz, Jean. 1982. *Homesick: My own story*. New York: G. P. Putnam's.

George, Jean Craighead. 1983. *A day in the desert*. New York: Thomas Y. Crowell.

———. 1972. *Julie of the wolves*. New York: Harper & Row.

Geras, Adele. 1990. *My grandmother's stories*. New York: Alfred A. Knopf.

Goennel, Heidi. 1989. *Sometimes I like to be alone*. Boston: Little, Brown.

Golenbock, Pater. 1990. *Teammates*. Orlando, FL: Harcourt Brace Jovanovich.

Gottlieb, Dale. 1991. *My stories—Hildy Calpurnia Rose*. New York: Alfred A. Knopf.

Graham, John. 1968. *A crowd of cows*. New York: Scholastic.

Graves, Ruth. 1986. *Once upon a time*. New York: G. P. Putnam's Sons.

Greenfield, Eloise. 1981. *Daydreamers*. New York: Dial.

———. 1975. *Me and Nessie*. New York: Harper & Row.

———. 1974. *Sister*. New York: HarperTrophy.

Greenfield, Eloise and Lessie Jones Little. 1979. *Childtimes*. New York: Thomas Y. Crowell.

Griffith, Helen V. 1986. *Georgia music*. New York: Mulberry Books.

Gwynne, Fred. 1988. *A little pigeon toad*. New York: Simon & Schuster.

Hailey, Kendall. 1989. *The day I became an autodidact: And the advice, adventure & acrimony that befell me thereafter*. New York: Dell.

Haley, Gail, E. 1970. *A story, a story*. New York: Aladdin.

Hall, Donald. 1984. *The man who lived alone*. Boston: David R. Godine.

———. 1979. *Ox-cart man*. New York: Viking Penguin.

Hautzig, Esther. 1969. *In school*. London: Macmillan.

Haynes, Betsy. 1990. *The Fabulous Five in Trouble*. New York: Bantam.

Hazen, Barbara Shook. 1979. *Tight times*. New York: Penguin.

Heide, Florence Pary and Judith Heide Gilliland. 1990. *The day of Ahmed secret*. New York: Lothrop, Lee & Shepard.

Heinrich, Bernard. 1990. *An owl in the house—a naturalist's diary* Boston: Little, Brown.

Heller, Nicholas. 1990 *The front hall carpet*. New York: Greenwillow.

Hendershot, Judith. 1987. *In coal country*. New York: Alfred A. Knopf.

Herberman, Ethan. 1989. *City kid's field guide.* New York: Simon & Schuster.

Homan, Felice. 1972. *Slake's limbo.* New York: Charles Scribner's Sons.

Howard, Jane. 1985. *When I'm sleepy.* New York: E. P. Dutton.

Howe, Deborah and James Howe. 1984. *Bunnicula.* New York: Atheneum.

Hyman, Trina Schart. 1981. *Self-portrait: Trina Schart Hyman.* New York: Harper & Row.

Jarrell, Randall. 1963. *The bat poet.* New York: Macmillan.

Johnson, Diane Johnston. 1990. *Bunkhouse journal.* New York: Charles Scribner's Sons.

Joseph, Lynn. 1991. *A wave in her pocket; stories from Trinidad.* New York: Clarion.

Juster, Norton. 1961. *The phantom tollbooth.* New York: Random House.

Kamen, Gloria. 1990. *Edward Lear, king of nonsense.* New York: Atheneum.

Keats, Ezra Jack. 1962. *Snowy day.* New York: Viking Penguin.

Kennedy, Richard. 1978. *Richard Kennedy's Collected stories.* New York: Harper & Row.

Kerr, M. E. 1972. *Dinky hocker shoots smack.* New York: Harper & Row.

Khalsa, Dayal. 1988. *My family vacation.* New York: Clarkson Potter.

———. 1986. *Tales of a gambling grandma.* New York: Clarkson Potter.

Kimmelman, Leslie. 1989. *Frannie's fruits.* New York: Harper & Row.

Kipling, Rudyard. 1989. *How the leopard got his spots.* Westport, CT: Rabbit Ears Books.

Kitamura, Satoshi. 1989. *UFO Diary.* New York: Farrar, Straus, & Giroux.

Klein, Robin. 1983. *Penny Polllard's diary.* Oxford: Oxford University Press.

Kojima, Naomi. 1980. *Mr. and Mrs. Thief.* New York: Thomas Y. Crowell.

Komaiko, Leah. 1990. *My perfect neighborhood.* New York: Harper & Row.

———. 1987. *Annie Bananie.* New York: Harper & Row.

———. 1987. *I like the music.* New York: Harper & Row.

Konigsburg, E. L. 1970. *From the mixed up files of Mrs. Basil E. Frankweiler.* New York: Atheneum.

Kumin, Maxine. 1964. *The beach before breakfast.* New York: G. P. Putnam's.

———. 1961. *A winter friend.* New York: G. P. Putnam's.

Kuskin, Karla. 1987. *Jerusalem shining still.* New York: Harper & Row.

———. 1986. *The Dallas titans get ready for bed.* New York: Harper & Row.

———. 1982. *The Philharmonic gets dressed.* New York: Harper & Row.

Lasky, Kathryn. 1986. *Pageant.* New York: Four Winds.

———. 1979. *My island grandma.* New York: Frederick Warne.

———. 1977. *Tugboats never sleep.* Boston: Little, Brown.

Lecourt, Nancy. 1991. *Abracadabra to zigzag.* New York: Lothrop, Lee & Shepard.

Lessac, Frane. 1985. *My little island.* New York: HarperTrophy.

Levinson, Riki. 1988. *Our home is the sea.* New York: E. P. Dutton.

————. 1985. *Watch the stars come out*. New York: E. P. Dutton.

Lewis, C. S. 1950. *The lion, the witch and the wardrobe*. New York: Macmillan.

Lindgren, Astrid. 1962. *The children of noisy village*. New York: Viking.

Lipsyte, Robert. 1981. *Summer rules*. New York: HarperCollins.

Little, Jean. 1987. *Little by little*. Ontario, Canada: Penguin.

————. 1986. *Hey world, here I am!* New York: Harper & Row.

Lobel, Arnold. 1970. *Frog and toad are friends*. New York: Harper & Row.

Lord Betty Bao. 1984. *In the year of the boar and Jackie Robinson*. New York: Harper-Collins.

Lowry, Lois. 1989. *Number the stars*. Boston: Houghton Mifflin.

————. 1980 *Autumn street*. New York: Dell.

————. 1979. *Anastasia Krupnik*. Boston: Houghton Mifflin.

Macaulay, David. 1980. *Unbuilding*. Boston: Houghton Mifflin.

MacCarthy, Patricia. 1989. *Animals galore*. New York: Dial.

MacLachlan, Patricia. 1985. *Sarah, plain and tall*. New York: Harper.

————. 1980. *Arthur, for the very first time*. New York: Harper & Row.

Martin, Ann. 1989. *Babysitter Club #29; Mallory and the mystery diary*. New York: Scholastic.

Martin, Bill Jr. 1983. *Brown bear, brown bear, what do you see?* New York: Henry Holt.

Martin, Bill Jr. and John Archambault. 1985. *The ghost eye tree*. New York: Holt, Rinehart and Winston.

————. 1966. *Knots on a counting rope*. New York: Henry Holt.

McCloskey, Robert. 1941. *Make way for duckling's*. New York: Viking Penguin.

————. 1940. *Lentil*. New York: Viking.

McLerran, Alice. 1991. *Roxaboxen*. New York: Lothrop, Lee & Shepard.

McNulty, Faith. 1963. *When a boy goes to bed at night*. New York: Alfred A. Knopf.

Meigs, Cornelia. 1933. *Invincible Louisa, the story of the author of Little Women*. Boston: Little, Brown.

Meltzer, Milton. 1991. *Starting from home: A writer's beginnings*. New York: Puffin.

Merrill, Jean. 1964. *The pushcart war*. New York: HarperCollins.

Miller, Montzalee. 1987. *My grandmother's cookie jar*. Los Angeles, CA: Price Stern Sloan.

Mills, Lauren. 1991. *The rag coat*. New York: Little, Brown.

Milne, A. A. 1958. *The world of Christopher Robin*. New York: Dutton Children's Books.

Munsch, Robert. 1972. *Love you forever*. Ontario, Canada: Firefly Books.

Murphy, Sirley Rousseau. 1974. *Poor Jenny, bright as a penny*. New York: Viking Penguin.

Naidoo, Beverly. 1988. *Journey to Jo'Burg: A South African story*. New York: Harper & Row.

Naylor, Phyllis Reynolds. 1978. *How I came to be a writer*. New York: Four Winds.

Nixon, Joan Lowery. 1988. *If you were a writer*. New York: Four Winds.

Oakley Graham. 1987. *The diary of a church mouse*. New York: Atheneum.

Orgel, Doris. 1970. *The uproar*. New York: McGraw-Hill.

Parish, Peggy. 1963. *Amelia Bedelia*. New York: HarperTrophy.

Paterson, Katherine. 1978. *The great Gilly Hopkins*. New York: Thomas Y. Crowell.

———. 1977. *Bridge to Terabithia*. New York: Thomas Y. Crowell.

Peck, Robert Newton. 1974. *Soup*. New York: Alfred A. Knopf.

Polacco, Patricia. 1988. *The keeping quilt*. New York: Simon & Schuster.

Pomerantz, Charlotte. 1989. *The chalk doll*. New York: J. B. Lippincott.

Rey, H. A. 1941. *Curious George*. Boston: Houghton Mifflin.

Ringgold, Faith. 1991. *Tar beach*. New York: Crown.

Roberts, Tom. 1990. *Goldilocks*. Westport, CT: Rabbit Ear Books.

Roberts, Tom, adaptor. 1990. *The Three Little Pigs*. Westport, CT: Rabbit Ear Books.

———. 1989. *The three billy goats gruff*. Westport, CT: Rabbit Ear Books.

Rockwell, Anne. 1970. *When the drum sang, an African folktale*. New York: Parents' Magazine.

Rukeyser, Muriel. 1961. *I go out*. New York: Harper & Row.

Russo, Marisabina. 1991. *A visit to Oma*. New York: Greenwillow.

Ryder, Joanne. 1991. *Hello, tree!* New York: Lodestar.

———. 1989. *Catching the wind*. New York: Morrow Junior Books.

Rylant, Cynthia. 1987. *Henry and Mudge*. New York: Macmillan.

———. 1985. *Every living thing*. New York: Aladdin.

———. 1985. *The relatives came*. New York: Bradbury.

———. 1982. *When I was young in the mountains*. New York: E. P. Dutton.

Schecter, Ben. 1989. *Grandma remembers*. New York: Harper & Row.

Schertle, Alice. 1990. *That's what I thought*. New York: Harper & Row.

Schlein, Miriam. 1989. *Pigeons*. New York: Thomas Y. Crowell.

Schweitzer, Byrd Baylor. 1989. *Amigo*. New York: Macmillan.

Seabrooke, Brenda. 1990. *Judy Scuppernog*. New York: Cobblehill.

Seiden, George. 1990. *The cricket in Times Square*. New York: Farrar, Straus, & Giroux.

Sendak, Maurice. 1963. *Where the wild things are*. New York: Harper & Row.

Seuss, Dr. 1989. *And to think that I saw it on Mulberry street*. New York: Random House.

Showers, Paul. 1991. *The listening walk*. New York: HarperCollins.

Shulevitz, Uri. 1978. *The treasure*. Toronto, Canada: Collins.

Shyer, Marlene Fanta. 1985. *Here I am an only child*. New York; Macmillan.

Sibley, Brian. 1989. *The land of Narnia.* New York: Harper & Row.

Slobodvinka, Esphyr. 1947. *Caps for sale.* New York: HarperCollins.

Smith, Doris Buchanan. 1973. *A taste of blackberries.* New York: Scholastic.

Smith, Robert Kimmel. 1987. *Mostly Michael.* New York: Delacorte.

———. 1984. *The war with grandpa.* New York: Delacorte.

Speare, Elizabeth George. 1958. *The witch of blackbird pond.* Boston: Houghton Mifflin.

Spier, Peter. 1972. *Crash! Bang! Boom!* New York: Doubleday.

———. 1971. *Gobble growl grunt.* New York: Doubleday.

Stanley, Diane. 1990. *The conversation club.* New York: Aladdin.

Steig, William. 1987. *CDB!* New York: Simon & Schuster.

Steptoe, John. 1987. *Mufaro's beautiful daughters; an African tale.* New York: Lothrop, Lee & Shepard.

———. 1969. *Stevie.* New York: Harper & Row.

Stern, Philip Van Doren. 1972. *Henry David Thoreau, writer and rebel.* New York: Thomas Y. Crowell.

Stevenson, James. 1986. *When I was nine.* New York: Greenwillow.

Stinson, Kathy. 1988. *Teddy Rabbit.* Toronto. Ontario: Annick.

Swift, Hildegarde H. and Lynd Ward. 1970. *The little red lighthouse and the great grey bridge.* Orlando, FL: Harcourt Brace Jovanovich.

Taylor, Sydney. 1951. *All of a kind family.* New York: Dell.

Terban, Marvin. 1990. *Punching the clock, funny actions idioms.* New York: Clarion.

———. 1989. *Super dupers, really funny real word.* New York: Clarion.

Townsend, Sue. 1982. *The growing pains of Adrian Mole.* New York: Avon.

Turner, Ann. 1987. *Nettie's trip south.* New York: Macmillan.

Ungerer, Tomi. 1960. *Emile.* New York: Harper & Row.

———. 1959. *Adelaide.* New York: Harper & Row.

———. 1958. *Crictor.* New York: Harper & Row.

Vance, Marguerite. 1966. *A rainbow for Robin.* New York: E. P. Dutton.

Vasiliu, Mircea. 1978. *A day at the beach.* New York: Random House.

Viorst, Judith. 1972. *Alexander and the terrible, horrible, no good, very bad day.* New York: Atheneum.

———. 1971. *The tenth good thing about Barney.* New York: Aladdin.

Voigt, Cynthia. 1981. *Homecoming.* New York: Random House.

Varley, Susan. 1984. *Badger's Parting Gifts.* New York: Lothrop.

Waber, Bernard. 1971. *Nobody is perfick.* Boston: Houghton Mifflin.

Walker, Alice. 1974. *Langston Hughes, American poet.* New York: Thomas Y. Crowell.

Wells, Rosemary. 1973. *Noisy Nora.* New York: Dial.

White, E. B. 1952. *Charlotte's web.* New York: HarperCollins.

———. 1945. *Stuart Little.* New York: Harper & Row.

Whitely, Opal. 1976. *Opal, the journal of an understanding heart.* Palo Alto, CA: Tioga.

Williams, Karen Lynn. 1990. *Baseball and Butterflies.* New York: Lothrop, Lee & Shepard.

Williams, Vera B. 1981. *Three days on a river in a red canoe.* New York: Greenwillow.

Williams, Vera B. and Jennifer Williams. 1990. *Stringbean's trip to the shining sea.* New York: William Morrow and Company, Inc.

Wilson, Beth P. 1990. *Jenny.* New York: Macmillan.

Yearling, Dell Young. 1987. *Share-a-story books.* New York: Dell Publishing.

Yolen, Jane. 1987. *Owl moon.* New York: Philomel Books.

Yorinks, Arthur. 1980. *Louis the fish.* New York: Farrar, Straus, & Giroux.

Yukio, Tsuchiya. 1951. *Faithful elephant, a true story of animals, people and war.* Boston: Houghton Mifflin.

Ziefert, Harriet. 1989. *Henry's wrong turn.* New York: Little, Brown.

Zolotow, Charlotte. 1987. *I like to be little.* New York: Harper & Row.

Poetry

Abrahamson, Richard. 1985. "Perfume and orange juice." *Language Arts,* September.

Agee, Rose. 1967. *How to eat a poem and other morsels.* New York: Random House.

Amedingen, E. M. 1984. *In grandparents' houses.* New York: Greenwillow.

Anonymous. 1989. "If all the seas were one sea." In *Book of a thousand poems.* New York: Peter Bedrick.

Behn, Harry. 1989. "Circles." In *Dilly dilly piccalilli: Poems for the very young,* ed. Myra Cohn Livingston. New York: MacMillan.

Booth, Philip. 1984. "The round." In *New coasts and strange harbors,* ed. Helen Hill and Agness Perkins. New York: Thomas Y. Crowell.

Brooks, Gendolyn. 1990. "Computer." In *The place my words are looking for,* ed. Paul Janeczko. New York: Bradbury.

Cassedy, Sylvia. 1987. *Roomrimes.* New York: Thomas Y. Crowell.

Ciardi, John. 1975. "Questions! Questions! Questions!" In *Fast & slow: poems for advanced children and beginning parents.* Boston: Houghton Mifflin.

Ciardi, John. 1962. *You read to me, I'll read to you.* New York: Harper & Row.

Clarke, Pauline. 1983. "My name is . . ." In *The Random House book of poetry for children,* ed. Jack Prelutsky. New York: Random House.

Cole, William. 1983. Bananananananana. In *The Random House book of poetry for children,* ed. Jack Prelutsky. New York: Random House.

de Regniers, Beatrice Schenk. 1989. "Keep a Poem in your Pocket." *Still as a star.* Boston: Little, Brown.

———. 1985. *Jack and the beanstalk retold in verse.* New York: Atheneum.

———. 1968. "I looked in the mirror." In *Piping down the valleys wild,* ed. Nancy Larrick. New York: Dell.

Dodat, Francois. 1897. "Ladybug." In *These small stones,* ed. Norma Farber and Myra Cohn Livingston. New York: Harper & Row.

Dickinson, Emily. 1983. "I'm nobody! Who are you?" In *The Random House book of poetry for children,* ed. Jack Prelutsky. New York: Random House.

Edens, Cooper. "The Peaceable Kingdom." In *Day and night and other dreams.* New York: Simon and Schuster.

Elledge, Scott. 1990. *Wider than the sky: Poems to grow up with.* New York: Harper & Row.

Field, Rachel. 1988. *General Store.* New York: Greenwillow.

———. 1983. "If once you have slept on an island." In *The Random House book of poetry for children,* ed. Jack Prelutsky. New York: Random House.

Fisher, Aileen. 1968. "June." In *Riping down the valleys wild; Poetry for the young of all ages.* New York: Delacourt.

Fleischman, Paul. 1988. *Joyful noise—poems for two voices.* New York: HarperCollins.

———. 1985. *I am Phoenix.* New York: Harper & Row.

Fraser, Kathleen. 1976. "Marbles." In *Potato chips and a slice of moon,* ed. Lee Bennett Hopkins and Misha Arenstein. New York: Scholastic.

———. 1989. "How Tuesday began." In *Crazy to be alive in such a strange world,* ed. Nancy Larrick. New York: M. Evans.

Frost, Robert. 1978. *Stopping by woods on a snowy evening.* New York: Dutton Children's Books.

Giovanni, Nikki. 1988. "Knoxville Tennessee" In *Sing a song of popcorn,* eds. Beatrice Schenk de Regniers, Eva Moore, Mary Michaels White and Jan Carr.

———. 1983. "The reason I like chocolate." In *The Random House book of poetry for children,* ed. Jack Pelutsky. New York: Random House.

Glenn, Mel. 1988. "Jonathan Sobel, pd. 5 room 26." In *Back to class: Poems by Mel Glenn.* New York: Clarion.

Greenfield, Eloise. 1978. "Aunt Roberta." In *Honey I love and other love poems.* New York: Thomas Y. Crowell.

———. 1978. "Keepsake." In *Honey I love and other love poems.* New York: Thomas Y. Crowell.

———. 1978. "Things." In *Honey I love and other love poems.* New York: Thomas Y. Crowell.

Greenfield, Eloise and Amos Ferguson. 1988. *Under the Sunday tree.* New York: Harper & Row.

Hoberman, Mary. 1983. "Clickbeetle." In *Random House book of poetry for children,* ed. Jack Prelutsky. New York: Random House.

Homan, Felice. 1974. "Who am I?" In *Room for me and a mountain lion,* ed. Nancy Larrick. New York: M. Evans.

Hopkins, Lee Bennett. 1980. *Morning, noon and nightime, too.* New York: Harper & Row.

Hughes, Langston., 1990. "April rain song." In *Wider than the sky: Poems to grow up with,* ed. Scott Elledge. New York: Harper & Row.

———. 1973. "Dream deferred." In *The Poetry of black America,* ed. Arnold Adoff. New York: Harper & Row.

Hughes, Ted. 1986. "Saints island." In *Flowers and insects—some birds and a pair of spiders.* New York: Alfred A. Knopf.

Jacobs, Frank. 1981. "If Walt Whitman had written Humpty Dumpty." In *Poem stew,* ed. William Cole. New York: Harper & Row.

Joseph, Lynn. 1990. *Coconut kind of day.* New York: Lothrop, Lee & Shepard.

Koch, Kenneth and Kate Farrell. 1985. *Talking to the sun—an illustrated anthology of poems for young people.* New York: The Metropolitan Museum of Art. Henry Holt.

Kuskin, Karla. 1990. "Being Lost." In *Good books, good times,* ed. Lee Bennett Hopkins. New York: Harper & Row.

———. 1980. Catherine. In *Dogs & dragons, trees & dreams.* New York: Harper & Row.

———. 1980. "I woke up this morning at quarter past seven." In *Dogs & dragons, trees & dreams.* New York: Harper & Row.

———. 1980. "Rules." In *Dogs & dragons, trees & dreams.* New York: Harper & Row.

———. 1975. *Near the window tree.* New York: Harper & Row.

La Gallienne, Richard. 1965. "I meant to do my work today." In *Arrow book of poetry,* ed. Ann McGovern. New York: Scholastic.

Lessac, Fane. 1987. *Caribbean canvas.* Philadelphia: J. B. Lippincott.

Little, Jean. 1980. "Plenty." In *Round slice of moon,* ed. Fran Newman. Ontario, Canada: Scholastic.

Livingston, Myra Cohn. 1987. "Math class." In *These small stones.* New York: Harper & Row.

———. 1985. "Fourth of July." In *Celebrations.* New York: Holiday House.

———. 1974. "Street song." In *the way things are and other poems.* New York: Atheneum.

MacCall, Ewan. 1987. "The first time I saw your face." In *Under all silences O shades of love,* ed. Ruth Gordon. New York: Harper & Row.

Mamchur, Carolyn. 1989. "Together." In *'Til all the stars have fallen,* ed. David Booth. London: Viking.

Mandell, Arlene. 1989. "Little girl grown." In *Metropolitan diary of New York Times,* 18 Jan.

Margolis, Richard. 1984. *Secrets of a small brother.* New York: Macmillan.

McNeil, Florence. 1989. "Squirrels in my notebook." In *'Til all the stars have fallen,* ed. David Booth. London: Viking Penguin.

Merriam, Eve. 1962. "Mean song." In *Potato chips and a slice of moon,* ed. Lee Bennett Hopkins and Misha Arenstein. New York: Scholastic.

The Metropolitan Museum of Art. 1987. *Go in and out the window.* New York: Henry Holt.

Milne, A. A. 1967. "Disobedience." In *The Christopher Robin book of verse.* New York: E. P. Dutton.

Moore, Lilian. 1969. "Wind song." In *Poems children will sit still for,* ed. Beatrice Schenk de Regmers, Eva Moore and Mary Michaels White. New York: Scholastic.

Moorison, Lillian. 1974. "Of kings and things." In *New coasts and strange harbors,* ed. Helen Hill and Agnes Perkins. New York: Thomas Y Crowell.

————. 1965. *Sprints and distances.* New York: Thomas Y. Crowell.

Neruda, Pablo. 1988. "The word." In *Lives on the line: The testimony of contemporary Latin American authors,* ed. Doris Meyer. Berkeley, CA: University of California Press.

Nicholas, Grace. 1988. *Come on into my tropical garden.* New York: J. B. Lippincott.

Olds, Sharon. 1984. "35/10." In *the dead and the living.* New York: Alfred A. Knopf.

Paxton, Tom. 1990. *Belling the cat and other Aesop's fables retold in verse.* New York: William Morrow.

Prelutsky, Jack. 1990. "Slow Sloth's slow song." In *Something big has been here.* New York: Greenwillow.

————. 1990. "I am growing a glorious garden." In *Something big has been here.* New York: Greenwillow.

————. 1990. "Slow Sloth's slow song." In *Something big has been here.* New York: Greenwillow.

————. 1990. "Twaddletalk Tuck." In *Something big has been here. New York: Greenwillow.*

Prince. Redcloud. 1983. "Now." In the sky is full of song, ed. Lee Bennett Hopkins. New York: Harper & Row.

Rich, Adrienne. 1989. "Living memory." In *Time's Power: Poems 1985–1988.* New York: W. W. Norton & Company.

Richards, Laura E. 1988. "Eletelephony." In *Sing a song of popcorn,* ed. Beatrice Schenk de Regniers, Eva Moore, Mary Michaels White and Jan Carr. New York: Scholastic.

Ridlon, Marci. 1969. "Bad day." In *That was summer.* New York: Follett Publishing Company.

————. 1969. "That was summer." In *That was summer.* New York: Follett Publishing Company.

————. 1976. "Catching quiet." In *Potato chips and a slice of moon,* ed. Lee Bennett Hopkins and Misha Arenstein.

Rosen, Michael. 1977. "I'm just going out for a moment." In *Wouldn't you like to know.* London: Andre Deutsch.

Rossetti, Christina. 1991. "What are heavy?" In *Fly away, fly away over the sea.* New York: North-South Books.

————. 1987. "Hurt no living thing." In *These small stones,* ed. New York: Harper & Row.

Rowlan, Alden. 1987. "Great things have happened." In *Going over to your place,* ed. Paul Janeczko. New York: Bradbury.

Sandburg, Carl. 1983. "Arithmetic." In *Random House book of poetry for children,* ed. Jack Prelutsky. New York: Random House.

Scarffe, Bronwen. 1987. "Double dutch." In *Going barefoot and other poems,* ed. Anne Hanzl and Yevonne Pollock. Gosford, Australia: Ashton Scholastic.

Soto, Gary. 1990. *A fire in my hands.* New York: Scholastic.

Stevens, Wallace. 1981. "Not idas about the thing but the thing itself." In *Harper anthology of poetry,* New York: Harper & Row.

Stevenson, Robert Louis. 1984. *The Moon.* New York: Harper & Row.

Straus, Gwen. 1990. *Trail of stones.* New York: Alfred A. Knopf.

Toushek, Gary. 1980. "Day at the beach." In *Round slice of moon.* Richmond Hill, Ontario: Scholastic.

Tsuda, Margaret. 1977. "Commitment in a city." In *Crazy to be alive in such a strange world,* ed. Nancy Larrick. New York: M. Evans.

Viorst, Judith. 1982. "Talking." In *If I were in charge of the world.* New York: Atheneum.

Watson, Clyde. 1971. *Father foxes penny rhymes.* New York: Thomas Y. Crowell.

Wilbur, Richard. 1973. *Opposites.* Orlando, FL, Harcourt Brace Jovanovich.

Wordsworth, William. 1959. "My heart leaps up when I behold." In *Time for poetry,* ed. May Hill Arbuthnot. Glenview, IL: Scott, Foresman.

Worth, Valerie. 1987. "dog." In *All the small poems.* New York: Farrar, Straus, & Giroux.

Zolotow, Charloto. 1970. "So will I." In *River winding.* New York: Thomas Y. Crowell.